50% OFF Online HiSET Prep Course!

Dear Customer,

We consider it an honor and a privilege that you chose our HiSET Study Guide. As a way of showing our appreciation and to help us better serve you, we have partnered with Mometrix Test Preparation to offer you **50% off their online HiSET Prep Course**. Many HiSET courses are needlessly expensive and don't deliver enough value. With their course, you get access to the best HiSET prep material, and **you only pay half price**.

Mometrix has structured their online course to perfectly complement your printed study guide. The HiSET Prep Course contains **in-depth lessons** that cover all the most important topics, over **1,950 practice questions** to ensure you feel prepared, **420+ review videos**, and more than **1,200 digital flashcards**, so you can study while you're on the go.

Online HiSET Prep Course

Topics Included:
- Language Arts - Reading
    - Literary Texts
- Language Arts - Writing
    - Conventions and Language Facility
- Mathematics
    - Measurement and Geometry
- Science
    - Physical Science
- Social Studies
    - American History

Course Features:
- HiSET Study Guide
    - Get content that complements our best-selling study guide.
- Full-Length Practice Tests
    - With over 1,950 practice questions, you can test yourself again and again.
- Mobile Friendly
    - If you need to study on the go, the course is easily accessible from your mobile device.
- HiSET Flashcards
    - Our course includes a flashcard mode with over 1,200 content cards to help you study.

To receive this discount, visit them at mometrix.com/university/hiset or simply scan this QR code with your smartphone. At the checkout page, enter the discount code: **TPBHISET50**

If you have any questions or concerns, please contact them at support@mometrix.com.

Sincerely,

 in partnership with

Online Resources

Included with your purchase are multiple online resources. This includes the practice tests in an interactive format and a convenient study timer to help you manage your time.

Instructions for accessing these resources can be found on the last page of this book.

HiSET® Prep Book 2025-2026
4 Practice Tests and HiSET Study Guide All Subjects
[9th Edition]

Lydia Morrison

Copyright © 2025 by TPB Publishing

All rights reserved. No part of this publication may be reproduced, distributed, or transmitted in any form or by any means, including photocopying, recording, or other electronic or mechanical methods, without the prior written permission of the publisher, except in the case of brief quotations embodied in critical reviews and certain other noncommercial uses permitted by copyright law.

Written and edited by TPB Publishing.

TPB Publishing is not associated with or endorsed by any official testing organization. TPB Publishing is a publisher of unofficial educational products. All test and organization names are trademarks of their respective owners. Content in this book is included for utilitarian purposes only and does not constitute an endorsement by TPB Publishing of any particular point of view.

Interested in buying more than 10 copies of our product? Contact us about bulk discounts:
bulkorders@studyguideteam.com

ISBN 13: 9781637750230

Table of Contents

Welcome 1

Quick Overview 2

Test-Taking Strategies 3

Introduction to the HiSET 7

Study Prep Plan for the HiSET 9

Math Reference Sheet 12

Language Arts: Reading 13

   Comprehension 13

   Inference and Interpretation 16

   Analysis 22

   Synthesis and Generalization 29

   Practice Quiz 34

   Answer Explanations 36

Language Arts: Writing 37

   Organization of Ideas 37

   Language Facility 40

   Writing Conventions 47

   Practice Quiz 60

   Answer Explanations 62

Mathematics 63

   Numbers and Operations on Numbers 63

   Measurement/Geometry 73

   Data Analysis/Probability/Statistics 86

Algebraic Concepts	98
Practice Quiz	126
Answer Explanations	128

Science **129**

Life Science	129
Physical Science	150
Earth Science	167
Science Process	183
Practice Quiz	190
Answer Explanations	191

Social Studies **192**

History	192
Civics/Government	207
Economics	220
Geography	228
Practice Quiz	243
Answer Explanations	245

HiSET Practice Test #1 .... **246**

Language Arts: Reading	246
Language Arts: Writing	257
Mathematics	274
Science	285
Social Studies	295

Answer Explanations #1 .... **303**

Language Arts: Reading	303
Language Arts: Writing	308

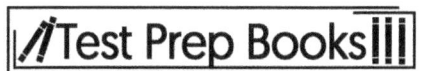

Mathematics	314
Science	324
Social Studies	330

HiSET Practice Tests #2, #3, and #4 338
Index 339
Online Resources 347

Welcome

Dear Reader,

Welcome to your new Test Prep Books study guide! We are pleased that you chose us to help you prepare for your exam. There are many study options to choose from, and we appreciate you choosing us. Studying can be a daunting task, but we have designed a smart, effective study guide to help prepare you for what lies ahead.

Whether you're a parent helping your child learn and grow, a high school student working hard to get into your dream college, or a nursing student studying for a complex exam, we want to help give you the tools you need to succeed. We hope this study guide gives you the skills and the confidence to thrive, and we can't thank you enough for allowing us to be part of your journey.

In an effort to continue to improve our products, we welcome feedback from our customers. We look forward to hearing from you. Suggestions, success stories, and criticisms can all be communicated by emailing us at info@studyguideteam.com.

Sincerely,

Test Prep Books Team

Quick Overview

As you draw closer to taking your exam, effective preparation becomes more and more important. Thankfully, you have this study guide to help you get ready. Use this guide to help keep your studying on track and refer to it often.

This study guide contains several key sections that will help you be successful on your exam. The guide contains tips for what you should do the night before and the day of the test. Also included are test-taking tips. Knowing the right information is not always enough. Many well-prepared test takers struggle with exams. These tips will help equip you to accurately read, assess, and answer test questions.

A large part of the guide is devoted to showing you what content to expect on the exam and to helping you better understand that content. In this guide are practice test questions so that you can see how well you have grasped the content. Then, answer explanations are provided so that you can understand why you missed certain questions.

Don't try to cram the night before you take your exam. This is not a wise strategy for a few reasons. First, your retention of the information will be low. Your time would be better used by reviewing information you already know rather than trying to learn a lot of new information. Second, you will likely become stressed as you try to gain a large amount of knowledge in a short amount of time. Third, you will be depriving yourself of sleep. So be sure to go to bed at a reasonable time the night before. Being well-rested helps you focus and remain calm.

Be sure to eat a substantial breakfast the morning of the exam. If you are taking the exam in the afternoon, be sure to have a good lunch as well. Being hungry is distracting and can make it difficult to focus. You have hopefully spent lots of time preparing for the exam. Don't let an empty stomach get in the way of success!

When traveling to the testing center, leave earlier than needed. That way, you have a buffer in case you experience any delays. This will help you remain calm and will keep you from missing your appointment time at the testing center.

Be sure to pace yourself during the exam. Don't try to rush through the exam. There is no need to risk performing poorly on the exam just so you can leave the testing center early. Allow yourself to use all of the allotted time if needed.

Remain positive while taking the exam even if you feel like you are performing poorly. Thinking about the content you should have mastered will not help you perform better on the exam.

Once the exam is complete, take some time to relax. Even if you feel that you need to take the exam again, you will be well served by some down time before you begin studying again. It's often easier to convince yourself to study if you know that it will come with a reward!

Test-Taking Strategies

1. Predicting the Answer

When you feel confident in your preparation for a multiple-choice test, try predicting the answer before reading the answer choices. This is especially useful on questions that test objective factual knowledge. By predicting the answer before reading the available choices, you eliminate the possibility that you will be distracted or led astray by an incorrect answer choice. You will feel more confident in your selection if you read the question, predict the answer, and then find your prediction among the answer choices. After using this strategy, be sure to still read all of the answer choices carefully and completely. If you feel unprepared, you should not attempt to predict the answers. This would be a waste of time and an opportunity for your mind to wander in the wrong direction.

2. Reading the Whole Question

Too often, test takers scan a multiple-choice question, recognize a few familiar words, and immediately jump to the answer choices. Test authors are aware of this common impatience, and they will sometimes prey upon it. For instance, a test author might subtly turn the question into a negative, or he or she might redirect the focus of the question right at the end. The only way to avoid falling into these traps is to read the entirety of the question carefully before reading the answer choices.

3. Looking for Wrong Answers

Long and complicated multiple-choice questions can be intimidating. One way to simplify a difficult multiple-choice question is to eliminate all of the answer choices that are clearly wrong. In most sets of answers, there will be at least one selection that can be dismissed right away. If the test is administered on paper, the test taker could draw a line through it to indicate that it may be ignored; otherwise, the test taker will have to perform this operation mentally or on scratch paper. In either case, once the obviously incorrect answers have been eliminated, the remaining choices may be considered. Sometimes identifying the clearly wrong answers will give the test taker some information about the correct answer. For instance, if one of the remaining answer choices is a direct opposite of one of the eliminated answer choices, it may well be the correct answer. The opposite of obviously wrong is obviously right! Of course, this is not always the case. Some answers are obviously incorrect simply because they are irrelevant to the question being asked. Still, identifying and eliminating some incorrect answer choices is a good way to simplify a multiple-choice question.

4. Don't Overanalyze

Anxious test takers often overanalyze questions. When you are nervous, your brain will often run wild, causing you to make associations and discover clues that don't actually exist. If you feel that this may be a problem for you, do whatever you can to slow down during the test. Try taking a deep breath or counting to ten. As you read and consider the question, restrict yourself to the particular words used by the author. Avoid thought tangents about what the author *really* meant, or what he or she was *trying* to say. The only things that matter on a multiple-choice test are the words that are actually in the question. You must avoid reading too much into a multiple-choice question, or supposing that the writer meant something other than what he or she wrote.

5. No Need for Panic

It is wise to learn as many strategies as possible before taking a multiple-choice test, but it is likely that you will come across a few questions for which you simply don't know the answer. In this situation, avoid panicking. Because most multiple-choice tests include dozens of questions, the relative value of a single wrong answer is small. As much as possible, you should compartmentalize each question on a multiple-choice test. In other words, you should not allow your feelings about one question to affect your success on the others. When you find a question that you either don't understand or don't know how to answer, just take a deep breath and do your best. Read the entire question slowly and carefully. Try rephrasing the question a couple of different ways. Then, read all of the answer choices carefully. After eliminating obviously wrong answers, make a selection and move on to the next question.

6. Confusing Answer Choices

When working on a difficult multiple-choice question, there may be a tendency to focus on the answer choices that are the easiest to understand. Many people, whether consciously or not, gravitate to the answer choices that require the least concentration, knowledge, and memory. This is a mistake. When you come across an answer choice that is confusing, you should give it extra attention. A question might be confusing because you do not know the subject matter to which it refers. If this is the case, don't eliminate the answer before you have affirmatively settled on another. When you come across an answer choice of this type, set it aside as you look at the remaining choices. If you can confidently assert that one of the other choices is correct, you can leave the confusing answer aside. Otherwise, you will need to take a moment to try to better understand the confusing answer choice. Rephrasing is one way to tease out the sense of a confusing answer choice.

7. Your First Instinct

Many people struggle with multiple-choice tests because they overthink the questions. If you have studied sufficiently for the test, you should be prepared to trust your first instinct once you have carefully and completely read the question and all of the answer choices. There is a great deal of research suggesting that the mind can come to the correct conclusion very quickly once it has obtained all of the relevant information. At times, it may seem to you as if your intuition is working faster even than your reasoning mind. This may in fact be true. The knowledge you obtain while studying may be retrieved from your subconscious before you have a chance to work out the associations that support it. Verify your instinct by working out the reasons that it should be trusted.

8. Key Words

Many test takers struggle with multiple-choice questions because they have poor reading comprehension skills. Quickly reading and understanding a multiple-choice question requires a mixture of skill and experience. To help with this, try jotting down a few key words and phrases on a piece of scrap paper. Doing this concentrates the process of reading and forces the mind to weigh the relative importance of the question's parts. In selecting words and phrases to write down, the test taker thinks about the question more deeply and carefully. This is especially true for multiple-choice questions that are preceded by a long prompt.

9. Subtle Negatives

One of the oldest tricks in the multiple-choice test writer's book is to subtly reverse the meaning of a question with a word like *not* or *except*. If you are not paying attention to each word in the question, you can easily be led astray by this trick. For instance, a common question format is, "Which of the following is...?" Obviously, if the question instead is, "Which of the following is not...?," then the answer will be quite different. Even worse, the test makers are aware of the potential for this mistake and will include one answer choice that would be correct if the question were not negated or reversed. A test taker who misses the reversal will find what he or she believes to be a correct answer and will be so confident that he or she will fail to reread the question and discover the original error. The only way to avoid this is to practice a wide variety of multiple-choice questions and to pay close attention to each and every word.

10. Reading Every Answer Choice

It may seem obvious, but you should always read every one of the answer choices! Too many test takers fall into the habit of scanning the question and assuming that they understand the question because they recognize a few key words. From there, they pick the first answer choice that answers the question they believe they have read. Test takers who read all of the answer choices might discover that one of the latter answer choices is actually *more* correct. Moreover, reading all of the answer choices can remind you of facts related to the question that can help you arrive at the correct answer. Sometimes, a misstatement or incorrect detail in one of the latter answer choices will trigger your memory of the subject and will enable you to find the right answer. Failing to read all of the answer choices is like not reading all of the items on a restaurant menu: you might miss out on the perfect choice.

11. Spot the Hedges

One of the keys to success on multiple-choice tests is paying close attention to every word. This is never truer than with words like *almost*, *most*, *some*, and *sometimes*. These words are called "hedges" because they indicate that a statement is not totally true or not true in every place and time. An absolute statement will contain no hedges, but

in many subjects, the answers are not always straightforward or absolute. There are always exceptions to the rules in these subjects. For this reason, you should favor those multiple-choice questions that contain hedging language. The presence of qualifying words indicates that the author is taking special care with his or her words, which is certainly important when composing the right answer. After all, there are many ways to be wrong, but there is only one way to be right! For this reason, it is wise to avoid answers that are absolute when taking a multiple-choice test. An absolute answer is one that says things are either all one way or all another. They often include words like *every*, *always*, *best*, and *never*. If you are taking a multiple-choice test in a subject that doesn't lend itself to absolute answers, be on your guard if you see any of these words.

12. Long Answers

In many subject areas, the answers are not simple. As already mentioned, the right answer often requires hedges. Another common feature of the answers to a complex or subjective question are qualifying clauses, which are groups of words that subtly modify the meaning of the sentence. If the question or answer choice describes a rule to which there are exceptions or the subject matter is complicated, ambiguous, or confusing, the correct answer will require many words in order to be expressed clearly and accurately. In essence, you should not be deterred by answer choices that seem excessively long. Oftentimes, the author of the text will not be able to write the correct answer without

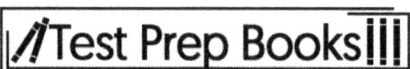

offering some qualifications and modifications. Your job is to read the answer choices thoroughly and completely and to select the one that most accurately and precisely answers the question.

13. Restating to Understand

Sometimes, a question on a multiple-choice test is difficult not because of what it asks but because of how it is written. If this is the case, restate the question or answer choice in different words. This process serves a couple of important purposes. First, it forces you to concentrate on the core of the question. In order to rephrase the question accurately, you have to understand it well. Rephrasing the question will concentrate your mind on the key words and ideas. Second, it will present the information to your mind in a fresh way. This process may trigger your memory and render some useful scrap of information picked up while studying.

14. True Statements

Sometimes an answer choice will be true in itself, but it does not answer the question. This is one of the main reasons why it is essential to read the question carefully and completely before proceeding to the answer choices. Too often, test takers skip ahead to the answer choices and look for true statements. Having found one of these, they are content to select it without reference to the question above. The savvy test taker will always read the entire question before turning to the answer choices. Then, having settled on a correct answer choice, he or she will refer to the original question and ensure that the selected answer is relevant. The mistake of choosing a correct-but-irrelevant answer choice is especially common on questions related to specific pieces of objective knowledge.

15. No Patterns

One of the more dangerous ideas that circulates about multiple-choice tests is that the correct answers tend to fall into patterns. These erroneous ideas range from a belief that B and C are the most common right answers, to the idea that an unprepared test-taker should answer "A-B-A-C-A-D-A-B-A." It cannot be emphasized enough that pattern-seeking of this type is exactly the WRONG way to approach a multiple-choice test. To begin with, it is highly unlikely that the test maker will plot the correct answers according to some predetermined pattern. The questions are scrambled and delivered in a random order. Furthermore, even if the test maker was following a pattern in the assignation of correct answers, there is no reason why the test taker would know which pattern he or she was using. Any attempt to discern a pattern in the answer choices is a waste of time and a distraction from the real work of taking the test. A test taker would be much better served by extra preparation before the test than by reliance on a pattern in the answers.

Introduction to the HiSET

Function of the Test

The High School Equivalency Test (HiSET) was introduced by the Educational Testing Service (ETS) in 2014 as an affordable alternative to the GED exam. It is intended for individuals who have not received a high school diploma as a way to demonstrate that they have knowledge and skills equivalent to someone who has successfully graduated from high school. While the GED exam has long been offered nationwide, the HiSET is thus far available only in certain states: California, Colorado, Hawaii, Illinois, Iowa, Louisiana, Maine, Massachusetts, Mississippi, Missouri, Montana, Nevada, New Hampshire, New Jersey, New Mexico, North Carolina, Oklahoma, Pennsylvania, Tennessee, and Wyoming. Additionally, each state's rules relating to the HiSET may vary.

The test is available in both English and Spanish, but the large majority of test takers take it in English.

Test Administration

The HiSET is administered at various community colleges and testing centers in the jurisdictions in which it is currently accepted. The test is typically available on any day that a given test center is open for business. Students who pass the test receive a high school equivalency certification. Students who do not pass may take it up to two more times within one year to attempt to pass.

The cost of the HiSET is determined by the individual states in which it is offered. The states in turn often allow the individual testing centers to set the price of the test. Some states charge for each individual subsection of the test, while others charge one price to take the whole thing. In the end, the typical total cost for taking the entire test is usually in the vicinity of $30 to $50.

ETS will provide reasonable accommodations for documented disabilities including but not limited to attention deficit/hyperactivity disorder, psychological or psychiatric disorders, learning and other cognitive disabilities, physical disorders/chronic health disabilities, intellectual disabilities, and hearing and visual impairment.

Test Format

The content of the HiSET exam is intended to cover the fundamental material that a student would gain mastery over during a typical high school education. It is broken down into five sections that are summarized below. A test taker can take one section at a time, or schedule several back-to-back. The test can be taken either by computer or in a pencil-and-paper form, and in either English or Spanish. Test takers can answer questions in any order they choose.

Section	Questions	Time
Language Arts- Reading	50	65 minutes
Language Arts- Writing	61	120 minutes
Mathematics	55	90 minutes
Science	60	80 minutes
Social Studies	60	70 minutes

Scoring

In order to pass the HiSET, test takers must get at least the minimum passing score on each of the five sections, the minimum passing score on the essay portion of the Writing section, and also get at least the minimum passing overall score. The minimum score on each section is an 8, the minimum score on the essay portion of the Writing section is a 2, and the overall minimum score is a 45.

Note that not all questions will be scored. Some questions are experimental and are being tested out. However, you have no way of knowing which are real and which are not, so be sure to do your best on every question.

The score is based on the total number of correct answers on the scored questions, with no deductions for incorrect responses, so there is no guessing penalty. Make sure you answer every question! If you begin to run out of time, just mark something down to at least give yourself a chance.

Recent/Future Developments

When the HiSET was created in 2014, it was intended as an alternative or replacement for the GED test in states that chose to adopt it. In 2016, ETS changed the structure of the Writing portion of the exam. As a result, students may now switch back and forth between the essay and multiple-choice portions of the exam as they like. This permits test takers who get through the multiple-choice questions quickly to spend more time on the essay, or vice-versa. ETS also adjusted the essay prompt such that it now includes two opposing arguments, one of which the test taker must adopt and defend.

Study Prep Plan for the HiSET

1 **Schedule** - Use one of our study schedules below or come up with one of your own.

2 **Relax** - Test anxiety can hurt even the best students. There are many ways to reduce stress. Find the one that works best for you.

3 **Execute** - Once you have a good plan in place, be sure to stick to it.

One Week Study Schedule

Day 1	Language Arts: Reading
Day 2	Mathematics
Day 3	Science
Day 4	Earth Science
Day 5	Social Studies
Day 6	HiSET Practice Test #1
Day 7	Take Your Exam!

Two Week Study Schedule

Day 1	Language Arts: Reading	Day 8	Physical Science
Day 2	Synthesis and Generalization	Day 9	Earth Science
Day 3	Writing Conventions	Day 10	Social Studies
Day 4	Mathematics	Day 11	Economics
Day 5	Measurement/Geometry	Day 12	HiSET Practice Test #1
Day 6	Data Analysis/Probability/Statistics	Day 13	Practice Test #2
Day 7	Science	Day 14	Take Your Exam!

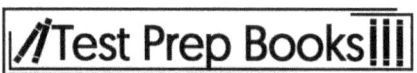

Study Prep Plan for the HiSET

One Month Study Schedule					
Day 1	Language Arts: Reading	Day 11	Probabilities of Single and Compound Events	Day 21	Interactions of the Earth-Moon-Sun System
Day 2	Analysis	Day 12	Algebraic Concepts	Day 22	Social Studies
Day 3	Synthesis and Generalization	Day 13	Solving Quadratic Equations	Day 23	The Structure and Functions of Different...
Day 4	Language Arts: Writing	Day 14	Graphing Functions	Day 24	Geography
Day 5	Style, Tone, and Mood	Day 15	Domain and Range of a Function	Day 25	Economic, Political, and Social Factors
Day 6	Using Reference Sources	Day 16	Science	Day 26	Answer Explanations #4
Day 7	Mathematics	Day 17	Relationships Between Structure...	Day 27	Practice Test #2
Day 8	Measurement/Geometry	Day 18	Physical Science	Day 28	Practice Test #3
Day 9	The Pythagorean Theorem	Day 19	Principles of Light, Heat, Electricity...	Day 29	Practice Test #4
Day 10	Data Analysis/Probability/Statistics	Day 20	Earth Science	Day 30	Take Your Exam!

Build your own prep plan by visiting:

testprepbooks.com/prep

As you study for your test, we'd like to take the opportunity to remind you that you are capable of great things! With the right tools and dedication, you truly can do anything you set your mind to. The fact that you are holding this book right now shows how committed you are. In case no one has told you lately, you've got this! Our intention behind including this coloring page is to give you the chance to take some time to engage your creative side when you need a little brain-break from studying. As a company, we want to encourage people like you to achieve their dreams by providing good quality study materials for the tests and certifications that improve careers and change lives. As individuals, many of us have taken such tests in our careers, and we know how challenging this process can be. While we can't come alongside you and cheer you on personally, we can offer you the space to recall your purpose, reconnect with your passion, and refresh your brain through an artistic practice. We wish you every success, and happy studying!

Math Reference Sheet

Symbol	Phrase
+	added to, increased by, sum of, more than
-	decreased by, difference between, less than, take away
×	multiplied by, 3 (4, 5 . . .) times as large, product of
÷	divided by, quotient of, half (third, etc.) of
=	is, the same as, results in, as much as
x, t, n, etc.	a variable which is an unknown value or quantity
<	is under, is below, smaller than, beneath
>	is above, is over, bigger than, exceeds
≤	no more than, at most, maximum; less than or equal to
≥	no less than, at least, minimum; greater than or equal to
√	square root of, exponent divided by 2

Geometry	Description
$P = 2l + 2w$	for perimeter of a rectangle
$P = 4 \times s$	for perimeter of a square
$P = a + b + c$	for perimeter of a triangle
$A = \frac{1}{2} \times b \times h = \frac{bh}{2}$	for area of a triangle
$A = b \times h$	for area of a parallelogram
$A = \frac{1}{2} \times h(b_1 + b_2)$	for area of a trapezoid
$A = \frac{1}{2} \times a \times P$	for area of a regular polygon
$C = 2 \times \pi \times r$	for circumference (perimeter) of a circle
$A = \pi \times r^2$	for area of a circle
$c^2 = a^2 + b^2; c = \sqrt{a^2 + b^2}$	for finding the hypotenuse of a right triangle
$SA = 2xy + 2yz + 2xz$	for finding surface area
$V = \frac{1}{3}xyh$	for finding volume of a rectangular pyramid
$V = \frac{4}{3}\pi r^3; \frac{1}{3}\pi r^2 h; \pi r^2 h$	for volume of a sphere; a cone; and a cylinder

Radical Expressions	Description
$\sqrt[n]{a} = a^{\frac{1}{n}}; \sqrt[n]{a^m} = (\sqrt[n]{a})^m = a^{\frac{m}{n}}$	a is the radicand, n is the index, m is the exponent
$\sqrt{x^2} = (x^2)^{\frac{1}{2}} = x$	to convert square root to exponent
$a^m \times a^n = a^{m+n}$	multiplying radicands with exponents
$(a^m)^n = a^{m \times n}$	multiplying exponents
$(a \times b)^m = a^m \times b^m$	parentheses with exponents

Property	Addition	Multiplication
Commutative	$a + b = b + a$	$a \times b = b \times a$
Associative	$(a + b) + c = a + (b + c)$	$(a \times b) \times c = a \times (b \times c)$
Identity	$a + 0 = a; 0 + a = a$	$a \times 1 = a; 1 \times a = a$
Inverse	$a + (-a) = 0$	$a \times \frac{1}{a} = 1; a \neq 0$
Distributive	$a(b + c) = ab + ac$	

Data	Description
Mean	equal to the total of the values of a data set, divided by the number of elements in the data set
Median	middle value in an odd number of ordered values of a data set, or the mean of the two middle values in an even number of ordered values in a data set
Mode	the value that appears most often
Range	the difference between the highest and the lowest values in the set

Graphing	Description
(x, y)	ordered pair, plot points in a graph
$y = mx + b$	slope-intercept form; m represents the slope of the line and b represents the y-intercept
$f(x)$	read as f of x, which means it is a function of x
(x_2, y_2) and (x_2, y_2)	two ordered pairs used to determine the slope of a line
$m = \frac{y_2 - y_1}{x_2 - x_1}$	to find the slope of the line, m, for ordered pairs
$Ax + By = C$	standard form of an equation, also for solving a system of equations through the elimination method
$M = (\frac{x_1 + x_2}{2}, \frac{y_1 + y_2}{2})$	for finding the midpoint of an ordered pair
$y = ax^2 + bx + c$	quadratic function for a parabola
$y = a(x - h)^2 + k$	quadratic function for a parabola with vertex
$y = ab^x; y = a \times b^x$	function for exponential curve
$y = ax^2 + bx + c$	standard form of a quadratic function
$x = \frac{-b}{2a}$	for finding axis of symmetry in a parabola; given quadratic formula in standard form
$f = \sqrt{\frac{\Sigma(x - \bar{x})^2}{n - 1}}$	function for standard deviation of the sample; where $\bar{x}$ = sample mean and n = sample size

Proportions and Percentage	Description
$\frac{gallons}{cost} = \frac{gallons}{cost}; \frac{7 \text{ gallons}}{\$14.70} = \frac{x}{\$20}$	written as equal ratios with a variable representing the missing quantity
$\frac{y_1}{x_1} = \frac{y_2}{x_2}$	for direct proportions
$(y_1)(x_1) = (y_2)(x_2)$	for indirect proportions
$\frac{change}{original \ value} \times 100 = percent \ change$	for finding percentage change in value
$\frac{new \ quantity - old \ quantity}{old \ quantity} \times 100$	for calculating the increase or decrease in percentage

Language Arts: Reading

Comprehension

Understanding Explicit Details

Readers want to draw a conclusion about what the author has presented. Drawing a conclusion will help the reader to understand what the writer intended as well as whether he or she agrees with what the author has said. There are a few ways to determine the logical conclusion, but careful reading is the most important. The passage should be read a few times, and readers should highlight or take notes on the details that they deem important to the meaning of the piece. Readers may draw a conclusion that is different than what the writer intended, or they may draw more than one conclusion. Readers should look carefully at the details to see if their conclusion matches up with what the writer has presented and intended for readers to understand.

Textual evidence can help readers to draw a conclusion about a passage. **Textual evidence** refers to information such as facts and examples that support the main point; it will likely come from outside sources and can be in the form of quoted or paraphrased material. Details should be precise, descriptive, and factual. Readers should look to this evidence and its credibility and validity in relation to the main idea to draw a conclusion about the writing.

The author may state the conclusion directly in the passage. Inferring the author's conclusion is useful, especially when it is not overtly stated, but inferences should not outweigh the information that is directly stated. Alternatively, when readers are trying to draw a conclusion about a text, it may not always be directly stated.

As mentioned before, summary is another effective way to draw a conclusion from a passage. Summary is a shortened version of the original text, written in one's own words. It should focus on the main points of the original text, including only the relevant details. It's important to be brief but thorough in a summary. While the summary should always be shorter than the original passage, it should still retain the meaning of the original source.

Like summary, paraphrasing can also help a reader to fully understand a part of a reading. Paraphrase calls for the reader to take a small part of the passage and to say it in their own words. Paraphrase is more than rewording the original passage, though. It should be written in one's own way, while still retaining the meaning of the original source. When a reader's goal is to write something in their own words, deeper understanding of the original source is required. Again, applying summary and paraphrase to the passages during the test may not be the most efficient use of the test taker's time. However, these tools should be considered when one is practicing comprehending passages. Test takers who are familiar with carefully selecting important aspects of the passage will benefit from this experience on test day.

Meaning of Words and Phrases

Another useful vocabulary skill is being able to understand meaning in context. A word's **context** refers to other words and information surrounding it, which can have a big impact on how readers interpret that word's meaning. Of course, many words have more than one definition. For example, consider the meaning of the word "engaged." The first definition that comes to mind might be "promised to be married," but consider the following sentences:

    a. The two armies engaged in a conflict that lasted all night.

    b. The three-hour lecture flew by because students were so engaged in the material.

    c. The busy executive engaged a new assistant to help with his workload.

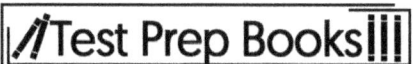

Were any of those sentences related to marriage? In fact, "engaged" has a variety of other meanings. In these sentences, respectively, it can mean: "battled," "interested or involved," and "appointed or employed." Readers may wonder how to decide which definition to apply. The appropriate meaning is prioritized based on context. For example, sentence C mentions "executive," "assistant," and "workload," so readers can assume that "engaged" has something to do with work—in which case, "appointed or employed" is the best definition for this context. Context clues can also be found in sentence A. Words like "armies" and "conflicts" show that this sentence is about a military situation, so in this context, "engaged" is closest in meaning to "battled." By using context clues—the surrounding words in the sentence—readers can easily select the most appropriate definition.

Context clues can also help readers when they don't know *any* meanings for a certain word. Test writers will deliberately ask about unfamiliar vocabulary to measure your ability to use context to make an educated guess about a word's meaning.

Which of the following is the closest in meaning to the word "loquacious" in the following sentence?

The *loquacious* professor was notorious for always taking too long to finish his lectures.
    a. knowledgeable
    b. enthusiastic
    c. approachable
    d. talkative

Even if the word "loquacious" seems completely new, it's possible to utilize context to make a good guess about the word's meaning. Grammatically, it's apparent that "loquacious" is an adjective that modifies the noun "professor"—so "loquacious" must be some kind of quality or characteristic. A clue in this sentence is "taking too long to finish his lectures." Readers should then consider qualities that might cause a professor's lectures to run long. Perhaps he's "disorganized," "slow," or "talkative"—all words that might still make sense in this sentence. Choice *D*, therefore, is a logical choice for this sentence—the professor talks too much, so his lectures run late. In fact, "loquacious" means "talkative or wordy."

One way to use context clues is to think of potential replacement words before considering the answer choices. You can also turn to the answer choices first and try to replace each of them in the sentence to see if the sentence is logical and retains the same meaning.

Another way to use context clues is to consider clues in the word itself. Most students are familiar with prefixes, suffixes, and root words—the building blocks of many English words. A little knowledge goes a long way when it comes to these components of English vocabulary, and these words can point readers in the right direction when they need help finding an appropriate definition.

Word Choices

Just as one word may have different meanings, the same meaning can be conveyed by different words or synonyms. However, there are very few synonyms that have *exactly* the same definition. Rather, there are slight nuances in usage and meaning. In this case, a writer's **diction**, or word choice, is important to the meaning meant to be conveyed.

Many words have a surface *denotation* and a deeper *connotation*. A word's **denotation** is the literal definition of a word that can be found in any dictionary (an easy way to remember this is that "denotation" and "dictionary definition" all begin with the letter "D"). For example, if someone looked up the word "snake" in the dictionary, they'd learn that a snake is a common reptile with scales, a long body, and no limbs.

A word's **connotation** refers to its emotional and cultural associations, beyond its literal definition. Some connotations are universal, some are common within a particular cultural group, and some are more personal. Let's go back to the word "snake." A reader probably already knows its denotation—a slithering animal—but readers should also take a moment to consider its possible connotations. For readers from a Judeo-Christian culture, they might associate a snake with the serpent from the Garden of Eden who tempts Adam and Eve into eating the forbidden fruit. In this case, a snake's connotations might include deceit, danger, and sneakiness.

Consider the following character description:

> He slithered into the room like a snake.

Does this sound like a character who can be trusted? It's the connotation of the word "snake" that implies untrustworthiness. Connotative language, then, helps writers to communicate a deeper, more emotional meaning.

Read the following excerpt from "The Lamb," a poem by William Blake.

> Little lamb, who made thee?
> Dost thou know who made thee,
> Gave thee life, and bid thee feed
> By the stream and o'er the mead;
> Gave thee clothing of delight,
> Softest clothing, woolly, bright;
> Gave thee such a tender voice,
> Making all the vales rejoice?
> Little lamb, who made thee?
> Dost thou know who made thee?

Think about the connotations of a "lamb." Whereas a snake might make readers think of something dangerous and dishonest, a lamb tends to carry a different connotation: innocence and purity. Blake's poem contains other emotional language—"delight," "softest," "tender," "rejoice"—to support this impression.

Some words have similar denotations but very different connotations. "Weird" and "unique" can both describe something distinctive and unlike the norm. But they convey different emotions:

> You have such a weird fashion sense!

> You have such a unique fashion sense!

Which sentence is a compliment? Which sentence is an insult? "Weird" generally has more negative connotations, whereas "unique" is more positive. In this way, connotative language is a powerful way for writers to evoke emotion.

A writer's diction also informs their tone. **Tone** refers to the author's attitude toward their subject. A writer's tone might be critical, curious, respectful, dismissive, or any other possible attitude. The key to understanding tone is focusing not just on *what* is said, but on *how* it's said.

> a. Although the latest drug trial did not produce a successful vaccine, medical researchers are one step further on the path to eradicating this deadly virus.

> b. Doctors faced yet another disappointing setback in their losing battle against the killer virus; their most recent drug trial has proved as unsuccessful as the last.

Both sentences report the same information: the latest drug trial was a failure. However, each sentence presents this information in a different way, revealing the writer's tone. The first sentence has a more hopeful and confident tone, downplaying the doctors' failure ("although" it failed) and emphasizing their progress ("one step further").

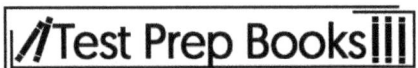

Language Arts: Reading

The second sentence has a decidedly more pessimistic and defeatist tone, using phrases like "disappointing setback" and "losing battle." The details a writer chooses to include can also help readers to identify their attitude towards their subject matter.

Identifying emotional or connotative language can be useful in determining the tone of a text. Readers can also consider questions such as, "Who is the speaker?" or "Who is their audience?" (Remember, particularly in fiction, that the speaker or narrator may not be the same person as the author.) For example, in an article about military conflict written by a notable anti-war activist, readers might expect their tone to be critical, harsh, or cynical. If they are presented with a poem written between newlyweds, readers might expect the tone to be loving, sensitive, or infatuated. If the tone seems wildly different from what's expected, consider if the writer is using **irony**. When a writer uses irony, they say one thing but imply the opposite meaning.

Inference and Interpretation

Inferences from the Text

Readers should be able to make **inferences**. Making an inference requires the reader to read between the lines and look for what's *implied* rather than what's directly stated. Using information that is known from the text, the reader is able to make a logical assumption about information that isn't directly stated but is probably true. Read the following passage:

"Hey, do you want to meet my new puppy?" Jonathan asked.

"Oh, I'm sorry but please don't—" Jacinta began to protest, but before she could finish Jonathan had already open the passenger side door of his car and a perfectly white ball of fur came bouncing towards Jacinta.

"Isn't he the cutest?" beamed Jonathan.

"Yes—achoo!—he's pretty—aaaachooo!!—adora—aaa—aaaachoo!" Jacinta managed to say in between sneezes. "But if you don't mind, I—I—achoo!—need to go inside."

Which of the following can be inferred from Jacinta's reaction to the puppy?
   a. She hates animals.
   b. She is allergic to dogs.
   c. She prefers cats to dogs.
   d. She is angry at Jonathan.

In order to make an inference, the reader must first consider the information presented and then form an idea about what is probably true. Based on the details in the passage, what's the best answer? Important details include the tone of Jacinta's dialogue, which is polite and apologetic, as well as her reaction itself, which is a long string of sneezes. Choices *A* and *D* both express strong emotions ("hates" and "angry") that aren't evident in Jacinta's speech or actions. Choice *C* mentions cats, but there isn't anything in the passage to indicate Jacinta's feelings about those animals. Choice *B* is the most logical choice. As she began sneezing as soon as the dog approached her, it makes sense to guess that Jacinta might be allergic to dogs. So even though Jacinta never directly states, "Sorry, I'm allergic to dogs!" using the clues in the passage, it's still reasonable to guess this is true.

Making inferences is crucial for readers because literary texts often avoid presenting complete and direct information about characters' thoughts or feelings, leaving the reader to interpret clues in the text. In order to make inferences, readers should ask:

- What details are presented in the text?
- Is there any important information that seems to be missing?
- Based on the information that the author does include, what else is probably true?
- Is this inference reasonable based on what is already known?

Drawing Conclusions Not Explicitly Present in the Text

It's also useful to infer meaning from informative texts. Scientists and researchers make inferences every day in order to develop new theories based on facts and observations. Readers of informative texts should also understand how inferences are applied in academic research. Generally speaking, there are two main types of reasoning—*deductive* and *inductive*. An inference based on **deductive reasoning** considers a principle that is generally believed to be true and then applies it to a specific situation ("All English majors love reading. Annabelle is an English major. Therefore, I can infer that Annabelle loves reading."). **Inductive reasoning** makes an inference by using specific evidence to make a general inference ("Trina, Arnold, and Uchenna are all from Florida. Trina, Arnold, and Uchenna all love to swim. Therefore, I can infer that people from Florida usually love swimming."). Both deductive and inductive reasoning use what is *known* to be true to make a logical guess about what is *probably* true.

Inferring the Traits, Feelings, and Motives of Characters

Inferences are useful in gaining a deeper understanding of characters in a narrative. Readers can use the same strategies outlined above—paying attention to details and using them to make reasonable guesses about the text—to read between the lines and get a more complete picture of how (and why) characters are thinking, feeling, and acting. Read the following passage from O. Henry's story "The Gift of the Magi":

> One dollar and eighty-seven cents. That was all. And sixty cents of it was in pennies. Pennies saved one and two at a time by bulldozing the grocer and the vegetable man and the butcher until one's cheeks burned with the silent imputation of parsimony that such close dealing implied. Three times Della counted it. One dollar and eighty-seven cents. And the next day would be Christmas.
>
> There was clearly nothing to do but flop down on the shabby little couch and howl. So Della did it.

These paragraphs introduce the reader to the character Della. Even though the author doesn't include a direct description of Della, the reader can already form a general impression of her personality and emotions. One detail that should stick out to the reader is repetition: "one dollar and eighty-seven cents." This amount is repeated twice in the first paragraph, along with other descriptions of money: "sixty cents of it was in pennies," "pennies saved one and two at a time." The story's preoccupation with money parallels how Della herself is constantly thinking about her finances—"three times Della counted" her meager savings. Already the reader can guess that Della is having money problems. Next, think about her emotions.

The first paragraph describes haggling over groceries "until one's cheeks burned"—another way to describe blushing. People tend to blush when they are embarrassed or ashamed, so readers can infer that Della is ashamed by her financial situation. This inference is also supported by the second paragraph, when she flops down and howls on her "shabby little couch." Clearly, she's in distress. Without saying, "Della has no money and is embarrassed to be poor," O. Henry is able to communicate the same impression to readers through his careful inclusion of details.

A character's **motive** is their reason for acting a certain way. Usually, characters are motivated by something that they want. In the passage above, why is Della upset about not having enough money? There's an important detail at the end of the first paragraph: "the next day would be Christmas." Why is money especially important around

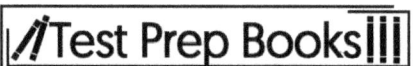

Christmas? Christmas is a holiday when people exchange gifts. If Della is struggling with money, she's probably also struggling to buy gifts. So a shrewd reader should be able to guess that Della's motivation is wanting to buy a gift for someone—but she's currently unable to afford it, leading to feelings of shame and frustration.

In order to understand characters in a text, readers should keep the following questions in mind:

- What words does the author use to describe the character? Are these words related to any specific emotions or personality traits (for example, characteristics like rude, friendly, unapproachable, or innocent)?
- What does the character say? Does their dialogue seem to be straightforward, or are they hiding some thoughts or emotions?
- What actions can be observed from this character? How do their actions reflect their feelings?
- What does the character want? What do they do to get it?

Interpreting Information Presented in Different Formats

Information is often presented in different formats. One of the most common ways to express data is in a table. The primary reason for plugging data into a table is to make interpretation more convenient. It's much easier to look at the table than to analyze results in a narrative paragraph. When analyzing a table, pay close attention to the title, variables, and data.

For example, the following theoretical antibiotic study can be analyzed. The study has 6 groups, named A through F, and each group receives a different dose of medicine. The results of the study are listed in the table below.

Results of Antibiotic Studies		
Group	Dosage of Antibiotics in milligrams (mg)	Efficacy (% of participants cured)
A	0 mg	20%
B	20 mg	40%
C	40 mg	75%
D	60 mg	95%
E	80 mg	100%
F	100 mg	100%

Tables generally list the title immediately above the data. The title should succinctly explain what is listed below. Here, "Results of Antibiotic Studies" informs the audience that the data pertains to the results of a scientific study on antibiotics.

Identifying the variables at play is one of the most important parts of interpreting data. Remember, the independent variable is intentionally altered, and its change is independent of the other variables. Here, the dosage of antibiotics administered to the different groups is the independent variable. The study is intentionally manipulating the strength of the medicine to study the related results. Efficacy is the dependent variable since its results *depend* on a different variable, the dose of antibiotics. Generally, the independent variable will be listed before the dependent variable in tables.

Also, pay close attention to the variables' labels. Here, the dose is expressed in milligrams (mg) and efficacy in percentages (%). Keep an eye out for questions referencing data in a different unit of measurement, or questions asking for a raw number when only the percentage is listed.

Now that the nature of the study and variables at play have been identified, the data itself needs be interpreted. Group A did not receive any of the medicine. As discussed earlier, Group A is the control, as it reflects the amount of people cured in the same timeframe without medicine. It's important to see that efficacy positively correlates with the dosage of medicine. A question using this study might ask for the lowest dose of antibiotics to achieve 100% efficacy. Although Group E and Group F both achieve 100% efficacy, it's important to note that Group E reaches 100% with a lower dose.

Interpreting Graphs

Graphs provide a visual representation of data. The variables are placed on the two axes. The bottom of the graph is referred to as the horizontal axis or X-axis. The left-hand side of the graph is known as the vertical axis or Y-axis. Typically, the independent variable is placed on the X-axis, and the dependent variable is located on the Y-axis. Sometimes, the X-axis is a timeline, and the dependent variables for different trials or groups have been measured throughout points in time; time is still an independent variable but is not always immediately thought of as the independent variable being studied.

The most common types of graphs are the bar graph and the line graph.

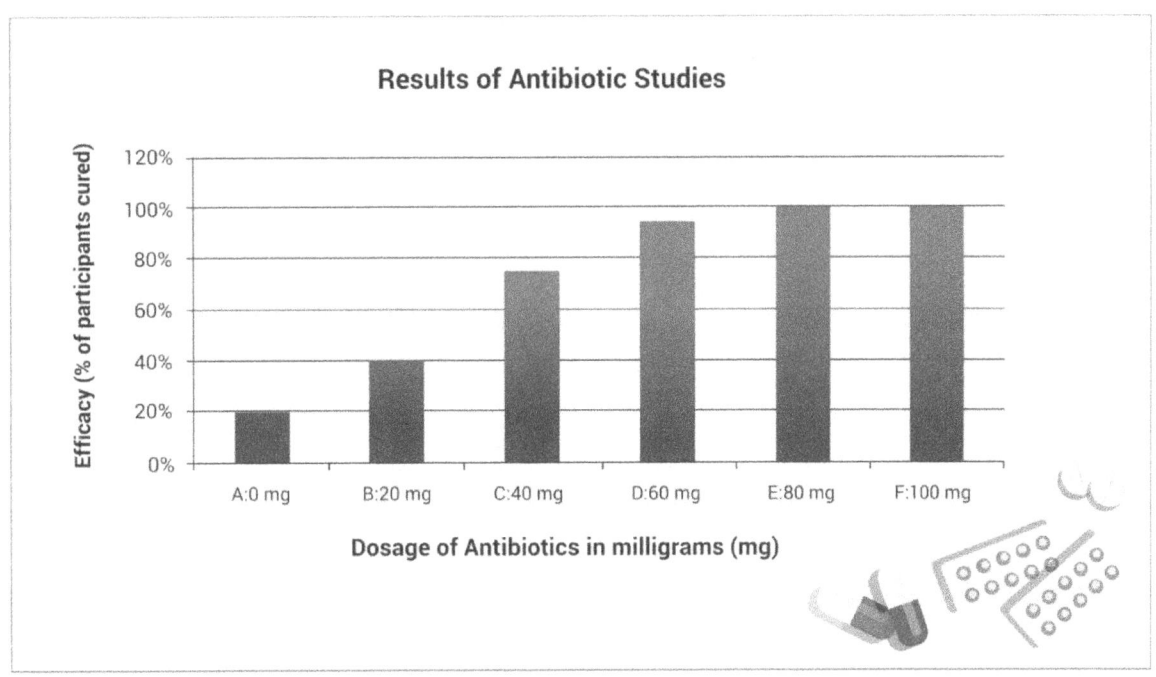

The **bar graph** below expresses the data from the table entitled "Results of Antibiotic Studies." To interpret the data for each group in the study, look at the top of their bars and read the corresponding efficacy on the Y-axis.

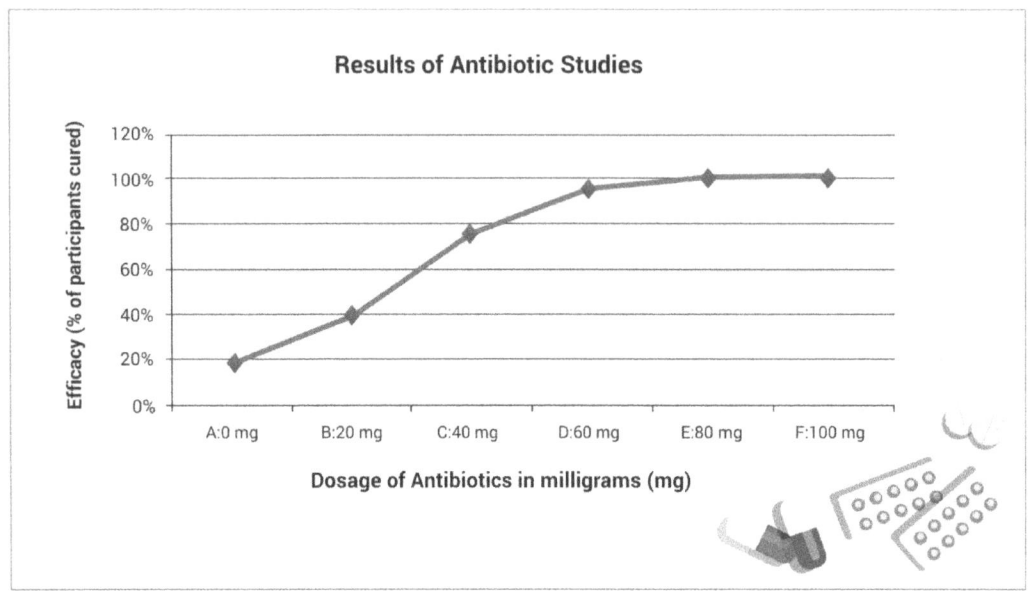

Here, the same data is expressed on a **line graph**. The points on the line correspond with each data entry. Reading the data on the line graph works like the bar graph. The data trend is measured by the slope of the line.

Interpreting Nonliteral Language

It's important to be able to recognize and interpret **figurative**, or non-literal, language. Literal statements rely directly on the denotations of words and express exactly what's happening in reality. Figurative language uses non-literal expressions to present information in a creative way. Consider the following sentences:

a. His pillow was very soft, and he fell asleep quickly.

b. His pillow was a fluffy cloud, and he floated away on it to the dream world.

Sentence A is literal, employing only the real meanings of each word. Sentence B is figurative. It employs a metaphor by stating that his pillow was a cloud. Of course, he isn't actually sleeping on a cloud, but the reader can draw on images of clouds as light, soft, fluffy, and relaxing to get a sense of how the character felt as he fell asleep. Also, in sentence B, the pillow becomes a vehicle that transports him to a magical dream world. The character isn't literally floating through the air—he's simply falling asleep! But by utilizing figurative language, the author creates a scene of peace, comfort, and relaxation that conveys stronger emotions and more creative imagery than the purely literal sentence. While there are countless types of figurative language, there are a few common ones that any reader should recognize.

Simile and *metaphor* are comparisons between two things, but their formats differ slightly. A **simile** says that two things are *similar* and makes a comparison using "like" or "as"—A is like B, or A is as [some characteristic] as B— whereas a metaphor states that two things are exactly the same—A is B. In both cases, simile and **metaphor** invite the reader to think more deeply about the characteristics of the two subjects and consider where they overlap. An example of metaphor can be found in the above sentence about the sleeper ("His pillow was a fluffy cloud"). For an example of simile, look at the first line of Robert Burns' famous poem:

My love is like a red, red rose

This is comparison using "like," and the two things being compared are love and a rose. Some characteristics of a rose are that it's fragrant, beautiful, blossoming, colorful, vibrant—by comparing his love to a rose, Burns asks the reader to apply these qualities to his love. In this way, he implies that his love is also fresh, blossoming, and brilliant.

Similes can also compare things that appear dissimilar. Here's a song lyric from Florence and the Machine:

> Happiness hit her like a bullet in the back

"Happiness" has a very positive connotation, but getting "a bullet in the back" seems violent and aggressive, not at all related to happiness. By using an unexpected comparison, the writer forces readers to think more deeply about the comparison and ask themselves how could getting shot be similar to feeling happy. "A bullet in the back" is something that she doesn't see coming; it's sudden and forceful; and presumably, it has a strong impact on her life. So, in this way, the author seems to be saying that unexpected happiness made a sudden and powerful change in her life.

Another common form of figurative language is **personification**, when a non-human object is given human characteristics. William Blake uses personification here:

> ... the stars threw down their spears,
>
> And watered heaven with their tears

He imagines the stars as combatants in a heavenly battle, giving them both action (throwing down their spears) and emotion (the sadness and disappointment of their tears). Personification helps to add emotion or develop relationships between characters and non-human objects. In fact, most people use personification in their everyday lives:

> My alarm clock betrayed me! It didn't go off this morning!
>
> The last piece of chocolate cake was staring at me from the refrigerator.

Next is **hyperbole**, a type of figurative language that uses extreme exaggeration. Sentences like, "I love you to the moon and back," or "I will love you for a million years," are examples of hyperbole. They aren't literally true—unfortunately, people cannot jump to outer space or live for a million years—but they're creative expressions that communicate the depth of feeling of the author.

Another way that writers add deeper meaning to their work is through *allusions*. An **allusion** is a reference to something from history, literature, or another cultural source. When the text is from a different culture or a time period, readers may not be familiar with every allusion. However, allusions tend to be well-known because the author wants the reader to make a connection between what's happening in the text and what's being referenced.

> I can't believe my best friend told our professor that I was skipping class to finish my final project! What a Judas!

This sentence contains a Biblical allusion to Judas, a friend and follower of Jesus who betrayed Jesus to the Romans. In this case, the allusion to Judas is used to give a deeper impression of betrayal and disloyalty from a trusted friend. Commonly used allusions in Western texts may come from the Bible, Greek or Roman mythology, or well-known literature such as Shakespeare. By familiarizing themselves with these touchstones of history and culture, readers can be more prepared to recognize allusions.

Analysis

Topic, Main Idea, and Theme

In order to understand any text, readers first must determine the **topic**, or what the text is about. In non-fiction writing, the topic can generally be expressed in a few words. For example, a passage might be about college education, moving to a new neighborhood, or dog breeds. Slightly more specific information is found in the **main idea**, or what the writer wants readers to know about the topic. An article might be about the history of popular dog breeds; another article might tell how certain dog breeds are unfairly stereotyped. In both cases, the topic is the same—dog breeds—but the main ideas are quite different.

Each writer has a distinct purpose for writing and a different set of details for what they want us to know about dog breeds. When a writer expresses their main idea in one sentence, this is known as a **thesis statement**. If a writer uses a thesis statement, it can generally be found at the beginning of the passage. Finally, the most specific information in a text is in the **supporting details**. An article about dog breed stereotyping might discuss a case study of pit bulls and provide statistics about how many dog attacks are caused by pit bulls versus other breeds.

Below is a diagram showcasing a topic with the main idea and supporting details. The topic is a single word (Cheetahs). The main idea tells us *what about* cheetahs the essay will be discussing. The supporting details offer proof that the main idea is true.

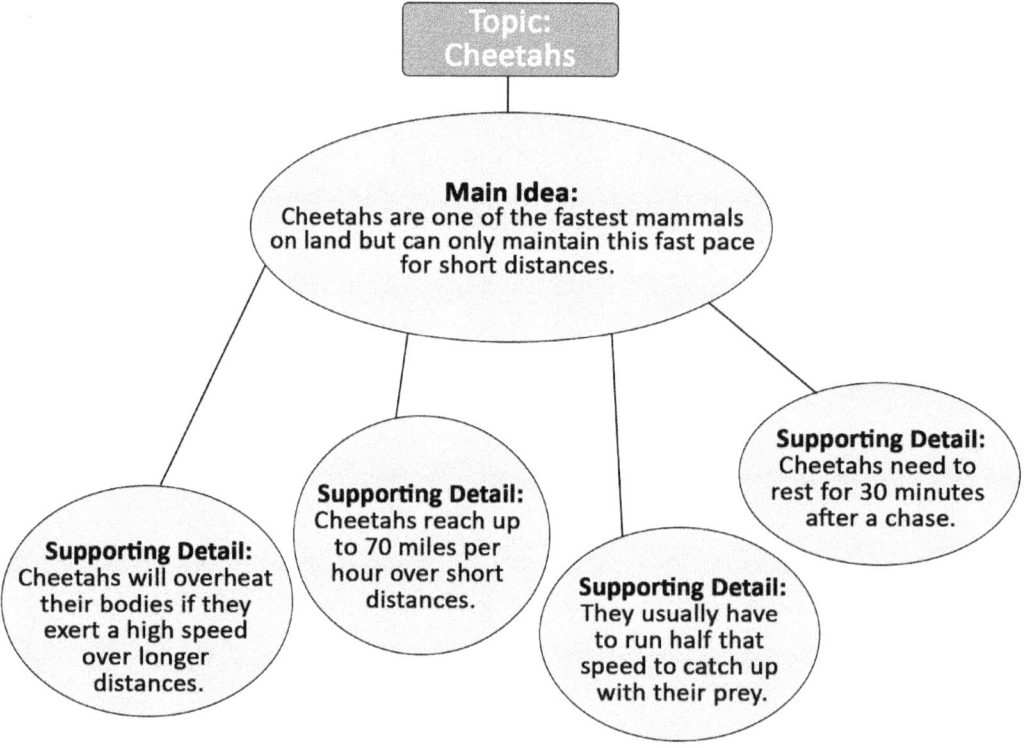

In contrast to informative writing, literary texts contain *themes*. A **theme** is a general way to describe the ideas and questions raised in a piece of literature. Like a topic, a theme can often be expressed in just one word or a few words rather than a full sentence. However, due to the complex nature of literature, most texts contain more than one theme. Some examples of literary themes include: isolation, sacrifice, vengeance. A text's theme might also explore the relationship between two contrasting ideas: ignorance versus knowledge, nature versus technology, science versus religion.

A theme generally expresses a relatively broad and abstract idea about the text—so don't confuse a text's theme with its subject. Both theme and subject can answer the question, "What's the story about?" but the subject answers the question in a concrete way while the theme answers more abstractly. For example, the subject of *Hamlet* is Hamlet's investigation of his father's death (a concrete idea of what happens in the story). However, its themes—that is, the ideas explored through the story—include indecision and revenge, fundamental concepts that unite the events of the story. Because the theme is usually abstract, it might seem difficult to identify. Readers can ask themselves several questions to get a better idea of the theme:

- What observations does the writer make about human behavior?
- How do specific events of this story relate to society in general?
- What forces drive the characters' actions and decisions?
- How did the characters change or what did they learn during the story?

Identifying the Author's Purpose

When it comes to an author's writing, readers should always identify a **position** or **stance**. No matter how objective a text may seem, readers should assume the author has preconceived beliefs. One can reduce the likelihood of accepting an invalid argument by looking for multiple articles on the topic, including those with varying opinions. If several opinions point in the same direction and are backed by reputable peer-reviewed sources, it's more likely that the author has a valid argument. Positions that run contrary to widely held beliefs and existing data should invite scrutiny. There are exceptions to the rule, so readers should be careful consumers of information.

While themes, symbols, and motifs are buried deep within the text and can sometimes be difficult to infer, an author's **purpose** is usually obvious from the beginning. There are four purposes of writing: to inform, to persuade, to describe, and to entertain. **Informative** writing presents facts in an accessible way. **Persuasive** writing appeals to emotions and logic to inspire the reader to adopt a specific stance. Readers should be wary of this type of writing, as it can mask a lack of objectivity with powerful emotion. **Descriptive** writing is designed to paint a picture in the reader's mind, while texts that **entertain** are often narratives designed to engage and delight the reader.

The various writing styles are usually blended, with one purpose dominating the rest. A persuasive text, for example, might begin with a humorous tale to make readers more receptive to the persuasive message, or a recipe in a cookbook designed to inform might be preceded by an entertaining anecdote that makes the recipes more appealing.

Author's Position and Response to Different Viewpoints

If an author presents a differing opinion or a counterargument in order to refute it, the reader should consider how and why the information is being presented. It is meant to strengthen the original argument and shouldn't be confused with the author's intended conclusion, but it should also be considered in the reader's final evaluation.

Authors can exhibit bias if they ignore the opposing viewpoint or present their side in an unbalanced way. A strong argument considers the opposition and finds a way to refute it. Critical readers should look for an unfair or one-sided presentation of the argument and be skeptical, as a bias may be present. Even if this bias is unintentional, if it exists in the writing, the reader should be wary of the validity of the argument. Readers should also look for the use of stereotypes, which refer to specific groups. Stereotypes are often negative connotations about a person or place and should always be avoided. When a critical reader finds stereotypes in a piece of writing, they should be critical of the argument, and consider the validity of anything the author presents. Stereotypes reveal a flaw in the writer's thinking and may suggest a lack of knowledge or understanding about the subject.

Inferring the Author's Purpose in the Passage

In nonfiction writing, authors employ argumentative techniques to present their opinion to readers in the most convincing way. First of all, persuasive writing usually includes at least one type of appeal: an appeal to logic (**logos**), emotion (**pathos**), or credibility and trustworthiness (**ethos**). When a writer appeals to logic, they are asking readers to agree with them based on research, evidence, and an established line of reasoning. An author's argument might also appeal to readers' emotions, perhaps by including personal stories and anecdotes (a short narrative of a specific event). A final type of appeal—appeal to authority—asks the reader to agree with the author's argument on the basis of their expertise or credentials. Consider three different approaches to arguing the same opinion:

Logic (Logos)

Below is an example of an appeal to logic. The author uses evidence to disprove the logic of the school's rule (the rule was supposed to reduce discipline problems; the number of problems has not been reduced; therefore, the rule is not working) and he or she calls for its repeal.

> Our school should abolish its current ban on campus cell phone use. The ban was adopted last year as an attempt to reduce class disruptions and help students focus more on their lessons. However, since the rule was enacted, there has been no change in the number of disciplinary problems in class. Therefore, the rule is ineffective and should be done away with.

Emotion (Pathos)

An author's argument might also appeal to readers' emotions, perhaps by including personal stories and anecdotes. The next example presents an appeal to emotion. By sharing the personal anecdote of one student and speaking about emotional topics like family relationships, the author invokes the reader's empathy in asking them to reconsider the school rule.

> Our school should abolish its current ban on campus cell phone use. If students aren't able to use their phones during the school day, many of them feel isolated from their loved ones. For example, last semester, one student's grandmother had a heart attack in the morning. However, because he couldn't use his cell phone, the student didn't know about his grandmother's condition until the end of the day—when she had already passed away and it was too late to say goodbye. By preventing students from contacting their friends and family, our school is placing undue stress and anxiety on students.

Credibility (Ethos)

Finally, an appeal to authority includes a statement from a relevant expert. In this case, the author uses a doctor in the field of education to support the argument. All three examples begin from the same opinion—the school's phone ban needs to change—but rely on different argumentative styles to persuade the reader.

> Our school should abolish its current ban on campus cell phone use. According to Dr. Bartholomew Everett, a leading educational expert, "Research studies show that cell phone usage has no real impact on student attentiveness. Rather, phones provide a valuable technological resource for learning. Schools need to learn how to integrate this new technology into their curriculum." Rather than banning phones altogether, our school should follow the advice of experts and allow students to use phones as part of their learning.

Rhetorical Questions

Another commonly used argumentative technique is asking **rhetorical questions**, questions that do not actually require an answer but that push the reader to consider the topic further.

> I wholly disagree with the proposal to ban restaurants from serving foods with high sugar and sodium contents. Do we really want to live in a world where the government can control what we eat? I prefer to make my own food choices.

Here, the author's rhetorical question prompts readers to put themselves in a hypothetical situation and imagine how they would feel about it.

Language Arts: Reading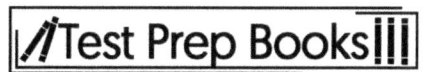

Analyzing Individuals, Events, and Ideas Over the Course of a Text

Transitions are the glue that holds the writing together. They function to purposefully incorporate new topics and supporting details in a smooth and coherent way. Transitions and the corresponding structure they create can be used to determine how individuals, events, and ideas change and develop over the course of the text.

Transition words can be categorized based on the relationships they create between ideas:

- **General order**: signaling elaboration of an idea to emphasize a point—e.g., *for example, for instance, to demonstrate, including, such as, in other words, that is, in fact, also, furthermore, likewise, and, truly, so, surely, certainly, obviously, doubtless*

- **Chronological order**: referencing the time frame in which the main event or idea occurs—e.g., *before, after, first, while, soon, shortly thereafter, meanwhile*

- **Numerical order/order of importance**: indicating that related ideas, supporting details, or events will be described in a sequence, possibly in order of importance—e.g., *first, second, also, finally, another, in addition, equally important, less importantly, most significantly, the main reason, last but not least*

- **Spatial order**: referring to the space and location of something or where things are located in relation to each other—e.g., *inside, outside, above, below, within, close, under, over, far, next to, adjacent to*

- **Cause and effect order**: signaling a causal relationship between events or ideas—e.g., *thus, therefore, since, resulted in, for this reason, as a result, consequently, hence, for, so*

- **Compare and contrast order**: identifying the similarities and differences between two or more objects, ideas, or lines of thought—e.g., *like, as, similarly, equally, just as, unlike, however, but, although, conversely, on the other hand, on the contrary*

- **Summary order**: indicating that a particular idea is coming to a close—e.g., *in conclusion, to sum up, in other words, ultimately, above all*

Style, Structure, Mood, and Tone

Readers should be able to identify and analyze the components of a writer's **style**. Think about someone's fashion style—a person might dress casually or formally; they might wear trendy clothes or classic clothes; they might prefer simple looks or flashy ones. And the way a person styles their fashion often determines the impression they give to other people. Similarly, writers combine elements of structure, diction, and figurative and connotative language to create their own style.

Structure refers to how a writer organizes ideas. In literature, a text may be either *prose* or *poetry*. Poetry relies on careful word choice (especially in terms of sound and emotional meaning) and rhythm in order to communicate a special feeling or idea. Contrary to the popular assumption, poetry doesn't have to rhyme or follow a strict structure. In fact, there are two types of poetic form: **open form** and **closed form**. In closed form, the poet follows a predictable and repetitive structure, perhaps by using a fixed number of syllables in each line or repeating the same rhyme scheme.

Examples of closed-form structure include sonnets and haiku, both of which require the poet to follow an established pattern of rhythm or rhyme. Open-form poetry doesn't have restrictions on length, the number of syllables or pattern of stress in each line (also known as meter), or the rhyme pattern. Open-form poetry has a structure, but it's more flexible and open to the creative whims of the poet. When a poet uses open form, changes in structure can reflect changes in emotion. For example, if a poem starts out with blunt, brief lines but then develops into long and complex lines, it might represent the speaker becoming more open and expressive of emotions that they had previously been reluctant to share.

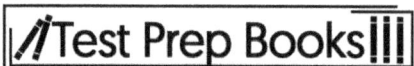

Prose is regular written language without any meter or rhythmic form. Literary prose includes novels, short stories, and memoirs. An author may choose prose over poetry when they want to communicate in colloquial language, or when they want to convey information that is more straightforward (but of course, both poetry and prose can be emotional and creative). It's also possible to combine prose and poetry. In Shakespeare's plays, for example, some characters speak in metered lines while other characters speak in prose. This separation may indicate the topic under discussion.

For example, in *Julius Caesar*, Brutus' speech is in prose, while Marc Antony's speech is written in iambic pentameter, a common poetic meter. Antony's speech begins with "Friends, Romans, countrymen, lend me your ears; / I come to bury Caesar, not to praise him." The cadence and stress of the language in Antony's speech makes for a more powerful listening device compared to Brutus' opening, "Romans, countrymen, and friends! Listen to my reasons and be silent so you can hear." In this way, employing prose or poetry can influence the impression that readers get from a text or drama. The crowd, in *Julius Caesar*, is persuaded by Marc Antony's speech in the end, for all its rhetorical glory.

There are also different story structures, or ways for the writer to present their narrative. A story can be either **linear** (told in the same order that events happened) or **non-linear** (the events are presented to the reader out of order). In a non-linear structure, the author may use flashbacks, when the timeline of the story shifts backwards to reveal earlier events. Non-linear storytelling is common in mystery or suspense writing, where the author keeps some information or events hidden from the reader until later in the story.

An author's style can also come from *diction*, or word choice. Just like a person's fashion style can be casual or formal depending on the event, an author's writing style can be anywhere from conversational to academic, elevated to colloquial, reflecting the audience and subject matter. For example, a chemistry textbook is going to contain more academic language and scientific terminology than a newspaper article, which is likely to contain common expressions and easier vocabulary. **Colloquial language** refers to the informal language of normal speech, and may include elements of non-standard pronunciation or grammar (words like "y'all," for example). Colloquialisms can often be found in "local color" pieces where the writer wants the reader to feel directly involved in the everyday lives and conversations of people or characters in the text.

Diction also contributes to the *tone* of the text. Keys to recognizing an author's tone include paying attention to any connotative or emotional language as well as what types of details and information are included (or if any important information seems to be missing). If an article about a proposal to build a new highway only includes information about how the highway will increase traffic congestion and negatively impact the environment, readers can feel the author's critical tone towards the subject. On the other hand, if the article also mentions research about how the highway could direct more customers to local businesses and boost the town's economy, the author's tone will probably seem more balanced.

A text's **mood** is the general feeling or atmosphere created by the author's descriptions and imagery (and, again, it relies on diction and selection of details). **Imagery** refers to all of the details in a text that appeal to any of the five senses; it's how the author helps draw a picture in the reader's mind. Imagine a story that starts with, "It was a dark and stormy night..." and includes descriptions of the howling wind outside, the dim flicker of candlelight, the mysterious creak of unknown footsteps coming upstairs. All of this imagery comes together to create a mood of creepiness and mystery.

Literary Devices

A **rhetorical device** is the phrasing and presentation of an idea that reinforces and emphasizes a point in an argument. A rhetorical device is often quite memorable. One of the more famous uses of a rhetorical device is in John F. Kennedy's 1961 inaugural address: "Ask not what your country can do for you, ask what you can do for your

Language Arts: Reading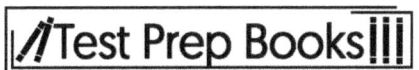

country." The contrast of ideas presented in the phrasing is an example of the rhetorical device of antimetabole. Some other common examples are provided below, but test takers should be aware that this is not a complete list.

Device	Definition	Example
Alliteration	Repeating the same beginning sound or letter in a phrase for emphasis	The busy baby babbled.
Allusion	A reference to a famous person, event, or significant literary text as a form of significant comparison	"We are apt to shut our eyes against a painful truth, and listen to the song of that siren till she transforms us into beasts." Patrick Henry
Anaphora	The repetition of the same words at the beginning of successive words, phrases, or clauses, designed to emphasize an idea	"We shall not flag or fail. We shall go on to the end. We shall fight in France, we shall fight on the seas and oceans, we shall fight with growing confidence ... we shall fight in the fields and in the streets, we shall fight in the hills. We shall never surrender." Winston Churchill
Antithesis	A part of speech where a contrast of ideas is expressed by a pair of words that are opposite of each other.	"That's one small step for man, one giant leap for mankind." Neil Armstrong
Foreshadowing	Giving an indication that something is going to happen later in the story	I wasn't aware at the time, but I would come to regret those words.
Hyperbole	Using exaggeration not meant to be taken literally	The girl weighed less than a feather.
Idiom	Using words with predictable meanings to create a phrase with a different meaning	The world is your oyster.
Imagery	Appealing to the senses by using descriptive language	The sky was painted with red and pink and streaked with orange.
Metaphor	Comparing two things as if they are the same	He was a giant teddy bear.
Onomatopoeia	Using words that imitate sound	The tire went off with a bang and a crunch.
Parallelism	A syntactical similarity in a structure or series of structures used for impact of an idea, making it memorable	"A penny saved is a penny earned." Ben Franklin
Personification	Attributing human characteristics to an object or an animal	The house glowered menacingly with a dark smile.

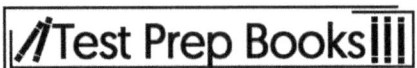

Language Arts: Reading

Device	Definition	Example
Rhetorical question	A question posed that is not answered by the writer though there is a desired response, most often designed to emphasize a point	"Can anyone look at our reduced standing in the world today and say, 'Let's have four more years of this?'" Ronald Reagan
Simile	Comparing two things using "like" or "as"	Her hair was like gold.
Symbolism	Using symbols to represent ideas and provide a different meaning	The ring represented the bond between us.
Understatement	A statement meant to portray a situation as less important than it actually is to create an ironic effect	"The war in the Pacific has not necessarily developed in Japan's favor." Emperor Hirohito, surrendering Japan in World War II

Sarcasm

Depending on the tone of voice or the words used, sarcasm can be expressed in many different ways. **Sarcasm** is defined as a bitter or ambiguous declaration that intends to cut or taunt. Most of the ways we use sarcasm is saying something and not really meaning it. In a way, sarcasm is a contradiction that is understood by both the speaker and the listener to convey the opposite meaning. For example, let's say Bobby is struggling to learn how to play the trumpet. His sister, Gloria, walks in and tells him: "What a great trumpet player you've become!" This is a sort of verbal irony known as sarcasm. Gloria is speaking a contradiction, but Bobby and Gloria both know the truth behind what she's saying: that Bobby is not a good trumpet player. Sarcasm can also be accompanied by nonverbal language, such as a smirk or a head tilt. Remember that sarcasm is not always clear to the listener; sometimes sarcasm can be expressed by the speaker but lost on the listener.

Irony

Irony is a device that authors use when pitting two contrasting items or ideas against each other in order to create an effect. It's frequently used when an author wants to employ humor or convey a sarcastic tone. Additionally, it's often used in fictional works to build tension between characters, or between a particular character and the reader. An author may use **verbal irony** (sarcasm), **situational irony** (where actions or events have the opposite effect than what's expected), and **dramatic irony** (where the reader knows something a character does not). Examples of irony include:

- Dramatic Irony: An author describing the presence of a hidden killer in a murder mystery, unbeknownst to the characters but known to the reader.

- Situational Irony: An author relating the tale of a fire captain who loses her home in a five-alarm conflagration.

- Verbal Irony: This is where an author or character says one thing but means another. For example, telling a police officer "Thanks a lot" after receiving a ticket.

Understatement

Making an **understatement** means making a statement that gives the illusion of something being smaller than it actually is. Understatement is used, in some instances, as a humorous rhetorical device. Let's say that there are two friends. One of the friends, Kate, meets the other friend's, Jasmine's, boyfriend. Jasmine's boyfriend, in Kate's opinion, is attractive, funny, and intelligent. After Kate meets her friend's boyfriend, Kate says to Jasmine, "You could do worse." Kate and Jasmine both know from Kate's tone that this means Kate is being ironic—Jasmine could do much, much worse, because her boyfriend is considered a "good catch." The understatement was a rhetorical device used by Kate to let Jasmine know she approves.

Synthesis and Generalization

Drawing Conclusions and Making Generalizations

As readers are presented with new information, they should organize it, make sense of it, and reflect on what they learned from the text. Readers draw conclusions at the end of a text by bringing together all of the details, descriptions, facts, and/or opinions presented by the author and asking, "What did I gain from reading this text? How have my ideas or emotions changed? What was the author's overall purpose for writing?" In this case, a **conclusion** is a unifying idea or final thought about the text that the reader can form after they are done reading. As discussed earlier, sometimes writers are very explicit in stating what conclusions should be drawn from a text and what readers are meant to have learned. However, more often than not, writers simply present descriptions or information and then leave it up to readers to draw their own conclusions. As with making inferences, though, readers always need to base their conclusions on textual evidence rather than simply guessing or making random statements.

> When the school district's uniform policy was first introduced fifteen years ago, parents and students alike were incredibly enthusiastic about it. Some of the most appealing arguments in favor of enforcing school uniforms was to create an equal learning environment for all students, to eliminate the focus on fashion and appearance, and to simplify students' morning routine by removing the need to pick a different outfit every day. However, despite this promising beginning, the uniform policy has steadily lost favor over the years. First of all, schools did not notice a significant drop in examples of bullying at school, and students continue to report that they feel judged on their appearance based on things like weight and hairstyle. This seems to indicate that uniforms have not been particularly effective at removing the social pressure that teens feel to appear a certain way in front of their peers. Also, many parents have complained that the school's required uniform pieces like jackets, sweaters, and neckties can only be purchased from one specific clothing shop. Because this retailer has cornered the market on school uniforms, they are operating under a total monopoly, and disgruntled parents feel that they are being grossly overcharged for school clothing for their children. The uniform policy is set to be debated at the upcoming school board meeting, and many expect it to be overturned.

After reading this article, a reader might conclude any of the following: that ideas that start with popular support might become unpopular over time; or that there are several compelling counterarguments to the benefits of school uniforms; or that this school district is open to new ideas but also open to criticism. While each conclusion is slightly different, they are all based on information and evidence from the article, and therefore all are plausible. Each conclusion sums up what the reader learned from the passage and what overall idea the writer seems to be communicating.

Another way for readers to make sense of information in a text is to make **generalizations**. This is somewhat related to the concept of inductive reasoning, by which readers move from specific evidence to a more general idea. When readers generalize, they take the specific content of a text and apply it to a larger context or to a different situation. Let's make a generalization from the topic, the bystander effect:

> A bystander is simply a person who watches something happen. Paradoxically, the more people who witness an accident happen, the less likely each individual is to actually intervene and offer assistance. This is known as the bystander effect. Psychologists attribute the bystander effect to something called "diffusion of responsibility." If one individual witnesses an accident, that single person feels the whole burden of responsibility to respond to the accident. However, if there are many witnesses, each person feels that

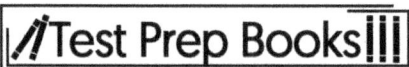

Language Arts: Reading

responsibility has been divided amongst many people, so their individual sense of responsibility is much lower and they are less likely to offer help.

This article describes one very specific psychological phenomenon known as the "bystander effect." However, based on this specific information, a reader could form a more general psychological statement such as, "Humans sometimes behave differently when they are alone and when they are in a group."

It's also possible to make generalizations from literary texts. This is a particularly useful reading skill when evaluating the collective works of a particular writer or when forming a general characterization of texts from a particular genre or time period. For example, after reading a handful of novels by Jane Austen, all of which feature clever female protagonists and contain several examples of cynical or unflattering depictions of marriage, a reader can form a general impression of Jane Austen's thoughts on women's social roles. An overarching generalization from these novels might be that, "Education is just as important for women as marriage," or "Marriage isn't a guarantee of happiness or satisfaction." Being able to form generalizations is an important step in drawing connections and establishing relationships between texts.

Making Predictions

When readers make **predictions**, they try to anticipate what will happen next in the text. Think about how weather forecasters make predictions for future weather conditions. It's not purely guesswork. Rather, they gather a wide variety of relevant data, analyze the information they've collected, and also compare it with previous weather patterns. Finally, they're able to make a well-researched prediction with a high rate of probability. Readers must do the same when making predictions in a text—rather than simply guessing, they draw information from earlier in the text and use preexisting knowledge to form a prediction that's reasonably likely to be true.

In literary texts, authors tend to give clues that guide readers through the narrative. One method is *foreshadowing*, where the author hints at what will happen next in the story. Consider this line from *Romeo and Juliet* in which Juliet desires to learn more about Romeo.

She says to her nurse:

> Go ask his name.—If he be married.
>
> My grave is like to be my wedding bed.

At this point in the play, Juliet's lines simply mean that she would be sorely disappointed to learn that Romeo was already attached to another woman. However, for readers who already know how the play ends, this sentence carries another level of meaning—Juliet's marital choices will go hand in hand with her death. In this way, Shakespeare foreshadows the tragic end of Juliet's love story at the very moment it begins.

Of course, authors sometimes give false hints that lead readers to dead ends. This type of misdirection is especially commonplace in genres like mystery and suspense, where the author wants to keep the reader guessing until the very end. A distracting hint that turns out to be false is known as a **red herring**. However, if readers are aware that certain genres are likely to contain red herrings, then readers can be more cautious in evaluating hints. If a clue seems too obvious, it might be a red herring! In a roundabout way, then, red herrings can actually *help* readers make predictions by forcing them to look beyond the most obvious details.

In addition to clues sprinkled throughout the text, readers can also make predictions by considering the tone and mood of a text. For example, if a story has an overall gloomy mood or its diction creates a tone that is melancholy and foreboding, readers will expect that dark or depressing events will follow. On the other hand, if the tone is playful and lighthearted, readers are less likely to expect tragedy and might instead predict a comic or happy outcome. If the outcome of the story is vastly different from what either readers or the story's characters themselves are expecting, the author is probably using irony.

It's also possible to make predictions in non-literary texts. Consider a persuasive article that opens with the following thesis statement:

> There are countless reasons why closing down the city's only public dog park is a bad idea for local citizens.

Readers can expect that the rest of the essay will contain evidence that supports the author's opinion. The same is also true of informative texts. Imagine a scientific article that contains this sentence:

> Surprising new evidence challenges long-held beliefs about the cognitive capabilities of non-human animals.

In the paragraphs that follow, readers might expect to find any of the following: background on previously accepted theories of animal cognition, description of new scientific research or experimentation, and interpretation and discussion of the experiment's results. By making these predictions whenever they encounter a new text, readers will be more prepared to understand new information and opinions. Also, making predictions about information is especially useful when readers have a limited amount of time to read a text for relevant details. By reading either the thesis statement of the article or the topic sentences of each paragraph, readers can then make logical predictions about what information might be discussed later without having to read the entire text first.

Compare and Contrast

In order to understand the relationship between ideas, readers should be able to *compare* and *contrast*. Comparing two things means identifying their similarities, while contrasting two things means finding their differences. Recall the excerpt from "The Lamb" by William Blake:

> Little lamb, who made thee?
> Dost thou know who made thee,
> Gave thee life, and bid thee feed
> By the stream and o'er the mead;
> Gave thee clothing of delight,
> Softest clothing, woolly, bright;
> Gave thee such a tender voice,
> Making all the vales rejoice?
> Little lamb, who made thee?
> Dost thou know who made thee?

Consider that poem alongside an excerpt from another work by Blake called "The Tyger."

> Tyger! Tyger! burning bright
> In the forests of the night,
> What immortal hand or eye
> Could frame thy fearful symmetry?
> […]
> What the hammer? what the chain?
> In what furnace was thy brain?
> What the anvil? what dread grasp
> Dare its deadly terrors clasp?
> When the stars threw down their spears,
> And watered heaven with their tears,

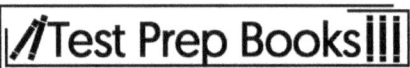

Did he smile his work to see?
Did he who made the Lamb make thee?

These poems have quite a few things in common. Each poem's subject is an animal—a lamb and a tiger, respectively—and each poem addresses the same question to the animal: "Who created you?" In fact, both poems are formed primarily of questions.

However, the poems also exhibit many differences. For example, it's easy to contrast the tone and word choice in each poem. Whereas "The Lamb" uses words with positive and gentle connotations to create a tone of innocence and serenity, "The Tyger" gives a completely different impression. Some strongly connotative words that stand out include "night," "fearful," and "deadly terrors," all of which contribute to a tone that is tense and full of danger.

The two poems address the same question from two different perspectives: who created the world and all of its creatures? "The Lamb" considers all of the sweet and delightful things that exist, leaving "The Tyger" to ponder the problem of why evil exists. In fact, Blake relies on the contrast between the two poems to fully communicate his dilemma over the paradox of creation—"Did he who make the Lamb make thee?" Although the poems present a strong contrast to one another, it's also possible to find similarities in their subject matter.

Authors often intentionally use contrast in order to ask readers to delve deeper into the qualities of the two things being compared. When an author deliberately places two things (characters, settings, etc.) side-by-side for readers to compare, it's known as *juxtaposition*. An example of juxtaposition can be found in Emily Bronte's *Wuthering Heights*, a novel in which the protagonist Cathy is caught in a love triangle between two romantic interests, Heathcliff and Edgar Linton, who are complete opposites. Cathy compares her feelings for each man in her memorable speech:

> My love for Linton is like the foliage in the woods: time will change it, I'm well aware, as winter changes the trees. My love for Heathcliff resembles the eternal rocks beneath: a source of little visible delight, but necessary. Nelly, I *am* Heathcliff! He's always, always in my mind: not as a pleasure, any more than I am always a pleasure to myself, but as my own being.

When these two characters are placed next to each other, it's easier for readers to grasp their notable characteristics. Edgar is gentle and sophisticated in comparison to Heathcliff, who is rough and wild. Here, Cathy also juxtaposes her feelings about each character. Her love for Edgar is fresh and harmless, like the new spring leaves on trees; but come winter, it will fade away. Her love for Heathcliff might be less conventionally appealing, like the rocks that form the earth; but, just like those rocks, that love forms the foundation of Cathy's being and is essential to her life. By juxtaposing these two men, Cathy is better able to express her thoughts about them.

Analyzing Information From Multiple Sources

When professors ask students to write a thesis, they expect students to base their essay on more than one source of information. When scholars delve into a research project, they too consult more than one source. In any academic endeavor, it's essential to look to *many* sources of information to get a comprehensive and well-rounded view of the subject matter. Getting information from multiple texts, though, requires readers to synthesize their content—that is, to combine ideas from various sources and express it in an organized way.

In order to synthetize information, readers first need to understand the relationship between the different sources. One way to do so is comparing and contrasting, as described above. Comparison and contrast is also useful in evaluating non-literary sources. For example, if readers want to learn more about a controversial issue, they might decide to read articles from both sides of the argument, compare differences in the arguments on each side, and identify any areas of overlap or agreement. This will allow readers to arrive at a more balanced conclusion.

In addition to synthesizing information from persuasive sources with different opinions, readers can also combine information from different types of texts—for example, from entertaining and informative texts. Readers who are interested in medieval religious life in Europe, for example, might read a text on medieval history by modern academics, a sociological research article about the role of religion in society, and a piece of literature from the Middle Ages such as Chaucer's *The Canterbury Tales*. By reading fiction from that time period, readers can look at one writer's perspective on religious activities in their world; and by reading non-fiction texts by modern researchers, readers can further enhance their background knowledge of the subject.

Practice Quiz

Questions 1–5 are based upon the following passage:

> Three years ago, I think there were not many bird-lovers in the United States who believed it possible to prevent the total extinction of both egrets from our fauna. All the known rookeries accessible to plume-hunters had been totally destroyed. Two years ago, the secret discovery of several small, hidden colonies prompted William Dutcher, President of the National Association of Audubon Societies, and Mr. T. Gilbert Pearson, Secretary, to attempt the protection of those colonies. With a fund contributed for the purpose, wardens were hired and duly commissioned. As previously stated, one of those wardens was shot dead in cold blood by a plume hunter. The task of guarding swamp rookeries from the attacks of money-hungry desperadoes, to whom the accursed plumes were worth their weight in gold, is a very chancy proceeding. There is now one warden in Florida who says that "before they get my rookery they will first have to get me."
>
> Thus far, the protective work of the Audubon Association has been successful. Now there are 20 colonies, which contain, all told, about 5,000 egrets and about 120,000 herons and ibises which are guarded by the Audubon wardens. One of the most important is on Bird Island, a mile out in Orange Lake, Central Florida, and it is ably defended by Oscar E. Baynard. To-day, the plume hunters who do not dare to raid the guarded rookeries are trying to study out the lines of flight of the birds, to and from their feeding-grounds, and shoot them in transit. Their motto is "Anything to beat the law, and get the plumes." It is there that the state of Florida should take part in the war.
>
> The success of this campaign is attested by the fact that last year a number of egrets were seen in eastern Massachusetts—for the first time in many years. And so to-day the question is, can the wardens continue to hold the plume-hunters at bay?

Excerpt from *Our Vanishing Wildlife* by William T. Hornaday

1. The author's use of first-person pronouns in the following text does NOT have which of the following effects? Three years ago, I think there were not many bird-lovers in the United States who believed it possible to prevent the total extinction of both egrets from our fauna.

    a. The phrase *I think* acts as a sort of hedging, where the author's tone is less direct and/or absolute.
    b. It allows the reader to more easily connect with the author.
    c. It encourages the reader to empathize with the egrets.
    d. It distances the reader from the text by overemphasizing the story.

2. What is on Bird Island?
    a. Hunters selling plumes
    b. An important bird colony
    c. Bird Island Battle between the hunters and the wardens
    d. An important egret with unique plumes

3. What is the main purpose of the passage?
    a. To persuade the audience to act in preservation of the bird colonies
    b. To show the effect hunting egrets has had on the environment
    c. To argue that the preservation of bird colonies has had a negative impact on the environment
    d. To demonstrate the success of the protective work of the Audubon Association

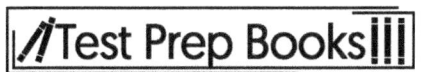

Language Arts: Reading

4. According to the passage, why are hunters trying to study the lines of flight of the birds?
    a. To study ornithology, which requires knowing the lines of flight that birds take
    b. To help wardens preserve the lives of the birds
    c. To have a better opportunity to hunt the birds
    d. To build their homes under the lines of flight because they believe it brings good luck

5. As it is used in the first paragraph, the word *commissioned* most nearly means:
    a. Appointed
    b. Compelled
    c. Beguiled
    d. Fortified

See answers on the next page.

Answer Explanations

1. D: The use of "I" could serve to have a "hedging" effect, allow the reader to connect with the author in a more personal way, and cause the reader to empathize more with the egrets. However, it doesn't distance the reader from the text, making Choice D the answer to this question.

2. B: Bird Island is home to an important bird colony. The previous sentence is describing "20 colonies" of birds, so what follows should be a bird colony. Choice A may be true, but we have no evidence of this in the text. Choice C does touch on the tension between the hunters and wardens, but there is no official "Bird Island Battle" mentioned in the text. Choice D does not exist in the text.

3. D: The main purpose of the passage is the text mentions several different times how and why the Audubon Association has been successful and gives examples to back this fact. Choice A is incorrect because the passage doesn't mention the need for people to take action. Likewise, Choices B and C are not mentioned in the text.

4. C: To have a better opportunity to hunt the birds. Choice A might be true in a general sense, but it is not relevant to the context of the text. Choice B is incorrect because the hunters are not studying lines of flight to help wardens, but to hunt birds. Choice D is incorrect because nothing in the text mentions that hunters are trying to build homes underneath lines of flight of birds for good luck.

5. A: The word *commissioned* most nearly means *appointed*. Choice B, *compelled*, means forced. Choice C, *beguiled*, means entertained. Choice D, *fortified*, means defended.

Language Arts: Writing

Organization of Ideas

Good writing is not merely a random collection of sentences. No matter how well written, sentences must relate and coordinate appropriately with one another. If not, the writing seems random, haphazard, and disorganized. Therefore, good writing must be organized, where each sentence fits a larger context and relates to the sentences around it.

Even if the writer includes plenty of information to support their point, the writing is only coherent when the information is in a logical order. **Logical sequencing** is really just common sense, but it's an important writing technique. First, the writer should introduce the main idea, whether for a paragraph, a section, or the entire piece. Second, they should present evidence to support the main idea by using transitional language. This shows the reader how the information relates to the main idea and the sentences around it. The writer should then take time to interpret the information, making sure necessary connections are obvious to the reader. Finally, the writer can summarize the information in a closing section.

Note: Though most writing follows this pattern, it isn't a set rule. Sometimes writers change the order for effect. For example, the writer can begin with a surprising piece of supporting information to grab the reader's attention, and then transition to the main idea. Thus, if a passage doesn't follow the logical order, don't immediately assume it's wrong. However, most writing usually settles into a logical sequence after a nontraditional beginning.

Introductions and Conclusions

Examining the writer's strategies for introductions and conclusions puts the reader in the right mindset to interpret the rest of the text. Look for methods the writer might use for **introductions** such as:

- Stating the main point immediately, followed by outlining how the rest of the piece supports this claim.

- Establishing important, smaller pieces of the main idea first, and then grouping these points into a case for the main idea.

- Opening with a quotation, anecdote, question, seeming paradox, or other piece of interesting information, and then using it to lead to the main point.

- Whatever method the writer chooses, the introduction should make their intention clear, establish their voice as a credible one, and encourage a person to continue reading.

Conclusions tend to follow a similar pattern. In them, the writer restates their main idea a final time, often after summarizing the smaller pieces of that idea. If the introduction uses a quote or anecdote to grab the reader's attention, the conclusion often makes reference to it again. Whatever way the writer chooses to arrange the conclusion, the final restatement of the main idea should be clear and simple for the reader to interpret. Finally, conclusions shouldn't introduce any new information.

Relevance of Content

A reader must be able to evaluate the argument or point the author is trying to make and determine if it is adequately supported. The first step is to determine the main idea. The **main idea** is what the author wants to say about a specific topic. The next step is to locate the supporting details. An author uses **supporting details** to illustrate the main idea. These are the details that provide evidence or examples to help make a point. Supporting details often appear in the form of quotations, paraphrasing, or analysis. Test takers should then examine the text to make sure the author connects details and analysis to the main point. These steps are crucial to understanding the text and evaluating how well the author presents their argument and evidence. The following graphic demonstrates the connection between the main idea and the supporting details.

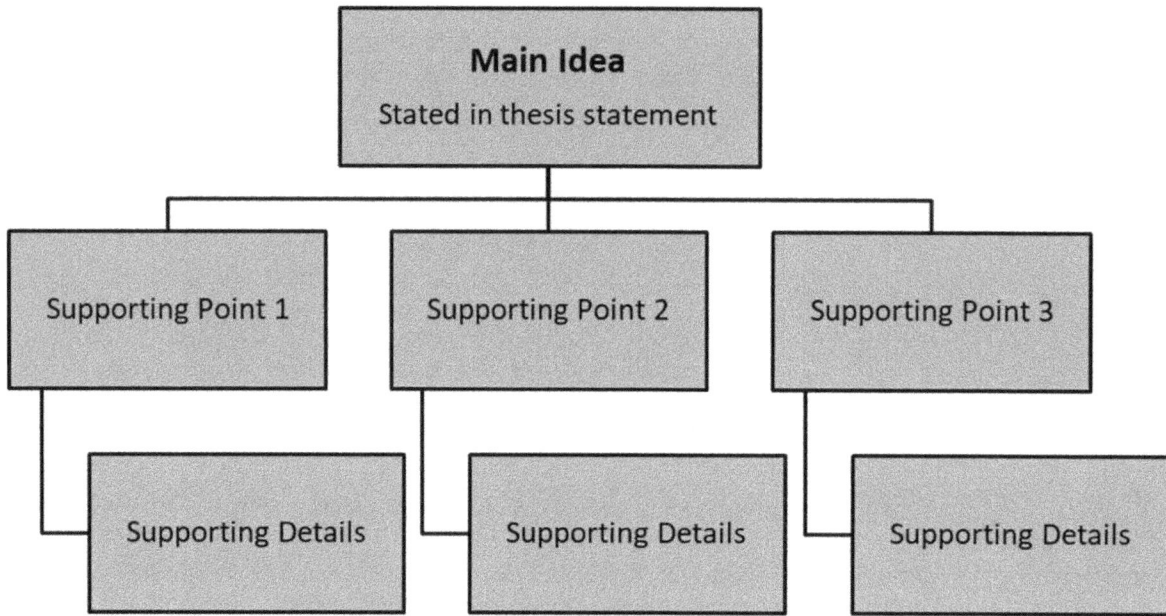

It is important to evaluate the author's supporting details to be sure that they are credible, provide evidence of the author's point, and directly support the main idea. Critical readers examine the facts used to support an author's argument and check those facts against other sources to be sure they are correct. They also check the validity of the sources used to be sure those sources are credible, academic, and/or peer reviewed. A strong argument uses valid, measurable facts to support ideas.

Analyzing Organizational Structure

Depending on what the author is attempting to accomplish, certain formats or text structures work better than others. For example, a sequence structure might work for narration but not for identifying similarities and differences between concepts. Similarly, a comparison-contrast structure is not useful for narration. It's the author's job to put the right information in the correct format.

Readers should be familiar with the five main literary structures:

1. **Sequence structure** (sometimes referred to as the order structure) is when the order of events proceed in a predictable order. In many cases, this means the text goes through the plot elements: exposition, rising action, climax, falling action, and resolution. Readers are introduced to characters, setting, and conflict in the exposition. In the rising action, there's an increase in tension and suspense. The climax is the height of tension and the point of no return. Tension decreases during the falling action. In the resolution, any conflicts presented in the exposition are solved, and the story concludes. An informative text that is structured sequentially will often go in order from one step to the next.

2. In the **problem-solution structure**, authors identify a potential problem and suggest a solution. This form of writing is usually divided into two paragraphs and can be found in informational texts. For example, cell phone, cable, and satellite providers use this structure in manuals to help customers troubleshoot or identify problems with services or products.

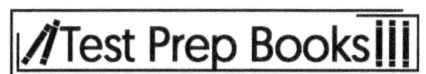

Language Arts: Writing

3. When authors want to discuss similarities and differences between separate concepts, they arrange thoughts in a **comparison-contrast paragraph structure**. **Venn diagrams** are an effective graphic organizer for comparison-contrast structures because they feature two overlapping circles that can be used to organize similarities and differences. A comparison-contrast essay organizes one paragraph based on similarities and another based on differences. A comparison-contrast essay can also be arranged with the similarities and differences of individual traits addressed within individual paragraphs. Words such as *however*, *but*, and *nevertheless* help signal a contrast in ideas.

4. **Descriptive writing** structure is designed to appeal to your senses. Much like an artist who constructs a painting, good descriptive writing builds an image in the reader's mind by appealing to the five senses: sight, hearing, taste, touch, and smell. However, overly descriptive writing can become tedious; whereas sparse descriptions can make settings and characters seem flat. Good authors strike a balance by applying descriptions only to passages, characters, and settings that are integral to the plot.

5. Passages that use the **cause and effect structure** are simply asking *why* by demonstrating some type of connection between ideas. Words such as *if, since, because, then, or consequently* indicate a cause-and-effect relationship. By switching the order of a complex sentence, the writer can rearrange the emphasis on different clauses. Saying, *If Sheryl is late, we'll miss the dance*, is different from saying *We'll miss the dance if Sheryl is late*. One emphasizes Sheryl's tardiness while the other emphasizes missing the dance. Paragraphs can also be arranged in a cause and effect format. Since the format—before and after—is sequential, it is useful when authors wish to discuss the impact of choices. Researchers often apply this paragraph structure to the scientific method.

Forming Paragraphs

A good *paragraph* should have the following characteristics:

- Be logical with organized sentences
- Have a *unified* purpose within itself
- Use sentences as *building blocks*
- Be a *distinct section* of a piece of writing
- Present a *single theme* introduced by a *topic sentence*
- Maintain a *consistent flow* through subsequent, relevant, well-placed sentences
- *Tell a story* of its own or have its own purpose, yet connect with what is written before and after
- Enlighten, entertain, and/or inform

Though certainly not set in stone, the length should be a consideration for the reader's sake, not merely for the sake of the topic. When paragraphs are especially short, the reader might experience an irregular, uneven effect; when they're much longer than 250 words, the reader's attention span, and probably their retention, is challenged. While a paragraph can technically be a sentence long, a good rule of thumb is for paragraphs to be at least three sentences long and no more than ten sentence long. An optimal word length is 100 to 250 words.

Recognizing Logical Transitions

The writer should act as a guide, showing the reader how all the sentences fit together. Consider this example concerning seat belts:

> Seat belts save more lives than any other automobile safety feature. Many studies show that airbags save lives as well. Not all cars have airbags. Many older cars don't. Air bags aren't entirely reliable. Studies show that in 15 percent of accidents, airbags don't deploy as designed. Seat belt malfunctions are extremely rare.

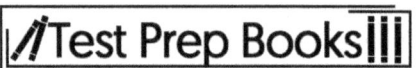

Language Arts: Writing

There's nothing wrong with any of these sentences individually, but together they're disjointed and difficult to follow. The best way for the writer to communicate information is through the use of transition words. Here are examples of transition words and phrases that tie sentences together, enabling a more natural flow:

- To show causality: *as a result*, *therefore*, and *consequently*
- To compare and contrast: *however*, *but*, and *on the other hand*
- To introduce examples: *for example*, *namely*, and *including*
- To show order of importance: *foremost*, *primarily*, *secondly*, and *lastly*

Note that this is not a complete list of transitions. There are many more that can be used; however, most fit into these or similar categories. The important point is that the words should clearly show the relationship between sentences, supporting information, and the main idea.

Here is an update to the previous example using transition words. These changes make it easier to read and bring clarity to the writer's points:

> Seat belts save more lives than any other automobile safety feature. Many studies show that airbags save lives as well; however, not all cars have airbags. For example, some older cars don't. Furthermore, air bags aren't entirely reliable. For example, studies show that in 15 percent of accidents, airbags don't deploy as designed, but, on the other hand, seat belt malfunctions are extremely rare.

Also, be prepared to analyze whether the writer is using the best transition word or phrase for the situation. Take this sentence for example: "As a result, seat belt malfunctions are extremely rare." This sentence doesn't make sense in the context above because the writer is trying to show the contrast between seat belts and airbags, not the causality.

Language Facility

Sentence Fluency

Learning and utilizing the mechanics of structure will encourage effective, professional results, and adding some creativity will elevate one's writing to a higher level.

First, let's review the basic elements of sentences.

A **sentence** is a set of words that make up a grammatical unit. The words must have certain elements and be spoken or written in a specific order to constitute a complete sentence that makes sense.

> 1. A sentence must have a *subject* (a noun or noun phrase). The subject tells whom or what the sentence is addressing (i.e., what it is about).
>
> 2. A sentence must have an *action* or *state of being* (*a verb*). To reiterate: A verb forms the main part of the predicate of a sentence. This means that it explains what the noun is doing.
>
> 3. A sentence must convey a complete thought.

Sometimes a sentence has two ideas that work together. For example, say the writer wants to make the following points:

> Seat belt laws have saved an estimated 50,000 lives.
>
> More lives are saved by seat belts every year.

Language Arts: Writing

These two ideas are directly related and appear to be of equal importance. Therefore they can be joined with a simple "and" as follows:

Seat belt laws have saved an estimated 50,000 lives, and more lives are saved by seat belts every year.

The word *and* in the sentence helps the two ideas work together or, in other words, it "coordinates" them. It also serves as a junction where the two ideas come together, better known as a **conjunction**. Therefore, the word *and* is known as a **coordinating conjunction** (a word that helps bring two equal ideas together). Now that the ideas are joined together by a conjunction, they are known as **clauses**. Other coordinating conjunctions include *or*, *but*, and *so*.

Sometimes, however, two ideas in a sentence are *not* of equal importance:

Seat belt laws have saved an estimated 50,000 lives.

Many more lives could be saved with stronger federal seat belt laws.

In this case, combining the two with a coordinating conjunction (*and*) creates an awkward sentence:

Seat belt laws have saved an estimated 50,000 lives, and many more lives could be saved with stronger federal seat belt laws.

Now the writer uses a word to show the reader which clause is the most important (or the "boss") of the sentence:

Although seat belt laws have saved an estimated 50,000 lives, many more lives could be saved with stronger federal seat belt laws.

In this example, the second clause is the key point that the writer wants to make, and the first clause works to set up that point. Since the first clause "works for" the second, it's called the **subordinate clause**. The word *although* tells the reader that this idea isn't as important as the clause that follows. This word is called the **subordinating conjunction**. Other subordinating conjunctions include *after*, *because*, *if*, *since*, *unless*, and many more. As mentioned before, it's easy to spot subordinate clauses because they don't stand on their own (as shown in this previous example):

Although seat belt laws have saved an estimated 50,000 lives.

This is not a complete thought. It needs the other clause (called the **independent clause**) to make sense. On the test, when asked to choose the best subordinating conjunction for a sentence, look at the surrounding text. Choose the word that best allows the sentence to support the writer's argument.

Conjunctions are vital words that connect words, phrases, thoughts, and ideas. Conjunctions show relationships between components. There are two types: coordinating and subordinating.

Coordinating conjunctions are the primary class of conjunctions placed between words, phrases, clauses, and sentences that are of equal grammatical rank; the coordinating conjunctions are *for*, *and*, *nor*, *but*, *or*, *yet*, and *so*. A useful memorization trick is to remember that all the first letters of these conjunctions collectively spell the word *fanboys*.

I need to go shopping, *but* I must be careful to leave enough money in the bank.
She wore a black, red, *and* white shirt.

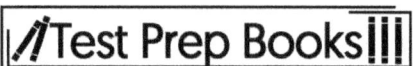

Subordinating conjunctions are the secondary class of conjunctions. They connect two unequal parts, one main (or independent) and the other subordinate (or dependent). I must go to the store *even though* I do not have enough money in the bank.

Because I read the review, I do not want to go to the movie.

Notice that the presence of subordinating conjunctions makes clauses dependent. *I read the review* is an independent clause, but *because* makes the clause dependent. Thus, it needs an independent clause to complete the sentence.

Parallel Structure

Parallel structure usually has to do with lists. Look at the following sentence and spot the mistake:

Increased seat belt legislation has been supported by the automotive industry, the insurance industry, and doctors.

Many people don't see anything wrong, but the word *doctors* breaks the sentence's parallel structure. The previous items in the list refer to an industry as a singular noun, so every item in the list must follow that same format:

Increased seat belt legislation has been supported by the automotive industry, the insurance industry, and the healthcare industry.

Another common mistake in parallel structure might look like this:

Before the accident, Maria enjoyed swimming, running, and played soccer.

Here, the words "played soccer" break the parallel structure. To correct it, the writer must change the final item in the list to match the format of the previous two:

Before the accident, Maria enjoyed swimming, running, and playing soccer.

Types of Sentences

All sentences contain the same basic elements: a subject and a verb. The **subject** is who or what the sentence is about; the **verb** describes the subject's action or condition. However, these elements, subjects and verbs, can be combined in different ways. The following graphic describes the different types of sentence structures.

Sentence Structure	Independent Clauses	Dependent Clauses
Simple	1	0
Compound	2 or more	0
Complex	1	1 or more
Compound-Complex	2 or more	1 or more

A **simple sentence** expresses a complete thought and consists of one subject and verb combination:

The children ate pizza.

The subject is *children*. The verb is *ate*.

Either the subject or the verb may be *compound*—that is, it could have more than one element:

The children and their parents ate pizza.

The children *ate pizza and watched a movie.*

All of these are still simple sentences. Despite having either compound subjects or compound verbs, each sentence still has only one subject and verb combination.

Compound sentences combine two or more simple sentences to form one sentence that has multiple subject-verb combinations:

The children ate pizza, and *their parents watched a movie.*

This structure is comprised of two independent clauses: (1) *the children ate pizza* and (2) *their parents watched a movie*. Compound sentences join different subject-verb combinations using a comma and a coordinating conjunction.

I called my mom**,** *but* she didn't answer the phone.

The weather was stormy**,** *so* we canceled our trip to the beach.

A **complex sentence** consists of an independent clause and one or more dependent clauses. Dependent clauses join a sentence using *subordinating conjunctions*. Some examples of subordinating conjunctions are *although, unless, as soon as, since, while, when, because, if,* and *before*.

I missed class yesterday *because* my mother was ill.

Before traveling to a new country, you need to exchange your money to the local currency.

The order of clauses determines their punctuation. If the dependent clause comes first, it should be separated from the independent clause with a comma. However, if the complex sentence consists of an independent clause followed by a dependent clause, then a comma is not always necessary.

A **compound-complex sentence** can be created by joining two or more independent clauses with at least one dependent clause:

After the earthquake struck, thousands of homes were destroyed, and many families were left without a place to live.

The first independent clause in the compound structure includes a dependent clause—*after the earthquake struck*. Thus, the structure is both complex and compound.

Other possible components of a sentence include descriptive words (adjectives or adverbs) that provide additional information called phrases or dependent clauses to the sentence but are not themselves complete sentences; independent clauses add more information to the sentence but could stand alone as their own sentence.

There isn't an overabundance of absolutes in grammar, but here is one: every sentence in the English language falls into one of four categories.

- Declarative: a simple statement that ends with a period

    The price of milk per gallon is the same as the price of gasoline.

- Imperative: a command, instruction, or request that ends with a period

    Buy milk when you stop to fill up your car with gas.

- Interrogative: a question that ends with a question mark

    Will you buy the milk?

- Exclamatory: a statement or command that expresses emotions like anger, urgency, or surprise and ends with an exclamation mark

    Buy the milk now!

Idiomatic Usage

A **figure of speech** (sometimes called an **idiom**) is a rhetorical device. It's a phrase that is not intended to be taken literally.

When the writer uses a figure of speech, their intention must be clear if it's to be used effectively. Some phrases can be interpreted in a number of ways, causing confusion for the reader. Look for clues to the writer's true intention to determine the best replacement. Likewise, some figures of speech may seem out of place in a more formal piece of writing. To show this, here is another example involving seat belts:

Seat belts save more lives than any other automobile safety feature. Many studies show that airbags save lives as well, however not all cars have airbags. For example, some older cars don't. In addition, air bags aren't entirely reliable. For example, studies show that in 15 percent of accidents, airbags don't deploy as designed, but, on the other hand, seat belt malfunctions happen once in a blue moon.

Most people know that "once in a blue moon" refers to something that rarely happens. However, because the rest of the paragraph is straightforward and direct, using this figurative phrase distracts the reader. In this example, the earlier version is much more effective.

Now it's important to take a moment and review the meaning of the word *literally*. This is because it's one of the most misunderstood and misused words in the English language. **Literally** means that something is exactly what it says it is, and there can be no interpretation or exaggeration. Unfortunately, *literally* is often used for emphasis as in the following example:

This morning, I literally couldn't get out of bed.

This sentence meant to say that the person was extremely tired and wasn't able to get up. However, the sentence can't *literally* be true unless that person was tied down to the bed, paralyzed, or affected by a strange situation that the writer (most likely) didn't intend. Here's another example:

I literally died laughing.

The writer tried to say that something was very funny. However, unless they're writing this from beyond the grave, it can't *literally* be true.

Note that this doesn't mean that writers can't use figures of speech. The colorful use of language and idioms make writing more interesting and draw in the reader. However, for these kinds of expressions to be used correctly, they cannot include the word *literally*.

Language Arts: Writing

Style, Tone, and Mood

Style, tone, and mood are often thought to be the same thing. Though they're closely related, there are important differences to keep in mind. The easiest way to do this is to remember that style "creates and affects" tone and mood. More specifically, style is how the writer uses words to create the desired tone and mood for their writing.

Style

Style can include any number of technical writing choices. A few examples of style choices include:

- Sentence Construction: When presenting facts, does the writer use shorter sentences to create a quicker sense of the supporting evidence, or do they use longer sentences to elaborate and explain the information?

- Technical Language: Does the writer use jargon to demonstrate their expertise in the subject, or do they use ordinary language to help the reader understand things in simple terms?

- Formal Language: Does the writer refrain from using contractions such as *won't* or *can't* to create a more formal tone, or do they use a colloquial, conversational style to connect to the reader?

- Formatting: Does the writer use a series of shorter paragraphs to help the reader follow a line of argument, or do they use longer paragraphs to examine an issue in great detail and demonstrate their knowledge of the topic?

On the test, examine the writer's style and how their writing choices affect the way the text comes across.

Tone

Tone refers to the writer's attitude toward the subject matter. Tone conveys how the writer feels about characters, situations, events, ideas, etc.

A lot of nonfiction writing has a neutral tone, which is an important tone for the writer to take. A neutral tone demonstrates that the writer is presenting a topic impartially and letting the information speak for itself. On the other hand, nonfiction writing can be just as effective and appropriate if the tone isn't neutral. For example, let's look at the seat belt example again:

> Seat belts save more lives than any other automobile safety feature. Many studies show that airbags save lives as well; however, not all cars have airbags. For example, some older cars don't. Furthermore, air bags aren't entirely reliable. For example, studies show that in 15 percent of accidents airbags don't deploy as designed, but, on the other hand, seat belt malfunctions are extremely rare. The number of highway fatalities has plummeted since laws requiring seat belt usage were enacted.

In this passage, the writer mostly chooses to retain a neutral tone when presenting information. If the writer would instead include their own personal experience of losing a friend or family member in a car accident, the tone would change dramatically. The tone would no longer be neutral and would show that the writer has a personal stake in the content, allowing them to interpret the information in a different way. When analyzing tone, consider what the writer is trying to achieve in the text and how they *create* the tone using style.

Mood

Mood refers to the feelings and atmosphere that the writer's words create for the reader. Like tone, many nonfiction texts can have a neutral mood. To return to the previous example, if the writer would choose to include information about a person they know being killed in a car accident, the text would suddenly carry an emotional component that is absent in the previous example. Depending on how they present the information, the writer can

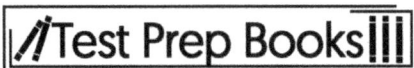

create a sad, angry, or even hopeful mood. When analyzing the mood, consider what the writer wants to accomplish and whether the best choice was made to achieve that end.

Analyzing Nuances in Words

Language is not as simple as one word directly correlated to one meaning. Rather, one word can express a vast array of diverse meanings, and similar meanings can be expressed through different words. However, there are very few words that express exactly the same meaning. For this reason, it is important to be able to pick up on the nuances of word meaning.

Many words contain two levels of meaning: connotation and denotation as discussed previously in the informational texts and rhetoric section. A word's **denotation** is its most literal meaning—the definition that can readily be found in the dictionary. A word's *connotation* includes all of its emotional and cultural associations.

In literary writing, authors rely heavily on connotative meaning to create mood and characterization. The following are two descriptions of a rainstorm:

- A. The rain slammed against the windowpane, and the wind howled through the fireplace. A pair of hulking oaks next to the house cast eerie shadows as their branches trembled in the wind.
- B. The rain pattered against the windowpane, and the wind whistled through the fireplace. A pair of stately oaks next to the house cast curious shadows as their branches swayed in the wind.

Description A paints a creepy picture for readers with strongly emotional words like *slammed*, connoting force and violence. *Howled* connotes pain or wildness, and *eerie* and *trembled* connote fear. Overall, the connotative language in this description serves to inspire fear and anxiety.

However, as can be seen in description B, swapping out a few key words for those with different connotations completely changes the feeling of the passage. *Slammed* is replaced with the more cheerful *pattered*, and *hulking* has been swapped out for *stately*. Both words imply something large, but *hulking* is more intimidating whereas *stately* is more respectable. *Curious* and *swayed* seem more playful than the language used in the earlier description. Although both descriptions represent roughly the same situation, the nuances of the emotional language used throughout the passages create a very different sense for readers.

Selective choice of language can also be extremely impactful in other forms of writing, such as editorials or persuasive texts. By choosing words that carry specific connotations, writers reveal their biases and opinions while trying to inspire feelings and actions in readers:

- A. Parents won't stop complaining about standardized tests.
- B. Parents continue to raise concerns about standardized tests.

Readers should be able to identify the nuance in meaning between these two sentences. The first one carries a more negative feeling, implying that parents are being bothersome or whiny. Readers of the second sentence, though, might come away with the feeling that parents are concerned and involved in their children's education. Again, the aggregate of even subtle cues can combine to give a specific emotional impression to readers, so from an early age, students should be aware of how language can be used to influence readers' opinions.

Another form of non-literal expression can be found in **figures of speech**. As with connotative language, figures of speech tend to be shared within a cultural group and may be difficult to pick up on for learners outside of that group. In some cases, a figure of speech may be based on the literal denotation of the words it contains, but in other cases, a figure of speech is far removed from its literal meaning. A case in point is **irony**, where what is said is the exact opposite of what is meant:

> The new tax plan is poorly planned, based on faulty economic data, and unable to address the financial struggles of middle-class families. Yet legislators remain committed to passing this brilliant proposal.

When the writer refers to the proposal as brilliant, the opposite is implied—the plan is "faulty" and "poorly planned." By using irony, the writer means that the proposal is anything but brilliant by using the word in a non-literal sense.

Another figure of speech is **hyperbole**—extreme exaggeration or overstatement. Statements like "I love you to the moon and back" or "Let's be friends for a million years" utilize hyperbole to convey a greater depth of emotion, without literally committing oneself to space travel or a life of immortality.

Figures of speech may sometimes use one word in place of another. **Synecdoche**, for example, uses a part of something to refer to its whole. The expression "Don't hurt a hair on her head!" implies protecting more than just an individual hair, but rather her entire body. "The art teacher is training a class of Picassos" uses Picasso, one individual notable artist, to stand in for the entire category of talented artists. Another figure of speech using word replacement is **metonymy**, where a word is replaced with something closely associated to it. For example, news reports may use the word *Washington* to refer to the American government or *the crown* to refer to the British monarch.

Writing Conventions

Verbs, Modifiers, and Pronouns

Verbs

Within the human skeleton, the constant motion of the inner workings of organs may be likened to the verb of a sentence in the grammar skeleton. The **verb** is the part of speech that describes an action, state of being, or occurrence.

A verb forms the main part of a predicate of a sentence. This means that the verb explains what the noun (person, place, or thing) is doing. A simple example is "Time flies." The verb *flies* explains what the action of the noun, *time*, is doing. This example is a *main* verb.

Auxiliary (helping) verbs are forms of the words *have, do,* and *be,* as well as other auxiliary verbs called **modals**. Modals and semi-modals (modal phrases) express ability, possibility, permission, or obligation. Modals and semi-modal examples are *can/could/be able to, may/might, shall/should, must/have to,* and *will/would.* "I *should* go to the store."

Particles are minor function words like *not, in, out, up,* or *down* that become part of the verb itself. "I might *not*."

Participles are words formed from verbs that are used to modify a noun (or noun phrase), or verb (or verb phrase), or to make a compound verb form. "He is *speaking*."

Verbs have five basic forms: the *base* form, the *-s* form, the *-ing* form, the *past* form, and the *past participle* form.

The *past* forms are either *regular* (*love/loved; hate/hated*) or *irregular* because they don't end by adding the common past tense suffix "-ed" (*go/went; fall/fell; set/set*). *To be* is an irregular verb with eight forms.

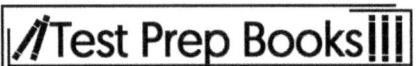

Language Arts: Writing

Pronouns

A word used in place of a noun is known as a **pronoun**. Pronouns are words like *I, mine, hers,* and *us.*

Pronouns can be split into different classifications (see below) which make them easier to learn; however, it's not important to memorize the classifications.

- Personal pronouns: refer to people, places, things, etc.
- First person: we, I, our, mine
- Second person: you, yours
- Third person: he, them
- Possessive pronouns: demonstrate ownership (mine, his, hers, its, ours, theirs, yours)
- Interrogative pronouns: ask questions (what, which, who, whom, whose)
- Relative pronouns: include the five interrogative pronouns and others that are relative (whoever, whomever, that, when, where)
- Demonstrative pronouns: replace something specific (this, that, those, these)
- Reciprocal pronouns: indicate something was done or given in return (each other, one another)
- Indefinite pronouns: have a nonspecific status (anybody, whoever, someone, everybody, somebody)

Indefinite pronouns such as *anybody, whoever, someone, everybody,* and *somebody* command a singular verb form, but others such as *all, none,* and *some* could require a singular or plural verb form.

An **antecedent** is the noun to which a pronoun refers; it needs to be written or spoken before the pronoun is used. For many pronouns, antecedents are imperative for clarity. In particular, many of the personal, possessive, and demonstrative pronouns need antecedents. Otherwise, it would be unclear who or what someone is referring to when they use a pronoun like *he* or *this*.

Pronoun reference means that the pronoun should refer clearly to one, clear, unmistakable noun (the antecedent).

Pronoun-antecedent agreement refers to the need for the antecedent and the corresponding pronoun to agree in gender, person, and number. Here are some examples:

The *kidneys* (plural antecedent) are part of the urinary system. *They* (plural pronoun) serve several roles.

The kidneys are part of the *urinary system* (singular antecedent). *It* (singular pronoun) is also known as the renal system.

The subjective pronouns —*I, you, he/she/it, we, they,* and *who*—are the subjects of the sentence.

Example: *They* have a new house.

The **objective pronouns**—*me, you* (singular), *him/her, us, them,* and *whom*—are used when something is being done for or given to someone; they are objects of the action.

Example: The teacher has an apple for *us.*

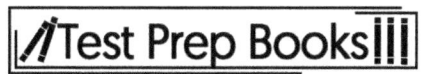

Language Arts: Writing

The **possessive pronouns**—*mine, my, your, yours, his, hers, its, their, theirs, our,* and *ours*—are used to denote that something (or someone) belongs to someone (or something).

Example: It's *their* chocolate cake.

Even Better Example: It's *my* chocolate cake!

One of the greatest challenges and worst abuses of pronouns concerns *who* and *whom*. Just knowing the following rule can eliminate confusion. *Who* is a subjective-case pronoun used only as a subject or subject complement. *Whom* is only objective-case and, therefore, the object of the verb or preposition.

Who is going to the concert?

You are going to the concert with *whom*?

Hint: When using *who* or *whom*, think of whether someone would say *he* or *him*. If the answer is *he*, use *who*. If the answer is *him*, use *whom*. This trick is easy to remember because *he* and *who* both end in vowels, and *him* and *whom* both end in the letter *M*.

Modifier Placement

Modifiers are words or phrases (often adjectives or nouns) that add detail to, explain, or limit the meaning of other parts of a sentence. Look at the following example:

A big pine tree is in the yard.

In the sentence, the words *big* (an adjective) and *pine* (a noun) modify *tree* (the head noun).

All related parts of a sentence must be placed together correctly. *Misplaced* and *dangling modifiers* are common writing mistakes. In fact, they're so common that many people are accustomed to seeing them and can decipher an incorrect sentence without much difficulty.

Since *modifiers* refer to something else in the sentence (*big* and *pine* refer to *tree* in the example above), they need to be placed close to what they modify. If a modifier is so far away that the reader isn't sure what it's describing, it becomes a *misplaced modifier*. For example:

Seat belts almost saved 5,000 lives in 2009.

It's likely that the writer means that the total number of lives saved by seat belts in 2009 is close to 5,000. However, due to the misplaced modifier (*almost*), the sentence actually says there are 5,000 examples when seat belts *almost saved lives*. In this case, the position of the modifier is actually the difference between life and death (at least in the meaning of the sentence). A clearer way to write the sentence is:

Seat belts saved almost 5,000 lives in 2009.

Now that the modifier is close to the 5,000 lives it references, the sentence's meaning is clearer.

Another common example of a misplaced modifier occurs when the writer uses the modifier to begin a sentence. For example:

Having saved 5,000 lives in 2009, Senator Wilson praised the seat belt legislation.

It seems unlikely that Senator Wilson saved 5,000 lives on her own, but that's what the writer is saying in this sentence. To correct this error, the writer should move the modifier closer to the intended object it modifies. Here are two possible solutions:

Having saved 5,000 lives in 2009, the seat belt legislation was praised by Senator Wilson.

Senator Wilson praised the seat belt legislation, which saved 5,000 lives in 2009.

When choosing a solution for a misplaced modifier, look for an option that places the modifier close to the object or idea it describes.

A modifier must have a target word or phrase that it's modifying. Without this, it's a *dangling modifier*. Dangling modifiers are usually found at the beginning of sentences:

After passing the new law, there is sure to be an improvement in highway safety.

This sentence doesn't say anything about who is passing the law. Therefore, "After passing the new law" is a dangling modifier because it doesn't modify anything in the sentence. To correct this type of error, determine what the writer intended the modifier to point to:

After passing the new law, legislators are sure to see an improvement in highway safety.

"After passing the new law" now points to *legislators*, which makes the sentence clearer and eliminates the dangling modifier.

Maintaining Grammatical Agreement

In English writing, certain words connect to other words. People often learn these connections (or *agreements*) as young children and use the correct combinations without a second thought. However, the questions on the test dealing with agreement probably aren't simple ones.

Subject-Verb Agreement

Which of the following sentences is correct?

A large crowd of protesters was on hand.

A large crowd of protesters were on hand.

Many people would say the second sentence is correct, but they'd be wrong. However, they probably wouldn't be alone. Most people just look at two words: *protesters were*. Together they make sense. They sound right. The problem is that the verb *were* doesn't refer to the word *protesters*. Here, the word *protesters* is part of a prepositional phrase that clarifies the actual subject of the sentence (*crowd*). Take the phrase "of protesters" away and re-examine the sentences:

A large crowd was on hand.

A large crowd were on hand.

Without the prepositional phrase to separate the subject and verb, the answer is obvious. The first sentence is correct. On the test, look for confusing prepositional phrases when answering questions about subject-verb agreement. Take the phrase away, and then recheck the sentence.

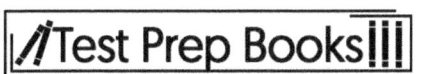

Language Arts: Writing

Noun Agreement

Nouns that refer to other nouns must also match in number. Take the following example:

> John and Emily both served as an intern for Senator Wilson.

Two people are involved in this sentence: John and Emily. Therefore, the word *intern* should be plural to match. Here is how the sentence should read:

> John and Emily both served as interns for Senator Wilson.

Pronouns are used to replace nouns so sentences don't have a lot of unnecessary repetition. This repetition can make a sentence seem awkward as in the following example:

> Seat belts are important because seat belts save lives, but seat belts can't do so unless seat belts are used.

Replacing some of the nouns (*seat belts*) with a pronoun (*they*) improves the flow of the sentence:

> Seat belts are important because they save lives, but they can't do so unless they are used.

A pronoun should agree in number (singular or plural) with the noun that precedes it. Another common writing error is the shift in *noun-pronoun agreement*. Here's an example:

> When people are getting in a car, he should always remember to buckle his seatbelt.

The first half of the sentence talks about a plural (*people*), while the second half refers to a singular person (*he* and *his*). These don't agree, so the sentence should be rewritten as:

> When people are getting in a car, they should always remember to buckle their seatbelt.

Fragments and Run-Ons

A **sentence fragment** is a failed attempt to create a complete sentence because it's missing a required noun or verb. Fragments don't function properly because there isn't enough information to understand the writer's intended meaning. For example:

> Seat belt use corresponds to a lower rate of hospital visits, reducing strain on an already overburdened healthcare system. Insurance claims as well.

Look at the last sentence: *Insurance claims as well*. What does this mean? This is a fragment because it has a noun but no verb, and it leaves the reader guessing what the writer means about insurance claims. Many readers can probably infer what the writer means, but this distracts them from the flow of the writer's argument. Choosing a suitable replacement for a sentence fragment may be one of the questions on the test. The fragment is probably related to the surrounding content, so look at the overall point the writer is trying to make and choose the answer that best fits that idea.

Remember that sometimes a fragment can *look* like a complete sentence or have all the nouns and verbs it needs to make sense. Consider the following two examples:

> Seat belt use corresponds to a lower rate of hospital visits.

> Although seat belt use corresponds to a lower rate of hospital visits.

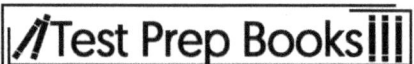

Both examples above have nouns and verbs, but only the first sentence is correct. The second sentence is a fragment, even though it's actually longer. The key is the writer's use of the word *although*. Starting a sentence with *although* turns that part into a *subordinate clause* (more on that next). Keep in mind that one doesn't have to remember that it's called a subordinate clause on the test. Just be able to recognize that the words form an incomplete thought and identify the problem as a sentence fragment.

A **run-on sentence** is, in some ways, the opposite of a fragment. It contains two or more sentences that have been improperly forced together into one. An example of a run-on sentence looks something like this:

Seat belt use corresponds to a lower rate of hospital visits it also leads to fewer insurance claims.

Here, there are two separate ideas in one sentence. It's difficult for the reader to follow the writer's thinking because there is no transition from one idea to the next. On the test, choose the best way to correct the run-on sentence.

Here are two possibilities for the sentence above:

Seat belt use corresponds to a lower rate of hospital visits. It also leads to fewer insurance claims.

Seat belt use corresponds to a lower rate of hospital visits, but it also leads to fewer insurance claims.

Both solutions are grammatically correct, so which one is the best choice? That depends on the point that the writer is trying to make. Always read the surrounding text to determine what the writer wants to demonstrate, and choose the option that best supports that thought.

Another type of run-on occurs when writers use inappropriate punctuation:

This winter has been very cold, some farmers have suffered damage to their crops.

Though a comma has been added, this sentence is still not correct. When a comma alone is used to join two independent clauses, it is known as a *comma splice*. Without an appropriate conjunction, a comma cannot join two independent clauses by itself.

Capitalization, Punctuation, and Spelling

Capitalization

- Capitalize the first word in a sentence and the first word in a quotation:

    The realtor showed them the house.

    Robert asked, "When can we get together for dinner again?"

- Capitalize proper nouns and words derived from them:

    We are visiting Germany in a few weeks.

    We will stay with our German relatives on our trip.

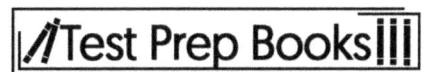

- Capitalize days of the week, months of the year, and holidays:

    The book club meets the last Thursday of every month.

    The baby is due in June.

    I decided to throw a Halloween party this year.

- Capitalize the main words in titles (referred to as *title case*), but not the articles, conjunctions, or prepositions:

    A Raisin in the Sun

    To Kill a Mockingbird

- Capitalize directional words that are used as names, but not when referencing a direction:

    The North won the Civil War.

    After making a left, go north on Rt. 476.

    She grew up on the West Coast.

    The winds came in from the west.

- Capitalize titles that go with names:

    Mrs. McFadden   Sir Alec Guinness   Lt. Madeline Suarez

- Capitalize familial relationships when referring to a *specific* person:

    I worked for my Uncle Steven last summer.

    Did you work for your uncle last summer?

Punctuation

Periods (.) are used to end a sentence that is a statement (*declarative*) or a command (*imperative*). They should not be used in a sentence that asks a question or is an exclamation. Periods are also used in abbreviations, which are shortened versions of words.

- Declarative: The boys refused to go to sleep.
- Imperative: Walk down to the bus stop.
- Abbreviations: Joan Roberts, M.D., Apple Inc., Mrs. Adamson
- If a sentence ends with an abbreviation, it is inappropriate to use two periods. It should end with a single period after the abbreviation.

    The chef gathered the ingredients for the pie, which included apples, flour, sugar, etc.

Question marks *(?)* are used with direct questions (*interrogative*). An *indirect question* can use a period:

Interrogative: When does the next bus arrive?

Indirect Question: I wonder when the next bus arrives.

An **exclamation point** *(!)* is used to show strong emotion or can be used as an *interjection*. This punctuation should be used sparingly in formal writing situations.

What an amazing shot!

Whoa!

In a sentence, **colons** are used before a list, a summary or elaboration, or an explanation related to the preceding information in the sentence:

There are two ways to reserve tickets for the performance: by phone or in person.

One thing is clear: students are spending more on tuition than ever before.

As these examples show, a colon must be preceded by an independent clause. However, the information after the colon may be in the form of an independent clause or in the form of a list.

Semicolons can be used in two different ways—to join ideas or to separate them. In some cases, semicolons can be used to connect what would otherwise be stand-alone sentences. Each part of the sentence joined by a semicolon must be an independent clause. The use of a semicolon indicates that these two independent clauses are closely related to each other:

The rising cost of childcare is one major stressor for parents; healthcare expenses are another source of anxiety.

Classes have been canceled due to the snowstorm; check the school website for updates.

Semicolons can also be used to divide elements of a sentence in a more distinct way than simply using a comma. This usage is particularly useful when the items in a list are especially long and complex and contain other internal punctuation.

Retirees have many modes of income: some survive solely off their retirement checks; others supplement their income through part time jobs, like working in a supermarket or substitute teaching; and others are financially dependent on the support of family members, friends, and spouses.

Dashes are used to set apart groups of words. The em dash (—) is useful because it can separate phrases that would otherwise be in parenthesis, or it can stand in for a colon. The en dash (–) is typically used either to represent a time span or range.

Quotation marks are found wherever there is a direct quote or phrase that needs to be set apart from the other text. They can also be used to indicate the title of a short work.

An **ellipsis** is comprised of three periods which is used to denote something that is missing or has been removed.

Spelling

Both spoken and written words have rhythm that might be defined as **inflection**. This serves to help writers in their choice of words, expression, and correct spelling. When creating original works, do at least one reading aloud. Some inflection is intrinsic to the words, some are added by writers, and some will be inferred when later read. If the written words are not spelled correctly, then what the author intended is not conveyed. Use rhythm as a spelling tool.

Saying and listening to a word serves as the beginning of knowing how to spell it. Keep these subsequent guidelines in mind, remembering there are often exceptions, because the English language is replete with them.

Guideline #1: Syllables must have a vowel

Every syllable in every English word has a vowel. Examples: d*o*g, h*a*yst*a*ck, *a*nsw*e*r*i*ng, *a*bst*e*nt*i*o*u*s (the longest word that uses the five vowels in order), and s*i*mpl*e*.

In addition to this vowel guideline is a built-in bonus: Guideline #1 helps one see whether the word looks right.

Guideline #2: The silent final -e

The final word example in Guideline #1, s*i*mpl*e,* provides the opportunity to see another guideline with multiple types:

- Because every syllable has a vowel, words like *simple* require the final silent -*e*.

- In a word that has a vowel-consonant-e combination like the short, simple word at*e*, the silent –*e* at the end shapes the sound of the earlier vowel. The technical term for this is it "makes the vowel say its name." There are thousands of examples of this guideline; just for starters, look at cut*e,* mat*e,* and tot*e*.

- Let's *dance*...after we leave the *range!* Look what the final silent –*e* does for the –*c* and –*g*: each provides the word's soft sound.

- Other than to *rev* a car's engine, are there other words that ends in a –*v?* How about a word that ends in a –*u?* Well some like their cheese ble*u,* there's one, but, while there are more (well, okay, *you*), they are few and far between, and consider words having the ending of the letter –*i*. Yes, English words generally do not end in –*v's,* –*u's,* and –*i's,* so silent –*e* to the rescue! Note that it does not change the pronunciation. Examples: believ*e,* lov*e,* and activ*e*; blu*e*, and tru*e*; and two very important –*i* examples, browni*e* and cooki*e*. (Exceptions to this rule are generally words from other languages.)

Guideline #3: The long and short of it

When the vowel has a short vowel sound as in *mad* or *bed,* only the single vowel is needed. If the word has a long vowel sound, add another vowel, either alongside it or separated by a consonant: bed/b*ead*; mad/m*ade.* When the second vowel is separated by two spaces—*madder*—it does not affect the first vowel's sound.

Guideline #4: What about the –fixes (pre- and suf-)?

A *prefix* is a word, letter, or number that is placed before another. It adjusts or qualifies the root word's meaning. When written alone, prefixes are followed by a dash to indicate that the root word follows. Some of the most common prefixes are the following:

Prefix	Meaning	Example
dis-	not or opposite of	disabled
in-, im-, il-, ir-	not	illiterate
re-	again	return
un-	not	unpredictable
anti-	against	antibacterial
fore-	before	forefront
mis-	wrongly	misunderstand
non-	not	nonsense
over-	more than normal	overabundance
pre-	before	preheat
super-	above	superman

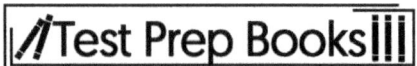

Language Arts: Writing

A **suffix** is a letter or group of letters added at the end of a word to form another word. The word created from the root and suffix is either a different tense of the same root (*help* + *ed* = *helped*) or a new word (*help* + *ful* = *helpful*). When written alone, suffixes are preceded by a dash to indicate that the root word comes before.

Some of the most common suffixes are the following:

Suffix	Meaning	Example
ed	makes a verb past tense	wash*ed*
ing	makes a verb a present participle verb	wash*ing*
ly	to make characteristic of	love*ly*
s/es	to make more than one	chair*s*, box*es*
able	can be done	deplor*able*
al	having characteristics of	comic*al*
est	comparative	great*est*
ful	full of	wonder*ful*
ism	belief in	commun*ism*
less	without	faith*less*
ment	action or process	accomplish*ment*
ness	state of	happ*iness*
ize, ise	to render, to make	steril*ize*, advert*ise*
cede/ceed/sede	go	con*cede*, pro*ceed*, super*sede*

Here are some helpful tips:

- When adding a suffix that starts with a vowel (for example, *-ed*) to a one-syllable root whose vowel has a short sound and ends in a consonant (for example, *stun*), double the final consonant of the root (*n*).

    stun + ed = stun*n*ed

Exception: If the past tense verb ends in *x* such as *box*, do not double the *x*.

    box + ed = boxed

- If adding a suffix that starts with a vowel (*-er*) to a multi-syllable word ending in a consonant (*begin*), double the consonant (*n*).

    begin + er = begin*n*er

- If a short vowel is followed by two or more consonants in a word such as *i+t+c+h = itch*, do <u>not</u> double the last consonant.

    itch + ed = itched

- If adding a suffix that starts with a vowel (*-ing*) to a word ending in *e* (for example, *name*), that word's final *e* is generally (but not always) dropped.

    name + ing = naming
    exception: manage + able = manageable

56

Language Arts: Writing

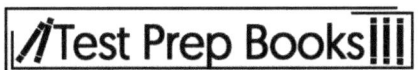

- If adding a suffix that starts with a consonant (-*ness*) to a word ending in *e* (*complete*), the *e* generally (but not always) remains.

    complete + ness = completeness
    exception: judge + ment = judgment

- There is great diversity on handling words that end in *y*. For words ending in a vowel + *y*, nothing changes in the original word.

    play + ed = played

- For words ending in a consonant + *y*, change the *y* to *i* when adding any suffix except for *–ing*.

    marry + ed = married
    marry + ing = marrying

Guideline #5: Which came first, the –i or the –e?
"When the letter 'c' you spy, put the 'e' before the 'i.' (Do not be) dec*ei*ved; when the letter 's' you see, put the 'i' before the 'e' (or you might be under) s*ie*ge." This old adage still holds up today regarding words where the "c" and "s" *precede* the "i." Another variation is, "*'i'* before *'e'* except after *'c'* or when sounded as *'a'* as in *neighbor* or *weigh.*" Keep in mind that these are only guidelines and that there are always exceptions to every rule.

Guideline #6: Vowels in the right order
A different helpful ditty is, "When two vowels go walking, the first one does the talking." Usually, when two vowels are in a row, the first one often has a long vowel sound and the other is silent. An example is *team*.

When having difficulty spelling words, determine a strategy to help. Work on pronunciations, play word games like Scrabble or Words with Friends, and consider using phonics (sounding words out by slowly and surely stating each syllable). Try using repetition and memorization and picturing the words. Try memory aids like making up silly things. See what works best. For disorders such as dyslexia, know that there are accommodations to help.

Use computer spellcheck; however, do not *rely on* computer spellcheck.

Using Reference Sources

Reference materials are indispensable tools for beginners and experts alike. Becoming a competent English communicator doesn't necessarily mean memorizing every single rule about spelling, grammar, or punctuation—it means knowing where and how to find accurate information about the rules of English usage. Students of English have a wide variety of references materials available to them, and, in an increasingly digitized world, more and more of these materials can be found online or as easily-accessible phone applications. Educators should introduce students to different types of reference materials as well as when and how to use them.

Dictionary
Dictionaries are readily available in print and digital formats. A dictionary offers a wealth of information to users. First, in the absence of spell checking software, a **dictionary** can be used to identify correct spelling and to determine the word's pronunciation—often written using the International Phonetic Alphabet (IPA). Dictionaries are best known for their explanations of words' meanings, as a single word can have multiple definitions. A dictionary organizes these definitions based on their parts of speech and then arranges them from most to least commonly used meanings or from oldest to most modern usage. Many dictionaries also offer information about a word's etymology and usage. With all these functions, then, a dictionary is a basic, essential tool in many situations. Students can turn to a dictionary when they encounter an unfamiliar word or when they see a familiar word used in a new way.

There are many dictionaries to choose from, but perhaps the most highly respected source is the *Oxford English Dictionary* (OED). The OED is a historical dictionary, and as such, all entries include quotes of the word as it has been used throughout history. Users of the OED can get a deeper sense of a word's evolution over time and in different parts of the world. Another standard dictionary in America is *Merriam-Webster*.

Thesaurus

Whereas a dictionary entry lists a word's definitions, a **thesaurus** entry lists a word's *synonyms* and *antonyms*—i.e., words with similar and opposite meanings, respectively. A dictionary can be used to find out what a word means and where it came from, and a thesaurus can be used to understand a word's relationship to other words. A **thesaurus** can be a powerful vocabulary building tool. By becoming familiar with synonyms and antonyms, students will be more equipped to use a broad range of vocabulary in their speech and writing. It is often advantageous to consult a thesaurus side-by-side with a dictionary because most words do not have exact synonyms, and a thesaurus may list several words with slight nuances of meaning. A **dictionary** can help determine if one word is more appropriate than another in a given context. Some digital sources, such as Dictionary.com, integrate a dictionary and a thesaurus.

Generally, though, a thesaurus is a useful tool to help writers add variety and precision to their word choice. Consulting a thesaurus can help students elevate their writing to an appropriate academic level by replacing vague or overused words with more expressive or academic ones. Also, word processors often offer a built-in thesaurus, making it easy for writers to look up synonyms and vary word choice as they work.

Glossary

Like dictionaries, **glossaries** also offer explanations of terms. However, while a dictionary attempts to cover every word in a language, a glossary only focuses on terms relevant to a specific field. Also, a glossary entry is more likely to offer a longer explanation of a term and its relevance within that field. Glossaries are often found at the back of textbooks or other nonfiction publications in order to explain new or unfamiliar terms to readers. A glossary may also be an entire book on its own that covers all of the essential terms and concepts within a particular profession, field, or other specialized area of knowledge. For learners seeking general definitions of terms from any context, then, a dictionary is an appropriate reference source, but for students of specialized fields, a glossary will usually provide more in-depth information.

Style Manual

Many rules of English usage are standard, but other rules may be more subjective. An example can be seen in the following structures:

A. I went to the store and bought eggs, milk, and bread.
B. I went to the store and bought eggs, milk and bread.

The final comma in a list before *and* or *or* is known as an **Oxford comma** or serial comma. It is, recommended in some styles, but not in others. To determine the appropriate use of the Oxford comma, writers can consult a style manual.

A **style manual** is a comprehensive collection of guidelines for language use and document formatting. Some fields refer to a common style guide—e.g., the Associated Press or **AP Stylebook**, a standard in American journalism. Individual organizations may rely on their own house style. Regardless, the purpose of a style manual is to ensure uniformity across all documents. Style manuals explain things such as how to format titles, when to write out numbers or use numerals, and how to cite sources. Because there are many different style guides, students should know how and when to consult an appropriate guide. The **Chicago Manual of Style** is common in the publication of books and academic journals. The **Modern Language Association style (MLA)** is another commonly used academic style format, while the **American Psychological Association style (APA)** may be used for scientific publications.

Familiarity with using a style guide is particularly important for students who are college bound or pursuing careers in academic or professional writing.

In the examples above, the Oxford comma is recommended by the Chicago Manual of Style, so sentence A would be correct if the writer is using this style. But the comma is not recommended by the *AP Stylebook*, so sentence B would be correct if the writer is using the AP style.

General Grammar and Style References

Any language arts textbook should offer general grammatical and stylistic advice to students, but there are a few well-respected texts that can also be used for reference. *Elements of Style* by **William Strunk** is regularly assigned to students as a guide on effective written communication, including how to avoid common usage mistakes and how to make the most of parallel structure. *Garner's Modern American Usage* by **Bryan Garner** is another text that guides students on how to achieve precision and understandability in their writing. Whereas other reference sources discussed above tend to address specific language concerns, these types of texts offer a more holistic approach to cultivating effective language skills.

Electronic Resources

With print texts, it is easy to identify the authors and their credentials, as well as the publisher and their reputation. With electronic resources like websites, though, it can be trickier to assess the reliability of information. Students should be alert when gathering information from the Internet. Understanding the significance of website *domains*—which include identification strings of a site—can help. Website domains ending in *.edu* are educational sites and tend to offer more reliable research in their field. A *.org* ending tends to be used by nonprofit organizations and other community groups, *.com* indicates a privately-owned website, and a *.gov* site is run by the government. Websites affiliated with official organizations, research groups, or institutes of learning are more likely to offer relevant, fact-checked, and reliable information.

Practice Quiz

Questions 1–5 are based on the following passage:

In our essay and class discussion, (1) <u>we came to talking about</u> mirrors. It was an excellent class in which we focused on an article written by Salman Rushdie that compared the homeland to a mirror. (2) <u>Essentially this mirror is an metaphor for us and our homeland.</u> (3) <u>When we look at our reflection we see the culture, our homeland staring back at us.</u> An interesting analogy, but the conversation really began when we read that Rushdie himself stated that the cracked mirror is more valuable than a whole one. But why?
(4) <u>After reflecting on the passage I found the answer to be simple.</u> The analogy reflects the inherent nature of human individuality. The cracks in the mirror represent different aspects of our own being. Perhaps it is our personal views, our hobbies, or our differences with other people, but (5) <u>whatever it is that makes us unique defines us, even while we are part of a big culture.</u> (6) <u>What this tells us is that we can have a homeland, but ultimately we ourselves are each different in it.</u>

Just because one's (7) <u>mirror is cracked, the individuals isn't disowned</u> from the actual, physical homeland and culture within. It means that the homeland is uniquely perceived by the (8) <u>individual beholding it and that there are in fact many aspects</u> to culture itself. Like the various cracks, a culture has religion, language, and many other factors that form to make it whole. What this idea does is invite the viewer to accept their own view of their culture as a whole.
Like in Chandra's *Love and Longing in Bombay*, a single homeland has many stories to tell. Whether one is a cop or a retired war veteran, the individual will perceive the different aspects of the world with unduplicated eyes. (9) <u>Rushdie, seems to be urging his readers</u> to love their culture but to not be pressured by the common crowd. Again, the cracks represent differences which could easily be interpreted as views about the culture, so what this is saying is to accept the culture but accept oneself as well.

From the essay "Portals to Homeland: Mirrors"

1. Which of the following would be the best replacement for the underlined portion of the sentence reproduced below?

   In our essay and class discussion, (1) <u>we came to talking about</u> mirrors.

   a. NO CHANGE
   b. we are talking about
   c. we talked about
   d. we came to talk about

2. Which of the following would be the best replacement for the underlined portion of the sentence reproduced below?

   (2) <u>Essentially this mirror is an metaphor for us and our homeland.</u>

   a. NO CHANGE
   b. Essentially this mirror is a metaphor for us and our homeland.
   c. Essentially this mirror is any metaphor for us and our homeland.
   d. Essentially this mirror is an metaphor, for us and our homeland.

Language Arts: Writing

3. Which of the following would be the best replacement for the underlined portion of the sentence reproduced below?

(3) When we look at our reflection we see the culture, our homeland staring back at us.
a. When we look at our reflection, we see the culture, our homeland, staring back at us.
b. When we look at our reflection we see our culture our homeland staring back at us.
c. When we look at our reflection we saw our culture, our homeland, staring back at us.
d. When we look at our reflection, we see the culture, our homeland staring back at us.

4. Which of the following would be the best replacement for the underlined portion of the sentence reproduced below?

(4) After reflecting on the passage I found the answer to be simple.

a. NO CHANGE
b. After reflecting on the passage; I found the answer to be simple.
c. After reflecting on the passage I finding the answer to be simple.
d. After reflecting on the passage, I found the answer to be simple.

5. Which of the following would be the best replacement for the underlined portion of the sentence reproduced below?

Perhaps it is our personal views, our hobbies, or our differences with other people, but (5) whatever it is that makes us unique defines us, even while we are part of a big culture.

a. NO CHANGE
b. whatever it is, that makes us unique, defines us, even while we are part of a big culture.
c. whatever it is that makes us unique defines us, even while we are part of a bigger culture.
d. whatever it is that makes us unique defines us, even though we are part of a big culture.

See answers on the next page.

Answer Explanations

1. C: The original phrase and Choice *D* are grammatically incorrect. Choice *B* is grammatically correct, but it should be in the past tense, as we can tell from the next sentence: It was an excellent class in which we focused on an article written by Salman Rushdie that compared the homeland to a mirror. Therefore, Choice *C* is the best choice.

2. B: The original sentence uses *an* before metaphor instead of *a*. Choice *C* incorrectly changes *an* to *any*. Choice *D* adds an unnecessary comma.

3. A: Choice *B* omits all of the commas. Choice *C* incorrectly changes the present tense *see* to the past tense *saw* and does not include the comma after *reflection*. Choice *D* does not include the comma after *homeland*. Choice *A* is the only answer choice with all of the appropriate commas.

4. D: The original sentence lacks the necessary comma after the dependent clause. Choice *B* uses a semicolon where a comma is needed. Choice *C* is also missing the required comma and incorrectly changes *found* to *finding*.

5. C: Choice *C* is correct because the other answer choices use the word *big*, which is incorrect in this context. The sentence needs the comparative adjective *bigger* in order to communicate the author's assessment of how people relate to others on a grand scale. Also, Choice *B* inserts unnecessary commas, and Choice *D* subtly alters the original meaning.

Mathematics

Numbers and Operations on Numbers

Properties of Operations with Real Numbers, Including Rational and Irrational Numbers

The mathematical number system is made up of two general types of numbers: real and complex. **Real numbers** are both irrational and rational numbers, while **complex numbers** are those composed of both a real number and an imaginary one. Imaginary numbers are the result of taking the square root of -1, and $\sqrt{-1} = i$.

The real number system is often explained using a Venn diagram similar to the one below. After a number has been labeled as a real number, further classification occurs when considering the other groups in this diagram. If a number is a never-ending, non-repeating decimal, it falls in the irrational category. Otherwise, it is rational. More information on these types of numbers is provided in the previous section. Furthermore, if a number does not have a fractional part, it is classified as an integer, such as -2, 75, or zero. Whole numbers are an even smaller group that only includes positive integers and zero. The last group of natural numbers is made up of only positive integers, such as 2, 56, or 12.

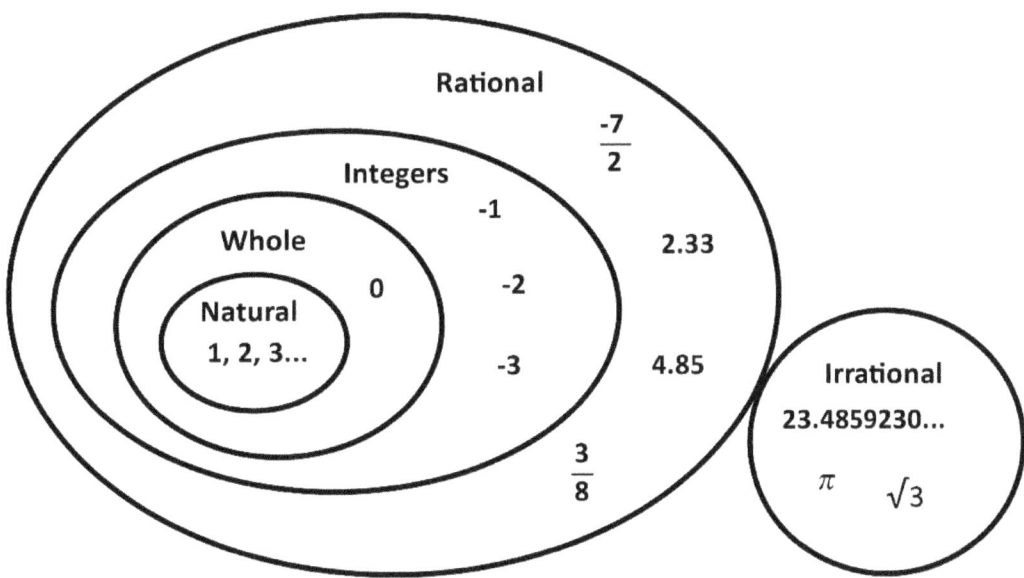

Real numbers can be compared and ordered using the number line. If a number falls to the left on the real number line, it is less than a number on the right. For example, $-2 < 5$ because -2 falls to the left of zero, and 5 falls to the right. Numbers to the left of zero are negative while those to the right are positive.

Complex numbers are made up of the sum of a real number and an imaginary number. Some examples of complex numbers include $6 + 2i$, $5 - 7i$, and $-3 + 12i$. Adding and subtracting complex numbers is similar to collecting like terms. The real numbers are added together, and the imaginary numbers are added together. For example, if the problem asks to simplify the expression $6 + 2i - 3 + 7i$, the 6 and (-3) are combined to make 3, and the $2i$ and $7i$ combine to make $9i$. Multiplying and dividing complex numbers is similar to working with exponents.

One rule to remember when multiplying is that:

$$i \times i = -1$$

For example, if a problem asks to simplify the expression $4i(3 + 7i)$, the $4i$ should be distributed throughout the 3 and the $7i$. This leaves the final expression $12i - 28$. The 28 is negative because $i \times i$ results in a negative number. The last type of operation to consider with complex numbers is the conjugate. The **conjugate** of a complex number is a technique used to change the complex number into a real number. For example, the conjugate of $4 - 3i$ is $4 + 3i$. Multiplying $(4 - 3i)(4 + 3i)$ results in $16 + 12i - 12i + 9$, which has a final answer of $16 + 9 = 25$.

The order of operations—**PEMDAS**—simplifies longer expressions with real or imaginary numbers. Each operation is listed in the order of how they should be completed in a problem containing more than one operation. Parenthesis can also mean grouping symbols, such as brackets and absolute value. Then, exponents are calculated. Multiplication and division should be completed from left to right, and addition and subtraction should be completed from left to right. The following shows step-by-step how an expression is simplified using the order of operations:

$$25 \div (8 - 3)^2 - 1$$

$$25 \div (5)^2 - 1$$

$$25 \div 25 - 1$$

$$1 - 1$$

$$0$$

Simplification of another type of expression occurs when radicals are involved. As explained previously, root is another word for radical. For example, the following expression is a radical that can be simplified: $\sqrt{24x^2}$. First, the number must be factored out to the highest perfect square. Any perfect square can be taken out of a radical. Twenty-four can be factored into 4 and 6, and 4 can be taken out of the radical. $\sqrt{4} = 2$ can be taken out, and 6 stays underneath. If $x > 0$, x can be taken out of the radical because it is a perfect square. The simplified radical is $2x\sqrt{6}$. An approximation can be found using a calculator.

There are also properties of numbers that are true for certain operations. The **commutative property** allows the order of the terms in an expression to change while keeping the same final answer. Both addition and multiplication can be completed in any order and still obtain the same result. However, order does matter in subtraction and division. The **associative property** allows any terms to be "associated" by parenthesis and retain the same final answer. For example, $(4 + 3) + 5 = 4 + (3 + 5)$. Both addition and multiplication are associative; however, subtraction and division do not hold this property. The **distributive property** states that $a(b + c) = ab + ac$. It is a property that involves both addition and multiplication, and the a is distributed onto each term inside the parentheses.

Integers can be factored into prime numbers. To **factor** is to express as a product. For example, $6 = 3 \times 2$, and $6 = 6 \times 1$. Both are factorizations, but the expression involving the factors of 3 and 2 is known as a **prime factorization** because it is factored into a product of two **prime numbers**—integers which do not have any factors other than themselves and 1. A **composite number** is a positive integer that can be divided into at least one other integer other than itself and 1, such as 6. Integers that have a factor of 2 are even, and if they are not divisible by 2, they are odd. Finally, a **multiple** of a number is the product of that number and a counting number—also known as a **natural number**. For example, some multiples of 4 are 4, 8, 12, 16, etc.

Properties of Rational and Irrational Numbers

All real numbers can be separated into two groups: rational and irrational numbers. **Rational numbers** are any numbers that can be written as a fraction, such as $\frac{1}{3}$, $\frac{7}{4}$, and -25. Alternatively, **irrational numbers** are those that

Mathematics

cannot be written as a fraction, such as numbers with never-ending, non-repeating decimal values. Many irrational numbers result from taking roots, such as $\sqrt{2}$ or $\sqrt{3}$. An irrational number may be written as:

$$34.5684952\ldots$$

The ellipsis (…) represents the line of numbers after the decimal that does not repeat and is never-ending.

When rational and irrational numbers interact, there are different types of number outcomes. For example, when adding or multiplying two rational numbers, the result is a rational number. No matter what two fractions are added or multiplied together, the result can always be written as a fraction. The following expression shows two rational numbers multiplied together:

$$\frac{3}{8} \times \frac{4}{7} = \frac{12}{56}$$

The product of these two fractions is another fraction that can be simplified to $\frac{3}{14}$.

As another interaction, rational numbers added to irrational numbers will always result in irrational numbers. No part of any fraction can be added to a never-ending, non-repeating decimal to make a rational number. The same result is true when multiplying a rational and irrational number. Taking a fractional part of a never-ending, non-repeating decimal will always result in another never-ending, non-repeating decimal. An example of the product of rational and irrational numbers is shown in the following expression: $2 \times \sqrt{7}$.

The last type of interaction concerns two irrational numbers, where the sum or product may be rational or irrational depending on the numbers being used. The following expression shows a rational sum from two irrational numbers:

$$\sqrt{3} + (6 - \sqrt{3}) = 6$$

The product of two irrational numbers can be rational or irrational. A rational result can be seen in the following expression:

$$\sqrt{2} \times \sqrt{8} = \sqrt{2 \times 8} = \sqrt{16} = 4$$

An irrational result can be seen in the following:

$$\sqrt{3} \times \sqrt{2} = \sqrt{6}$$

Rewriting Expressions Involving Radicals and Rational Exponents

Exponents are used in mathematics to express a number or variable multiplied by itself a certain number of times. For example, x^3 means x is multiplied by itself three times. In this expression, x is called the *base*, and 3 is the *exponent*. Exponents can be used in more complex problems when they contain fractions and negative numbers.

Fractional exponents can be explained by looking first at the inverse of exponents, which are *roots*. Given the expression x^2, the square root can be taken, $\sqrt{x^2}$, cancelling out the 2 and leaving x by itself, if x is positive. Cancellation occurs because $\sqrt{x}$ can be written with exponents, instead of roots, as $x^{\frac{1}{2}}$. The numerator of 1 is the exponent, and the denominator of 2 is called the root (which is why it's referred to as **square root**). Taking the square root of x^2 is the same as raising it to the $\frac{1}{2}$ power. Written out in mathematical form, it takes the following progression:

$$\sqrt{x^2} = (x^2)^{\frac{1}{2}} = x$$

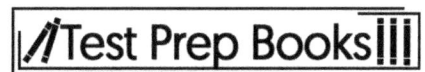

From properties of exponents, $2 \times \frac{1}{2} = 1$ is the actual exponent of x. Another example can be seen with $x^{\frac{4}{7}}$. The variable x, raised to four-sevenths, is equal to the seventh root of x to the fourth power: $\sqrt[7]{x^4}$. In general,

$$x^{\frac{1}{n}} = \sqrt[n]{x}$$

and

$$x^{\frac{m}{n}} = \sqrt[n]{x^m}$$

Negative exponents also involve fractions. Whereas y^3 can also be rewritten as $\frac{y^3}{1}$, y^{-3} can be rewritten as $\frac{1}{y^3}$. A negative exponent means the exponential expression must be moved to the opposite spot in a fraction to make the exponent positive. If the negative appears in the numerator, it moves to the denominator. If the negative appears in the denominator, it is moved to the numerator. In general, $a^{-n} = \frac{1}{a^n}$, and a^{-n} and a^n are reciprocals.

Take, for example, the following expression:

$$\frac{a^{-4}b^2}{c^{-5}}$$

Since a is raised to the negative fourth power, it can be moved to the denominator. Since c is raised to the negative fifth power, it can be moved to the numerator. The b variable is raised to the positive second power, so it does not move.

The simplified expression is as follows:

$$\frac{b^2 c^5}{a^4}$$

In mathematical expressions containing exponents and other operations, the order of operations must be followed. **PEMDAS** states that exponents are calculated after any parenthesis and grouping symbols but before any multiplication, division, addition, and subtraction.

Scientific Notation

Scientific Notation is used to represent numbers that are either very small or very large. For example, the distance to the sun is approximately 150,000,000,000 meters. Instead of writing this number with so many zeros, it can be written in scientific notation as 1.5×10^{11} meters. The same is true for very small numbers, but the exponent becomes negative. If the mass of a human cell is 0.000000000001 kilograms, that measurement can be easily represented by 1.0×10^{-12} kilograms. In both situations, scientific notation makes the measurement easier to read and understand. Each number is translated to an expression with one digit in the tens place times an expression corresponding to the zeros.

When two measurements are given and both involve scientific notation, it is important to know how these interact with each other:

- In addition and subtraction, the exponent on the ten must be the same before any operations are performed on the numbers. For example, $(1.3 \times 10^4) + (3.0 \times 10^3)$ cannot be added until one of the exponents on the ten is changed. The 3.0×10^3 can be changed to 0.3×10^4, then the 1.3 and 0.3 can be added. The answer comes out to be 1.6×10^4.

Mathematics

- For multiplication, the first numbers can be multiplied and then the exponents on the tens can be added. Once an answer is formed, it may have to be converted into scientific notation again depending on the change that occurred.

- The following is an example of multiplication with scientific notation:
$$(4.5 \times 10^3) \times (3.0 \times 10^{-5}) = 13.5 \times 10^{-2}$$

- Since this answer is not in scientific notation, the decimal is moved over to the left one unit, and 1 is added to the ten's exponent. This results in the final answer: 1.35×10^{-1}.

- For division, the first numbers are divided, and the exponents on the tens are subtracted. Again, the answer may need to be converted into scientific notation form, depending on the type of changes that occurred during the problem.

- **Order of magnitude** relates to scientific notation and is the total count of powers of 10 in a number. For example, there are 6 orders of magnitude in 1,000,000. If a number is raised by an order of magnitude, it is multiplied times 10. Order of magnitude can be helpful in estimating results using very large or small numbers. An answer should make sense in terms of its order of magnitude.

- For example, if area is calculated using two dimensions with 6 orders of magnitude, because area involves multiplication, the answer should have around 12 orders of magnitude. Also, answers can be estimated by rounding to the largest place value in each number. For example, 5,493,302×2,523,100 can be estimated by 5×3 = 15 with 12 orders of magnitude.

Reasoning Quantitatively and Using Units to Solve Problems

It is important to be able to reason quantitatively when working with mathematical problems. In some ways, mathematics can be thought of as a foreign language. As one gains fluency, they should develop the ability to correctly represent a given problem, work through the procedures to find a solution, and take pause throughout the process to evaluate the logic behind the steps and intermediate answers found.

The meaning behind the numbers involved, including their units and magnitude, should be considered as the values are manipulated. For example, if a problem is investigating the speed at which a car traveled, students should be mindful that the units should be in miles per hour or kilometers per hour. Also, they should consider logical driving speeds. It is important to not only memorize formulas and procedures, but to understand the meaning and purpose behind them so that they are correctly applied to various situations. Whenever possible, the calculated solution should be verified for accuracy before moving onto the next problem. To accomplish this, the inverse operation or procedure can sometimes be applied.

As a simple example, if asked to calculate the product of nine and four ($9 \times 4 = 36$), the answer can be double-checked by using the inverse operation: ($\frac{36}{9} = 4$). When it is not possible to rely on this method of double-checking answers, one should consider if the answer makes sense logically. This ability showcases a deeper understanding of the mathematical principles at play. As another example, if a problem is asking for the total length of fencing needed to enclose a small vegetable garden, it is reasonable that the answer will be a certain amount of feet. Any calculated solutions that include units of measurement that differ from this (inches, miles, square feet, etc.) can be immediately disregarded because they would not be logical. Solutions to quantitative problems should be verified as reasonable to prevent careless mistakes and unnecessary errors and to ensure that the proper procedures and calculations are carried out.

Dimensional analysis is the process of converting between different units using equivalent measurement statements. For example, running a 5K is the same as running approximately 3.1 miles. This conversion can be found by knowing that 1 kilometer is equal to approximately 0.62 miles.

The following calculation shows how to convert kilometers into miles. The original units need to be opposite one another in each of the two fractions: one in the original amount and one in the denominator of the conversion factor. This specific example consists of 5 km being multiplied times the conversion factor .62 mi/km. By design, quantities in kilometers are opposite one another and therefore cancel, leaving 3.11 miles as the converted result.

$$5\text{km} \times \left(\frac{0.62 \text{miles}}{1 \text{km}}\right) = 3.11 \text{ miles}$$

Units are also important throughout formulas in calculating quantities such as volume and area. To find the volume of a pyramid, the following formula is used: $V = \frac{1}{3}Bh$. B is the area of the base, and h is the height. In the example shown below, two of the same type of dimension are composed of two different units. All dimensions must be converted to the same units before plugging values into the formula for volume.

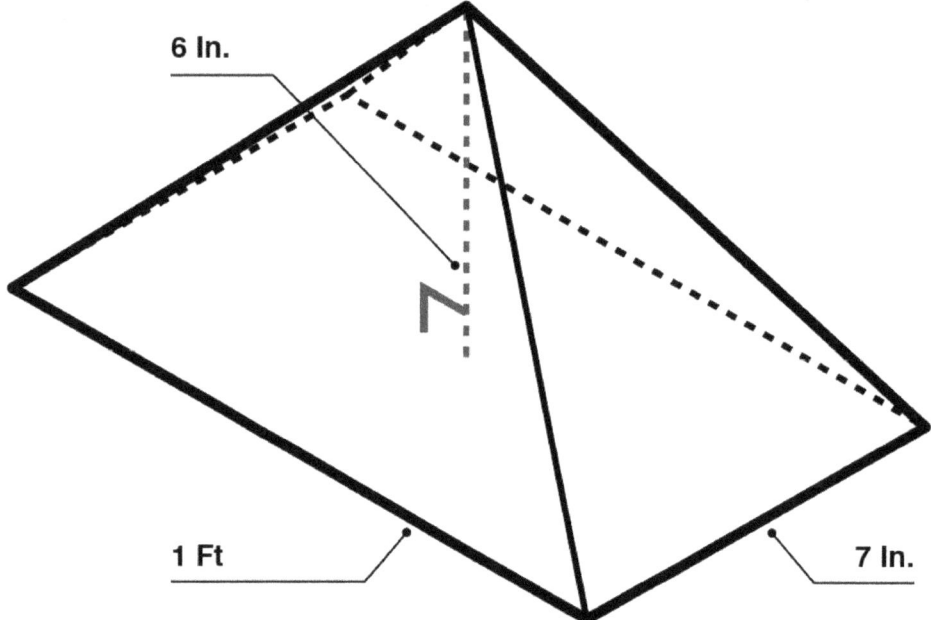

In this case, all lengths will be converted to inches. To find the area of the base, it's necessary to convert 1 ft. to 12 inches. Then, the area of the base can be calculated as $B = 12 \text{ in} \times 7 \text{ in} = 84 \text{ in}^2$. B can then be substituted into the volume formula as follows: $V = \frac{1}{3}(84 \text{ in}^2)(6 \text{ in}) = 168 \text{ in}^3$.

Formulas are a common situation in which units need to be interpreted and used. However, graphs can also carry meaning through units. The following graph is an example. It represents a graph of the position of an object over time. The m axis represents the number of meters the object is from the starting point at time s, in seconds. Interpreting this graph, the origin shows that at time zero seconds, the object is zero meters away from the starting point. As the time increases to one second, the position increases to five meters away. This trend continues until 6 seconds, where the object is 30 meters away from the starting position. After this point in time—since the graph remains horizontal from 6 to 10 seconds—the object must have stopped moving.

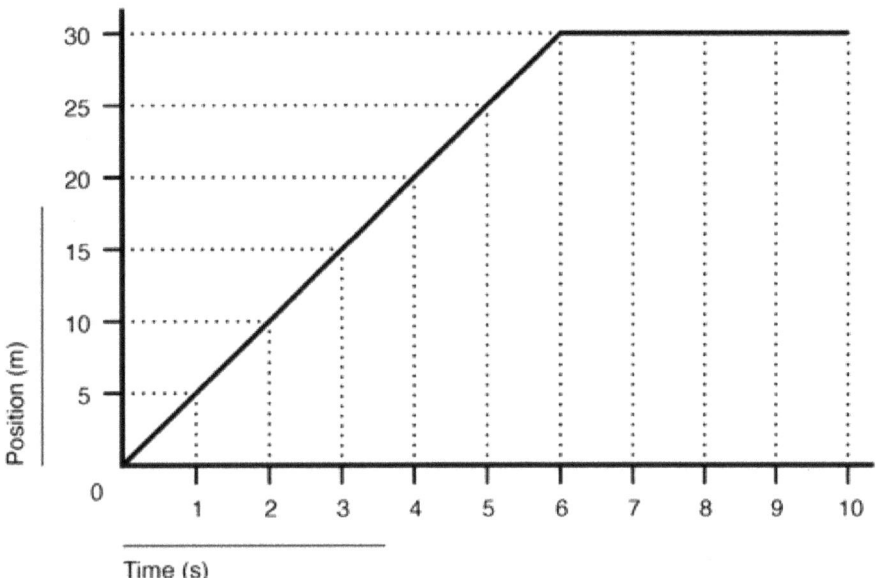

When solving problems with units, it's important to consider the reasonableness of the answer. If conversions are used, it's helpful to have an estimated value to compare the final answer to. This way, if the final answer is too distant from the estimate, it will be obvious that a mistake was made.

Choosing a Level of Accuracy Appropriate to Limitations on Measurement

Precision and accuracy are used to describe groups of measurements. **Precision** describes a group of measures that are very close together, regardless of whether the measures are close to the true value. **Accuracy** describes how close the measures are to the true value. The following graphic illustrates the different combinations that may occur with different groups of measures:

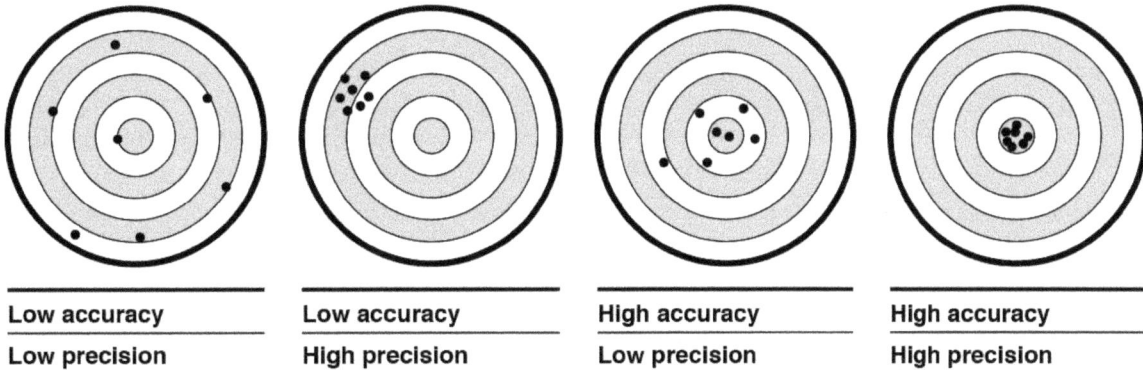

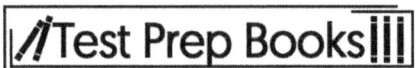

Since accuracy refers to the closeness of a value to the true measurement, the level of accuracy depends on the object measured and the instrument used to measure it. This will vary depending on the situation. If measuring the mass of a set of dictionaries, kilograms may be used as the units. In this case, it is not vitally important to have a high level of accuracy. If the measurement is a few grams away from the true value, the discrepancy might not make a big difference in the problem.

In a different situation, the level of accuracy may be more significant. Pharmacists need to be sure they are very accurate in their measurements of medicines that they give to patients. In this case, the level of accuracy is vitally important and not something to be estimated. In the dictionary situation, the measurements were given as whole numbers in kilograms. In the pharmacist's situation, the measurements for medicine must be taken to the milligram and sometimes further, depending on the type of medicine.

When considering the accuracy of measurements, the error in each measurement can be shown as absolute and relative. **Absolute error** tells the actual difference between the measured value and the true value. The **relative error** tells how large the error is in relation to the true value. There may be two problems where the absolute error of the measurements is 10 grams. For one problem, this may mean the relative error is very small because the measured value is 14,990 grams, and the true value is 15,000 grams. Ten grams in relation to the true value of 15,000 is small: 0.06%. For the other problem, the measured value is 290 grams, and the true value is 300 grams. In this case, the 10-gram absolute error means a high relative error because the true value is smaller. The relative error is $\frac{10}{300} = 0.03$, or 3%.

Solving Multistep Real-World and Mathematical Problems Involving Rational Numbers in Any Form

Ratios are used to show the relationship between two quantities. The ratio of oranges to apples in the grocery store may be 3 to 2. That means that for every 3 oranges, there are 2 apples. This comparison can be expanded to represent the actual number of oranges and apples, such as 36 oranges to 24 apples. Another example may be the number of boys to girls in a math class. If the ratio of boys to girls is given as 2 to 5, that means there are 2 boys to every 5 girls in the class. Ratios can also be compared if the units in each ratio are the same. The ratio of boys to girls in the math class can be compared to the ratio of boys to girls in a science class by stating which ratio is higher and which is lower.

Rates are used to compare two quantities with different units. **Unit rates** are the simplest form of rate. With unit rates, the denominator in the comparison of two units is one. For example, if someone can type at a rate of 1,000 words in 5 minutes, then their unit rate for typing is $\frac{1,000}{5} = 200$ words in one minute or 200 words per minute. Any rate can be converted into a unit rate by dividing to make the denominator one. 1,000 words in 5 minutes has been converted into the unit rate of 200 words per minute.

Ratios and rates can be used together to convert rates into different units. For example, if someone is driving 50 kilometers per hour, that rate can be converted into miles per hour by using a ratio known as the **conversion factor**. Since the given value contains kilometers and the final answer needs to be in miles, the ratio relating miles to kilometers needs to be used. There are 0.62 miles in 1 kilometer. This, written as a ratio and in fraction form, is

$$\frac{0.62 \text{ miles}}{1 \text{ km}}$$

To convert 50 km/hour into miles per hour, the following conversion needs to be set up:

$$\frac{50 \text{ km}}{1 \text{ hour}} \times \frac{0.62 \text{ miles}}{1 \text{ km}} = 31 \text{ miles per hour}$$

The ratio between two similar geometric figures is called the **scale factor**. In the following example, there are two similar triangles. The scale factor from figure A to figure B is 2 because the length of the corresponding side of the larger triangle, 14, is twice the corresponding side on the smaller triangle, 7.

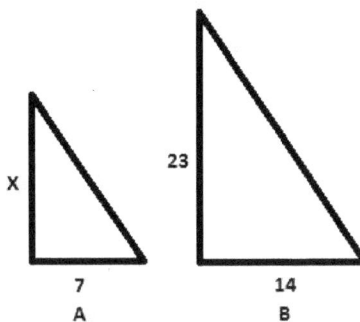

This scale factor can also be used to find the value of X. Since the scale factor from small to large is 2, the larger number, 23, can be divided by 2 to find the missing side: $X = 11.5$. The scale factor can also be represented in the equation $2A = B$ because two times the lengths of A gives the corresponding lengths of B. This is the idea behind similar triangles.

Much like a scale factor can be written using an equation like $2A = B$, a **proportional relationship** is represented by the equation $Y = kX$. X and Y are proportional because as values in X increase, the values in Y also increase. A relationship that is inversely proportional can be represented by the equation $Y = \frac{k}{X}$, where the value of Y decreases as the value of X increases and vice versa.

The following graph represents these two types of relationships between x and y. The grey line represents a proportional relationship because the y-values increase as the x-values increase. The black line represents an inversely-proportional relationship because the y-values decrease as the x-values increase.

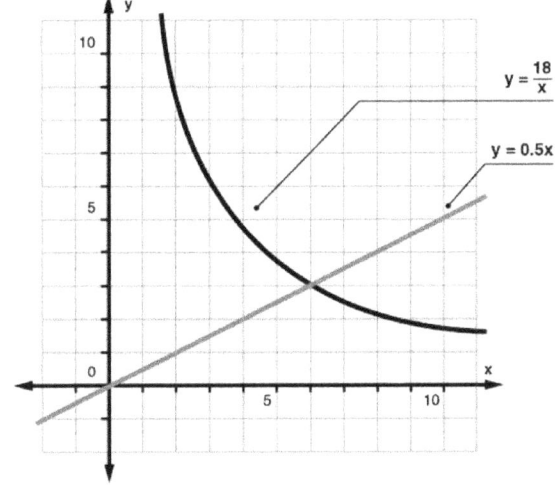

Proportional reasoning can be used to solve problems involving ratios, percentages, and averages. Ratios can be used in setting up proportions and solving them to find unknowns. For example, if someone averages 10 pages of math homework completed in 3 nights, how long would it take him or her to complete 22 pages? Both ratios can be

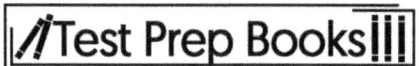

written as fractions. The second ratio would contain the unknown. The following proportion represents this problem where x is the unknown number of nights:

$$\frac{10 \text{ pages}}{3 \text{ nights}} = \frac{22 \text{ pages}}{x \text{ nights}}$$

Solving this proportion entails cross-multiplying and results in the following equation: $10x = 22 \times 3$. Simplifying and solving for x results in the exact solution: $x = 6.6$ nights. The result would be rounded up to 7 because the homework would actually be completed on the 7th night.

The following problem uses ratios involving percentages:

If 20% of the class is girls and 30 students are in the class, how many girls are in the class?

To set up this problem, it is helpful to use the common proportion: $\frac{\%}{100} = \frac{is}{of}$. Within the proportion, % is the percentage of girls, 100 is the total percentage of the class, *is* is the number of girls, and *of* is the total number of students in the class. Most percentage problems can be written using this language. To solve this problem, the proportion should be set up as $\frac{20}{100} = \frac{x}{30}$, then solved for x. Cross-multiplying results in the equation $20 \times 30 = 100x$, which results in the solution $x = 6$. There are 6 girls in the class.

Ratios can be used to solve problems that concern length, volume, and other units. If the following graphic of a cone is given, the problem may ask for the volume to be found.

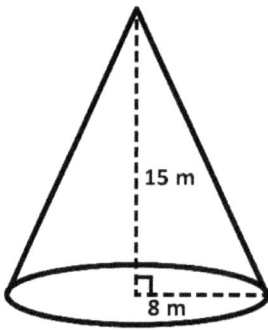

Referring to the formulas provided on the test, the volume of a cone is given as: $V = \pi r^2 \frac{h}{3}$, where r is the radius, and h is the height. Plugging $r = 8$ and $h = 15$ from the graphic into the formula, the following is obtained: $V = \pi(8^2)\frac{15}{3}$. Therefore, the volume of the cone is found to be 1,005.3 m³. Sometimes, answers in different units are sought. If this problem wanted the answer in liters, 1,005.3 m³ would need to be converted. Using the equivalence statement 1 m³ = 1,000 L, the following ratio would be used to solve for liters: $1{,}005.3 \text{ m}^3 \times \frac{1{,}000 \text{ L}}{1 \text{ m}^3}$. Cubic meters in the numerator and denominator cancel each other out, and the answer is converted to 1,005,300 liters, or 1.0053×10^6 L.

Other conversions can also be made between different given and final units. If the temperature in a pool is 30°C, what is the temperature of the pool in degrees Fahrenheit? To convert these units, an equation is used relating Celsius to Fahrenheit. The following equation is used: $T_{°F} = 1.8 T_{°C} + 32$. Plugging in the given temperature and solving the equation for T yields the result: $T_{°F} = 1.8(30) + 32 = 86°F$. Units in both the metric system and U.S. customary system are widely used.

Measurement/Geometry

Using Transformations to Show Congruence or Similarity

Transformations in the Plane

A **transformation** occurs when a shape is altered in the plane where it exists. There are three major types of transformation: translations, reflections, and rotations. A **translation** consists of shifting a shape in one direction. A **reflection** results when a shape is transformed over a line to its mirror image. Finally, a **rotation** occurs when a shape moves in a circular motion around a specified point. The object can be turned clockwise or counterclockwise and, if rotated 360 degrees, returns to its original location.

Distance and Angle Measure

The three major types of transformations preserve distance and angle measurement. The shapes stay the same, but they are moved to another place in the plane. Therefore, the distance between any two points on the shape doesn't change. Also, any original angle measure between two line segments doesn't change. However, there are transformations that don't preserve distance and angle measurements, including those that don't preserve the original shape. For example, transformations that involve stretching and shrinking shapes don't preserve distance and angle measures. In these cases, the input variables are multiplied by either a number greater than one (*stretch*) or less than one (*shrink*).

Rigid Motion

A **rigid motion** is a transformation that preserves distance and length. Every line segment in the resulting image is congruent to the corresponding line segment in the pre-image. Congruence between two figures means a series of transformations (or a rigid motion) can be defined that maps one of the figures onto the other. Basically, two figures are congruent if they have the same shape and size.

Dilation

A shape is dilated, or a **dilation** occurs, when each side of the original image is multiplied by a given scale factor. If the scale factor is less than 1 and greater than 0, the dilation contracts the shape, and the resulting shape is smaller. If the scale factor equals 1, the resulting shape is the same size, and the dilation is a rigid motion. Finally, if the scale factor is greater than 1, the resulting shape is larger and the dilation expands the shape. The **center of dilation** is the point where the distance from it to any point on the new shape equals the scale factor times the distance from the center to the corresponding point in the pre-image. Dilation isn't an isometric transformation because distance isn't preserved. However, angle measure, parallel lines, and points on a line all remain unchanged. The following figure is an example of translation, rotation, dilation, and reflection:

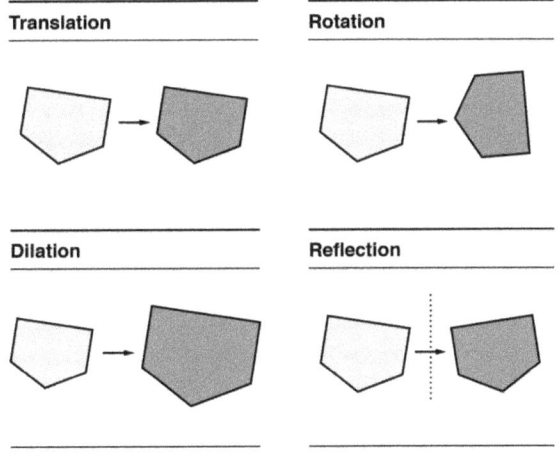

Determining Congruence

Two figures are **congruent** if there is a rigid motion that can map one figure onto the other. Therefore, all pairs of sides and angles within the image and pre-image must be congruent. For example, in triangles, each pair of the three sides and three angles must be congruent. Similarly, in two four-sided figures, each pair of the four sides and four angles must be congruent.

To prove theorems about triangles, basic definitions involving triangles (e.g., equilateral, isosceles, etc.) need to be known. Proven theorems concerning lines and angles can be applied to prove theorems about triangles. Common theorems to be proved include: the sum of all angles in a triangle equals 180 degrees; the sum of the lengths of two sides of a triangle is greater than the length of the third side; the base angles of an isosceles triangle are congruent; the line segment connecting the midpoint of two sides of a triangle is parallel to the third side and its length is half the length of the third side; and the medians of a triangle all meet at a single point.

Triangle Congruence

There are five theorems to show that triangles are congruent when it's unknown whether each pair of angles and sides are congruent. Each theorem is a shortcut that involves different combinations of sides and angles that must be true for the two triangles to be congruent. For example, **side-side-side (SSS)** states that if all sides are equal, the triangles are congruent. **Side-angle-side (SAS)** states that if two pairs of sides are equal and the included angles are congruent, then the triangles are congruent.

Similarly, **angle-side-angle (ASA)** states that if two pairs of angles are congruent and the included side lengths are equal, the triangles are congruent. **Angle-angle-side (AAS)** states that two triangles are congruent if they have two pairs of congruent angles and a pair of corresponding equal side lengths that aren't included. Finally, **hypotenuse-leg (HL)** states that if two right triangles have equal hypotenuses and an equal pair of shorter sides, then the triangles are congruent. An important item to note is that **angle-angle-angle (AAA)** is not enough information to have congruence. It's important to understand why these rules work by using rigid motions to show congruence between the triangles with the given properties. For example, three reflections are needed to show why *SAS* follows from the definition of congruence.

Similarity for Two Triangles

If two angles of one triangle are congruent with two angles of a second triangle, the triangles are similar. This is because, within any triangle, the sum of the angle measurements is 180 degrees. Therefore, if two are congruent, the third angle must also be congruent because their measurements are equal. Three congruent pairs of angles mean that the triangles are similar.

Proving Congruence and Similarity

The criteria needed to prove triangles are congruent involves both angle and side congruence. Both pairs of related angles and sides need to be of the same measurement to use congruence in a proof. The criteria to prove similarity in triangles involves proportionality of side lengths. Angles must be congruent in similar triangles; however, corresponding side lengths only need to be a constant multiple of each other. Once similarity is established, it can be used in proofs as well. Relationships in geometric figures other than triangles can be proven using triangle congruence and similarity. If a similar or congruent triangle can be found within another type of geometric figure, their criteria can be used to prove a relationship about a given formula. For example, a rectangle can be broken up into two congruent triangles.

Mathematics

Properties of Polygons and Circles

A **polygon** is a closed two-dimensional figure consisting of three or more sides. Polygons can be either convex or concave. A polygon that has interior angles all measuring less than 180° is convex. A concave polygon has one or more interior angles measuring greater than 180°. Examples are shown below.

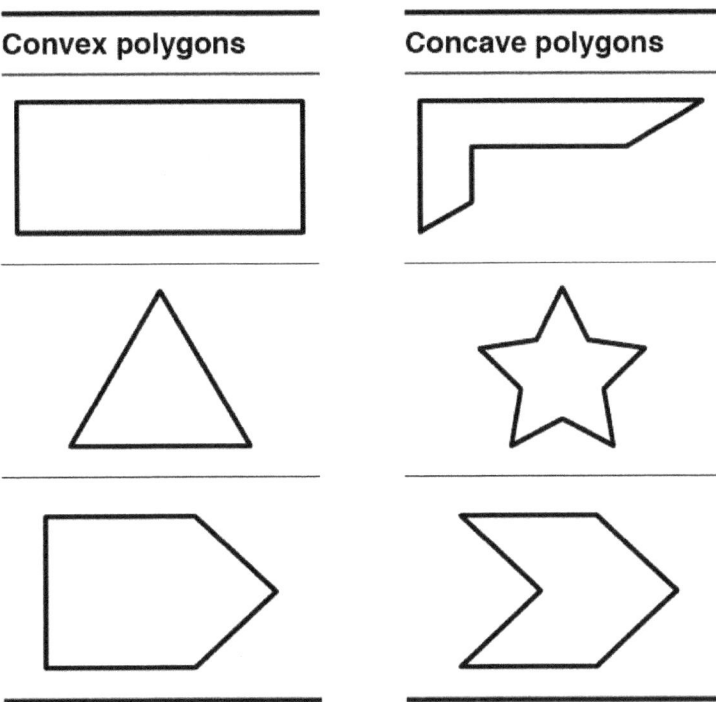

Polygons can be classified by the number of sides (also equal to the number of angles) they have. The following are the names of polygons with a given number of sides or angles:

# of sides	3	4	5	6	7	8	9	10
Name of polygon	Triangle	Quadrilateral	Pentagon	Hexagon	Septagon (or heptagon)	Octagon	Nonagon	Decagon

Equiangular polygons are polygons in which the measure of every interior angle is the same. The sides of equilateral polygons are always the same length. If a polygon is both equiangular and equilateral, the polygon is defined as a regular polygon. Examples are shown below.

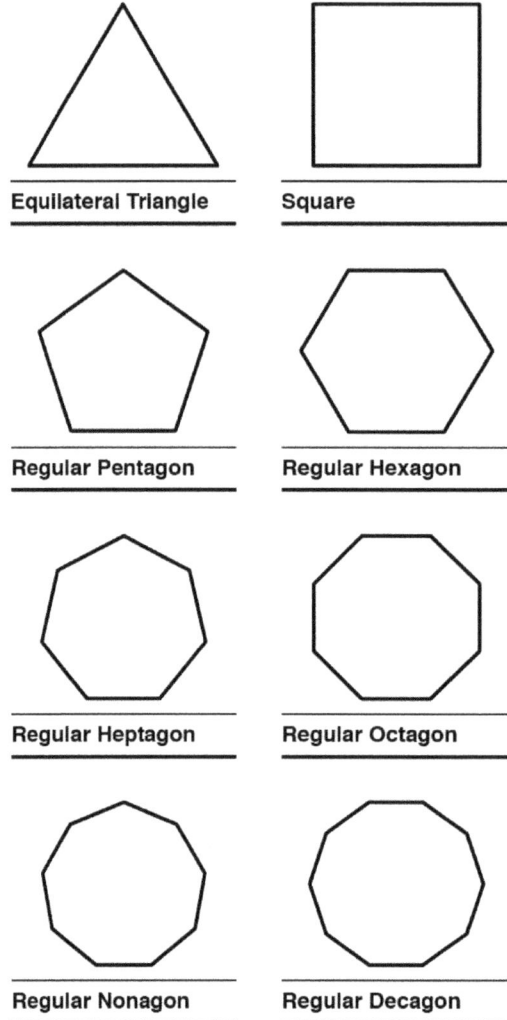

Triangles can be further classified by their sides and angles. A triangle with its largest angle measuring 90° is a **right triangle**.

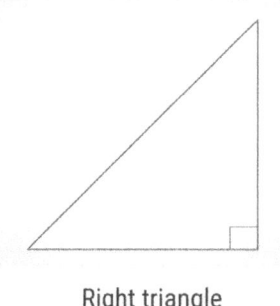

Right triangle

A triangle with the largest angle less than 90° is an **acute triangle**. A triangle with the largest angle greater than 90° is an obtuse triangle.

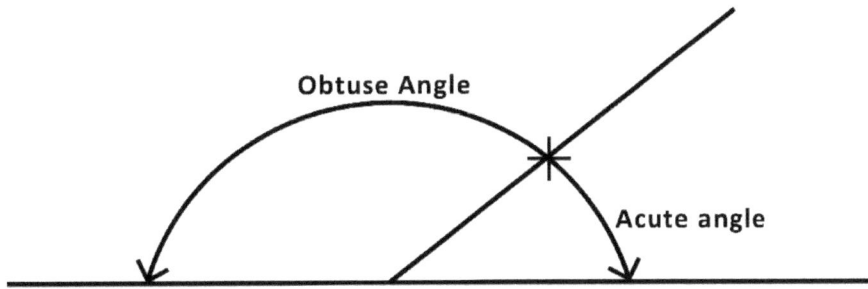

A triangle consisting of two equal sides and two equal angles is an **isosceles triangle**. A triangle with three equal sides and three equal angles is an **equilateral triangle**. A triangle with no equal sides or angles is a **scalene triangle**.

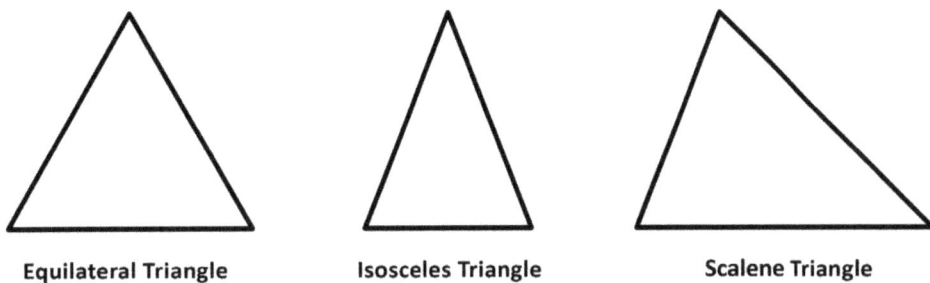

Quadrilaterals can be further classified according to their sides and angles. A quadrilateral with exactly one pair of parallel sides is called a **trapezoid**. A quadrilateral that shows both pairs of opposite sides parallel is a **parallelogram**. Parallelograms include rhombuses, rectangles, and squares. A **rhombus** has four equal sides. A

rectangle has four equal angles (90° each). A **square** has four 90° angles and four equal sides. Therefore, a square is both a rhombus and a rectangle.

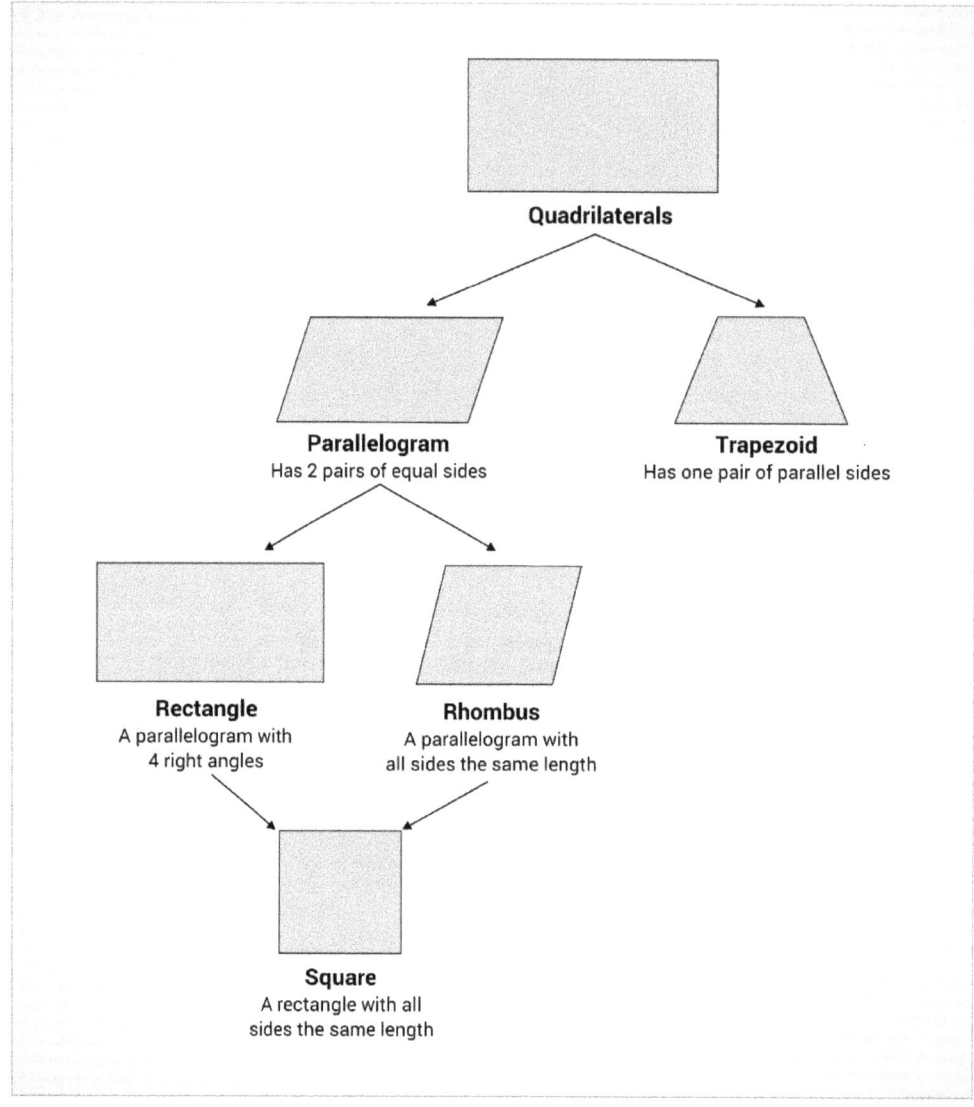

There are many key facts related to geometry that are applicable. The sum of the measures of the angles of a triangle are 180°, and for a quadrilateral, the sum is 360°. Rectangles and squares each have four right angles. A *right angle* has a measure of 90°.

Mathematics

Perimeter

The **perimeter** is the distance around a figure or the sum of all sides of a polygon.

The *formula for the perimeter of a square* is four times the length of a side. For example, the following square has side lengths of 5 meters:

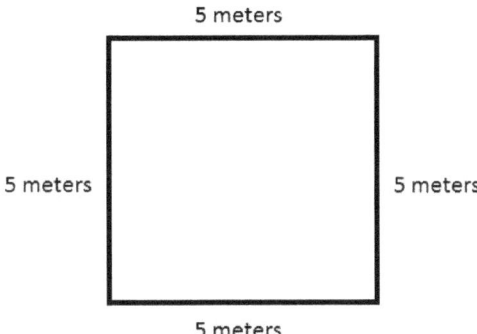

The perimeter is 20 meters because 4 times 5 is 20.

The *formula for a perimeter of a rectangle* is the sum of twice the length and twice the width. For example, if the length of a rectangle is 10 inches and the width 8 inches, then the perimeter is 36 inches because:

$$P = 2l + 2w$$

$$2(10) + 2(8)$$

$$20 + 16 = 36 \text{ inches}$$

Area

The **area** is the amount of space inside of a figure, and there are formulas associated with area.

The **area of a triangle** is the product of $\frac{1}{2}$ the base and height. For example, if the base of the triangle is 2 feet and the height is 4 feet, then the area is 4 square feet. The following equation shows the formula used to calculate the area of the triangle:

$$A = \tfrac{1}{2}bh = \tfrac{1}{2}(2)(4) = 4 \text{ square feet}$$

The **area of a square** is the length of a side squared. For example, if the side of a square is 5 centimeters, then the area is 25 square centimeters. The formula for this example is $A = s^2 = 5^2 = 25$ square centimeters.

The **area of a trapezoid** is $\frac{1}{2}$ the height times the sum of the bases. For example, if the length of the bases are 2.5 and 3 feet and the height 3.5 feet, then the area is 9.625 square feet. The following formula shows how the area is calculated:

$$A = \frac{1}{2}h(b_1 + b_2)$$

$$\frac{1}{2}(3.5)(2.5 + 3)$$

$$\frac{1}{2}(3.5)(5.5) = 9.625 \text{ square feet}$$

The perimeter of a figure is measured in single units, while the area is measured in square units.

If a quadrilateral is inscribed in a circle, the sum of its opposite angles is 180 degrees. Consider the quadrilateral $ABCD$ centered at the point O:

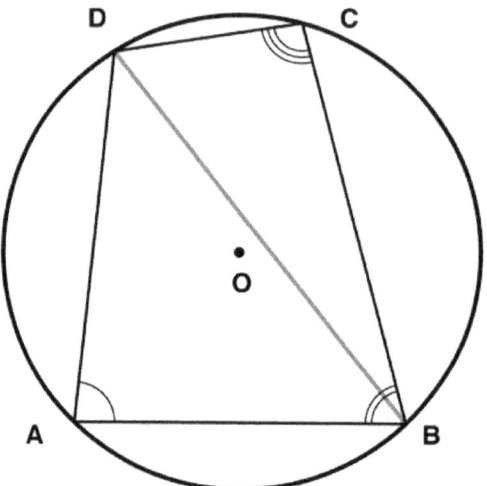

Each of the four line segments within the quadrilateral is a chord of the circle. Consider the diagonal DB. Angle DAB is an inscribed angle leaning on the arc DCB. Therefore, angle DAB is half the measure of the arc DCB. Conversely, angle DCB is an inscribed angle leaning on the arc DAB. Therefore, angle DCB is half the measure of the arc DAB. The sum of arcs DCB and DAB is 360 degrees because they make up the entire circle. Therefore, the sum of angles DAB and DCB equals half of 360 degrees, which is 180 degrees.

Degrees are used to express the size of an angle. A complete circle is represented by 360°, and a half circle is represented by 180°. In addition, a right angle fills one quarter of a circle and is represented by 90°.

The equation used to find the area of a circle is $A = \pi r^2$. For example, if a circle has a radius of 5 centimeters, the area is computed by substituting 5 for the radius: $(5)^2$. Using this reasoning, to find half of the area of a circle, the formula is $A = 0.5\pi r^2$. Similarly, to find the quarter of an area of a circle, the formula is $A = 0.25\pi r^2$. To find any fractional area of a circle, a student can use the formula $A = \frac{C}{360}\pi r^2$, where C is the number of degrees of the central angle of the sector.

Other related concepts for circles include the diameter and circumference. *Circumference* is the distance around a circle. The formula for circumference is $C = 2\pi r$. The *diameter* of a circle is the distance across a circle through its center point. The formula for circumference can also be thought of as $C = dr$ where d is the circle's diameter, since the diameter of a circle is $2r$.

A **circle** can be defined as the set of all points that are the same distance (known as the radius, r) from a single point C (known as the center of the circle). The center has coordinates (h, k), and any point on the circle can be labelled with coordinates (x, y).

As shown below, a right triangle is formed with these two points:

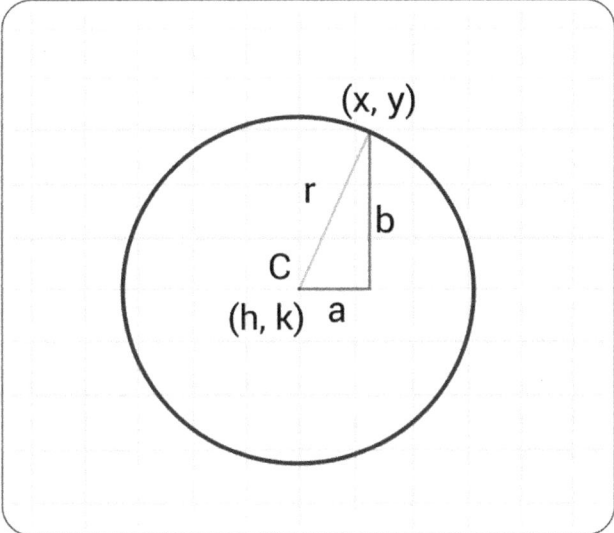

The **Pythagorean theorem** states that $a^2 + b^2 = r^2$. However, a can be replaced by $|x - h|$ and b can be replaced by $|y - k|$ by using the *distance formula* which is:

$$d = \sqrt{(x_2 - x_1)^2 + (y_2 - y_1)^2}$$

That substitution results in:

$$(x - h)^2 + (y - k)^2 = r^2$$

This is the formula for finding the equation of any circle with a center (h, k) and a radius r. Note that sometimes C is used instead of r.

The Pythagorean Theorem

The **Pythagorean theorem** is an important relationship between the three sides of a right triangle. It states that the square of the side opposite the right triangle, known as the **hypotenuse** (denoted as c^2), is equal to the sum of the squares of the other two sides ($a^2 + b^2$). Thus, $a^2 + b^2 = c^2$.

The theorem can be seen in the following image:

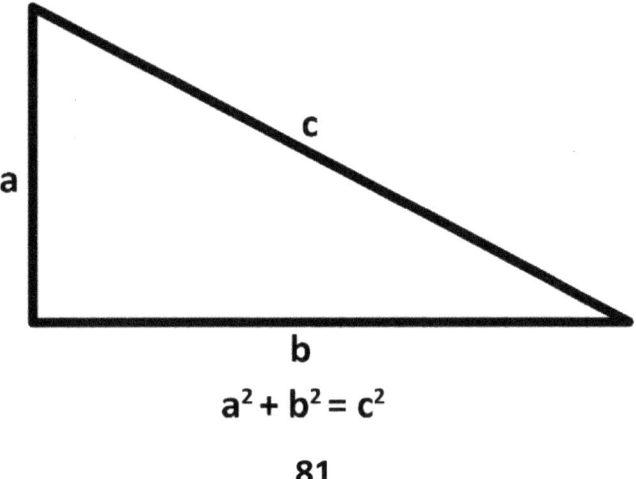

Both the trigonometric functions and the Pythagorean theorem can be used in problems that involve finding either a missing side or a missing angle of a right triangle. To do so, one must look to see what sides and angles are given and select the correct relationship that will help find the missing value. These relationships can also be used to solve application problems involving right triangles. Often, it's helpful to draw a figure to represent the problem to see what's missing.

As an example of the theorem, suppose that Shirley has a rectangular field that is 5 feet wide and 12 feet long, and she wants to split it in half using a fence that goes from one corner to the opposite corner. How long will this fence need to be? To figure this out, note that this makes the field into two right triangles, whose hypotenuse will be the fence dividing it in half. Therefore, the fence length is given by $\sqrt{5^2 + 12^2} = \sqrt{169} = 13$ feet long.

Similar and Congruent Triangles

Suppose that Lara is 5 feet tall and is standing 30 feet from the base of a light pole, and her shadow is 6 feet long. How high is the light on the pole? To figure this out, it helps to make a sketch of the situation:

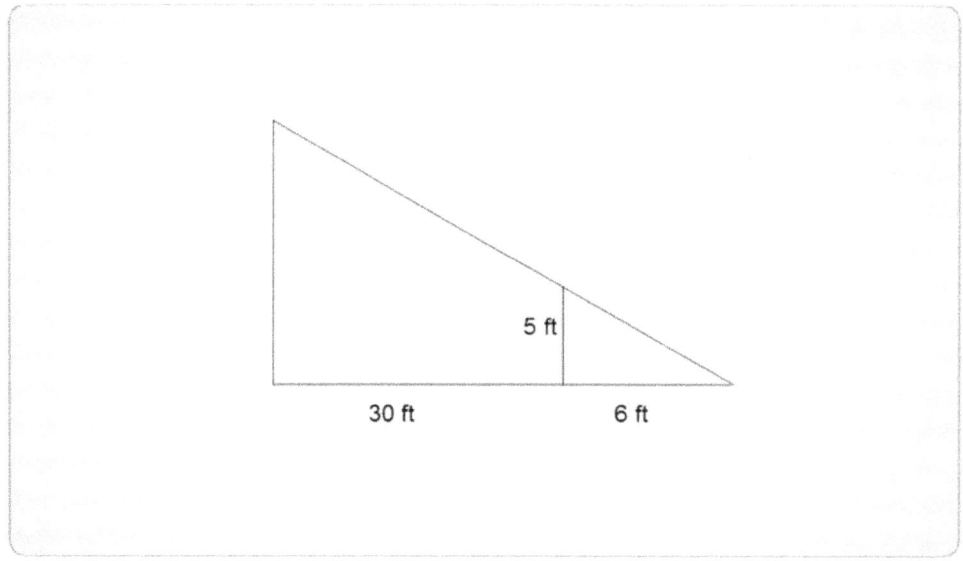

The light pole is the left side of the triangle. Lara is the 5-foot vertical line. Test takers should notice that there are two right triangles here, and that they have all the same angles as one another. Therefore, they form similar triangles. So, the ratio of proportionality between them must be found.

The bases of these triangles are known. The small triangle, formed by Lara and her shadow, has a base of 6 feet. The large triangle formed by the light pole along with the line from the base of the pole out to the end of Lara's shadow is $30 + 6 = 36$ feet long. So, the ratio of the big triangle to the little triangle is $\frac{36}{6} = 6$. The height of the little triangle is 5 feet. Therefore, the height of the big triangle will be $6 \times 5 = 30$ feet, meaning that the light is 30 feet up the pole.

Using Volume and Surface Area Formulas

Surface area and volume are two- and three-dimensional measurements. Surface area measures the total surface space of an object, like the six sides of a cube. Questions about surface area will ask how much of something is needed to cover a three-dimensional object, like wrapping a present. **Volume** is the measurement of how much space an object occupies, like how much space is in the cube. Volume questions will ask how much of something is

Mathematics

needed to completely fill the object. The most common surface area and volume questions deal with spheres, cubes, and rectangular prisms.

The formula for a cube's surface area is $SA = 6 \times s^2$, where s is the length of a side. A cube has 6 equal sides, so the formula expresses the area of all the sides. Volume is simply measured by taking the cube of the length, so the formula is $V = s^3$.

The surface area formula for a rectangular prism or a general box is $SA = 2(lw + lh + wh)$, where l is the length, h is the height, and w is the width. The volume formula is $V = l \times w \times h$, which is the cube's volume formula adjusted for the unequal lengths of a box's sides.

The formula for a sphere's surface area is $SA = 4\pi r^2$, where r is the sphere's radius. The surface area formula is the area for a circle multiplied by four. To measure volume, the formula is $V = \frac{4}{3}\pi r^3$.

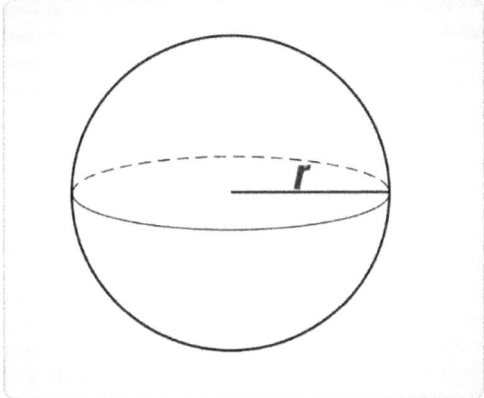

A **rectangular pyramid** is a figure with a rectangular base and four triangular sides that meet at a single vertex. If the rectangle has sides of lengths x and y, then the volume will be given by $V = \frac{1}{3}xyh$.

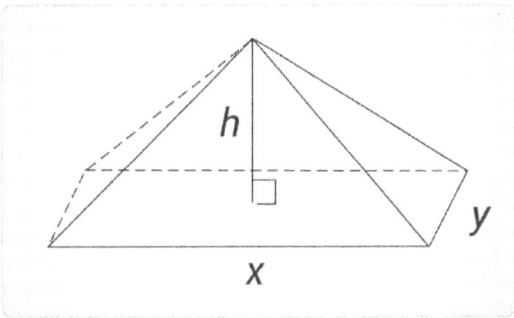

To find the surface area, the dimensions of each triangle must be known. However, these dimensions can differ depending on the problem in question. Therefore, there is no general formula for calculating total surface area.

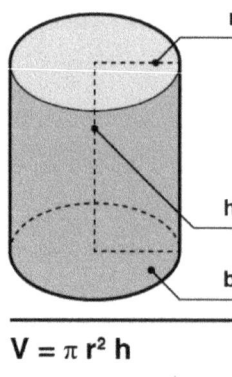

$$V = \pi r^2 h$$

The formula to find the volume of a cylinder is $\pi r^2 h$. This formula contains the formula for the area of a circle (πr^2) because the base of a cylinder is a circle. To calculate the volume of a cylinder, the slices of circles needed to build the entire height of the cylinder are added together. For example, if the radius is 5 feet and the height of the cylinder is 10 feet, the cylinder's volume is calculated by using the following equation: $\pi 5^2 \times 10$. Substituting 3.14 for π, the volume is 785 ft³.

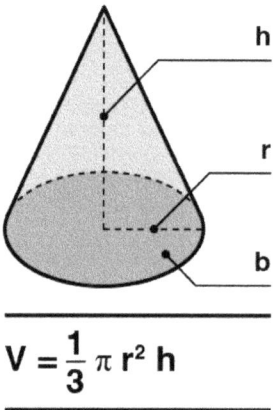

$$V = \frac{1}{3} \pi r^2 h$$

The formula used to calculate the volume of a cone is $\frac{1}{3}\pi r^2 h$. Essentially, the area of the base of the cone is multiplied by the cone's height. In a real-life example where the radius of a cone is 2 meters and the height of a cone is 5 meters, the volume of the cone is calculated by utilizing the formula $\frac{1}{3}\pi 2^2 \times 5$. After substituting 3.14 for π, the volume is 20.9 m³.

Concepts of Density

The **density** of a substance is the ratio of mass to area or volume. It's a relationship between the mass and how much space the object actually takes up. Knowing which units to use in each situation is crucial. Population density is an example of a real-life situation that's modeled by using density concepts. It involves calculating the ratio of the number of people to the number of square miles. The amount of material needed per a specific unit of area or volume is another application. For example, estimating the number of BTUs per cubic foot of a home is a measurement that relates to heating or cooling the house based on the desired temperature and the house's size.

Solving Problems Involving Angles

In geometry, a **line** connects two points, has no thickness, and extends indefinitely in both directions beyond each point. If the length is finite, it's known as a **line segment** and has two **endpoints**. A **ray** is the straight portion of a

Mathematics

line that has one endpoint and extends indefinitely in the other direction. An **angle** is formed when two rays begin at the same endpoint and extend indefinitely. The endpoint of an angle is called a **vertex**. **Adjacent angles** are two side-by-side angles formed from the same ray that have the same endpoint. Angles are measured in **degrees** or **radians**, which is a measure of **rotation**. A **full rotation** equals 360 degrees or 2π radians, which represents a circle. Half a rotation equals 180 degrees or π radians and represents a half-circle.

Subsequently, 90 degrees ($\frac{\pi}{2}$ radians) represents a quarter of a circle, which is known as a **right angle**. Any angle less than 90 degrees is an **acute angle**, and any angle greater than 90 degrees is an **obtuse angle**. Angle measurement is additive. When an angle is broken into two non-overlapping angles, the total measure of the larger angle equals the sum of the two smaller angles. Lines are **coplanar** if they're located in the same plane. Two lines are **parallel** if they are coplanar, extend in the same direction, and never cross. If lines do cross, they're labeled as **intersecting lines** because they "intersect" at one point. If they intersect at more than one point, they're the same line. **Perpendicular lines** are coplanar lines that form a right angle at their point of intersection.

Supplementary angles add up to 180 degrees. **Vertical angles** are two nonadjacent angles formed by two intersecting lines. For example, in the following picture, angles 4 and 2 are vertical angles and so are angles 1 and 3:

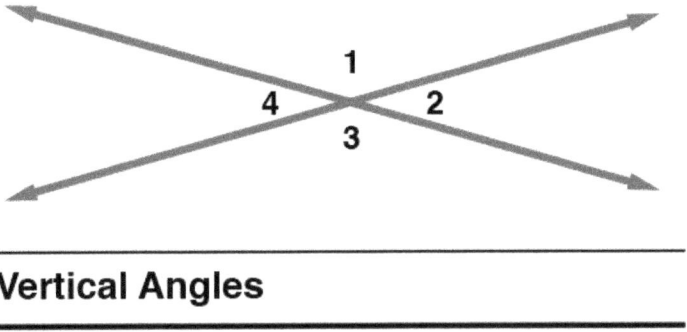

Vertical Angles

Corresponding angles are two angles in the same position whenever a straight line (known as a *transversal*) crosses two others. If the two lines are parallel, the corresponding angles are equal. In the following diagram, angles 1 and 3 are corresponding angles but aren't equal to each other:

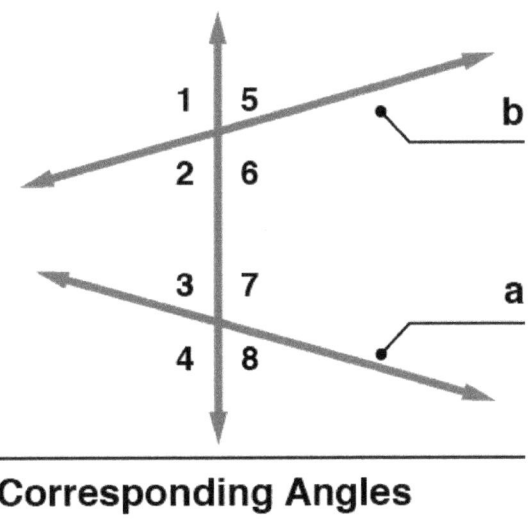

Corresponding Angles

Alternate interior angles are also a pair of angles formed when two lines are crossed by a transversal. They are opposite angles that exist inside of the two lines. In the corresponding angles diagram above, angles 2 and 7 are

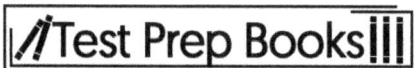

alternate interior angles, as well as angles 6 and 3. **Alternate exterior angles** are opposite angles formed by a transversal but, in contrast to interior angles, exterior angles exist outside the two original lines. Therefore, angles 1 and 8 are alternate exterior angles and so are angles 5 and 4. Finally, **consecutive interior angles** are pairs of angles formed by a transversal. These angles are located on the same side of the transversal and inside the two original lines. Therefore, angles 2 and 3 are a pair of consecutive interior angles, and so are angles 6 and 7. These definitions are instrumental in solving many problems that involve determining relationships between angles.

Data Analysis/Probability/Statistics

Summarizing and Interpreting Data, Making Predictions, and Solving Problems

Summarizing Data

Most statistics involve collecting a large amount of data, analyzing it, and then making decisions based on previously known information. These decisions also can be measured through additional data collection and then analyzed. Therefore, the cycle can repeat itself over and over. Representing the data visually is a large part of the process, and many plots on the real number line exist that allow this to be done. For example, a *dot plot* uses dots to represent data points above the number line. Also, a **histogram** represents a data set as a collection of rectangles, which illustrate the frequency distribution of the data. Finally, a **box plot** (also known as a *box and whisker plot*) plots a

Mathematics

data set on the number line by segmenting the distribution into four quartiles that are divided equally in half by the median. Here's an example of a box plot, a histogram, and a dot plot for the same data set:

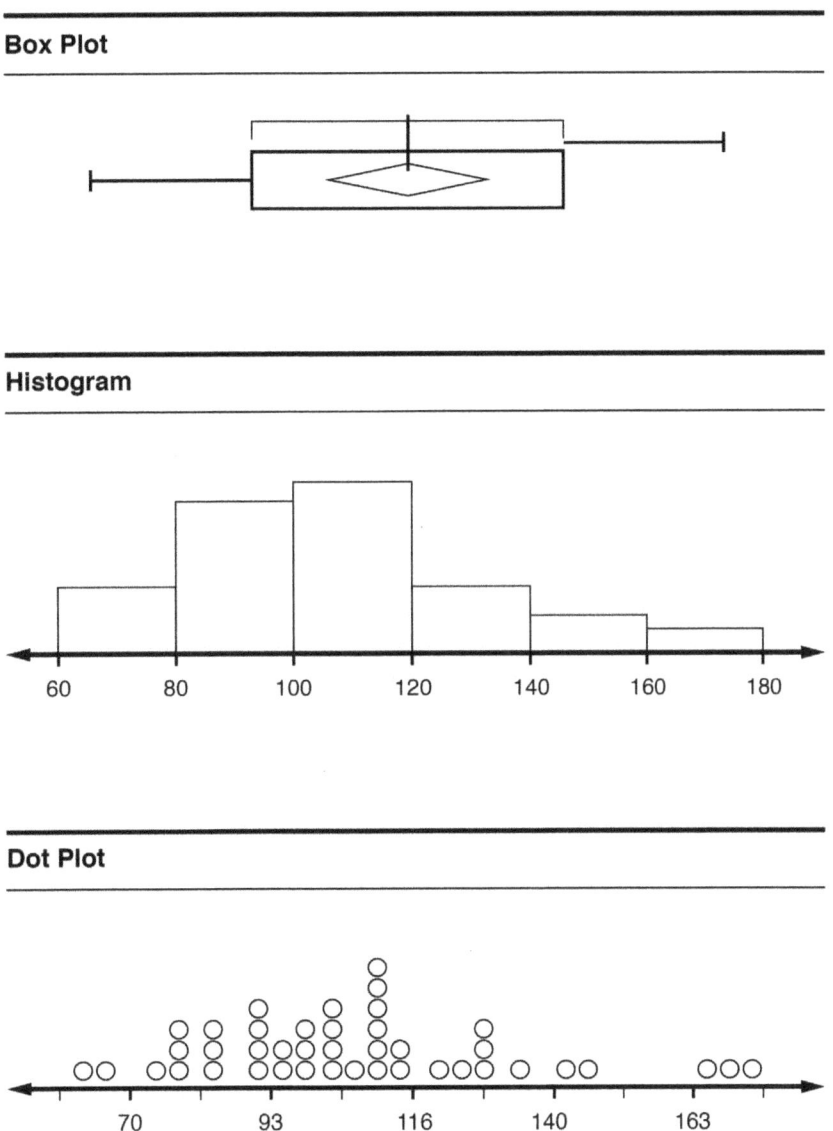

Interpreting Data

Comparing data sets within statistics can mean many things. The first way to compare data sets is by looking at the center and spread of each set. The center of a data set can mean two things: median or mean. The **median** is the halfway point of a data set, and it splits the data into two intervals. The **mean** is the average value of the data within a set. It's calculated by adding up all of the data in the set and dividing the total by the number of data points.

Outliers can significantly impact the mean. Additionally, two completely different data sets can have the same mean. For example, a data set with values ranging from zero to 100 and a data set with values ranging from 44 to 56 can both have means of 50. The first data set has a much wider range, which is known as the *spread* of the data. This measures how varied the data is within each set. Spread can be defined further as either interquartile range or standard deviation. The **interquartile range (IQR)** is the range of the middle 50 percent of the data set. This range can be seen in the large rectangle on a box plot. The **standard deviation** quantifies the amount of variation with respect to the mean. A lower standard deviation shows that the data set doesn't differ greatly from the mean. A larger standard deviation shows that the data set is spread out farther from the mean.

Given a data set X consisting of data points $(x_1, x_2, x_3, \ldots x_n)$, the *variance* of X is defined to be:

$$\frac{\sum_{i=1}^{n}(x_i - \bar{X})^2}{n}$$

This means that the variance of X is the average of the squares of the differences between each data point and the mean of X.

Given a data set X consisting of data points $(x_1, x_2, x_3, \ldots x_n)$, the **standard deviation** of X is defined to be:

$$s_x = \sqrt{\frac{\sum_{i=1}^{n}(x_i - \bar{X})^2}{n}}$$

x is each value in the data set, $\bar{x}$ is the mean, and n is the total number of data points in the set.

In other words, the standard deviation is the square root of the variance. Both the variance and the standard deviation are measures of how much the data tend to be spread out. When the standard deviation is low, the data points are mostly clustered around the mean. When the standard deviation is high, it generally indicates that the data are quite spread out, or else that there are a few substantial outliers.

As a simple example, compute the standard deviation for the data set (1, 3, 3, 5). The first step is to compute the mean, which is $\frac{1+3+3+5}{4} = \frac{12}{4} = 3$. Next, the variance of X is found with the formula:

$$\sum_{i=1}^{4}(x_i - \bar{X})^2 = (1-3)^2 + (3-3)^2 + (3-3)^2 + (5-3)^2$$

$$-2^2 + 0^2 + 0^2 + 2^2 = 8$$

Therefore, the variance is $\frac{8}{4} = 2$. Taking the square root, the standard deviation is found to be $\sqrt{2}$.

The shape of a data set is another way to compare two or more sets of data. If a data set isn't symmetric around its mean, it's said to be *skewed*. If the tail to the left of the mean is longer, it's said to be **skewed to the left**. In this case, the mean is less than the median. Conversely, if the tail to the right of the mean is longer, it's said to be **skewed to the right** and the mean is greater than the median. When classifying a data set according to its shape, its overall **skewness** is being discussed. If the mean and median are equal, the data set isn't **skewed**; it is **symmetric**, and is considered normally distributed.

An **outlier** is a data point that lies a great distance away from the majority of the data set. It also can be labeled as an extreme value. Technically, an outlier is any value that falls 1.5 times the IQR above the upper quartile or 1.5 times the IQR below the lower quartile. The effect of outliers in the data set is seen visually because they affect the mean. If there's a large difference between the mean and mode, outliers are the cause. The mean shows bias towards the outlying values. However, the median won't be affected as greatly by outliers.

Mathematics

Representing Data

Chart is a broad term that refers to a variety of ways to represent data.

To graph relations, the **Cartesian plane** is used. This means to think of the plane as being given a grid of squares, with one direction being the x-axis and the other direction the y-axis. Any point on the plane can be specified by saying how far to go along the x-axis and how far along the y-axis with a pair of numbers (x, y). Specific values for these pairs can be given names such as $C = (-1, 3)$. Negative values mean to move left or down; positive values mean to move right or up. The point where the axes cross one another is called the **origin**. The origin has coordinates $(0, 0)$ and is usually called O when given a specific label. An illustration of the Cartesian plane, along with the plotted points $(2, 1)$ and $(-1, -1)$, is below.

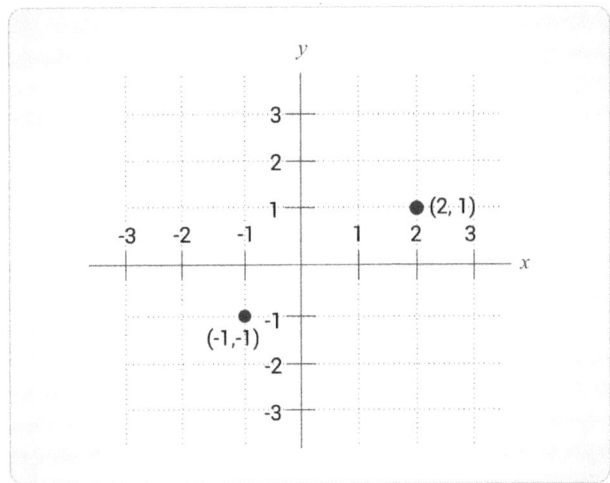

A **line plot** is a diagram that shows quantity of data along a number line. It is a quick way to record data in a structure similar to a bar graph without needing to do the required shading of a bar graph. Here is an example of a line plot:

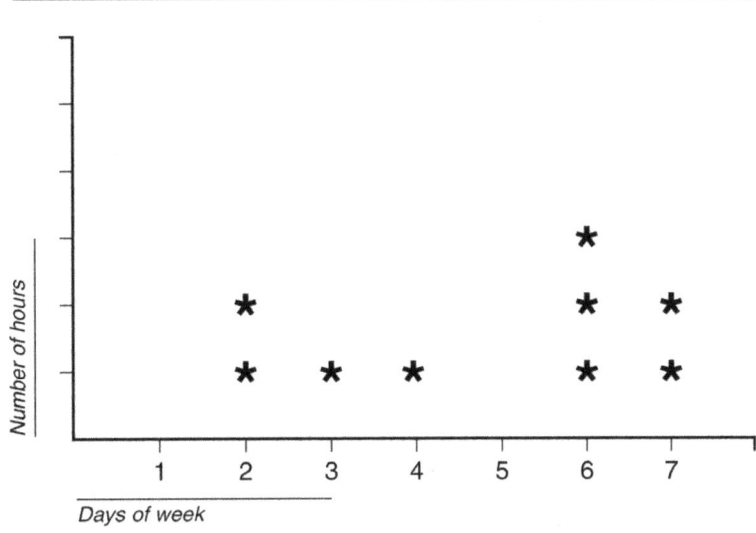

A **tally chart** is a diagram in which tally marks are utilized to represent data. Tally marks are a means of showing a quantity of objects within a specific classification. Here is an example of a tally chart:

Number of days with rain	Number of weeks
0			
1							
2										
3																
4						
5							
6						
7		

Data is often recorded using fractions, such as half a mile, and understanding fractions is critical because of their popular use in real-world applications. Also, it is extremely important to label values with their units when using data. For example, regarding length, the number 2 is meaningless unless it is attached to a unit. A measurement of 2 cm is much different than 2 miles.

A **picture graph** is a diagram that shows pictorial representations of data being discussed. The symbols used can represent a certain number of objects. Notice how each fruit symbol in the following graph represents a count of two fruits. One drawback of picture graphs is that they can be less accurate if each symbol represents a large number. For example, if each banana symbol represented ten bananas, and students consumed 22 bananas, it may be challenging to draw and interpret two and one-fifth bananas as a frequency count of 22.

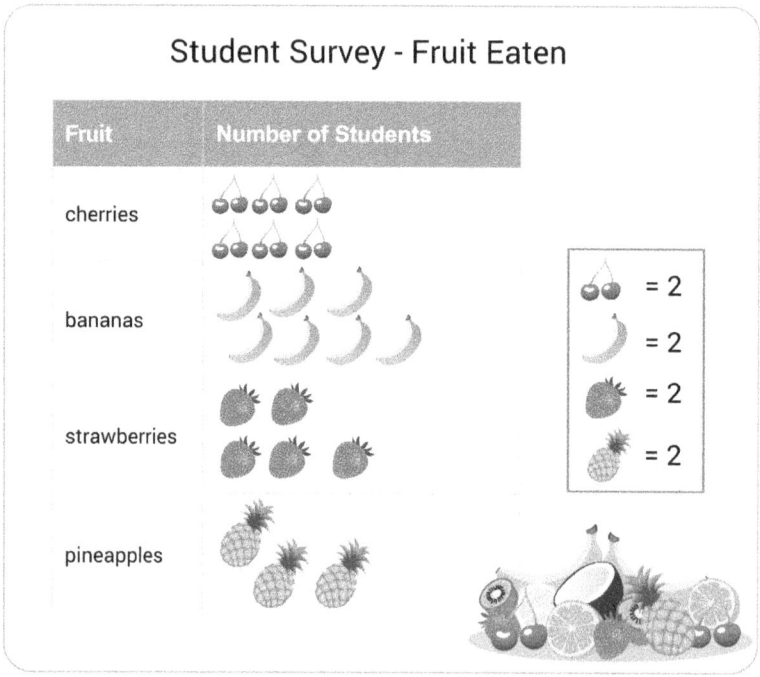

Mathematics

A **circle graph**, also called a **pie chart**, shows categorical data with each category representing a percentage of the whole data set. To make a circle graph, the percent of the data set for each category must be determined. To do so, the frequency of the category is divided by the total number of data points and converted to a percent. For example, if 80 people were asked what their favorite sport is and 20 responded basketball, basketball makes up 25% of the data ($\frac{20}{80} = 0.25 = 25\%$). Each category in a data set is represented by a *slice* of the circle proportionate to its percentage of the whole.

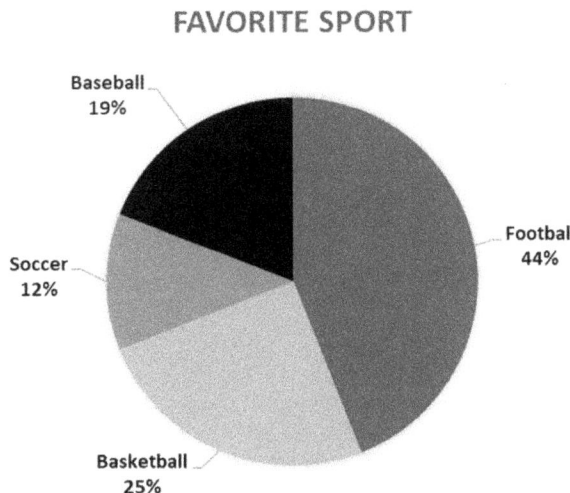

A **scatter plot** displays the relationship between two variables. Values for the independent variable, typically denoted by x, are paired with values for the dependent variable, typically denoted by y. Each set of corresponding values are written as an ordered pair (x, y). To construct the graph, a coordinate grid is labeled with the x-axis representing the independent variable and the y-axis representing the dependent variable. Each ordered pair is graphed.

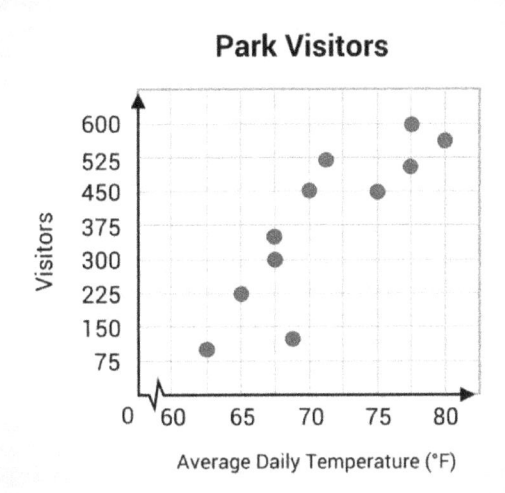

Like a scatter plot, a **line graph** compares two variables that change continuously, typically over time. Paired data values (ordered pairs) are plotted on a coordinate grid with the x- and y-axis representing the two variables. A line is drawn from each point to the next, going from left to right. A double line graph simply displays two sets of data that contain values for the same two variables. The double line graph below displays the profit for given years (two variables) for Company A and Company B (two data sets).

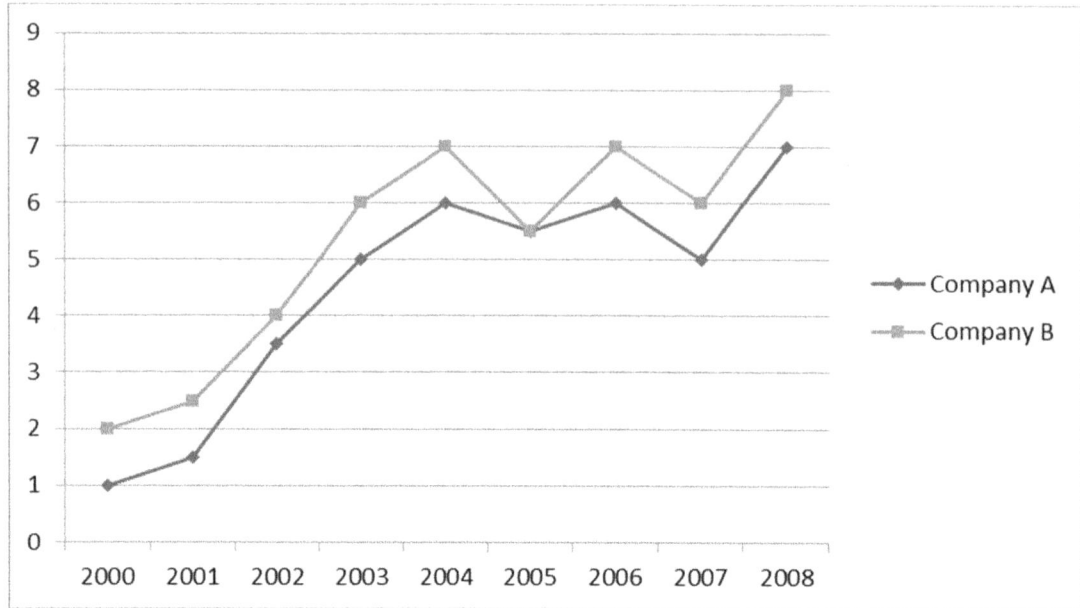

Choosing the appropriate graph to display a data set depends on what type of data is included in the set and what information must be shown.

Scatter plots and line graphs can be used to display data consisting of two variables. Examples include height and weight, or distance and time. A correlation between the variables is determined by examining the points on the graph. Line graphs are used if each value for one variable pairs with a distinct value for the other variable. Line graphs show relationships between variables.

Identifying Line of Best Fit

Regression lines are a way to calculate a relationship between the independent variable and the dependent variable. A straight line means that there's a linear trend in the data. Technology can be used to find the equation of this line (e.g., a graphing calculator or Microsoft Excel®). In either case, all of the data points are entered, and a line

Mathematics

is "fit" that best represents the shape of the data. Other functions used to model data sets include quadratic and exponential models. Here's an example of a data set and its regression line:

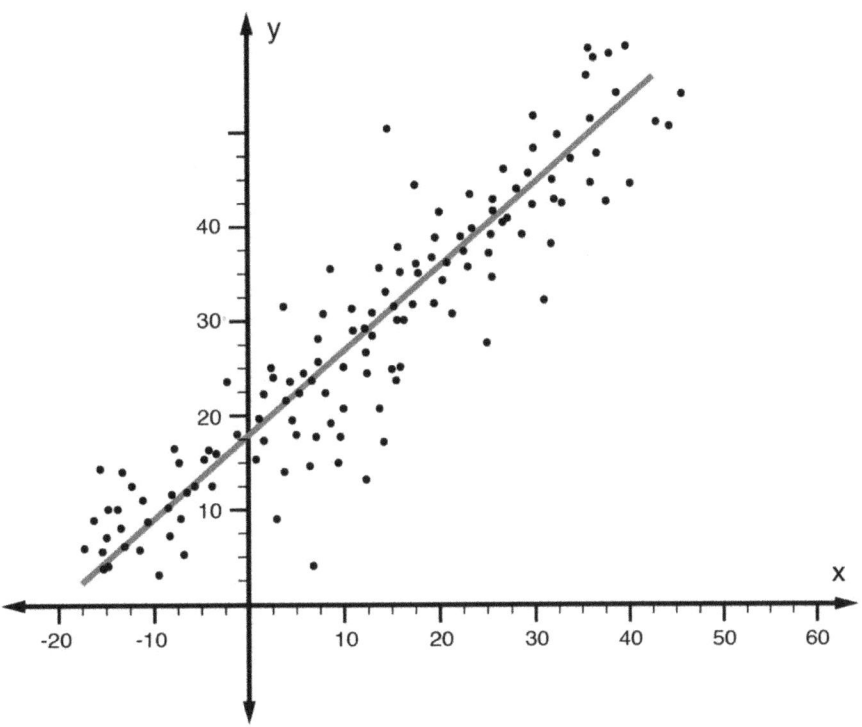

Estimating Data Points

Regression lines can be used to estimate data points not already given. For example, if an equation of a line is found that fit the temperature and beach visitor data set, its input is the average daily temperature and its output is the projected number of visitors. Thus, the number of beach visitors on a 100-degree day can be estimated. The output is a data point on the regression line, and the number of daily visitors is expected to be greater than on a 96-degree day because the regression line has a positive slope.

Interpreting the Regression Line

The formula for a regression line is $y = mx + b$, where m is the slope and b is the y-intercept. Both the slope and y-intercept are found in the **Method of Least Squares**, which is the process of finding the equation of the line through minimizing residuals. The **slope** represents the rate of change in y as x gets larger. Therefore, because y is the dependent variable, the slope actually provides the predicted values given the independent variable. The y-intercept is the predicted value for when the independent variable equals zero. In the temperature example, the y-intercept is the expected number of beach visitors for a very cold average daily temperature of zero degrees.

Probabilities of Single and Compound Events

A **simple event** consists of only one outcome. The most popular simple event is flipping a coin, which results in either heads or tails. A **compound event** results in more than one outcome and consists of more than one simple event. An example of a compound event is flipping a coin while tossing a die. The result is either heads or tails on the coin and a number from one to six on the die. The probability of a simple event is calculated by dividing the number of possible outcomes by the total number of outcomes.

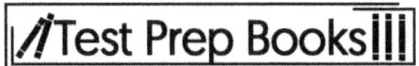

Therefore, the probability of obtaining heads on a coin is $\frac{1}{2}$, and the probability of rolling a 6 on a die is $\frac{1}{6}$. The probability of compound events is calculated using the basic idea of the probability of simple events. If the two events are independent, the probability of one outcome is equal to the product of the probabilities of each simple event. For example, the probability of obtaining heads on a coin and rolling a 6 is equal to $\frac{1}{2} \times \frac{1}{6} = \frac{1}{12}$. The probability of either A or B occurring is equal to the sum of the probabilities minus the probability that both A and B will occur. Therefore, the probability of obtaining either heads on a coin or rolling a 6 on a die is:

$$\frac{1}{2} + \frac{1}{6} - \frac{1}{12} = \frac{7}{12}$$

The two events aren't mutually exclusive because they can happen at the same time. If two events are mutually exclusive, and the probability of both events occurring at the same time is zero, the probability of event A or B occurring equals the sum of both probabilities. An example of calculating the probability of two mutually exclusive events is determining the probability of pulling a king or a queen from a deck of cards. The two events cannot occur at the same time.

Uniform and Non-Uniform Probability Models

A **uniform probability model** is one where each outcome has an equal chance of occurring, such as the probabilities of rolling each side of a die. A **non-uniform probability model** is one where each result has a different chance of taking place. In a uniform probability model, the conditional probability formulas for $P(B|A)$ and $P(A|B)$ can be multiplied by their respective denominators to obtain two formulas for $P(A \text{ and } B)$. Therefore, the multiplication rule is derived as:

$$P(A \text{ and } B) = P(A)P(B|A) = P(B)P(A|B)$$

In a model, if the probability of either individual event is known and the corresponding conditional probability is known, the multiplication rule allows the probability of the joint occurrence of A and B to be calculated.

Measuring Probabilities with Two-Way Frequency Tables

When measuring event probabilities, two-way frequency tables can be used to report the raw data and then used to calculate probabilities. If the frequency tables are translated into relative frequency tables, the probabilities presented in the table can be plugged directly into the formulas for conditional probabilities. By plugging in the correct frequencies, the data from the table can be used to determine if events are independent or dependent.

Differing Probabilities

The probability that event A occurs differs from the probability that event A occurs given B. When working within a given model, it's important to note the difference. $P(A|B)$ is determined using the formula $P(A|B) = \frac{P(A \text{ and } B)}{P(B)}$ and represents the total number of A's outcomes left that could occur after B occurs. $P(A)$ can be calculated without any regard for B. For example, the probability of a student finding a parking spot on a busy campus is different once class is in session.

The Addition Rule

The probability of event A or B occurring isn't equal to the sum of each individual probability. The probability that both events can occur at the same time must be subtracted from this total. This idea is shown in the *addition rule*:

$$P(A \text{ or } B) = P(A) + P(B) - P(A \text{ and } B)$$

The **addition rule** is another way to determine the probability of compound events that aren't mutually exclusive. If the events are mutually exclusive, the probability of both A and B occurring at the same time is 0.

Mathematics

Approximating the Probability of a Chance Event

Probability is a measure of how likely an event is to occur. Probability is written as a fraction between zero and one. If an event has a probability of zero, the event will never occur. If an event has a probability of one, the event will definitely occur. If the probability of an event is closer to zero, the event is unlikely to occur. If the probability of an event is closer to one, the event is more likely to occur. For example, a probability of $\frac{1}{2}$ means that the event is equally as likely to occur as it is not to occur. An example of this is tossing a coin. The probability of an event can be calculated by dividing the number of favorable outcomes by the number of total outcomes. For example, suppose you have 2 raffle tickets out of 20 total tickets sold. The probability that you win the raffle is calculated:

$$\frac{number\ of\ favorable\ outcomes}{total\ number\ of\ outcomes} = \frac{2}{20}$$

$$\frac{2}{20} = \frac{1}{10}\ (always\ reduce\ fractions)$$

Therefore, the probability of winning the raffle is $\frac{1}{10}$ or 0.1.

Chance is the measure of how likely an event is to occur, written as a percent. If an event will never occur, the event has a 0% chance. If an event will certainly occur, the event has a 100% chance. If an event will sometimes occur, the event has a chance somewhere between 0% and 100%. To calculate chance, probability is calculated, and the fraction is converted to a percent.

The probability of multiple events occurring can be determined by multiplying the probability of each event. For example, suppose you flip a coin with heads and tails, and roll a six-sided die numbered one through six. To find the probability that you will flip heads AND roll a two, the probability of each event is determined, and those fractions are multiplied. The probability of flipping heads is $\frac{1}{2}\left(\frac{1\ side\ with\ heads}{2\ sides\ total}\right)$, and the probability of rolling a two is $\frac{1}{6}\left(\frac{1\ side\ with\ a\ 2}{6\ total\ sides}\right)$. The probability of flipping heads AND rolling a 2 is:

$$\frac{1}{2} \times \frac{1}{6} = \frac{1}{12}$$

The above scenario with flipping a coin and rolling a die is an example of independent events. Independent events are circumstances in which the outcome of one event does not affect the outcome of the other event. Conversely, dependent events are ones in which the outcome of one event affects the outcome of the second event. Consider the following scenario: a bag contains 5 black marbles and 5 white marbles. What is the probability of picking 2 black marbles without replacing the marble after the first pick?

The probability of picking a black marble on the first pick is:

$$\frac{5}{10}\left(\frac{5\ black\ marbles}{10\ total\ marbles}\right)$$

Assuming that a black marble was picked, there are now 4 black marbles and 5 white marbles for the second pick. Therefore, the probability of picking a black marble on the second pick is:

$$\frac{4}{9}\left(\frac{4\ black\ marbles}{9\ total\ marbles}\right)$$

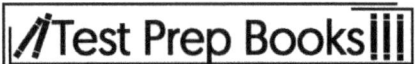

To find the probability of picking two black marbles, the probability of each is multiplied:

$$\frac{5}{10} \times \frac{4}{9} = \frac{20}{90} = \frac{2}{9}$$

Using Measures of Center to Draw Inferences About Populations

The center of a set of data (statistical values) can be represented by its mean, median, or mode. These are sometimes referred to as measures of central tendency.

Mean

The first property that can be defined for this set of data is the **mean**. This is the same as the average. To find the mean, add up all the data points, then divide by the total number of data points. For example, suppose that in a class of 10 students, the scores on a test were 50, 60, 65, 65, 75, 80, 85, 85, 90, 100. Therefore, the average test score will be:

$$\frac{50 + 60 + 65 + 65 + 75 + 80 + 85 + 85 + 90 + 100}{10} = 75.5$$

The mean is a useful number if the distribution of data is normal (more on this later), which means that the frequency of different outcomes has a single peak and is roughly equally distributed on both sides of that peak. However, it is less useful in some cases where the data might be split or where there are some *outliers*. **Outliers** are data points that are far from the rest of the data. For example, suppose there are 10 executives and 90 employees at a company. The executives make $1,000 per hour, and the employees make $10 per hour.

Therefore, the average pay rate will be:

$$\frac{\$1,000 \times 10 + \$10 \times 90}{100} = \$109 \text{ per hour}$$

In this case, this average is not very descriptive since it's not close to the actual pay of the executives or the employees.

Median

Another useful measurement is the **median**. In a data set, the median is the point in the middle. The middle refers to the point where half the data comes before it and half comes after, when the data is recorded in numerical order. For instance, these are the speeds of the fastball of a pitcher during the last inning that he pitched (in order from least to greatest):

$$90, 92, 93, 93, 95, 96, 97, 97, 97$$

There are nine total numbers, so the middle or *median* number is the 5th one, which is 95.

In cases where the number of data points is an even number, then the average of the two middle points is taken. In the previous example of test scores, the two middle points are 75 and 80. Since there is no single point, the average of these two scores needs to be found. The average is:

$$\frac{75 + 80}{2} = 77.5$$

The median is generally a good value to use if there are a few outliers in the data. It prevents those outliers from affecting the "middle" value as much as when using the mean.

Mathematics

Since an outlier is a data point that is far from most of the other data points in a data set, this means an outlier also is any point that is far from the median of the data set. The outliers can have a substantial effect on the mean of a data set, but they usually do not change the median or mode, or do not change them by a large quantity. For example, consider the data set (3, 5, 6, 6, 6, 8). This has a median of 6 and a mode of 6, with a mean of $\frac{34}{6} \approx 5.67$. Now, suppose a new data point of 1,000 is added so that the data set is now (3, 5, 6, 6, 6, 8, 1,000). The median and mode, which are both still 6, remain unchanged. However, the average is now $\frac{1,034}{7}$, which is approximately 147.7. In this case, the median and mode will be better descriptions for most of the data points.

Outliers in a given data set are sometimes the result of an error by the experimenter, but oftentimes, they are perfectly valid data points that must be taken into consideration.

Mode

One additional measure to describe a set of data is the **mode**. This is the data point that appears most frequently. If two or more data points all tie for the most frequent appearance, then each of them is considered a mode. In the case of the test scores, where the numbers were 50, 60, 65, 65, 75, 80, 85, 85, 90, 100, there are two modes: 65 and 85.

Using Statistics to Gain Information About a Population

Statistics involves making decisions and predictions about larger data sets based on smaller data sets. Basically, the information from one part or subset can help predict what happens in the entire data set or population at large. The entire process involves guessing, and the predictions and decisions may not be 100 percent correct all of the time; however, there is some truth to these predictions, and the decisions do have mathematical support. The smaller data set is called a **sample** and the larger data set (in which the decision is being made) is called a **population.** A **random sample** is used as the sample, which is an unbiased collection of data points that represents the population as well as it can. There are many methods of forming a random sample, and all adhere to the fact that every potential data point has a predetermined probability of being chosen. Statistical inference, based in probability theory, makes calculated assumptions about an entire population based on data from a sample set from that population.

A population is the entire set of people or things of interest. Suppose a study is intended to determine the number of hours of sleep per night for college females in the U.S. The population would consist of EVERY college female in the country. A sample is a subset of the population that may be used for the study. It would not be practical to survey every female college student, so a sample might consist of 100 students per school from 20 different colleges in the country. From the results of the survey, a sample statistic can be calculated. A sample statistic is a numerical characteristic of the sample data, including mean and variance. A sample statistic can be used to estimate a corresponding population parameter. A population parameter is a numerical characteristic of the entire population. Suppose the sample data had a mean (average) of 5.5. This sample statistic can be used as an estimate of the population parameter (average hours of sleep for every college female in the U.S.).

Confidence Intervals

A population parameter is usually unknown and therefore is estimated using a sample statistic. This estimate may be highly accurate or relatively inaccurate based on errors in sampling. A confidence interval indicates a range of values likely to include the true population parameter. These are constructed at a given confidence level, such as 95%. This means that if the same population is sampled repeatedly, the true population parameter would occur within the interval for 95% of the samples.

The accuracy of a population parameter based on a sample statistic may also be affected by measurement error, which is the difference between a quantity's true value and its measured value. Measurement error can be divided into random error and systematic error. An example of random error for the previous scenario would be a student

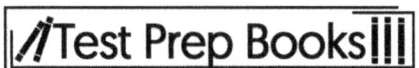

reporting 8 hours of sleep when she actually sleeps 7 hours per night. Systematic errors are those attributed to the measurement system. Suppose the sleep survey gave response options of 2, 4, 6, 8, or 10 hours. This would lead to systematic measurement error.

Algebraic Concepts

Interpreting Parts of an Expression

A **term** is either a number, a variable, or the product of the two. The **coefficient** is the number part of a term that is made up of a constant and a variable. Algebraic expressions are built out of monomials. A **monomial** is a variable raised to some power multiplied by a constant: ax^n, where a is any constant and n is a whole number. A constant is also a monomial.

A **polynomial** is a sum of monomials. Examples of polynomials include $3x^4 + 2x^2 - x - 3$ and $\frac{4}{5}x^3$. The latter is also a monomial. If the highest power of x is 1, the polynomial is called **linear**. If the highest power of x is 2, it is called *quadratic*.

Performing Arithmetic Operations on Polynomials and Rational Expressions

Addition and subtraction operations can be performed on polynomials with like terms. **Like terms** refers to terms that have the same variable and exponent. The two following polynomials can be added together by collecting like terms:

$$(x^2 + 3x - 4) + (4x^2 - 7x + 8)$$

The x^2 terms can be added as $x^2 + 4x^2 = 5x^2$. The x terms can be added as $3x + -7x = -4x$, and the constants can be added as $-4 + 8 = 4$. The following expression is the result of the addition:

$$5x^2 - 4x + 4$$

When subtracting polynomials, the same steps are followed, only subtracting like terms together.

Multiplication of polynomials can also be performed. Given the two polynomials, $(y^3 - 4)$ and $(x^2 + 8x - 7)$, each term in the first polynomial must be multiplied by each term in the second polynomial. The steps to multiply each term in the given example are as follows:

$$(y^3 \times x^2) + (y^3 \times 8x) + (y^3 \times -7) + (-4 \times x^2) + (-4 \times 8x) + (-4 \times -7)$$

Simplifying each multiplied part, yields:

$$x^2y^3 + 8xy^3 - 7y^3 - 4x^2 - 32x + 28$$

None of the terms can be combined because there are no like terms in the final expression. Any polynomials can be multiplied by each other by following the same set of steps, then collecting like terms at the end.

Polynomial Identities

Difference of squares refers to a binomial composed of the difference of two squares. For example, $a^2 - b^2$ is a difference of squares. It can be written $(a)^2 - (b)^2$, and it can be factored into $(a - b)(a + b)$. Recognizing the difference of squares allows the expression to be rewritten easily because of the form it takes. For some expressions, factoring consists of more than one step. When factoring, it's important to always check to make sure that the result cannot be factored further. If it can, then the expression should be split further. If it cannot be, the factoring step is complete, and the expression is completely factored.

A sum and difference of cubes is another way to factor a polynomial expression. When the polynomial takes the form of addition or subtraction of two terms that can be written as a cube, a formula is given. The following graphic shows the factorization of a difference of cubes:

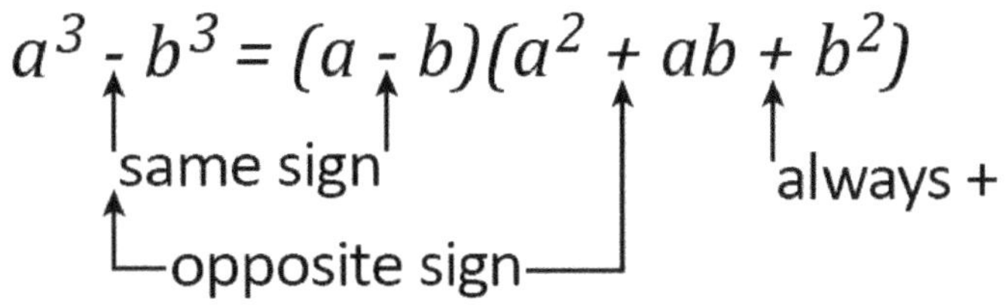

$$a^3 - b^3 = (a - b)(a^2 + ab + b^2)$$

where the first signs are the same sign, the middle connection is the opposite sign, and the last is always +.

This form of factoring can be useful in finding the zeros of a function of degree 3. For example, when solving $x^3 - 27 = 0$, this rule needs to be used. $x^3 - 27$ is first written as the difference two cubes, $(x)^3 - (3)^3$ and then factored into $(x - 3)(x^2 + 3x + 9)$. This expression may not be factored any further. Each factor is then set equal to zero. Therefore, one solution is found to be $x = 3$, and the other two solutions must be found using the quadratic formula. A sum of squares would have a similar process. The formula for factoring a sum of cubes is:

$$a^3 + b^3 = (a + b)(a^2 - ab + b^2)$$

The opposite of factoring is multiplying. Multiplying a square of a binomial involves the following rules:

$$(a + b)^2 = a^2 + 2ab + b^2$$

$$(a - b)^2 = a^2 - 2ab + b^2$$

The binomial theorem for expansion can be used when the exponent on a binomial is larger than 2, and the multiplication would take a long time. The binomial theorem is given as:

$$(a + b)^n = \sum_{k=0}^{n} \binom{n}{k} a^{n-k} b^k$$

where

$$\binom{n}{k} = \frac{n!}{k!(n-k)!}$$

The **Remainder Theorem** can be helpful when evaluating polynomial functions $P(x)$ for a given value of x. A polynomial can be divided by $(x - a)$, if there is a remainder of 0. This also means that $P(a) = 0$ and $(x - a)$ is a factor of $P(x)$. In a similar sense, if P is evaluated at any other number b, $P(b)$ is equal to the remainder of dividing $P(x)$ by $(x - b)$.

For example, consider:

$$P(x) = x^3 - 7x - 6$$

$$P(4) = 30 \text{ because}$$

$$
\begin{array}{r}
x^2 + 4x + 9 \\
x - 4 \overline{\smash{)} x^3 + 0x^2 - 7x - 6} \\
\underline{-x^3 + 4x^2 } \\
4x^2 - 7x - 6 \\
\underline{-4x^2 + 16x } \\
9x - 6 \\
\underline{-9x + 36} \\
30
\end{array}
$$

Rational Expressions

A fraction, or ratio, wherein each part is a polynomial, defines **rational expressions**. Some examples include $\frac{2x+6}{x}$, $\frac{1}{x^2-4x+8}$, and $\frac{z^2}{x+5}$. Exponents on the variables are restricted to whole numbers, which means roots and negative exponents are not included in rational expressions.

Rational expressions can be transformed by factoring. For example, the expression $\frac{x^2-5x+6}{(x-3)}$ can be rewritten by factoring the numerator to obtain $\frac{(x-3)(x-2)}{(x-3)}$. Therefore, the common binomial $(x-3)$ can cancel so that the simplified expression is $\frac{(x-2)}{1} = (x-2)$.

Additionally, other rational expressions can be rewritten to take on different forms. Some may be factorable in themselves, while others can be transformed through arithmetic operations. Rational expressions are closed under addition, subtraction, multiplication, and division by a nonzero expression. *Closed* means that if any one of these operations is performed on a rational expression, the result will still be a rational expression. The set of all real numbers is another example of a set closed under all four operations.

Adding and subtracting rational expressions is based on the same concepts as adding and subtracting simple fractions. For both concepts, the denominators must be the same for the operation to take place. For example, here are two rational expressions:

$$\frac{x^3 - 4}{(x-3)} + \frac{x+8}{(x-3)}$$

Since the denominators are both $(x-3)$, the numerators can be combined by collecting like terms to form:

$$\frac{x^3 + x + 4}{(x-3)}$$

If the denominators are different, they need to be made common (the same) by using the **Least Common Denominator (LCD)**. Each denominator needs to be factored, and the LCD contains each factor that appears in any one denominator the greatest number of times it appears in any denominator. The original expressions need to be multiplied times a form of 1, which will turn each denominator into the LCD. This process is like adding fractions with unlike denominators. It is also important when working with rational expressions to define what value of the variable makes the denominator zero. For this particular value, the expression is undefined.

Multiplication of rational expressions is performed like multiplication of fractions. The numerators are multiplied; then, the denominators are multiplied. The final fraction is then simplified. The expressions are simplified by factoring and canceling out common terms. In the following example, the numerator of the second expression can be factored first to simplify the expression before multiplying:

$$\frac{x^2}{(x-4)} \times \frac{x^2 - x - 12}{2}$$

$$\frac{x^2}{(x-4)} \times \frac{(x-4)(x+3)}{2}$$

The $(x-4)$ on the top and bottom cancel out:

$$\frac{x^2}{1} \times \frac{(x+3)}{2}$$

Then multiplication is performed, resulting in:

$$\frac{x^3 + 3x^2}{2}$$

Dividing rational expressions is similar to the division of fractions, where division turns into multiplying by a reciprocal. The following expression can be rewritten as a multiplication problem:

$$\frac{x^2 - 3x + 7}{x - 4} \div \frac{x^2 - 5x + 3}{x - 4}$$

$$\frac{x^2 - 3x + 7}{x - 4} \times \frac{x - 4}{x^2 - 5x + 3}$$

The $x - 4$ cancels out, leaving:

$$\frac{x^2 - 3x + 7}{x^2 - 5x + 3}$$

The final answers should always be completely simplified. If a function is composed of a rational expression, the zeros of the graph can be found from setting the polynomial in the numerator as equal to zero and solving. The values that make the denominator equal to zero will either exist on the graph as a hole or a vertical asymptote.

Writing Expressions in Equivalent Forms

Algebraic expressions are made up of numbers, variables, and combinations of the two, using mathematical operations. Expressions can be rewritten based on their factors. For example, the expression $6x + 4$ can be rewritten as $2(3x + 2)$ because 2 is a factor of both $6x$ and 4. More complex expressions can also be rewritten based on their factors. The expression $x^4 - 16$ can be rewritten as $(x^2 - 4)(x^2 + 4)$. This is a different type of factoring, where a difference of squares is factored into a sum and difference of the same two terms. With some expressions, the factoring process is simple and only leads to a different way to represent the expression. With others, factoring and rewriting the expression leads to more information about the given problem.

In the following quadratic equation, factoring the binomial leads to finding the zeros of the function:

$$x^2 - 5x + 6 = y$$

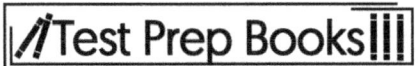

This equation factors into $(x-3)(x-2) = y$, where 2 and 3 are found to be the zeros of the function when y is set equal to zero. The zeros of any function are the x-values where the graph of the function on the coordinate plane crosses the x-axis.

Factoring an equation is a simple way to rewrite the equation and find the zeros, but factoring is not possible for every quadratic. Completing the square is one way to find zeros when factoring is not an option. The following equation cannot be factored:

$$x^2 + 10x - 9 = 0$$

The first step in this method is to move the constant to the right side of the equation, making it $x^2 + 10x = 9$. Then, the coefficient of x is divided by 2 and squared. This number is then added to both sides of the equation, to make the equation still true. For this example, $\left(\frac{10}{2}\right)^2 = 25$ is added to both sides of the equation to obtain:

$$x^2 + 10x + 25 = 9 + 25$$

This expression simplifies to $x^2 + 10x + 25 = 34$, which can then be factored into $(x+5)^2 = 34$. Solving for x then involves taking the square root of both sides and subtracting 5. This leads to two zeros of the function:

$$x = \pm\sqrt{34} - 5$$

Depending on the type of answer the question seeks, a calculator may be used to find exact numbers.

Given a quadratic equation in standard form— $ax^2 + bx + c = 0$—the sign of a tells whether the function has a minimum value or a maximum value. If $a > 0$, the graph opens up and has a minimum value. If $a < 0$, the graph opens down and has a maximum value. Depending on the way the quadratic equation is written, multiplication may need to occur before a max/min value is determined.

Exponential expressions can also be rewritten, just as quadratic equations. Properties of exponents must be understood. Multiplying two exponential expressions with the same base involves adding the exponents:

$$a^m a^n = a^{m+n}$$

Dividing two exponential expressions with the same base involves subtracting the exponents:

$$\frac{a^m}{a^n} = a^{m-n}$$

Raising an exponential expression to another exponent includes multiplying the exponents:

$$(a^m)^n = a^{mn}$$

The zero power always gives a value of 1: $a^0 = 1$. Raising either a product or a fraction to a power involves distributing that power:

$$(ab)^m = a^m b^m \text{ and } \left(\frac{a}{b}\right)^m = \frac{a^m}{b^m}$$

Finally, raising a number to a negative exponent is equivalent to the reciprocal including the positive exponent:

$$a^{-m} = \frac{1}{a^m}$$

Mathematics

Finding the Zeros of a Function

The **zeros of a function** are the points where its graph crosses the x-axis. At these points, $y = 0$. One way to find the zeros is to analyze the graph. If given the graph, the x-coordinates can be found where the line crosses the x-axis. Another way to find the zeros is to set $y = 0$ in the equation and solve for x. Depending on the type of equation, this could be done by using opposite operations, by factoring the equation, by completing the square, or by using the quadratic formula. If a graph does not cross the x-axis, then the function may have complex roots.

Solving Linear Equations and Inequalities in One Variable

The sum of a number and 5 is equal to -8 times the number. To find this unknown number, a simple equation can be written to represent the problem. Key words such as difference, equal, and times are used to form the following equation with one variable: $n + 5 = -8n$. When solving for n, opposite operations are used. First, n is subtracted from $-8n$ across the equals sign, resulting in $5 = -9n$. Then, -9 is divided on both sides, leaving $n = -\frac{5}{9}$. This solution can be graphed on the number line with a dot as shown below:

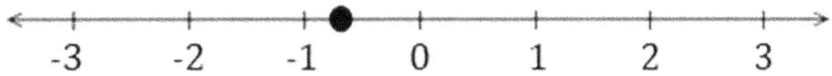

If the problem were changed to say, "The sum of a number and 5 is greater than -8 times the number," then an inequality would be used instead of an equation. Using key words again, *greater than* is represented by the symbol >. The inequality $n + 5 > -8n$ can be solved using the same techniques, resulting in $n < -\frac{5}{9}$. The only time solving an inequality differs from solving an equation is when a negative number is either multiplied times or divided by each side of the inequality. The sign must be switched in this case. For this example, the graph of the solution changes to the following graph because the solution represents all real numbers less than $-\frac{5}{9}$. Not included in this solution is $-\frac{5}{9}$ because it is a *less than* symbol, not *equal to*.

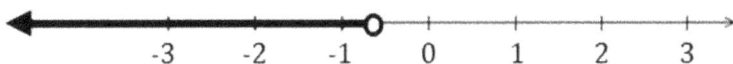

Equations and inequalities in two variables represent a relationship. Jim owns a car wash and charges $40 per car. The rent for the facility is $350 per month. An equation can be written to relate the number of cars Jim cleans to the money he makes per month. Let x represent the number of cars and y represent the profit Jim makes each month from the car wash. The equation $y = 40x - 350$ can be used to show Jim's profit or loss. Since this equation has two variables, the coordinate plane can be used to show the relationship and predict profit or loss for Jim. The following graph shows that Jim must wash at least nine cars to pay the rent, where $x = 9$. Anything nine cars and above yields a profit as shown in the value on the y-axis.

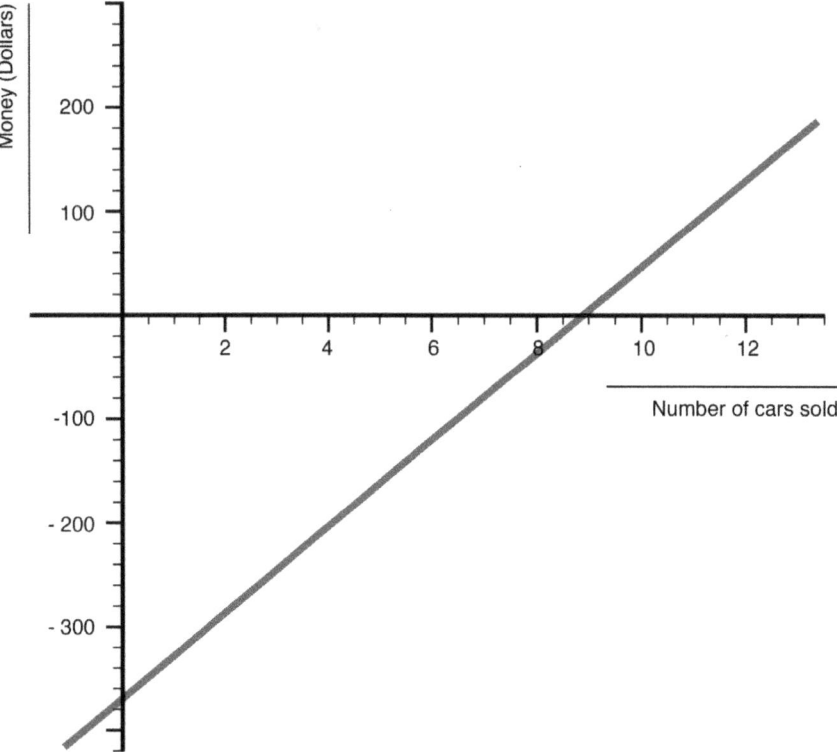

With a single equation in two variables, the solutions are limited only by the situation the equation represents. When two equations or inequalities are used, more constraints are added. For example, in a system of linear equations, there is often—although not always—only one answer. The point of intersection of two lines is the solution. For a system of inequalities, there are infinitely many answers.

The intersection of two solution sets gives the solution set of the system of inequalities. In the following graph, the darker shaded region is where two inequalities overlap. Any set of x and y found in that region satisfies both inequalities. The line with the positive slope is solid, meaning the values on that line are included in the solution.

Mathematics

The line with the negative slope is dotted, so the coordinates on that line are not included.

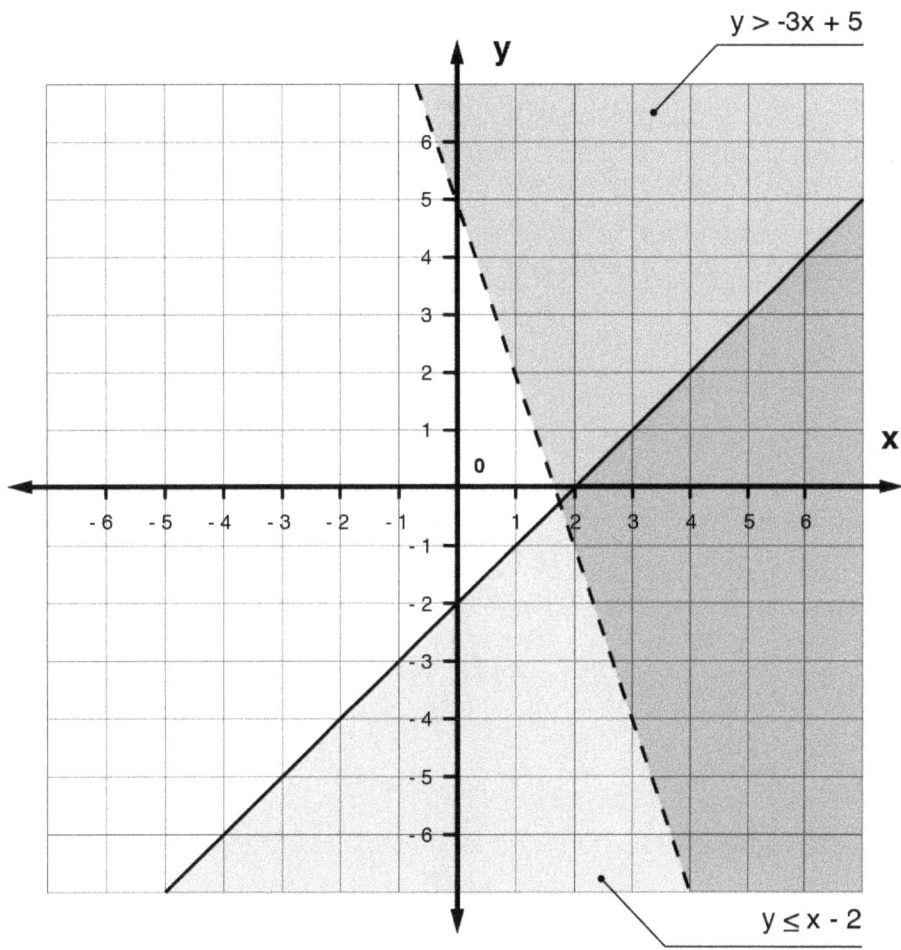

Formulas with two variables are equations used to represent a specific relationship. For example, the formula $d = rt$ represents the relationship between distance, rate, and time. If Bob travels at a rate of 35 miles per hour on his road trip from Westminster to Seneca, the formula $d = 35t$ can be used to represent his distance traveled in a specific length of time. Formulas can also be used to show different roles of the variables, transformed without any given numbers. Solving for r, the formula becomes $\frac{d}{t} = r$. The t is moved over by division so that *rate* is a function of distance and time.

The letters in an equation are variables as they stand for unknown quantities that you are trying to solve for. The numbers attached to the variables by multiplication are called coefficients. X is commonly used as a variable, though any letter can be used. For example, in $3x - 7 = 20$, the variable is $3x$, and it needs to be isolated. The numbers (also called constants) are -7 and 20. That means $3x$ needs to be on one side of the equals sign (either side is fine), and all the numbers need to be on the other side of the equals sign.

To accomplish this, the equation must be manipulated by performing opposite operations of what already exists. Remember that addition and subtraction are opposites and that multiplication and division are opposites. Any action taken to one side of the equation must be taken on the other side to maintain equality.

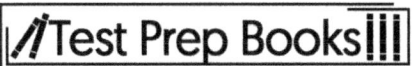

Therefore, since the 7 is being subtracted, it can be moved to the right side of the equation by adding seven to both sides:

$$3x - 7 = 20$$

$$3x - 7 + 7 = 20 + 7$$

$$3x = 27$$

Now that the variable $3x$ is on one side and the constants (now combined into one constant) are on the other side, the 3 needs to be moved to the right side. 3 and x are being multiplied together, so 3 needs to be divided from each side.

$$\frac{3x}{3} = \frac{27}{3}$$

$$x = 9$$

Now x has been completely isolated, and thus we know its value.

The solution is found to be $x = 9$. This solution can be checked for accuracy by plugging $x = 9$ in the original equation. After simplifying the equation, $20 = 20$ is found, which is a true statement:

$$3 \times 9 - 7 = 20$$

$$27 - 7 = 20$$

$$20 = 20$$

Equations that require solving for a variable (*algebraic equations*) come in many forms. Here are some more examples:

No coefficient attached to the variable:

$$x + 8 = 20$$

$$x + 8 - 8 = 20 - 8$$

$$x = 12$$

A fractional coefficient:

$$\frac{1}{2}z + 24 = 36$$

$$\frac{1}{2}z + 24 - 24 = 36 - 24$$

$$\frac{1}{2}z = 12$$

Now we multiply the fraction by its inverse:

$$\frac{2}{1} \times \frac{1}{2}z = 12 \times \frac{2}{1}$$

$$z = 24$$

Multiple examples of x:

$$14x + x - 4 = 3x + 2$$

All examples of x can be combined.

$$15x - 4 = 3x + 2$$

$$15x - 4 + 4 = 3x + 2 + 4$$

$$15x = 3x + 6$$

$$15x - 3x = 3x + 6 - 3x$$

$$12x = 6$$

$$\frac{12x}{12} = \frac{6}{12}$$

$$x = \frac{1}{2}$$

Solving Quadratic Equations

Equations with one variable can be solved using the addition principle and multiplication principle. If $a = b$, then $a + c = b + c$, and $ac = bc$. Given the equation $2x - 3 = 5x + 7$, the first step is to combine the variable terms and the constant terms. Using the principles, expressions can be added and subtracted onto and off both sides of the equals sign, so the equation turns into $-10 = 3x$. Dividing by 3 on both sides through the multiplication principle with $c = \frac{1}{3}$ results in the final answer of $x = \frac{-10}{3}$.

Some equations have a higher degree and are not solved by simply using opposite operations. When an equation has a degree of 2, completing the square is an option. For example, the quadratic equation $x^2 - 6x + 2 = 0$ can be rewritten by completing the square. The goal of completing the square is to get the equation into the form $(x - p)^2 = q$. Using the example, the constant term 2 first needs to be moved over to the opposite side by subtracting. Then, the square can be completed by adding 9 to both sides, which is the square of half of the coefficient of the middle term $-6x$. The current equation is $x^2 - 6x + 9 = 7$. The left side can be factored into a square of a binomial, resulting in $(x - 3)^2 = 7$. To solve for x, the square root of both sides should be taken, resulting in:

$$(x - 3) = \pm\sqrt{7}$$

$$x = 3 \pm \sqrt{7}$$

Other ways of solving quadratic equations include graphing, factoring, and using the quadratic formula. The equation $y = x^2 - 4x + 3$ can be graphed on the coordinate plane, and the solutions can be observed where it crosses the x-axis. The graph will be a parabola that opens up with two solutions at 1 and 3.

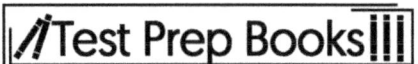

The equation can also be factored to find the solutions. The original equation, $y = x^2 - 4x + 3$ can be factored into $y = (x - 1)(x - 3)$. Setting this equal to zero, the x-values are found to be 1 and 3, just as on the graph. Solving by factoring and graphing are not always possible.

The method of completing the square can be used in finding another method, the quadratic formula. It can be used to solve any quadratic equation. This formula may be the longest method for solving quadratic equations and is commonly used as a last resort after other methods are ruled out.

It can be helpful in memorizing the formula to see where it comes from, so here are the steps involved.

The most general form for a quadratic equation is $ax^2 + bx + c = 0$.

First, dividing both sides by a leaves us with $x^2 + \frac{b}{a}x + \frac{c}{a} = 0$.

To complete the square on the left-hand side, $\frac{c}{a}$ can be subtracted on both sides to get:

$$x^2 + \frac{b}{a}x = -\frac{c}{a}$$

$(\frac{b}{2a})^2$ is then added to both sides.

This gives:

$$x^2 + \frac{b}{a}x + (\frac{b}{2a})^2 = (\frac{b}{2a})^2 - \frac{c}{a}$$

The left can now be factored and the right-hand side simplified to give:

$$(x + \frac{b}{2a})^2 = \frac{b^2 - 4ac}{4a}$$

Taking the square roots gives:

$$x + \frac{b}{2a} = \pm \frac{\sqrt{b^2 - 4ac}}{2a}$$

Solving for x yields the quadratic formula:

$$x = \frac{-b \pm \sqrt{b^2 - 4ac}}{2a}$$

Where a, b, and c are the coefficients in the original equation in standard form $y = ax^2 + bx + c$. For the above example,

$$x = \frac{4 \pm \sqrt{(-4)^2 - 4(1)(3)}}{2(1)}$$

$$\frac{4 \pm \sqrt{16 - 12}}{2} = \frac{4 \pm 2}{2} = 1, 3$$

The expression underneath the radical is called the **discriminant**. Without working out the entire formula, the value of the discriminant can reveal the nature of the solutions. If the value of the discriminant $b^2 - 4ac$ is positive, then

Mathematics

there will be two real solutions. If the value is zero, there will be one real solution. If the value is negative, the two solutions will be imaginary or complex. If the solutions are complex, it means that the parabola never touches the x-axis. An example of a complex solution can be found by solving the following quadratic: $y = x^2 - 4x + 8$. By using the quadratic formula, the solutions are found to be:

$$x = \frac{4 \pm \sqrt{(-4)^2 - 4(1)(8)}}{2(1)}$$

$$\frac{4 \pm \sqrt{16 - 32}}{2}$$

$$\frac{4 \pm \sqrt{-16}}{2} = 2 \pm 2i$$

The solutions both have a real part, 2, and an imaginary part, $2i$.

Solving Simple Rational and Radical Equations in One Variable

A **rational expression** is an expression that has the form $\frac{p(x)}{q(x)}$, where $p(x)$ and $q(x)$ are both polynomials. To solve equations or inequalities involving rational expressions, one typically rewrites the expression to get rid of the denominator; as a result, the problem becomes an equation or inequality involving polynomials. One can then apply the techniques mentioned above to complete the solution.

For example, consider the problem $\frac{3x+2}{x-4} = 2$. One can start by multiplying both sides of the equation by $x - 4$. This results in the equation $3x + 2 = 2x - 8$. Now this equation can be solved like any other linear equation. Subtracting $2x$ from both sides and subtracting 2 from both sides gives the solution $x = -10$.

When an equation or an inequality involves radicals, all the radicals must be moved to one side. Then, one can raise both sides to the appropriate power to get rid of the radicals. Remember that the quantity inside a square root must be non-negative. When dealing with inequalities, remember that multiplying both sides by a negative quantity reverses the direction of the inequality.

For example, $\sqrt{x+1} - 2 = 2$. The first step is to isolate the radical, so add 2 to both sides. This addition results in $\sqrt{x+1} = 4$. Square both sides, and the result is $x + 1 = 16$, or $x = 15$.

When dealing with multiple radicals, proceed by first isolating one radical, squaring both sides to remove it, and then repeating this process to remove the remaining radicals. Consider this equation:

$$\sqrt{3x - 1} + 1 = \sqrt{x + 1} + 2$$

Start by subtracting 1 from both sides, isolating the radical on the left, which results in:

$$\sqrt{3x - 1} = \sqrt{x + 1} + 1$$

Now square both sides:

$$3x - 1 = \left(\sqrt{x + 1} + 1\right)^2 = x + 1 + 2\sqrt{x + 1} + 1$$

or

$$3x - 1 = x + 2\sqrt{x + 1} + 2$$

Isolate the radical on the right: $2x - 3 = 2\sqrt{x+1}$. Now square both sides, which results in:

$$4x^2 - 12x + 9 = 4x + 4$$

This problem can now be solved by using the quadratic formula.

Solving Systems of Equations

A **system of equations** is a group of equations that have the same variables or unknowns. These equations can be linear, but they are not always so. Finding a solution to a system of equations means finding the values of the variables that satisfy each equation. For a linear system of two equations and two variables, there could be a single solution, no solution, or infinitely many solutions.

A **single solution** occurs when there is one value for x and y that satisfies the system. This is shown on the graph where the lines cross at exactly one point. When there is no solution, the lines are parallel and do not ever cross. With infinitely many solutions, the equations may look different, but they are the same line. One equation will be a multiple of the other, and on the graph, they lie on top of each other. These three types of systems of linear equations are shown below:

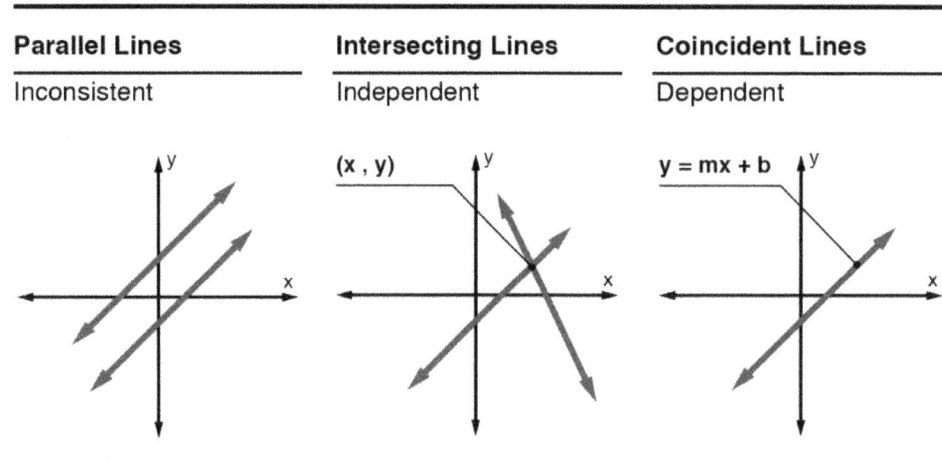

The process of elimination can be used to solve a system of equations. For example, the following equations make up a system: $x + 3y = 10$ and $2x - 5y = 9$. Immediately adding these equations does not eliminate a variable, but it is possible to change the first equation by multiplying the whole equation by -2. This changes the first equation to $-2x - 6y = -20$. The equations can be then added to obtain $-11y = -11$. Solving for y yields $y = 1$. To find the rest of the solution, 1 can be substituted in for y in either original equation to find the value of $x = 7$. The solution to the system is $(7, 1)$ because it makes both equations true, and it is the point in which the lines intersect. If the system is **dependent**—having infinitely many solutions—then both variables will cancel out when the elimination method is used, resulting in an equation that is true for many values of x and y. Since the system is dependent, both equations can be simplified to the same equation, or line.

A system can also be solved using **substitution**. This involves solving one equation for a variable and then plugging that solved equation into the other equation in the system. For example, $x - y = -2$ and $3x + 2y = 9$ can be solved using substitution. The first equation can be solved for x, where $x = -2 + y$. Then it can be plugged into the other equation, $3(-2 + y) + 2y = 9$. Solving for y yields $-6 + 3y + 2y = 9$, where $y = 3$. If $y = 3$, then $x = 1$. This solution can be checked by plugging in these values for the variables in each equation to see if it makes a true statement.

Finally, a solution to a system of equations can be found graphically. The solution to a linear system is the point or points where the lines cross. The values of x and y represent the coordinates (x, y) where the lines intersect. Using the same system of equations as above, they can be solved for y to put them in slope-intercept form, $y = mx + b$. These equations become $y = x + 2$ and $y = -\frac{3}{2}x + 4.5$. The slope is the coefficient of x, and the y-intercept is the constant value. This system with the solution is shown below:

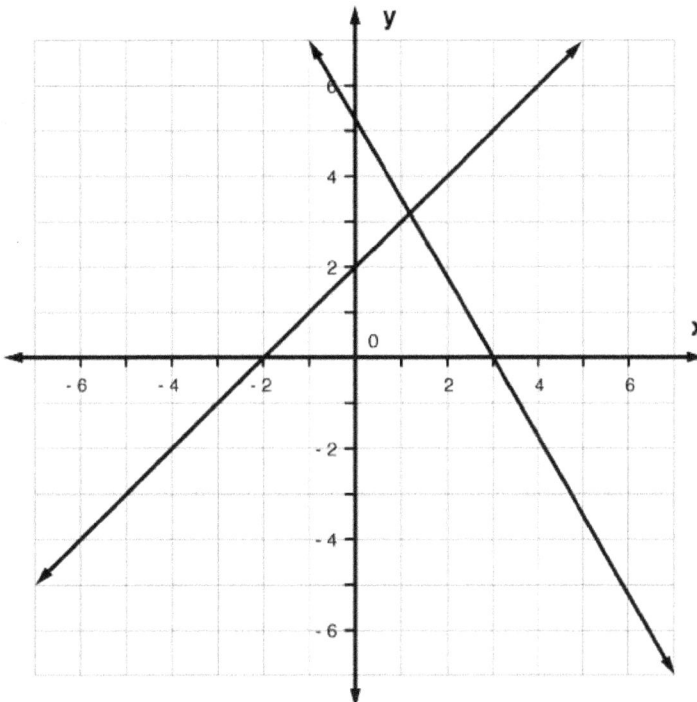

A **system of equations** may also be made up of a linear and a quadratic equation. These systems may have one solution, two solutions, or no solutions. The graph of these systems involves one straight line and one parabola. Algebraically, these systems can be solved by solving the linear equation for one variable and plugging that answer in to the quadratic equation. If possible, the equation can then be solved to find part of the answer. The graphing method is commonly used for these types of systems. On a graph, these two lines can be found to intersect at one point, at two points across the parabola, or at no points.

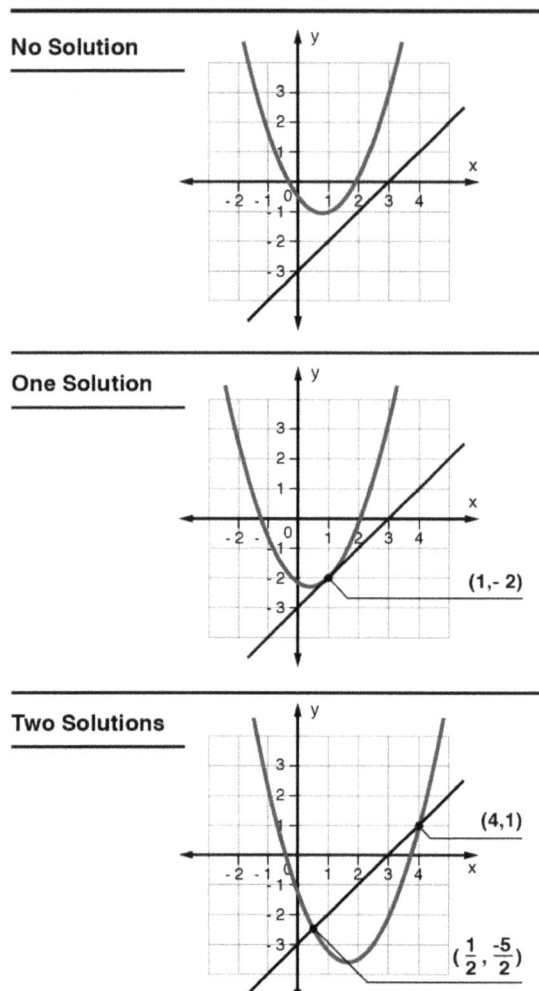

Matrices can also be used to solve systems of linear equations. Specifically, for systems, the coefficients of the linear equations in standard form are the entries in the matrix. Using the same system of linear equations as above, $x - y = -2$ and $3x + 2y = 9$, the matrix to represent the system is:

$$\begin{bmatrix} 1 & -1 \\ 3 & 2 \end{bmatrix} \begin{bmatrix} x \\ y \end{bmatrix} = \begin{bmatrix} -2 \\ 9 \end{bmatrix}$$

To solve this system using matrices, the inverse matrix must be found.

For a general 2x2 matrix, $\begin{bmatrix} a & b \\ c & d \end{bmatrix}$, the inverse matrix is found by the expression:

$$\frac{1}{ad - bc} \begin{bmatrix} d & -b \\ -c & a \end{bmatrix}$$

Mathematics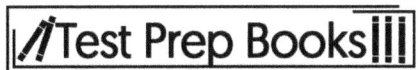

The inverse matrix for the given system above is:

$$\frac{1}{2--3}\begin{bmatrix} 2 & 1 \\ -3 & 1 \end{bmatrix} = \frac{1}{5}\begin{bmatrix} 2 & 1 \\ -3 & 1 \end{bmatrix}$$

The next step in solving is to multiply this identity matrix times the system matrix above. This is given by the following equation:

$$\frac{1}{5}\begin{bmatrix} 2 & 1 \\ -3 & 1 \end{bmatrix}\begin{bmatrix} 1 & -1 \\ 3 & 2 \end{bmatrix}\begin{bmatrix} x \\ y \end{bmatrix}$$

$$\begin{bmatrix} -2 \\ 9 \end{bmatrix}\begin{bmatrix} 2 & 1 \\ -3 & 1 \end{bmatrix}\frac{1}{5}$$

This simplifies to:

$$\frac{1}{5}\begin{bmatrix} 5 & 0 \\ 0 & 5 \end{bmatrix}\begin{bmatrix} x \\ y \end{bmatrix} = \frac{1}{5}\begin{bmatrix} 5 \\ 15 \end{bmatrix}$$

Solving for the solution matrix, the answer is:

$$\begin{bmatrix} 1 & 0 \\ 0 & 1 \end{bmatrix}\begin{bmatrix} x \\ y \end{bmatrix} = \begin{bmatrix} 1 \\ 3 \end{bmatrix}$$

Since the first matrix is the identity matrix, the solution is $x = 1$ and $y = 3$.

Finding solutions to systems of equations is essentially finding what values of the variables make both equations true. It is finding the input value that yields the same output value in both equations. For functions $g(x)$ and $f(x)$, the equation $g(x) = f(x)$ means the output values are being set equal. Solving for the value of x means finding the x-coordinate that gives the same output to both functions. For example, $f(x) = x + 2$ and $g(x) = -3x + 10$ is a system of equations. Setting $f(x) = g(x)$ yields the equation $x + 2 = -3x + 10$. Solving for x gives the x-coordinate $x = 2$ where the two lines cross. This value can also be found by using a table or a graph. On a table, both equations could be given the same inputs, and the outputs could be recorded to find the point(s) where the lines crossed. Any method of solving finds the same solution, but some methods are more appropriate for some systems of equations than others.

Graphing Functions

Different types of functions behave in different ways. A function is defined to be increasing over a subset of its domain if for all $x_1 \geq x_2$ in that interval, $f(x_1) \geq f(x_2)$. Also, a function is decreasing over an interval if for all $x_1 \geq x_2$ in that interval, $f(x_1) \leq f(x_2)$. A point in which a function changes from increasing to decreasing can also be labeled as the **maximum value** of a function if it is the largest point the graph reaches on the y-axis. A point in which a function changes from decreasing to increasing can be labeled as the minimum value of a function if it is the smallest point the graph reaches on the y-axis. Maximum values are also known as **extreme values**. The graph of a continuous function does not have any breaks or jumps in the graph. This description is not true of all functions. A radical function, for example, $f(x) = \sqrt{x}$, has a restriction for the domain and range because there are no real negative inputs or outputs for this function. The domain can be stated as $x \geq 0$, and the range is $y \geq 0$.

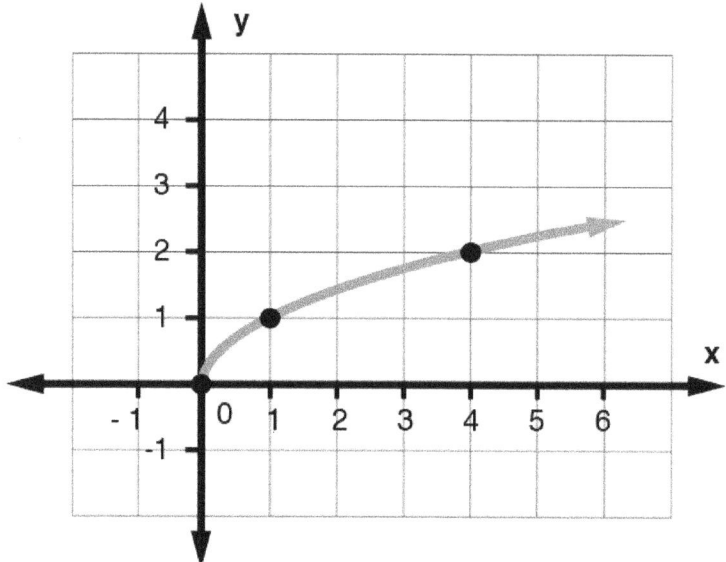

A piecewise-defined function also has a different appearance on the graph. In the following function, there are three equations defined over different intervals. It is a function because there is only one y-value for each x-value, passing the Vertical Line Test. The domain is all real numbers less than or equal to 6. The range is all real numbers greater than zero. From left to right, the graph decreases to zero, then increases to almost 4, and then jumps to 6.

From input values greater than 2, the input decreases just below 8 to 4, and then stops.

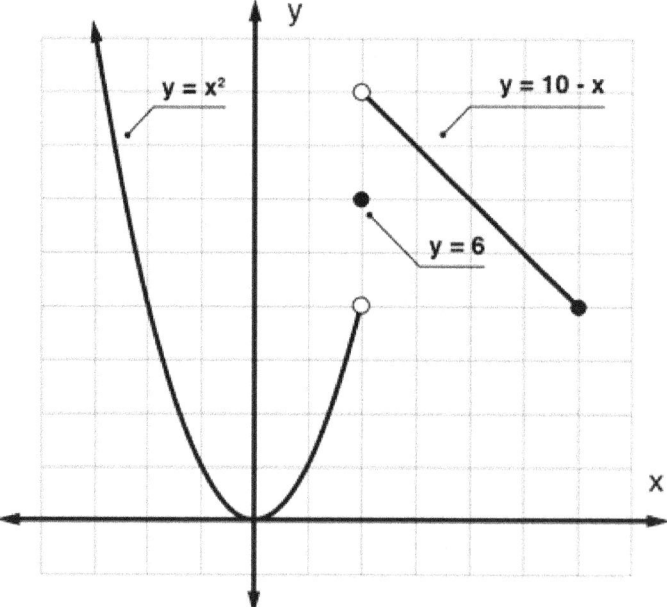

Logarithmic and exponential functions also have different behavior than other functions. These two types of functions are inverses of each other. The **inverse** of a function can be found by switching the place of x and y, and solving for y. When this is done for the exponential equation, $y = 2^x$, the function $y = \log_2 x$ is found. The general form of a **logarithmic function** is $y = \log_b x$, which says b raised to the y power equals x.

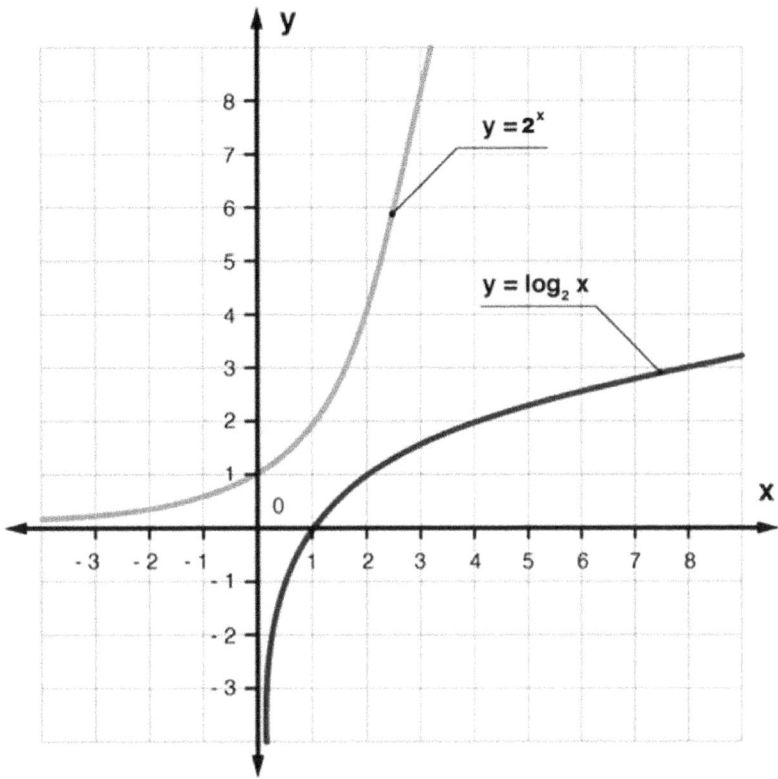

The thick black line on the graph above represents the logarithmic function $y = \log_2 x$. This curve passes through the point $(1, 0)$, just as all log functions do, because any value $b^0 = 1$. The graph of this logarithmic function starts very close to zero, but does not touch the y-axis. The output value will never be zero by the definition of logarithms. The thinner gray line seen above represents the exponential function $y = 2^x$. The behavior of this function is opposite the logarithmic function because the graph of an inverse function is the graph of the original function flipped over the line $y = x$. The curve passes through the point $(0, 1)$ because any number raised to the zero power is one. This curve also gets very close to the x-axis but never touches it because an exponential expression never has an output of zero. The x-axis on this graph is called a horizontal asymptote. An **asymptote** is a line that represents a boundary for a function. It shows a value that the function will get close to, but never reach.

Three common functions used to model different relationships between quantities are linear, quadratic, and exponential functions. Linear functions are the simplest of the three, and the independent variable x has an exponent of 1. Written in the most common form, $y = mx + b$, the coefficient of x indicates how fast the function grows at a constant rate, and the b-value denotes the starting point. A quadratic function has an exponent of 2 on the independent variable x. Standard form for this type of function is $y = ax^2 + bx + c$, and the graph is a parabola. These type functions grow at a changing rate. An exponential function has an independent variable in the exponent $y = ab^x$. The graph of these types of functions is described as *growth* or *decay*, based on whether the base, b, is greater than or less than 1. These functions are different from quadratic functions because the base stays constant. A common base is base e.

The following three functions model a linear, quadratic, and exponential function respectively: $y = 2x$, $y = x^2$, and $y = 2^x$. Their graphs are shown below. The first graph, modeling the linear function, shows that the growth is constant over each interval. With a horizontal change of 1, the vertical change is 2. It models constant positive growth. The second graph shows the quadratic function, which is a curve that is symmetric across the y-axis. The growth is not constant, but the change is mirrored over the axis. The last graph models the exponential function, where the horizontal change of 1 yields a vertical change that increases more and more with each iteration of horizontal change. The exponential graph gets very close to the x-axis, but never touches it, meaning there is an asymptote there. The y-value can never be zero because the base of 2 can never be raised to an input value that yields an output of zero.

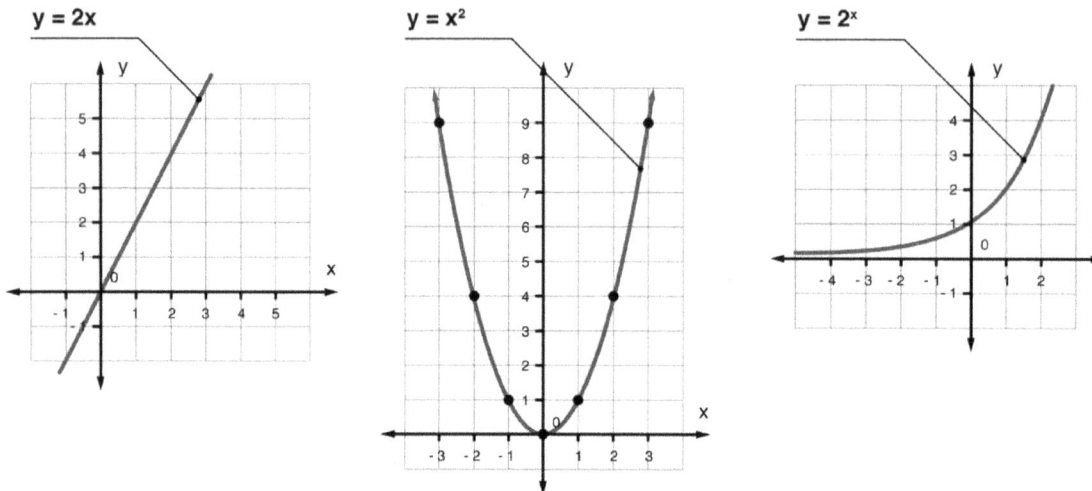

The three tables below show specific values for three types of functions. The third column in each table shows the change in the y-values for each interval. The first table shows a constant change of 2 for each equal interval, which matches the slope in the equation $y = 2x$. The second table shows an increasing change, but it also has a pattern. The increase is changing by 2 more each time, so the change is quadratic. The third table shows the change as factors of the base, 2. It shows a continuing pattern of factors of the base.

$y = 2x$		
x	y	Δy
1	2	
2	4	2
3	6	2
4	8	2
5	10	2

$y = x^2$		
x	y	Δy
1	1	
2	4	3
3	9	5
4	16	7
5	25	9

$y = 2^x$		
x	y	Δy
1	2	
2	4	2
3	8	4
4	16	8
5	32	16

Given a table of values, the type of function can be determined by observing the change in y over equal intervals. For example, the tables below model two functions. The changes in interval for the x-values is 1 for both tables. For the first table, the y-values increase by 5 for each interval. Since the change is constant, the situation can be described as a linear function. The equation would be:

$$y = 5x + 3$$

For the second table, the change for y is 20, 100, and 500, respectively. The increases are multiples of 5, meaning the situation can be modeled by an exponential function. The equation below models this situation:

$$y = 5^x + 3$$

$y = 5x + 3$	
x	y
1	8
2	13
3	18
4	23

$y = 5^x + 3$	
x	y
1	8
2	28
3	128
4	628

Quadratic equations can be used to model real-world area problems. For example, a farmer may have a rectangular field that he needs to sow with seed. The field has length $x + 8$ and width $2x$. The formula for area should be used: $A = lw$. Therefore,

$$A = (x + 8) \times 2x = 2x^2 + 16x$$

The possible values for the length and width can be shown in a table, with input x and output A. If the equation was graphed, the possible area values can be seen on the y-axis for given x-values.

Exponential growth and decay can be found in real-world situations. For example, if a piece of notebook paper is folded 25 times, the thickness of the paper can be found. To model this situation, a table can be used. The initial point is one-fold, which yields a thickness of 2 papers. For the second fold, the thickness is 4. Since the thickness doubles each time, the table below shows the thickness for the next few folds. Notice the thickness changes by the same factor each time. Since this change for a constant interval of folds is a factor of 2, the function is exponential. The equation for this is $y = 2^x$. For twenty-five folds, the thickness would be 33,554,432 papers.

x (folds)	y (paper thickness)
0	1
1	2
2	4
3	8
4	16
5	32

One exponential formula that is commonly used is the *interest formula*: $A = Pe^{rt}$. In this formula, interest is compounded continuously. A is the value of the investment after the time, t, in years. P is the initial amount of the investment, r is the interest rate, and e is the constant equal to approximately 2.718. Given an initial amount of $200 and a time of 3 years, if interest is compounded continuously at a rate of 6%, the total investment value can be found by plugging each value into the formula. The invested value at the end is $239.44. In more complex problems, the final investment may be given, and the rate may be the unknown. In this case, the formula becomes $239.44 = 200e^{r3}$. Solving for r requires isolating the exponential expression on one side by dividing by 200, yielding the equation $1.20 = e^{r3}$. Taking the natural log of both sides results in $\ln(1.2) = r3$. Using a calculator to evaluate the logarithmic expression, $r = 0.06 = 6\%$.

When working with logarithms and exponential expressions, it is important to remember the relationship between the two. In general, the logarithmic form is $y = \log_b x$ for an exponential form $b^y = x$. Logarithms and exponential functions are inverses of each other.

Finding the zeros of polynomial functions is the same process as finding the solutions of polynomial equations. These are the points at which the graph of the function crosses the x-axis. As stated previously, factors can be used to find the zeros of a polynomial function. The degree of the function shows the number of possible zeros. If the highest exponent on the independent variable is 4, then the degree is 4, and the number of possible zeros is 4. If there are complex solutions, the number of roots is less than the degree.

Given the function $y = x^2 + 7x + 6$, y can be set equal to zero, and the polynomial can be factored. The equation turns into $0 = (x + 1)(x + 6)$, where $x = -1$ and $x = -6$ are the zeros. Since this is a quadratic equation, the shape of the graph will be a parabola. Knowing that zeros represent the points where the parabola crosses the x-axis, the maximum or minimum point is the only other piece needed to sketch a rough graph of the function. By looking at the function in standard form, the coefficient of x is positive; therefore, the parabola opens *up*. Using the zeros and the minimum, the following rough sketch of the graph can be constructed:

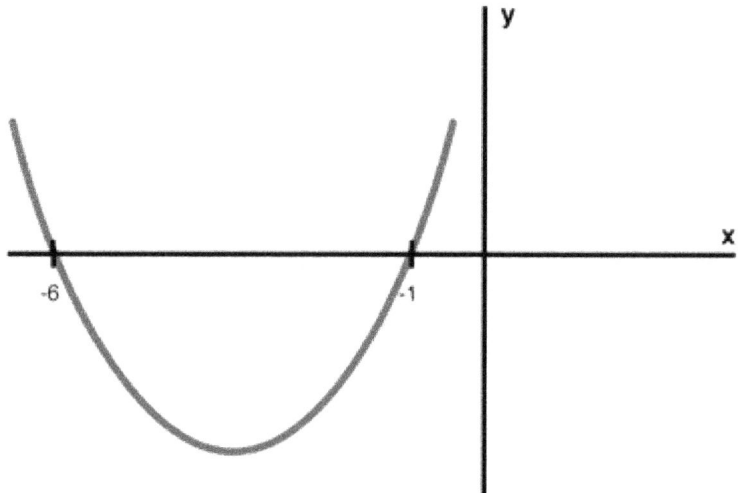

A quadratic function can be written in the standard form:

$$y = ax^2 + bx + c$$

It can be represented by a U-shaped graph called a parabola. The graph can either open up or open down (upside down U). The graph is symmetric about a vertical line, called the axis of symmetry. Corresponding points on the parabola are directly across from each other (same y-value) and are the same distance from the axis of symmetry (on either side). The axis of symmetry intersects the parabola at its vertex. For a quadratic function where the value of a is positive, as the inputs increase, the outputs increase until a certain value (maximum of the function) is reached. As inputs increase past the value that corresponds with the maximum output, the relationship reverses, and the outputs decrease. For a quadratic function where a is negative, as the inputs increase, the outputs (1) decrease, (2) reach a maximum, and (3) then increase.

Creating Equations and Inequalities

An algebraic expression is a statement about unknown quantities expressed in mathematical symbols. The statement *five times a number added to forty* is expressed as $5x + 40$. An equation is a statement in which two

Mathematics

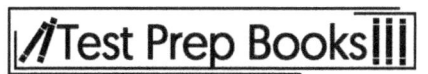

expressions (with at least one containing a variable) are equal to one another. The statement *five times a number added to forty is equal to ten* is expressed as $5x + 40 = 10$.

Real world scenarios can also be expressed mathematically. Suppose a job pays its employees $300 per week and $40 for each sale made. The weekly pay is represented by the expression $40x + 300$ where x is the number of sales made during the week.

Consider the following scenario: Bob had $20 and Tom had $4. After selling 4 ice cream cones to Bob, Tom has as much money as Bob. The cost of an ice cream cone is an unknown quantity and can be represented by a variable (x). The amount of money Bob has after his purchase is four times the cost of an ice cream cone subtracted from his original $20 → $20 - 4x$. The amount of money Tom has after his sale is four times the cost of an ice cream cone added to his original $4 → $4x + 4$. After the sale, the amount of money that Bob and Tom have is equal → $20 - 4x = 4x + 4$.

When expressing a verbal or written statement mathematically, it is vital to understand words or phrases that can be represented with symbols. The following are examples:

Symbol	Phrase
+	Added to; increased by; sum of; more than
−	Decreased by; difference between; less than; take away
×	Multiplied by; 3(4,5...) times as large; product of
÷	Divided by; quotient of; half (third, etc.) of
=	Is; the same as; results in; as much as; equal to
x, t, n, etc.	A number; unknown quantity; value of; variable

Use of Formulas

Formulas are mathematical expressions that define the value of one quantity, given the value of one or more different quantities. Formulas look like equations because they contain variables, numbers, operators, and an equal sign. All formulas are equations, but not all equations are formulas. A formula must have more than one variable. For example, $2x + 7 = y$ is an equation and a formula (it relates the unknown quantities x and y). However, $2x + 7 = 3$ is an equation but not a formula (it only expresses the value of the unknown quantity x).

Formulas are typically written with one variable alone (or isolated) on one side of the equal sign. This variable can be thought of as the *subject* in that the formula is stating the value of the *subject* in terms of the relationship between the other variables. Consider the distance formula: $distance = rate \times time$ or $d = rt$. The value of the subject variable d (distance) is the product of the variable r and t (rate and time). Given the rate and time, the distance traveled can easily be determined by substituting the values into the formula and evaluating.

The formula $P = 2l + 2w$ expresses how to calculate the perimeter of a rectangle (P) given its length (l) and width (w). To find the perimeter of a rectangle with a length of 3 ft and a width of 2 ft, these values are substituted into the formula for l and w: $P = 2(3 \text{ ft}) + 2(2 \text{ ft})$. Following the order of operations, the perimeter is determined to be 10 ft. When working with formulas such as these, including units is an important step.

Given a formula expressed in terms of one variable, the formula can be manipulated to express the relationship in terms of any other variable. In other words, the formula can be rearranged to change which variable is the *subject*. To solve for a variable of interest by manipulating a formula, the equation may be solved as if all other variables were numbers. The same steps for solving are followed, leaving operations in terms of the variables instead of calculating numerical values. For the formula $P = 2l + 2w$, the perimeter is the subject expressed in terms of the length and width. To write a formula to calculate the width of a rectangle, given its length and perimeter, the previous formula relating the three variables is solved for the variable w. If P and l were numerical values, this is a

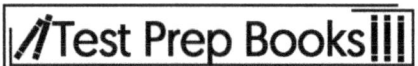

two-step linear equation solved by subtraction and division. To solve the equation $P = 2l + 2w$ for w, $2l$ is first subtracted from both sides: $P - 2l = 2w$. Then both sides are divided by 2: $\frac{P-2l}{2} = w$.

Functions and Function Notation, Interpreting Key Features of Graphs and Tables in Terms of Quantities

A **relation** is a set of input and output values that can be written as ordered pairs. A function is a relation in which each input is paired with exactly one output. A **function** is defined as a relationship between inputs and outputs where there is only one output value for a given input. As an example, the following function is in function notation: $f(x) = 3x - 4$. The $f(x)$ represents the output value for an input of x. If $x = 2$, the equation becomes:

$$f(2) = 3(2) - 4 = 6 - 4 = 2$$

The input of 2 yields an output of 2, forming the ordered pair $(2, 2)$. The following set of ordered pairs corresponds to the given function: $(2, 2), (0, -4), (-2, -10)$. The set of all possible inputs of a function is its **domain**, and all possible outputs is called the **range**. By definition, each member of the domain is paired with only one member of the range.

Functions can also be defined recursively. In this form, they are not defined explicitly in terms of variables. Instead, they are defined using previously-evaluated function outputs, starting with either $f(0)$ or $f(1)$. An example of a recursively-defined function is:

$$f(1) = 2, f(n) = 2f(n-1) + 2n, n > 1$$

The domain of this function is the set of all integers.

Functions can also be described as being even, odd, or neither. If $f(-x) = f(x)$, the function is even. For example, the function $f(x) = x^2 - 2$ is even. Plugging in $x = 2$ yields an output of $y = 2$. After changing the input to $x = -2$, the output is still $y = 2$. The output is the same for opposite inputs. Another way to observe an even function is by the symmetry of the graph. If the graph is symmetrical about the axis, then the function is even. If the graph is symmetric about the origin, then the function is odd. Algebraically, if $f(-x) = -f(x)$, the function is odd.

Also, a function can be described as periodic if it repeats itself in regular intervals. Common periodic functions are trigonometric functions. For example, $y = \sin x$ is a periodic function with period 2π because it repeats itself every 2π units along the x-axis.

Functions can be built out of the context of a situation. For example, the relationship between the money paid for a gym membership and the months that someone has been a member can be described through a function. If the one-time membership fee is $40 and the monthly fee is $30, then the function can be written $f(x) = 30x + 40$. The x-value represents the number of months the person has been part of the gym, while the output is the total money paid for the membership. The table below shows this relationship. It is a representation of the function because the initial cost is $40 and the cost increases each month by $30.

x (months)	y (money paid to gym)
0	40
1	70
2	100
3	130

Functions can also be built from existing functions. For example, a given function $f(x)$ can be transformed by adding a constant, multiplying by a constant, or changing the input value by a constant. The new function $g(x) = f(x) + k$ represents a vertical shift of the original function. In $f(x) = 3x - 2$, a vertical shift 4 units up would be:

$$g(x) = 3x - 2 + 4 = 3x + 2$$

Multiplying the function times a constant k represents a vertical stretch, based on whether the constant is greater than or less than 1. The function:

$$g(x) = kf(x) = 4(3x - 2) = 12x - 8$$

This represents a stretch.

Changing the input x by a constant forms the function:

$$g(x) = f(x + k) = 3(x + 4) - 2 = 3x + 12 - 2 = 3x + 10$$

This represents a horizontal shift to the left 4 units. If $(x - 4)$ was plugged into the function, it would represent a horizontal shift to the right.

A composition function can also be formed by plugging one function into another. In function notation, this is written:

$$(f \circ g)(x) = f(g(x))$$

For two functions $f(x) = x^2$ and $g(x) = x - 3$, the composition function becomes:

$$f(g(x)) = (x - 3)^2 = x^2 - 6x + 9$$

The composition of functions can also be used to verify if two functions are inverses of each other. Given the two functions $f(x) = 2x + 5$ and $g(x) = \frac{x-5}{2}$, the composition function can be found $(f \circ g)(x)$. Solving this equation yields:

$$f(g(x)) = 2\left(\frac{x - 5}{2}\right) + 5 = x - 5 + 5 = x$$

It also is true that $g(f(x)) = x$. Since the composition of these two functions gives a simplified answer of x, this verifies that $f(x)$ and $g(x)$ are inverse functions. The domain of $f(g(x))$ is the set of all x-values in the domain of $g(x)$ such that $g(x)$ is in the domain of $f(x)$. Basically, both $f(g(x))$ and $g(x)$ have to be defined.

To build an inverse of a function, $f(x)$ needs to be replaced with y, and the x- and y-values need to be switched. Then, the equation can be solved for y. For example, given the equation $y = e^{2x}$, the inverse can be found by

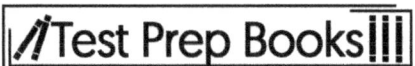

rewriting the equation $x = e^{2y}$. The natural logarithm of both sides is taken down, and the exponent is brought down to form the equation:

$$\ln(x) = \ln(e) \, 2y$$

$\ln(e) = 1$, which yields the equation $\ln(x) = 2y$. Dividing both sides by 2 yields the inverse equation

$$\frac{\ln(x)}{2} = y = f^{-1}(x)$$

The domain of an inverse function is the range of the original function, and the range of an inverse function is the domain of the original function. Therefore, an ordered pair (x, y) on either a graph or a table corresponding to $f(x)$ means that the ordered pair (y, x) exists on the graph of $f^{-1}(x)$. Basically, if $f(x) = y$, then $f^{-1}(y) = x$. For a function to have an inverse, it must be one-to-one. That means it must pass the *Horizontal Line Test*, and if any horizontal line passes through the graph of the function twice, a function is not one-to-one. The domain of a function that is not one-to-one can be restricted to an interval in which the function is one-to-one, to be able to define an inverse function.

Functions can also be formed from combinations of existing functions.

Given $f(x)$ and $g(x)$, the following can be built:

$$f + g$$

$$f - g$$

$$fg$$

$$\frac{f}{g}$$

The domains of $f + g$, $f - g$, and fg are the intersection of the domains of f and g. The domain of $\frac{f}{g}$ is the same set, excluding those values that make $g(x) = 0$.

For example, if:

$$f(x) = 2x + 3$$

$$g(x) = x + 1$$

then

$$\frac{f}{g} = \frac{2x + 3}{x + 1}$$

Its domain is all real numbers except -1.

Domain and Range of a Function

The domain and range of a function can be found visually by its plot on the coordinate plane. In the function $f(x) = x^2 - 3$, for example, the domain is all real numbers because the parabola stretches as far left and as far right as it can go, with no restrictions. This means that any input value from the real number system will yield an answer in the real number system. For the range, the inequality $y \geq -3$ would be used to describe the possible output values

Mathematics

because the parabola has a minimum at $y = -3$. This means there will not be any real output values less than -3 because -3 is the lowest value it reaches on the y-axis.

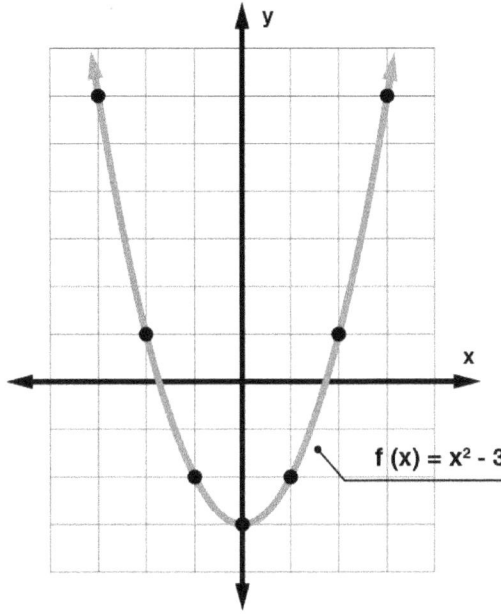

These same answers for domain and range can be found by observing a table. The table below shows that from input values $x = -2$ to $x = 2$, the output results in a minimum of -3. On each side of $x = 0$, the numbers increase, showing that the range is all real numbers greater than or equal to -3.

x (domain/input)	y (range/output)
-2	1
-1	-2
0	-3
-1	-2
2	1

Steps in Solving a Simple Equation

All equations, from the simple to more complex, involve a series of steps that build upon the solution found in the prior step. Sometimes, subsequent steps further manipulate the equation or apply an additional formula, while other times, steps simplify the solution obtained in the prior step or convert its units or presentation in one way or another. In the latter cases, solutions to the two steps are actually equivalent, but presented in different forms. In all situations, it is important to understand and be able to logically explain the reason behind each step involved in finding a solution to a given problem and why the given procedure was followed. To that end, one should verify that their obtained answer is reasonable for the provided problem and can defend its accuracy.

For example, when solving a linear equation, the desired result requires determining a numerical value for the unknown variable. If given a linear equation involving addition, subtraction, multiplication, or division, working backwards isolates the variable. Addition and subtraction are inverse operations, as are multiplication and division. Therefore, they can be used to cancel each other out.

The first steps to solving linear equations are distributing, if necessary, and combining any like terms on the same side of the equation. Sides of an equation are separated by an *equal* sign. Next, the equation is manipulated to show the variable on one side. Whatever is done to one side of the equation must be done to the other side of the equation to remain equal. Inverse operations are then used to isolate the variable and undo the order of operations backwards. Addition and subtraction are undone, then multiplication and division are undone.

For example, solve $4(t - 2) + 2t - 4 = 2(9 - 2t)$

Distributing: $4t - 8 + 2t - 4 = 18 - 4t$

Combining like terms: $6t - 12 = 18 - 4t$

Adding $4t$ to each side to move the variable: $10t - 12 = 18$

Adding 12 to each side to isolate the variable: $10t = 30$

Dividing each side by 10 to isolate the variable: $t = 3$

The answer can be checked by substituting the value for the variable into the original equation and ensuring that both sides calculate to be equal.

Calculating and Interpreting the Average Rate of Change of a Function

Rate of change for any line calculates the steepness of the line over a given interval. Rate of change is also known as the slope or rise/run. The rates of change for nonlinear functions vary depending on the interval being used for the function. The rate of change over one interval may be zero, while the next interval may have a positive rate of change. The equation plotted on the graph below, $y = x^2$, is a quadratic function and non-linear. The average rate of change from points $(0, 0)$ to $(1, 1)$ is 1 because the vertical change is 1 over the horizontal change of 1. For the next interval, $(1, 1)$ to $(2, 4)$, the average rate of change is 3 because the slope is $\frac{3}{1}$.

You can see that here:

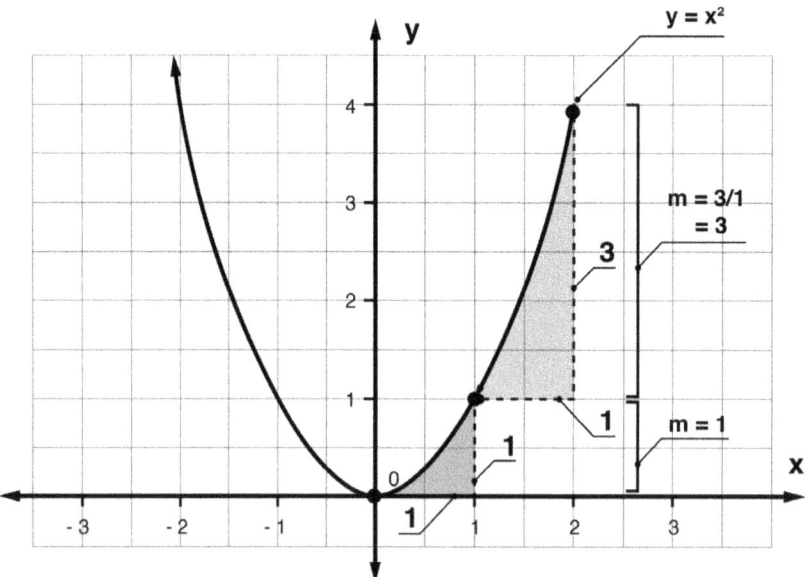

The rate of change for a linear function is constant and can be determined based on a few representations. One method is to place the equation in slope-intercept form: $y = mx + b$. Thus, m is the slope, and b is the y-intercept.

Mathematics

In the graph below, the equation is $y = x + 1$, where the slope is 1 and the y-intercept is 1. For every vertical change of 1 unit, there is a horizontal change of 1 unit. The x-intercept is -1, which is the point where the line crosses the x-axis.

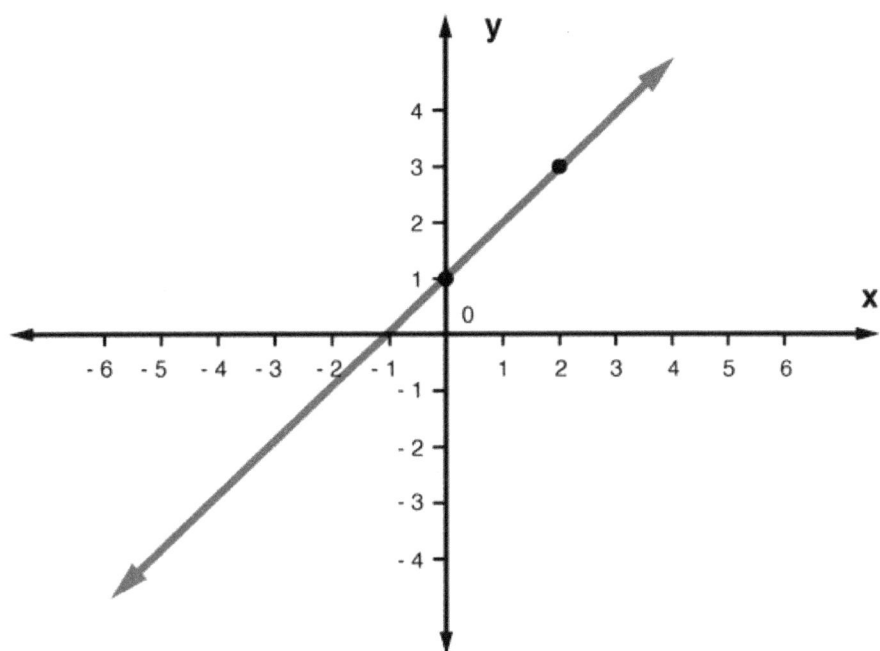

Practice Quiz

1. An accounting firm charted its income on the following pie graph. If the total income for the year was $500,000, how much income was received from Audit Services and Taxation Services?

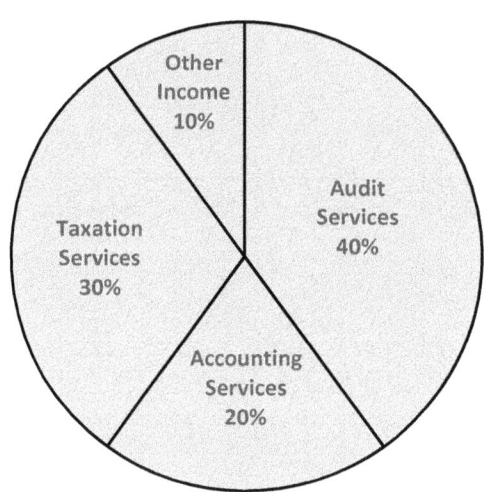

   a. $200,000
   b. $350,000
   c. $150,000
   d. $300,000

2. What are the roots of $x^2 + x - 2$?
   a. 1 and -2
   b. -1 and 2
   c. 2 and -2
   d. 9 and 13

3. What is the y-intercept of $y = x^{5/3} + (x-3)(x+1)$?
   a. 3.5
   b. 7.6
   c. -3
   d. -15.1

4. $(4x^2y^4)^{\frac{3}{2}}$ can be simplified to which of the following?
   a. $8x^3y^6$
   b. $4x^{\frac{5}{2}}y$
   c. $4xy$
   d. $32x^{\frac{7}{2}}y^{\frac{11}{2}}$

Mathematics

5. If $\sqrt{1 + x} = 4$, what is x?
    a. 10
    b. 15
    c. 20
    d. 25

See answers on the next page.

Answer Explanations

1. B: Audit Services makes up 40% of total income, and Taxation Services makes up 30%, so together they make up $40\% + 30\% = 70\%$ of total income. To find 70% of $500,000, change the percentage to a decimal and multiply: $0.7 \times \$500,000 = \$350,000$.

2. A: Finding the roots means finding the values of x that make the polynomial equal zero. The quadratic formula could be used, but in this case, it is possible to factor by hand since the numbers -1 and 2 add to 1 and multiply to -2. So, factor $x^2 + x - 2 = (x - 1)(x + 2) = 0$, then set each factor equal to zero. Solving for each value gives the values $x = 1$ and $x = -2$.

3. C: To find the y-intercept, substitute zero for x, which gives us:

$$y = 0^{\frac{5}{3}} + (0 - 3)(0 + 1) = 0 + (-3)(1) = -3$$

4. A: Simplify this to:

$$(4x^2 y^4)^{\frac{3}{2}} = 4^{\frac{3}{2}}(x^2)^{\frac{3}{2}}(y^4)^{\frac{3}{2}}$$

$$4^{\frac{3}{2}} = (\sqrt{4})^3 = 2^3 = 8$$

For the other, recall that the exponents must be multiplied; this yields:

$$8x^{2 \cdot \frac{3}{2}} y^{4 \cdot \frac{3}{2}} = 8x^3 y^6$$

5. F: Start by squaring both sides to get $1 + x = 16$. Then, subtract 1 from both sides to get $x = 15$.

Science

Life Science

Understand Organisms, Their Environments, and Their Life Cycles

There are several common traits among all living organisms, including:

- They are comprised of cells
- The contain DNA, the genetic code of life
- They grow and develop
- They reproduce
- They need food for energy
- They maintain homeostasis
- They react to their surroundings
- They evolve as a population

There are two types of cells that make up living things: simple bacterial cells (**prokaryotes**) and the complicated cells of protists, fungi, plants, and animals (**eukaryotes**). All of these have a set of instructions, DNA, which codes for the proteins that allow organisms to grow. In the case of bacteria and single-celled eukaryotes, there is simple development, such as creating structures like DNA, **ribosomes** (protein factories), and a cell membrane. Bacteria do not have complex development because they simply divide once and make a new organism; however, multicellular organisms develop more complex structures—for examples, humans have hearts, stomachs, brains, etc. A human starts as one fused cell called a **zygote**. In nine months, that zygote has developed so much that it has all the internal organs needed to support life.

Organisms cannot live without energy to fuel the necessary reactions to grow and develop. They get the energy they need either by making it themselves (if they are **producers/autotrophs** like plants) or consuming it (like animals and fungi) from an outside source. Not only do organisms use that food to grow and develop, but they also use it to stay healthy and maintain homeostasis. For example, the human body has a constant temperature of 98.6 degrees. If the temperature goes above that, the body starts to sweat to cool off. Much below that temperature, the body will shiver in order to generate energy to heat up. For survival, all organisms must be highly regulated to function, kind of like a car. Every single part has to work together in harmony in order to function properly.

Living things, such as humans, respond to their surroundings. If someone hears a loud noise, their head turns toward it. If something gets thrown at one's face, the person will blink. Even plants grow towards sunlight. Living things also evolve as a population. Humans today are nothing like our ancestors of long ago because as a species, humans had to continually adapt to the Earth's changing environment.

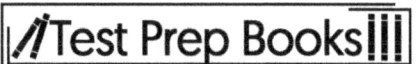

Life Cycle and Organism Interaction with Habitats

Human **development** starts when sperm fertilizes an egg to create a zygote, which will develop into an embryo. Pregnant women carry an **embryo** inside their bodies for nine months before giving birth to a live baby. The following table provides examples of various organisms' life cycles and how they differ from human development:

Chicken	Hens are female chickens, and they lay about one egg per day. If there is no rooster around to fertilize the egg, the egg never turns into a chick and instead becomes an egg that humans can eat. If a rooster is around, he mates with the female chicken and fertilizes the egg. Once the egg is fertilized, the tiny little embryo will start as a white dot adjacent to the yolk and **albumen** (egg white) and will develop for 21 days. The mother hen sits on her clutch of eggs to incubate them and keep them warm. She will turn the eggs to make sure the embryo doesn't stick to one side of the shell. The embryo continues to develop, using the egg white and yolk nutrients, and eventually develops an "egg tooth" on its beak that it uses to crack open the egg and hatch. Before it hatches, it even chirps to let the mom know of its imminent arrival.
Frog	Frogs mate similar to the way chickens do, and then lay eggs in a very wet area. Sometimes, the parents abandon the eggs and let them develop on their own. The eggs, like chickens', will hatch around 21 days later. Just like chickens, a frog develops from a yolk, but when it hatches, it continues to use the yolk for nutrients. A chicken hatches and looks like a cute little chick, but a baby frog is actually a **tadpole** that is barely developed. It can't even swim around right away, although eventually it will develop gills, a mouth, and a tail. After more time, it will develop teeth and tiny legs and continue to change into a fully grown frog. This type of development is called **metamorphosis.**
Fish	Most fish also lay eggs in the water, but unlike frogs, their swimming sperm externally fertilize the eggs. Like frogs, when fish hatch, they feed on a yolk sac and are called *larvae*. Once the larvae no longer feed on their yolk and can find their own nutrients, they are called **fry,** which are basically baby fish that grow into adulthood.
Butterfly	Like frogs, butterflies go through a process called **metamorphosis**, where they completely change into a different looking organism. After the process of mating and internal fertilization, the female finds the perfect spot to lay her eggs, usually a spot with lots of leaves. When the babies hatch from the eggs, they are in the larva form, which for butterflies is called a **caterpillar**. The larvae eat and eat and then go through a process like hibernation and form into a **pupa**, or a **chrysalis**. When they hatch from the chrysalises, the butterflies are in their adult form.
Bugs	After fertilization, other bugs go through **incomplete metamorphosis**, which involves three states: eggs that hatch, nymphs that look like little adults without wings and molt their exoskeleton over time, and adults.

All of these organisms depend on a proper environment for development, and that environment depends on their form. Frogs need water, caterpillars need leaves, and baby chicks need warmth to thrive and grow.

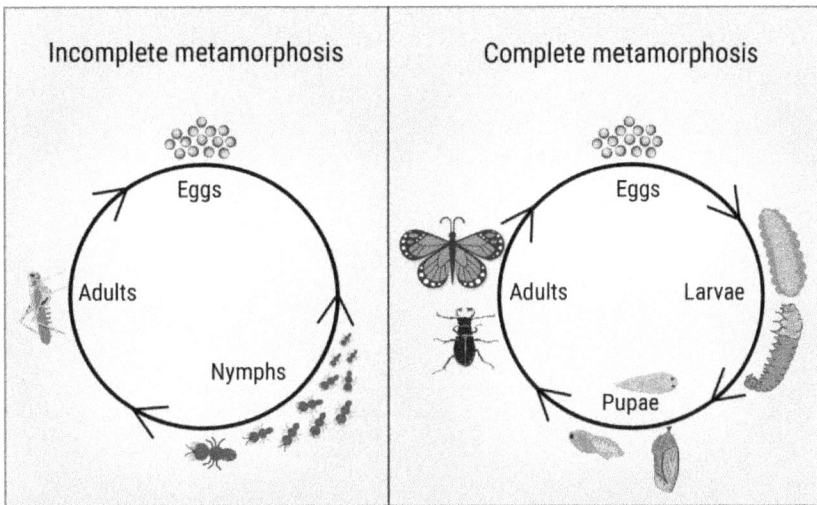

Interactions of Organisms and Their Environments

An **ecosystem** consists of all living (**community**) and nonliving components (abiotic factors) in an area. **Abiotic factors** include the atmosphere, soil, rocks, and water, which all have a role in sustaining life. The atmosphere provides the necessary gasses, soil contains nutrients for plants, rocks erode and affect topography, and water has many different roles.

An ecosystem not only involves living things interacting with nonliving things, but also involves the community interacting with each other. **Food chains** depict one type of community interaction, like the one shown here:

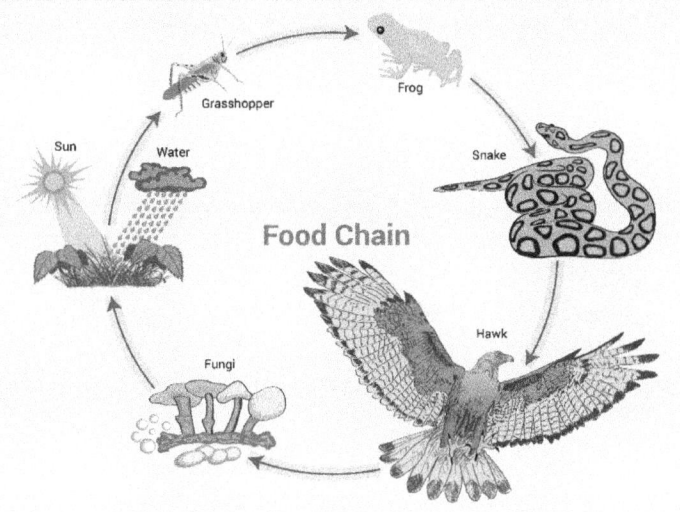

Food chains show the transfer of energy as one organism eats another. They also show an organism's eating habits. **Herbivores** eat plants and **carnivores** eat meat. A lion in grassland with no available animal prey will starve to death even though there is lots of grass because lions don't eat grass; that isn't their role in their habitat.

Food webs not only show predator-prey relationships, but they also show another relationship called **competition**.

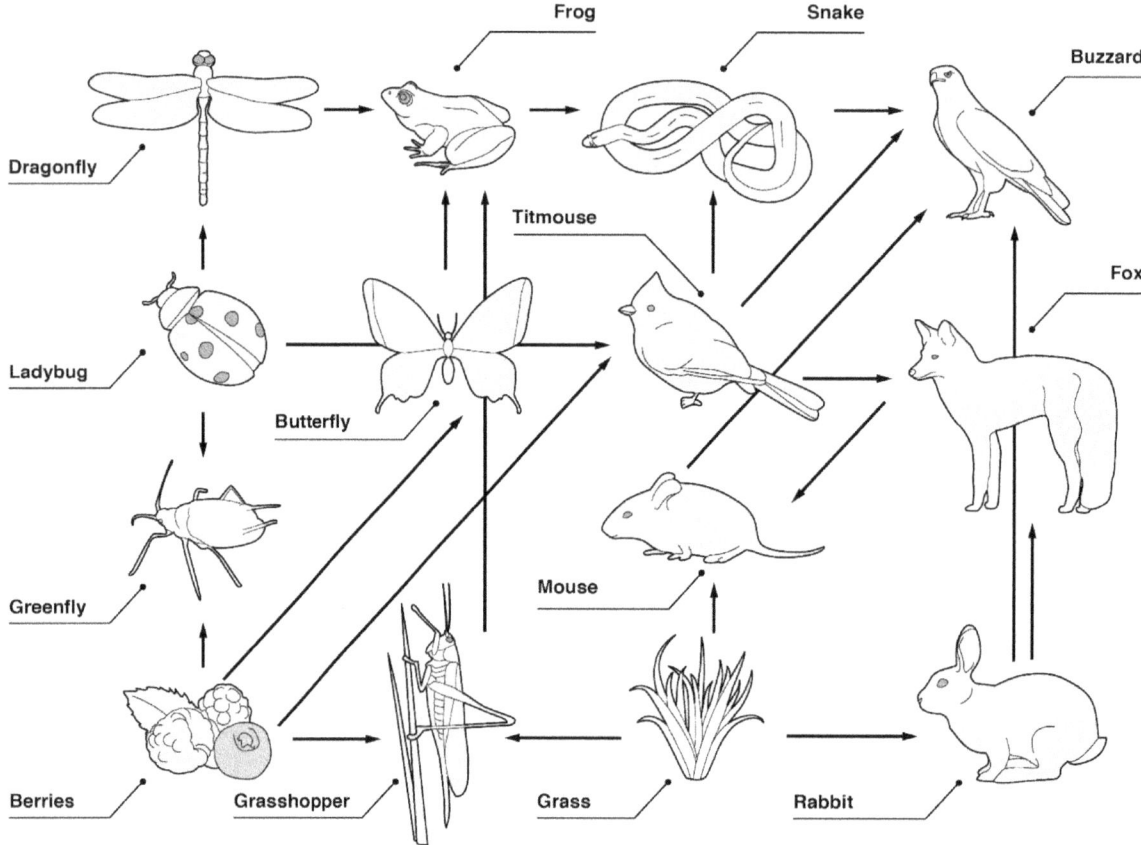

This food web shows that snakes and foxes are competing for titmice. If there is a scarcity of titmice, the snake and fox populations will decrease.

The final three types of community relationships all fall under the blanket term **symbiosis** and are described in the table below.

	Mutualism	**Commensalism**	**Parasitism**
Definition	Both organisms benefit from the relationship	One organism benefits from the relationship	One organism benefits from the relationship, and the other is harmed
Example	Birds and flowers	Whale and barnacle	Dog and flea

	Mutualism	Commensalism	Parasitism
Explanation	Birds get nectar. Plants get pollinated.	Barnacle gets a free ride and access to food. Whale doesn't care because the barnacle is just latched on and isn't hurting anything.	Flea sucks dog's blood and gets nutrients. Dog is itchy and gets its blood drained.

Inherited Traits, Learned Behaviors, and Organism Survival

Many characteristics are inherited from the DNA obtained from an individual's parents, including skin color, eye shape, hair color, and color-blindness, among others. Learned behavior isn't related to genetics and is a result of training. For example, a dog catching a stick is learned. The overall intelligence of the dog, however, has to do with its genes.

An organism's survival depends on its **fitness** relative to the environment, and any trait that helps it survive is called an **adaptation**. Whale blubber and shark teeth are examples of adaptations. Blubber keeps whales warm, and a shark's many teeth ensures it's better able to capture prey. Whales don't decide to grow blubber, and sharks don't decide to grow teeth. These characteristics have been inherited from their parents.

Understanding the Interdependence of Organisms

Population dynamics is the study of the composition of populations, including size, age, and the biological and environmental processes that cause changes. These can include immigration, emigration, births, and deaths.

Behavior

Different species within a population can act differently regarding their environment. Some species display **territoriality**, which is a specific type of competition that excludes other species from a given area. It can be shown through specific animal calls, intimidating behavior, or marking an area with scents, and is often a display of defense.

Intraspecific Relationships

Intraspecific relationships is a term that describes the competition and cooperation between organisms that belong to the same species. They may compete for the same food sources, or for mates that are necessary for their personal survival and reproduction. Stronger organisms may display dominance that allows them to reside at the top of a social hierarchy and obtain better food and higher quality mates. However, organisms may also cooperate with each other in order to benefit the larger group; for instance, they may divide laborious activities among themselves.

Community Ecology

An **ecological community** is a group of species that interact and live in the same location. Because of their shared environment, they tend to have a large influence on each other.

Niche

An **ecological niche** is the role that a species plays in its environment, including how it finds its food and shelter. It could be a predator of a different species, or prey for a larger species.

Species Diversity
Species diversity is the number of different species that cohabitate in an ecological community. It has two different facets: **species richness**, which is the general number of species, and **species evenness**, which accounts for the population size of each species.

Interspecific Relationships
Interspecific relationships include the interactions between organisms of different species. The following list defines the common relationships that can occur:

- **Commensalism**: One organism benefits while the other is neither benefited nor harmed
- **Mutualism**: Both organisms benefit
- **Parasitism**: One organism benefits and the other is harmed
- **Competition**: Two or more species compete for limited resources that are necessary for their survival
- **Predation (Predator-Prey)**: One species is a food source for another species

Ecosystems
An **ecosystem** includes all of the living organisms and nonliving components of an environment (each community) and their interactions with each other.

Biomes
A **biome** is a group of plants and animals that are found in many different continents and have the same characteristics because of the similar climates in which they live. Each biome is composed of all of the ecosystems in that area. Five primary types of biomes are aquatic, deserts, forests, grasslands, and tundra. The sum total of all biomes comprises the Earth's biosphere.

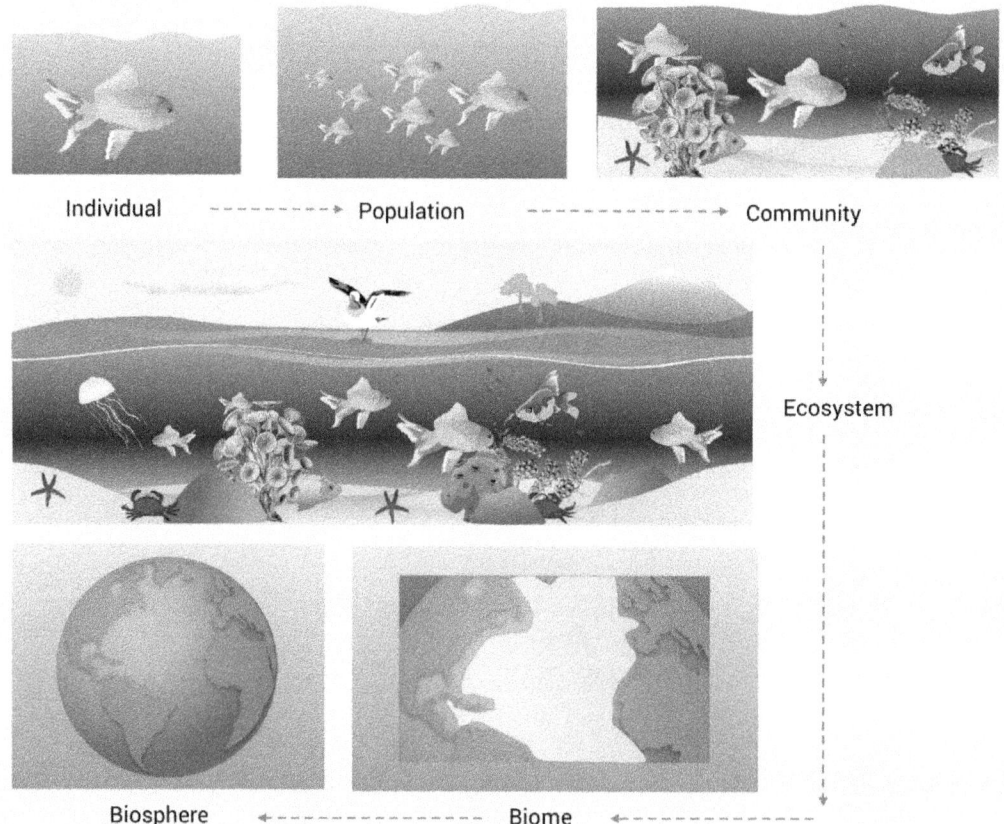

Stability and Disturbances

Ecological stability is the ability of an ecosystem to withstand changes that are occurring within it. With **regenerative stability**, an ecosystem may change, but then quickly return to its previous state. **Constant stability** occurs in ecosystems that remain unchanged despite the changes going on around them.

An **ecological disturbance** is a change in the environment that causes a larger change in the ecosystem. Smaller disturbances include fires and floods. Larger disturbances include the **climate change** that is currently occurring. Gas emissions from human activity are causing the atmosphere to warm up, which is changing the Earth's water systems and making weather more extreme. The increase in temperature is causing greater evaporation of the water sources on Earth, creating droughts and depleting natural water sources. This has also caused many of the Earth's glaciers to begin melting, which can change the salinity of the oceans.

Changes in the environment can cause an **ecological succession** to occur, which is the change in structure of the species that coexist in an ecological community. When the environment changes, resources available to the different species also change. For example, the formation of sand dunes or a forest fire would change the environment enough to allow a change in the social hierarchy of the coexisting species.

Energy Flow

Ecosystems are maintained by cycling the energy and nutrients that they obtain from external sources. The process can be diagramed in a **food web**, which represents the feeding relationship between species in a community. The different levels of the food web are called **trophic levels**. The first trophic level generally consists of plants, algae, and bacteria. The second trophic level consists of herbivores. The third trophic level consists of predators that eat herbivores. The trophic levels continue on to larger and larger predators. **Decomposers** are an important part of the food chain that are not at a specific trophic level. They eat decomposing things on the ground that other animals do not want to eat. This allows them to provide nutrients to their own predators.

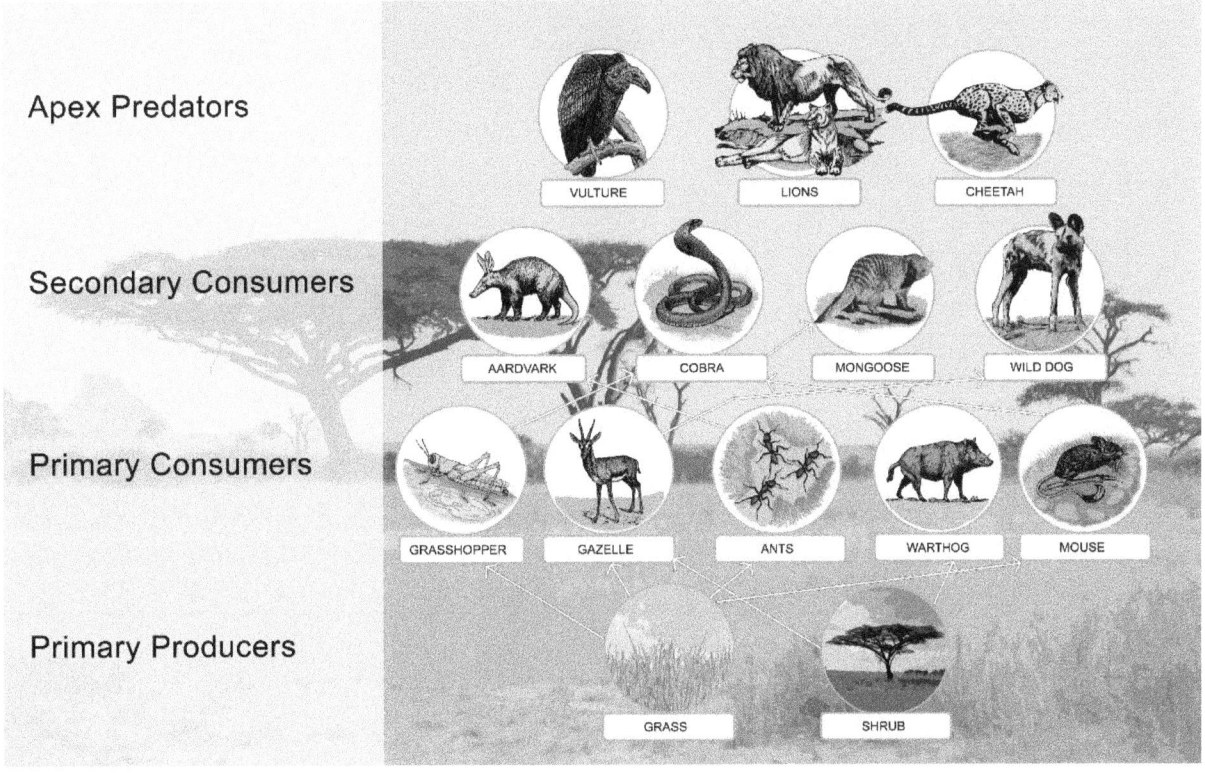

Biogeochemical Cycles

Biogeochemical cycles are the pathways by which chemicals move through the **biotic**, or biospheric, and **abiotic**, or atmospheric, parts of the Earth. The most important biogeochemical cycles include the water, carbon, and nitrogen cycles. **Water** goes through an evaporation, condensation, and precipitation cycle. **Nitrogen** makes up seventy-eight percent of the Earth's atmosphere and can affect the rate of many ecosystem processes, such as production of the primary producers at the first trophic level of the food web. The **carbon cycle** has many steps that are vitally important for sustaining life on Earth.

The water cycle:

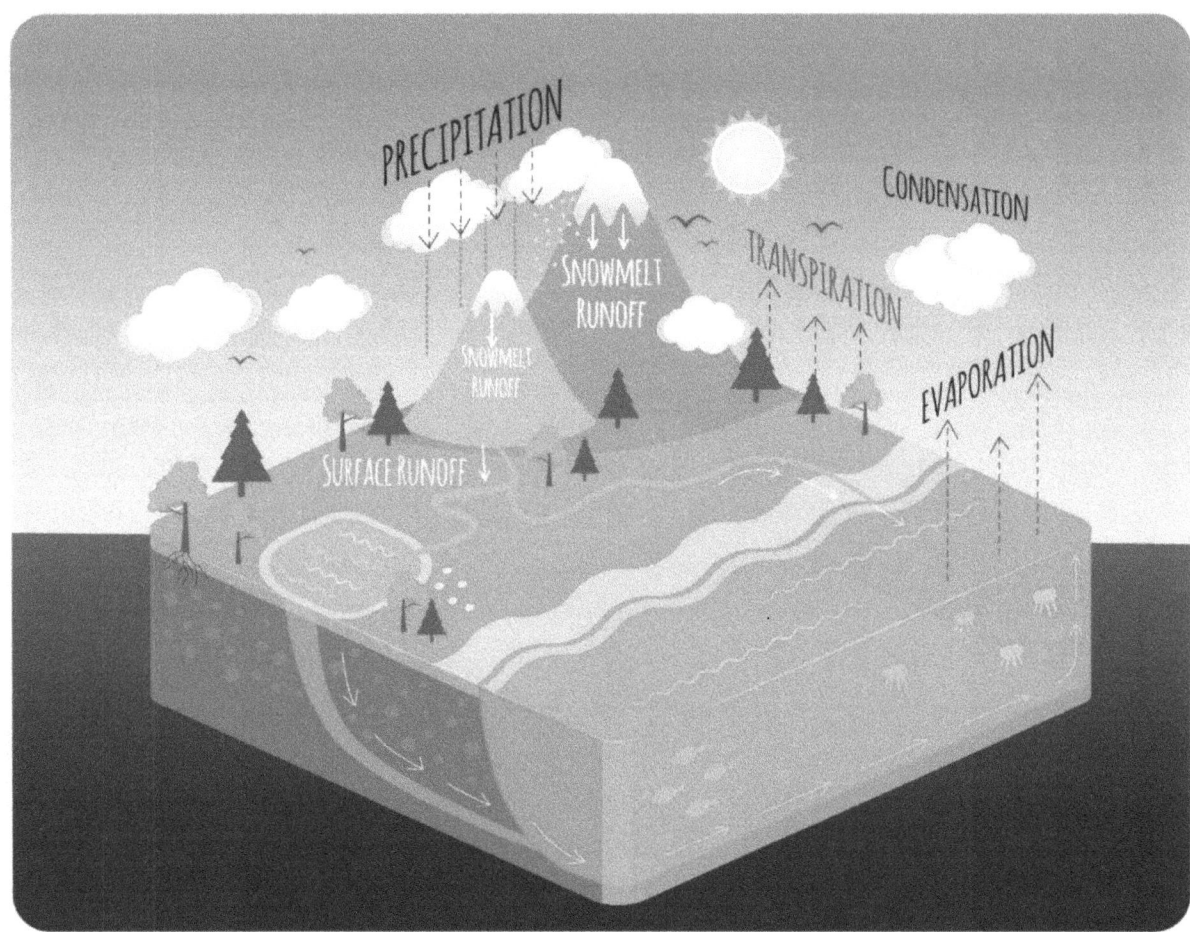

Below are illustrations for the nitrogen cycle and carbon cycle:

The Nitrogen Cycle

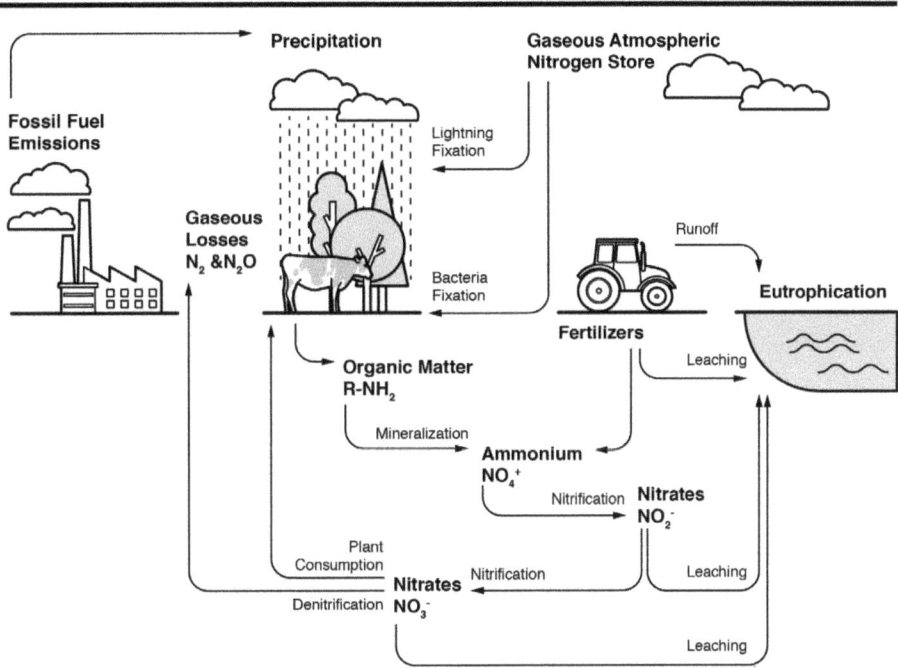

The Carbon Cycle

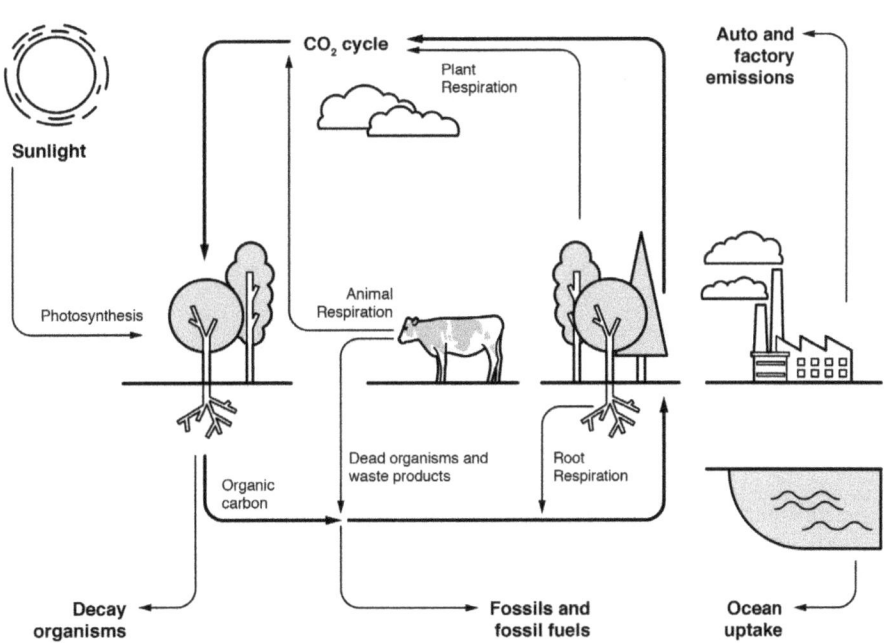

Relationships Between Structure and Function in Living Systems

Taxonomy is the science behind the biological names of organisms. Biologists often refer to organisms by their Latin scientific names to avoid confusion with common names, such as with fish. Jellyfish, crayfish, and silverfish all have the word "fish" in their name, but belong to three different species. In the eighteenth century, Carl Linnaeus invented a naming system for species that included using the Latin scientific name of a species, called the **binomial**, which has two parts: the **genus**, which comes first, and the **specific epithet**, which comes second. Similar species are grouped into the same genus. The Linnaean system is the commonly used taxonomic system today and, moving from comprehensive similarities to more general similarities, classifies organisms into their species, genus, family, order, class, phylum, and kingdom. **Homo sapiens** is the Latin scientific name for humans.

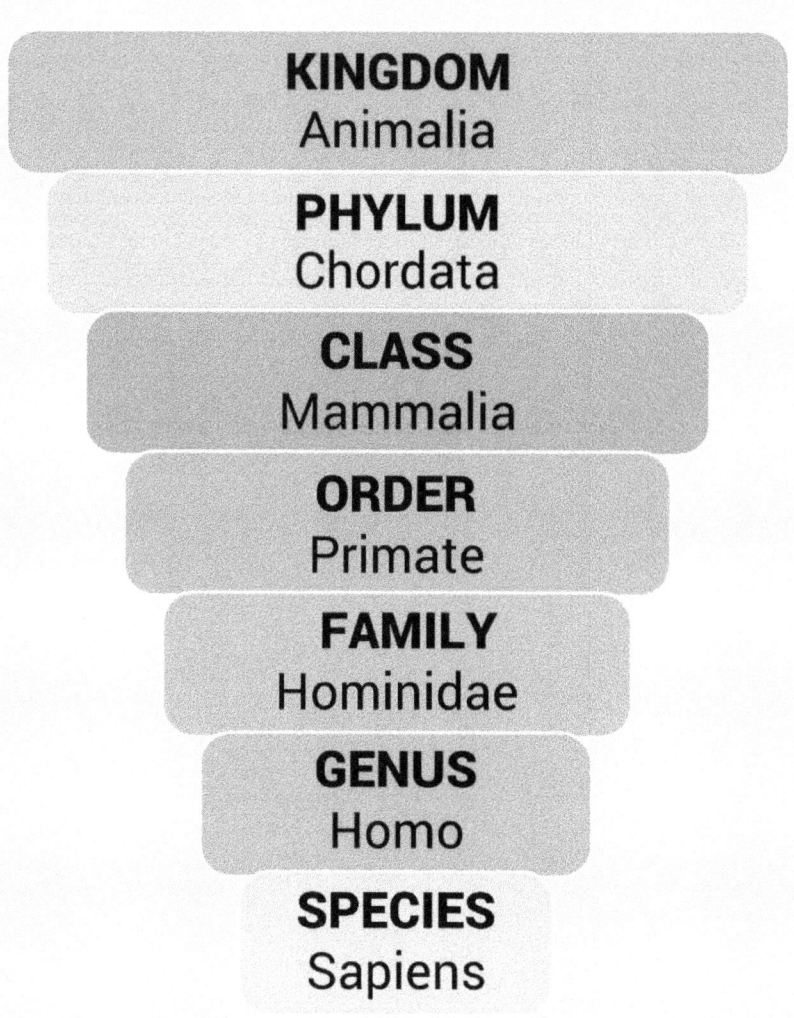

Phylogenetic trees are branching diagrams that represent the evolutionary history of a species. The branch points most often match the classification groups set forth by the Linnaean system. Using this system helps elucidate the relationship between different groups of organisms. The diagram below is that of an empty phylogenetic tree:

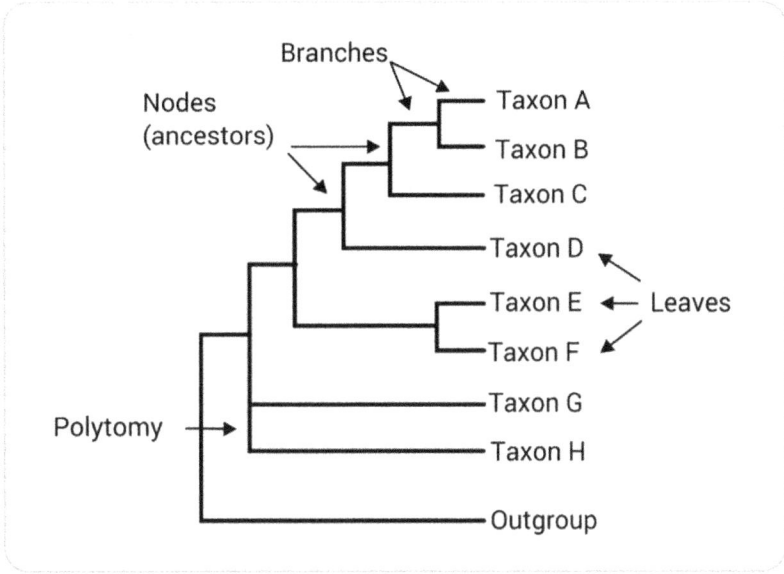

Each branch of the tree represents the divergence of two species from a common ancestor. For example, the coyote is known as Canis latrans and the gray wolf is known as Canis lupus. Their common ancestor, the Canis lepophagus, which is now extinct, is where their shared genus derived.

Characteristics of Bacteria, Animals, Plants, Fungi, and Protists

As discussed earlier, there are two distinct types of cells that make up most living organisms: prokaryotic and eukaryotic. Bacteria (and archaea) are classified as prokaryotic cells, whereas animal, plant, fungi, and protist cells are classified as eukaryotic cells.

Although animal cells and plant cells are both eukaryotic, they each have several distinguishing characteristics. **Animal cells** are surrounded by a plasma membrane, while **plant cells** have a cell wall made up of cellulose that provides more structure and an extra layer of protection for the cell. Animals use oxygen to breathe and give off carbon dioxide, while plants do the opposite—they take in carbon dioxide and give off oxygen. Plants also use light as a source of energy. Animals have highly developed sensory and nervous systems and the ability to move freely, while plants lack both abilities. Animals, however, cannot make their own food and must rely on their environment to provide sufficient nutrition, whereas plants do make their own food.

Fungal cells are typical eukaryotes, containing both a nucleus and membrane-bound organelles. They have a cell wall, similar to plant cells; however, they use oxygen as a source of energy and cannot perform photosynthesis. They also depend on outside sources for nutrition and cannot produce their own food. Of note, their cell walls contain **chitin**.

Protists are a group of diverse eukaryotic cells that are often grouped together because they do not fit into the categories of animal, plant, or fungal cells. They can be categorized into three broad categories: protozoa, protophyta, and molds. These three broad categories are essentially "animal-like," "plant-like," and "fungus-like," respectively. All of them are unicellular and do not form tissues. Besides this simple similarity, protists are a diverse group of organisms with different characteristics, life cycles, and cellular structures.

Major Structures of Plants and Their Functions

Characteristics of Vascular and Nonvascular Plants

Plants that have an extensive vascular transport system are called **vascular plants**. Those plants without a transport system are called **nonvascular plants**. Approximately ninety-three percent of plants that are currently living and reproducing are vascular plants. The cells that comprise the vascular tissue in vascular plants form tubes that transport water and nutrients through the entire plant. Nonvascular plants include mosses, liverworts, and hornworts. They do not retain any water; instead, they transport water using other specialized tissue. They have structures that look like leaves, but are actually just single sheets of cells without a cuticle or stomata.

Structure and Function of Roots, Leaves, and Stems

Roots are responsible for anchoring plants in the ground. They absorb water and nutrients and transport them up through the plant. **Leaves** are the main location of photosynthesis. They contain **stomata**, which are pores used for gas exchange, on their underside to take in carbon dioxide and release oxygen. **Stems** transport materials through the plant and support the plant's body. They contain **xylem**, which conducts water and dissolved nutrients upward through the plant, and **phloem**, which conducts sugars and metabolic products downward through the leaves.

Asexual and Sexual Reproduction

Plants can generate future generations through both asexual and sexual reproduction. Asexually, plants can go through an artificial reproductive technique called **budding**, in which parts from two or more plants of the same species are joined together with the hope that they will begin to grow as a single plant.

Sexual reproduction of flowers can happen in a couple of ways. **Angiosperms** are flowering plants that have seeds. The flowers have male parts that make pollen and female parts that contain ovules. Wind, insects, and other animals carry the pollen from the male part to the female part in a process called **pollination**. Once the ovules are pollinated, or fertilized, they develop into seeds that then develop into new plants. In many angiosperms, the flowers develop into fruit, such as oranges, or even hard nuts, which protect the seeds inside of them.

Nonvascular plants reproduce by sexual reproduction involving **spores**. Parent plants send out spores that contain a set of chromosomes. The spores develop into sperm or eggs, and fertilization is similar to that in humans. Sperm travel to the egg through water in the environment. An embryo forms and then a new plant grows from the embryo. Generally, this happens in damp places.

Growth

Germination is the process of a plant growing from a seed or spore, such as when a seedling sprouts from a seed or a sporeling grows from a spore. Plants then grow by **elongation**. Plant cell walls are modified by the hormone auxin, which allows for cell elongation. This process is regulated by light and phytohormones, which are plant hormones that regulate growth, so plants are often seen growing toward the sun.

Uptake and Transport of Nutrients and Water

Plant roots are responsible for bringing nutrients and water into the plant from the ground. The nutrients are not used as food for the plant, but rather to maintain the plant's health so that the plant can make its own food during photosynthesis. The xylem and phloem in the stem help with transport of water and other substances throughout the plant.

Responses to Stimuli

Because plants have limited mobility, they often respond to stimuli through changes in their growth behavior. **Tropism** is a response to stimuli that causes the plant to grow toward or away from the stimuli:

- **Phototropism**: A reaction to light that causes plants to grow toward the source of the light
- **Thermotropism**: A response to changes in temperature
- **Hydrotropism**: A response to a change in water concentration
- **Gravitropism**: A response to gravity that causes roots to follow the pull of gravity and grow downward, but also causes plant shoots to act against gravity and grow upward

Human Body Systems

Biological Molecules

Basic units of organic compounds are often called **monomers**. Repeating units of linked monomers are called **polymers**. The most important large molecules, or polymers, found in all living things can be divided into four categories: carbohydrates, lipids, proteins, and nucleic acids. This may be surprising since there is so much diversity in the outward appearance and physical abilities of living things present on Earth. Carbon (C), hydrogen (H), oxygen (O), nitrogen (N), sulfur (S), and phosphorus (P) are the major elements of most biological molecules. Carbon is a common backbone of large molecules because of its ability to form four covalent bonds.

Carbohydrates

Carbohydrates consist of sugars and polymers of sugars. The simplest sugar are **monosaccharide**, which have the empirical formula of CH_2O. The formula for the monosaccharide glucose, for example, is $C_6H_{12}O_6$. Glucose is an important molecule for cellular respiration, the process of cells extracting energy by breaking bonds through a series of reactions. The individual atoms are then used to rebuild new small molecules. **Polysaccharides** are made up of a few hundred to a few thousand monosaccharides linked together. These larger molecules have two major functions. The first is that they can be stored as starches, such as **glycogen**, and then broken down later for energy. Secondly, they may be used to form strong materials, such as **cellulose**, which is the firm wall that encloses plant cells, and **chitin**, the carbohydrate insects use to build exoskeletons.

Lipids

Lipids are a class of biological molecules that are **hydrophobic**, meaning they don't mix well with water. They are mostly made up of large chains of carbon and hydrogen atoms, termed **hydrocarbon chains**. When lipids mix with water, the water molecules bond to each other and exclude the lipids because they are unable to form bonds with the long hydrocarbon chains. The three most important types of lipids are fats, phospholipids, and steroids.

Fats are made up of two types of smaller molecules: glycerol and fatty acids. **Glycerol** is a chain of three carbon atoms, with a **hydroxyl group** attached to each carbon atom. A hydroxyl group is made up of an oxygen and hydrogen atom bonded together. **Fatty acids** are long hydrocarbon chains that have a backbone of sixteen or eighteen carbon atoms. The carbon atom on one end of the fatty acid is part of a **carboxyl group.** A carboxyl group is a carbon atom that uses two of its four bonds to bond to one oxygen atom (double bond) and uses another one of its bonds to link to a hydroxyl group.

Fats are made by joining three fatty acid molecules and one glycerol molecule.

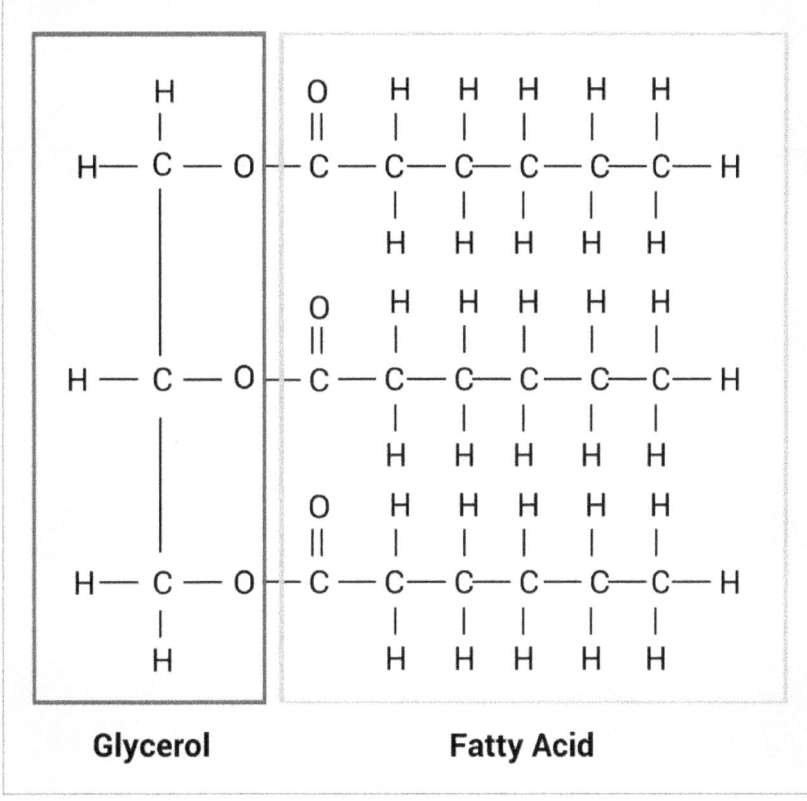

Glycerol **Fatty Acid**

Phospholipids are made of two fatty acid molecules linked to one glycerol molecule. A **phosphate group** is attached to a third hydroxyl group of the glycerol molecule. A phosphate group consists of a phosphate atom connected to four oxygen atoms and has an overall negative charge.

Phospholipids have an interesting structure because their fatty acid tails are hydrophobic, but their phosphate group heads are hydrophilic. When phospholipids mix with water, they create double-layered structures, called **bilayers,** that shield their hydrophobic regions from water molecules. Cell membranes are made of phospholipid bilayers, which allow the cells to mix with aqueous solutions outside and inside, while forming a protective barrier and a semi-permeable membrane around the cell.

Steroids are lipids that consist of four fused carbon rings. The different chemical groups that attach to these rings are what make up the many types of steroids. **Cholesterol** is a common type of steroid found in animal cell membranes. Steroids are mixed in between the phospholipid bilayer and help maintain the structure of the membrane and aids in cell signaling.

Proteins

Proteins are essential for most all functions in living beings. The term *protein* is derived from the Greek word *proteios*, meaning *first* or *primary*. All proteins are made from a set of twenty amino acids that are linked in unbranched polymers. The combinations are numerous, which accounts for the diversity of proteins. Amino acids are linked by peptide bonds, while polymers of amino acids are called **polypeptides**. These polypeptides, either individually or in linked combination with each other, fold up to form coils of biologically-functional molecules, called proteins.

There are four levels of protein structure: primary, secondary, tertiary, and quaternary. The **primary structure** is the sequence of amino acids, similar to the letters in a long word. The **secondary structure** is beta sheets, or alpha helices, formed by hydrogen bonding between the polar regions of the polypeptide backbone. **Tertiary structure** is the overall shape of the molecule that results from the interactions between the side chains linked to the polypeptide backbone. **Quaternary structure** is the overall protein structure that occurs when a protein is made up of two or more polypeptide chains.

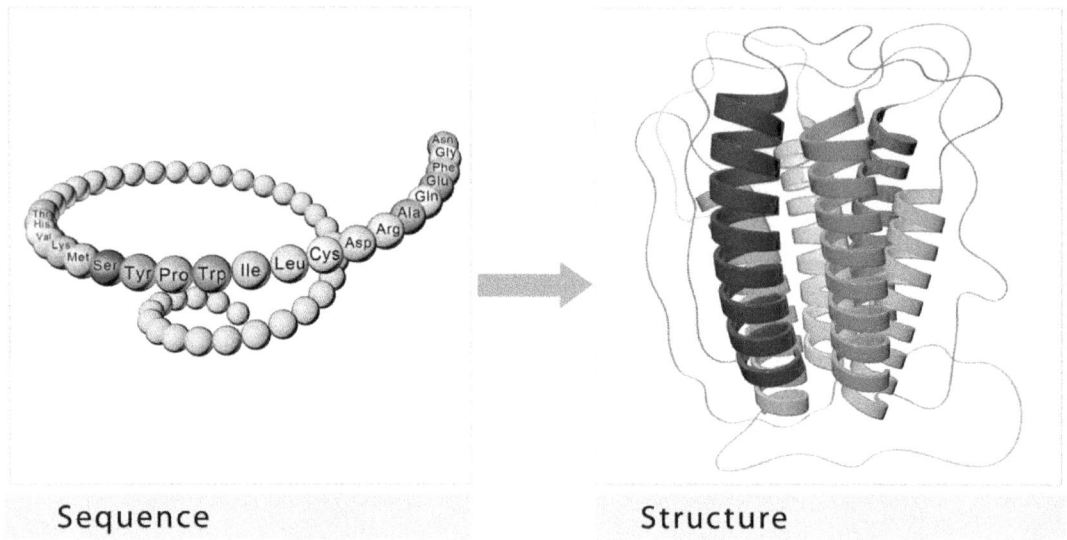

Sequence → Structure

Nucleic Acids

Nucleic acids can also be called **polynucleotides** because they are made up of chains of monomers called **nucleotides.** Nucleotides consist of a five-carbon sugar, a nitrogen-containing base, and a phosphate group. There are two types of nucleic acids: **deoxyribonucleic acid (DNA)** and **ribonucleic acid (RNA)**. Both DNA and RNA enable living organisms to pass on their genetic information and complex components to subsequent generations. While DNA is made up of two strands of nucleotides coiled together in a double-helix structure, RNA is made up of a single strand of nucleotides that folds onto itself.

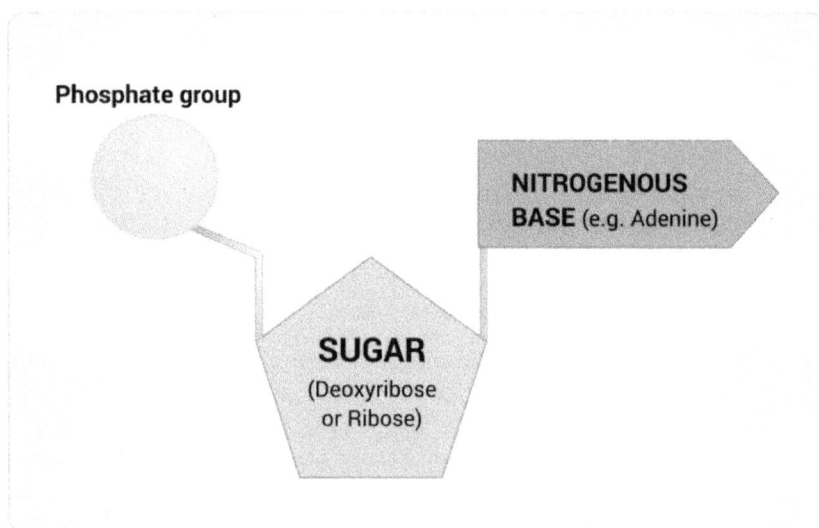

Science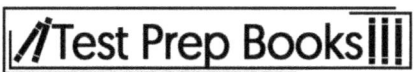

Metabolism

Metabolism is the set of chemical processes that occur within a cell for the maintenance of life. It includes both the synthesizing and breaking down of substances. A metabolic pathway begins with a molecule and ends with a specific product after going through a series of reactions, often involving an enzyme at each step. An **enzyme** is a protein that aids in the reaction. **Catabolic pathways** are metabolic pathways in which energy is released by complex molecules being broken down into simpler molecules. Contrast to catabolic pathways are **anabolic pathways**, which use energy to build complex molecules out of simple molecules. With cell metabolism, remember the **first law of thermodynamics**: Energy can be transformed, but it cannot be created or destroyed. Therefore, the energy released in a cell by a catabolic pathway is used up in anabolic pathways.

The reactions that occur within metabolic pathways are classified as either exergonic reactions or endergonic reactions. **Exergonic reactions** end in a release of free energy, while **endergonic reactions** absorb free energy from its surroundings. **Free energy** is the portion of energy in a system, such as a living cell, that can be used to perform work, such as a chemical reaction. It is denoted as the capital letter G and the change in free energy from a reaction or set of reactions is denoted as delta G (ΔG). When reactions do not require an input of energy, they are said to occur spontaneously. Exergonic reactions are considered spontaneous because they result in a negative delta G (−ΔG), where the products of the reaction have less free energy within them than the reactants. Endergonic reactions require an input of energy and result in a positive delta G (+ΔG), with the products of the reaction containing more free energy than the individual reactants. When a system no longer has free energy to do work, it has reached **equilibrium**. Since cells always work, they are no longer alive if they reach equilibrium.

Cells balance their energy resources by using the energy from exergonic reactions to drive endergonic reactions forward, a process called **energy coupling**. **Adenosine triphosphate**, or ATP, is a molecule that is an immediate source of energy for cellular work. When it is broken down, it releases energy used in endergonic reactions and anabolic pathways. ATP breaks down into adenosine diphosphate, or ADP, and a separate phosphate group, releasing energy in an exergonic reaction. As ATP is used up by reactions, it is also regenerated by having a new phosphate group added onto the ADP products within the cell in an endergonic reaction.

Enzymes are special proteins that help speed up metabolic reactions and pathways. They do not change the overall free energy release or consumption of reactions; they just make the reactions occur more quickly as it lowers the activation energy required. Enzymes are designed to act only on specific substrates. Their physical shape fits snugly onto their matched substrates, so enzymes only speed up reactions that contain the substrates to which they are matched.

The Cell

Cells are the basic structural and functional unit of all organisms. They are the smallest unit of matter that is living. While there are many single-celled organisms, most biological organisms are more complex and made up of many different types of cells. There are two distinct types of cells: prokaryotic and eukaryotic. **Prokaryotic cells** include bacteria, while **eukaryotic cells** include animal and plant cells. Both types of cells are enclosed by a cell membrane, which is selectively permeable. Selective permeability means essentially that it is a gatekeeper, allowing certain molecules and ions in and out, and keeping unwanted ones at bay, at least until they are ready for use. Both contain ribosomes, which are complexes that make protein inside the cell, and DNA. One major difference is that the DNA in eukaryotic cells are enclosed in a membrane-bound **nucleus**, where in prokaryotic cells, DNA is in the **nucleoid**, a region that is not enclosed by a membrane. Another major difference is that eukaryotic cells contain **organelles**, which are membrane-enclosed structures, each with a specific function, while prokaryotic cells do not have organelles.

Organelles Found in Eukaryotic Cells
The following cell organelles are found in both animal and plant cells unless otherwise noted:

Nucleus: The nucleus consists of three parts: nuclear envelope, nucleolus, and chromatin. The **nuclear envelope** is the double membrane that surrounds the nucleus and separates its contents from the rest of the cell. It is porous so substances can pass back and forth between the nucleus and the other parts of the cell. It is also continuous, with the endoplasmic reticulum that is present within the cytosol of the cell. The **nucleolus** is in charge of producing ribosomes. **Chromosomes are comprised of tightly coiled proteins, RNA, and DNA and are collectively called chromatin.**

Endoplasmic Reticulum (ER): The ER is a network of membranous sacs and tubes responsible for membrane synthesis and other metabolic and synthetic activities of the cell. There are two types of ER, rough and smooth. Rough ER is lined with ribosomes and is the location of protein synthesis. This provides a separate compartment for site-specific protein synthesis and is important for the intracellular transport of proteins. Smooth ER does not contain ribosomes and is the location of lipid synthesis.

Flagellum: The flagellum is found in protists and animal cells. It is a cluster of microtubules projected out of the plasma membrane and aids in cell motility.

Centrosome: The centrosome is the area of the cell where microtubules are created and organized for mitosis. Each centrosome contains two **centrioles.**

Cytoskeleton: The cytoskeleton in animal cells is made up of microfilaments, intermediate filaments, and microtubules. In plant cells, the cytoskeleton is made up of only microfilaments and microtubules. These structures reinforce the cell's shape and aid in cell movements.

Microvilli: Microvilli are found only in animal cells. They are protrusions in the cell membrane that increase the cell's surface area. They have a variety of functions, including absorption, secretion, and cellular adhesion.

Peroxisome: A peroxisome contains enzymes that are involved in many of the cell's metabolic functions, one of the most important being the breakdown of fatty acid chains. It produces hydrogen peroxide as a by-product of these processes and then converts the hydrogen peroxide to water.

Mitochondrion: The mitochondrion, considered the cell's powerhouse, is one of the most important structures for maintaining regular cell function. It is where cellular respiration occurs and where most of the cell's ATP is generated.

Lysosome: Lysosomes are found exclusively in animal cells. They are responsible for digestion and can hydrolyze macromolecules.

Golgi Apparatus: The Golgi apparatus is responsible for synthesizing, modifying, sorting, transporting, and secreting cell products. Because of its large size, it was one of the first organelles studied in detail.

Ribosomes: Ribosomes are found either free in the cytosol, bound to the rough ER, or bound to the nuclear envelope. They are also found in prokaryotes. Ribosomes make up a complex that forms proteins within the cell.

Plasmodesmata: Found only in plant cells, plasmodesmata are cytoplasmic channels, or tunnels, that go through the cell wall and connect the cytoplasm of adjacent cells.

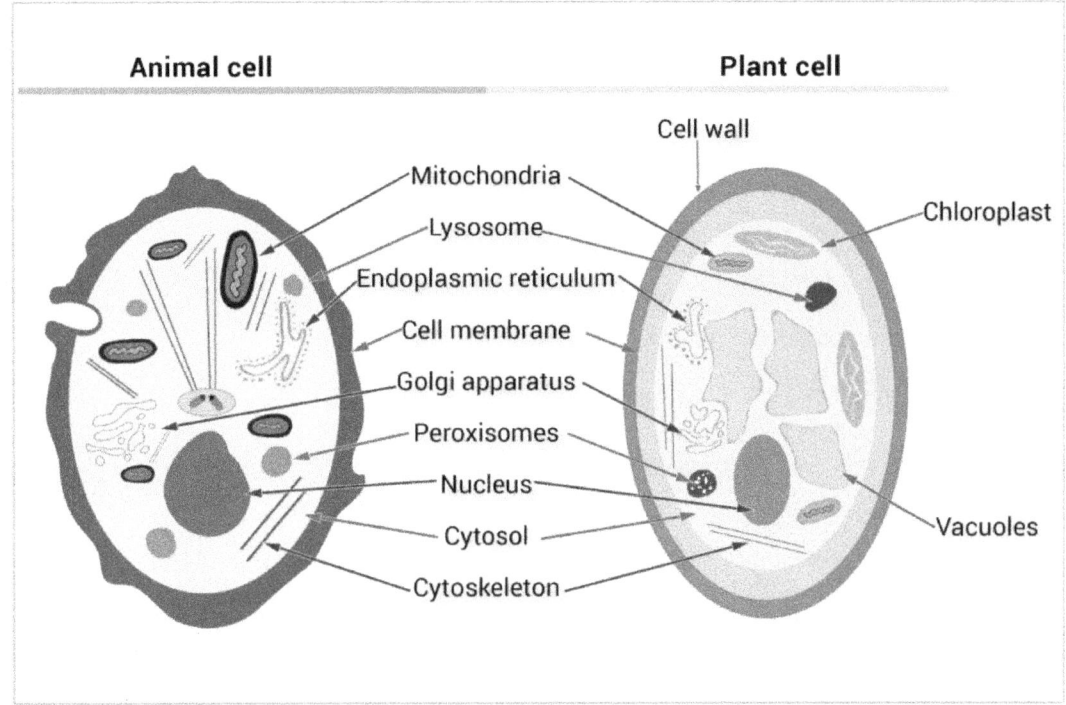

Chloroplast: Chloroplasts are found in protists, such as algae and plant cells. It is responsible for photosynthesis, which is the process of converting sunlight to chemical energy that is stored and used later to drive cellular activities.

Central Vacuole: A central vacuole is found only in plant cells, and is responsible for storage, breakdown of waste products, and hydrolysis of macromolecules.

Plasma Membrane: The plasma membrane is a phospholipid bilayer that encloses the cell. It is also found in prokaryotes.

Cell Wall: Cell walls are present in fungi, plant cells, and some protists. The cell wall is made up of strong fibrous substances, including cellulose (plants), chitin (fungi) and other polysaccharides, and protein. It is a layer outside of the plasma membrane that protects the cell from mechanical damage and helps maintain the cell's shape.

Cellular Respiration

Cellular respiration is a set of metabolic processes that converts energy from nutrients into ATP. Respiration can either occur aerobically, using oxygen, or anaerobically, without oxygen. While prokaryotic cells carry out respiration in the cytosol, most of the respiration in eukaryotic cells occurs in the mitochondria.

Cellular Reproduction

Cellular reproduction is the process that cells use to divide into two new cells. The ability of a multi-cellular organism to generate new cells to replace dying and damaged cells is vital for sustaining its life. There are two processes by which a cell can divide: mitosis and meiosis. In **mitosis,** the daughter cells produced from parental cell division are identical to each other and the parent. **Meiosis** produces genetically unique haploid cells due to two stages of cell division. Meiosis produces **haploid** cells, or **gametes** (sperm and egg cells), which only have one set of chromosomes. Humans are **diploid** because we have two sets of chromosomes – one from each parent. **Somatic** (body) cells are all diploid and are produced via mitosis.

Mitosis

Mitosis is the division of the genetic material in the nucleus of a cell, and is immediately followed by **cytokinesis**, which is the division of the cytoplasm of the cell. The two processes make up the mitotic phase of the cell cycle. Mitosis can be broken down into five stages: prophase, prometaphase, metaphase, anaphase, and telophase. Mitosis is preceded by **interphase**, where the cell spends the majority of its life while growing and replicating its DNA.

Prophase: During this phase, the mitotic spindles begin to form. They are made up of centrosomes and microtubules. As the microtubules lengthen, the centrosomes move farther away from each other. The nucleolus disappears and the chromatin fibers begin to coil up and form chromosomes. Two sister **chromatids**, which are two identical copies of one chromosome, are joined together at the centromere.

Prometaphase: The nuclear envelope begins to break down and the microtubules enter the nuclear area. Each pair of chromatin fibers develops a **kinetochore**, which is a specialized protein structure in the middle of the adjoined fibers. The chromosomes are further condensed.

Metaphase: The microtubules are stretched across the cell and the centrosomes are at opposite ends of the cell. The chromosomes align at the metaphase plate, which is a plane that is exactly between the two centrosomes. The centromere of each chromosome is attached to the kinetochore microtubules that are stretching from each centrosome to the metaphase plate.

Anaphase: The sister chromatids break apart, forming individual chromosomes. The two daughter chromosomes move to opposite ends of the cell. The microtubules shorten toward opposite ends of the cell as well. The cell elongates and, by the end of this phase, there is a complete set of chromosomes at each end of the cell.

Telophase: Two nuclei form at each end of the cell and nuclear envelopes begin to form around each nucleus. The nucleoli reappear and the chromosomes become less condensed. The microtubules are broken down by the cell and mitosis is complete.

Cytokinesis divides the cytoplasm by pinching off the cytoplasm, forming a cleavage furrow, and the two daughter cells then enter interphase, completing the cycle.

Plant cell mitosis is similar except that it lacks centromeres, and instead has a microtubule organizing center. Cytokinesis occurs with the formation of a cell plate.

Meiosis

Meiosis is a type of cell division in which the parent cell has twice as many sets of chromosomes as the daughter cells into which it divides. Although the first stage of meiosis involves the duplication of chromosomes, similar to that of mitosis, the parent cell in meiosis divides into four cells, as opposed to the two produced in mitosis.

Meiosis has the same phases as mitosis, except that they occur twice: once in meiosis I and again in meiosis II. The diploid parent has two sets of homologous chromosomes, one set from each parent. During meiosis I, each chromosome set goes through a process called **crossing over**, which jumbles up the genes on each chromatid. In anaphase one, the separated chromosomes are no longer identical and, once the chromosomes pull apart, each daughter cell is haploid (one set of chromosomes with two non-identical sister chromatids). Next, during meiosis II, the two intermediate daughter cells divide again, separating the chromatids, producing a total of four total haploid cells that each contains one set of chromosomes.

Genetics

Genetics is the study of heredity, which is the transmission of traits from one generation to the next, and hereditary variation. The chromosomes passed from parent to child contain hereditary information in the form of genes. Each gene has specific sequences of DNA that encode proteins, start pathways, and result in inherited traits. In the human life cycle, one haploid sperm cell joins one haploid egg cell to form a diploid cell. The diploid cell is the zygote, the first cell of the new organism, and from then on mitosis takes over and nine months later, there is a fully developed human that has billions of identical cells.

The monk Gregor Mendel is referred to as the father of genetics. In the 1860s, Mendel came up with one of the first models of inheritance, using peapods with different traits in the garden at his abbey to test his theory and develop his model. His model included three laws to determine which traits are inherited; his theories still apply today, after genetics has been studied more in depth.

1. The **Law of Dominance:** Each characteristic has two versions that can be inherited. The gene that encodes for the characteristic has two variations, or alleles, and one is dominant over the other.

2. The **Law of Segregation:** When two parent cells form daughter cells, the alleles segregate and each daughter cell only inherits one of the alleles from each parent.

3. The **Law of Independent Assortment:** Different traits are inherited independent of one another because in metaphase, the set of chromosomes line up in random fashion – mom's set of chromosomes do not line up all on the left or right, there is a random mix.

Dominant and Recessive Traits

Each gene has two **alleles**, one inherited from each parent. **Dominant alleles** are noted in capital letters (A) and **recessive alleles** are noted in lower case letters (a). There are three possible combinations of alleles among dominant and recessive alleles: AA, Aa (known as a heterozygote), and aa. Dominant alleles, when mixed with recessive alleles, will mask the recessive trait. The recessive trait would only appear as the phenotype when the allele combination is aa because a dominant allele is not present to mask it.

Although most genes follow the standard dominant/recessive rules, there are some genes that defy them. Examples include cases of co-dominance, multiple alleles, incomplete dominance, sex-linked traits, and polygenic inheritance.

In cases of **co-dominance**, both alleles are expressed equally. For example, blood type has three alleles: I^A, I^B, and i. I^A and I^B are both dominant to i, but co-dominant with each other. An I^AI^B has AB blood. With incomplete dominance, the allele combination Aa actually makes a third phenotype. An example: certain flowers can be red (AA), white (aa), or pink (Aa).

Punnett Square

For simple genetic combinations, a **Punnett square** can be used to assess the phenotypes of subsequent generations. In a 2 x 2 cell square, one parent's alleles are set up in columns and the other parent's alleles are in rows. The resulting allele combinations are shown in the four internal cells.

Mutations

Genetic **mutations** occur when there is a permanent alteration in the DNA sequence that codes for a specific gene. They can be small, affecting only one base pair, or large, affecting many genes on a chromosome. Mutations are classified as either hereditary, which means they were also present in the parent gene, or acquired, meaning they occurred after the genes were passed down from the parents. Although mutations are not common, they are an important aspect of genetics and variation in the general population.

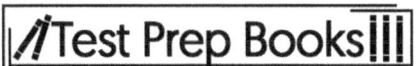

DNA

DNA is made of nucleotide and contains the genetic information of a living organism. It consists of two polynucleotide strands that are twisted and linked together in a double-helix structure. The polynucleotide strands are made up of four nitrogenous bases: adenine (A), thymine (T), guanine (G), and cytosine (C). Adenine and guanine are purines while thymine and cytosine are pyrimidines. These bases have specific pairings of A with T, and G with C. The bases are ordered so that these specific pairings will occur when the two polynucleotide strands coil together to form a DNA molecule. The two strands of DNA are described as antiparallel because one strand runs 5' → 3' while the other strand of the helix runs 3' → 5'.

Before chromosome replication and cell division can occur, DNA replication must happen in interphase. There are specific base pair sequences on DNA, called origins of replication, where DNA replication begins. The proteins that begin the replication process attach to this site and begin separating the two strands and creating a replication bubble. Each end of the bubble has a replication fork, which is a Y-shaped area of the DNA that is being unwound. Several types of proteins are important to the beginning of DNA replication. **Helicases** are enzymes responsible for untwisting the two strands at the replication fork. Single-strand binding proteins bind to the separated strands so that they do not join back together during the replication process. While part of the DNA is unwound, the remainder of the molecule becomes even more twisted in response. Topoisomerase enzymes help relieve this strain by breaking, untwisting, and rejoining the DNA strands.

Once the DNA strand is unwound, an initial primer chain of RNA from the enzyme primase is made to start replication. Replication of DNA can only occur in the 5' → 3' direction. Therefore, during replication, one strand of the DNA template creates the leading strand in the 5' → 3' direction and the other strand creates the lagging strand. While the leading strand is created efficiently and in one piece, the lagging strand is generated in fragments, called **Okazaki fragments**, then are pieced together to form a complete strand by DNA ligase. Following the primer chain of RNA, DNA polymerases are the enzymes responsible for extending the DNA chains by adding on base pairs.

Physical Science

Recognizing Physical Properties

Chemistry is the study of matter, including its properties and behavior. **Matter** is the material that the universe is made of; it is any object that occupies space and has mass. Despite the diversity of items found in the universe, matter is comprised of only about 100 substances, known as elements. Elements cannot be broken down into simpler substances. Hydrogen and oxygen are two examples of elements. When different elements join together, they form compounds. Water is a compound made from hydrogen and oxygen. Atoms and molecules are among the smallest forms of matter.

The physical and chemical properties of matter can help distinguish different substances. Physical properties include color, odor, density, and hardness. These are properties that can be observed without changing the substance's identity or composition. When a substance undergoes a physical change, its physical appearance changes but its composition remains the same. Chemical properties are those that describe the way a substance might change to form another substance. Examples of chemical properties are flammability, toxicity, and ability to oxidize. These properties are observed by changing the environment of the substance and seeing how the substance reacts. A substance's composition is changed when it undergoes a chemical change.

Many properties of matter can be measured quantitatively, meaning the measurement is associated with a number. When a property of matter is represented by a number, it is important to include the unit of measure, otherwise the number is meaningless. For example, saying a pencil measures 10 is meaningless. It could be referring to 10 of something very short or 10 of something very long. The correct measurement notation would be 10 centimeters, because a centimeter has a designated length. Other examples of properties of matter that can be measured quantitatively are mass, time, and temperature, among others.

Physical Properties vs. Chemical Properties
Both physical and chemical properties are used to sort and classify objects:

- Physical properties: refers to the appearance, mass, temperature, state, size, or color of an object or fluid; a physical change indicates a change in the appearance, mass, temperature, state, size or color of an object or fluid.

- Chemical properties: refers to the chemical makeup of an object or fluid; a chemical change refers to an alteration in the makeup of an object or fluid and forms a new solution or compound.

Differences Between Chemical and Physical Changes
A change in the physical form of matter, but not in its chemical identity, is known as a **physical change**. An example of a physical change is tearing a piece of paper in half. This changes the shape of the matter, but it is still paper.

Conversely, a **chemical change** alters the chemical composition or identity of matter. An example of a chemical change is burning a piece of paper. The heat necessary to burn the paper alters the chemical composition of the paper. This chemical change cannot be easily undone, since it has created at least one form of matter different than the original matter.

Reversible Change vs. Non-Reversible Change
Reversible change (physical change) is the changing of the size or shape of an object without altering its chemical makeup. Examples include the heating or cooling of water, change of state (solid, liquid, gas), the freezing of water into ice, or cutting a piece of wood in half.

When two or more materials are combined, it is called a mixture. Generally, a mixture can be separated out into the original components. When one type of matter is dissolved into another type of matter (a solid into a liquid or a liquid into another liquid), and cannot easily be separated back into its original components, it is called a solution.

States of matter refer to the form substances take such as solid, liquid, gas, or plasma. Solid refers to a rigid form of matter with a flexed shape and a fixed volume. Liquid refers to the fluid form of matter with no fixed shape and a fixed volume. Gas refers to an easily compressible fluid form of matter with no fixed shape that expands to fill any space available. Finally, plasma refers to an ionized gas where electrons flow freely from atom to atom.

> Examples: A rock is a solid because it has a fixed shape and volume. Water is considered to be a liquid because it has a set volume, but not a set shape; therefore, you could pour it into different containers of different shapes, as long as they were large enough to contain the existing volume of the water. Oxygen is considered to be a gas. Oxygen does not have a set volume or a set shape; therefore, it could expand or contract to fill a container or even a room. Gases in fluorescent lamps become plasma when electric current is applied to them.

Matter can change from one state to another in many ways, including through heating, cooling, or a change in pressure.

Changes of state are identified as:

- Melting: solid to liquid
- Sublimation: solid to gas
- Evaporation: liquid to gas
- Freezing: liquid to solid

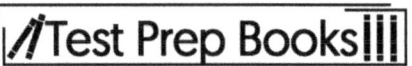

- Condensation: gas to liquid

Non-reversible change (chemical change): When one or more types of matter change and it results in the production of new materials. Examples include burning, rusting, and combining solutions. If a piece of paper is burned it cannot be turned back into its original state. It has forever been altered by a chemical change.

Concepts Relating to the Position and Motion of Objects

The proper use of tools and machinery depends on an understanding of basic physics, which includes the study of motion and the interactions of *mass*, *force*, and *energy*. These terms are used every day, but their exact meanings are difficult to define. In fact, they're usually defined in terms of each other.

The matter in the universe (atoms and molecules) is characterized in terms of its **mass**, which is measured in kilograms in the **International System of Units (SI)**. The amount of mass that occupies a given volume of space is termed **density**.

Mass occupies space, but it's also a component that inversely relates to acceleration when a force is applied to it. This **force** is the application of **energy** to an object with the intent of changing its position (mainly its acceleration).

To understand **acceleration**, it's necessary to relate it to displacement and velocity. The **displacement** of an object is simply the distance it travels. The **velocity** of an object is the distance it travels in a unit of time, such as miles per hour or meters per second:

$$Velocity = \frac{Distance\ Traveled}{Time\ Required}$$

There's often confusion between the words "speed" and "velocity." Velocity includes speed *and* direction. For example, a car traveling east and another traveling west can have the same speed of 30 miles per hour (mph), but their velocities are different. If movement eastward is considered positive, then movement westward is negative. Thus, the eastbound car has a velocity of 30 mph while the westbound car has a velocity of -30 mph.

The fact that velocity has a **magnitude** (speed) and a direction makes it a vector quantity. A **vector** is an arrow pointing in the direction of motion, with its length proportional to its magnitude.

Vectors can be added geometrically as shown below. In this example, a boat is traveling east at 4 *knots* (nautical miles per hour) and there's a current of 3 knots (thus a slow boat and a very fast current). If the boat travels in the same direction as the current, it gets a "lift" from the current and its speed is 7 knots. If the boat heads *into* the current, it has a forward speed of only 1 knot (4 knots − 3 knots = 1 knot) and makes very little headway.

As shown in the figure below, the current is flowing north across the boat's path. Thus, for every 4 miles of progress the boat makes eastward, it drifts 3 miles to the north.

Working with Velocity Vectors

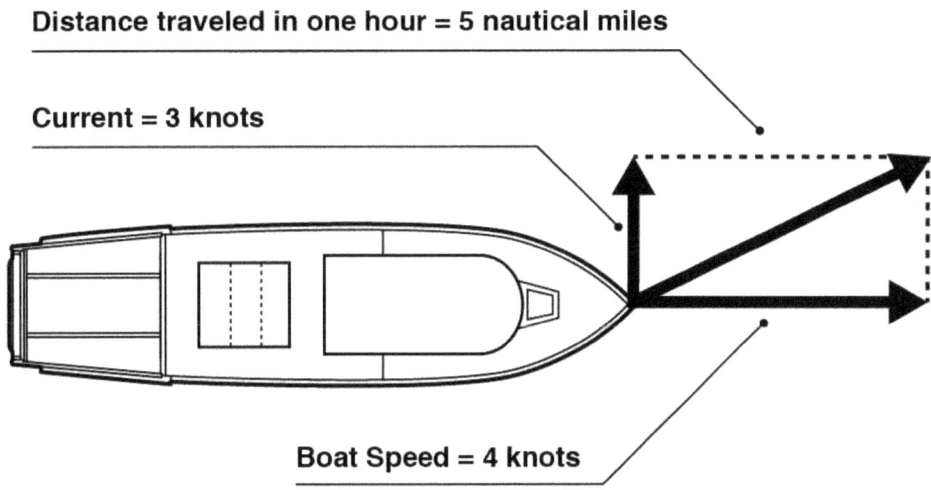

Distance traveled in one hour = 5 nautical miles

Current = 3 knots

Boat Speed = 4 knots

The total distance traveled is calculated using the *Pythagorean Theorem* for a right triangle, which should be memorized as follows:

$$a^2 + b^2 = c^2 \text{ or } c = \sqrt{a^2 + b^2}$$

Of course, the problem above was set up using a Pythagorean triple (3, 4, 5), which made the calculation easy.

Another example where velocity and speed are different is with a car traveling around a bend in the road. The speed is constant along the road, but the direction (and therefore the velocity) changes continuously.

The **acceleration** of an object is the change in its velocity in a given period of time:

$$Acceleration = \frac{Change \: in \: Velocity}{Time \: Required}$$

Newton's Laws

Isaac Newton's three laws of motion describe how the acceleration of an object is related to its mass and the forces acting on it. The three laws are:

- Unless acted on by a force, a body at rest tends to remain at rest; a body in motion tends to remain in motion with a constant velocity and direction.

- A force that acts on a body accelerates it in the direction of the force. The larger the force, the greater the acceleration; the larger the mass, the greater its inertia (resistance to movement and acceleration).

- Every force acting on a body is resisted by an equal and opposite force.

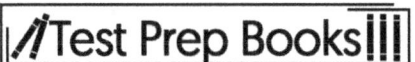

To understand Newton's laws, it's necessary to understand forces. These forces can push or pull on a mass, and they have a magnitude and a direction. Forces are represented by a vector, which is the arrow lined up along the direction of the force with its tip at the point of application. The magnitude of the force is represented by the length of the vector.

The figure below shows a mass acted on or "pushed" by two equal forces (shown here by vectors of the same length). Both vectors "push" along the same line through the center of the mass, but in opposite directions. What happens?

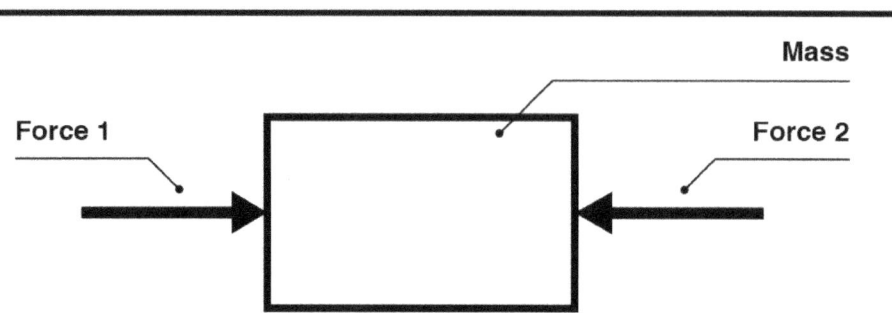

According to Newton's third law, every force on a body is resisted by an equal and opposite force. In the figure above, Force 1 acts on the left side of the mass. The mass pushes back. Force 2 acts on the right side, and the mass pushes back against this force too. The net force on the mass is zero, so according to Newton's first law, there's no change in the **momentum** (the mass times its velocity) of the mass. Therefore, if the mass is at rest before the forces are applied, it remains at rest. If the mass is in motion with a constant velocity, its momentum doesn't change. So, what happens when the net force on the mass isn't zero, as shown in the figure below?

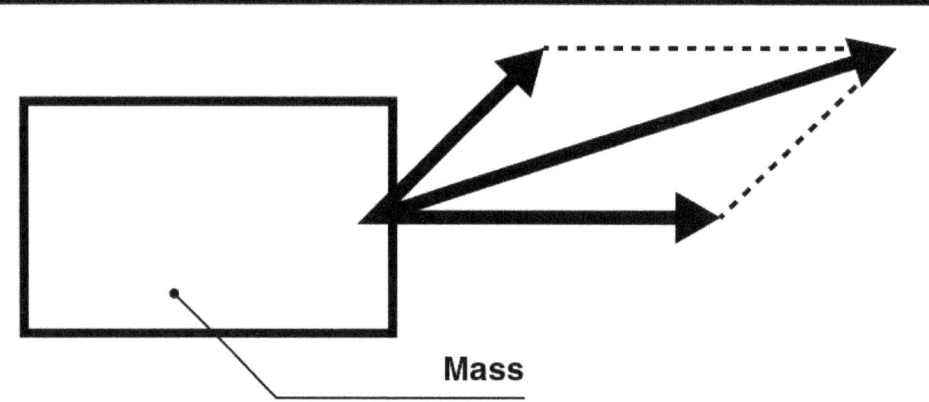

Notice that the forces are vector quantities and are added geometrically the same way that velocity vectors are manipulated.

Here in the figure above, the mass is pulled by two forces acting to the right, so the mass accelerates in the direction of the net force. This is described by Newton's second law:

$$Force = Mass \times Acceleration$$

The force (measured in *newtons*) is equal to the product of the mass (measured in kilograms) and its acceleration (measured in meters per second squared or meters per second, per second). A better way to look at the equation is dividing through by the mass:

$$Acceleration = \frac{Force}{Mass}$$

This form of the equation makes it easier to see that the acceleration of an object varies directly with the net force applied and inversely with the mass. Thus, as the mass increases, the acceleration is reduced for a given force. To better understand, think of how a baseball accelerates when hit by a bat. Now imagine hitting a cannonball with the same bat and the same force. The cannonball is more massive than the baseball, so it won't accelerate very much when hit by the bat.

In addition to forces acting on a body by touching it, gravity acts as a force at a distance and causes all bodies in the universe to attract each other. The *force of gravity (F_g)* is proportional to the masses of the two objects (m and M) and inversely proportional to the square of the distance (r^2) between them (and G is the proportionality constant).

This is shown in the following equation:

$$F_g = G \frac{mM}{r^2}$$

The force of **gravity** is what causes an object to fall to Earth when dropped. Understanding gravity helps explain the difference between mass and weight. Mass is a property of an object that remains the same while it's intact, no matter where it's located. A 10-kilogram cannonball has the same mass on Earth as it does on the moon. On Earth, it weighs 98.1 newtons because of the attractive force of gravity, so it accelerates at 9.81 m/s². However, on the moon, the same cannonball has a weight of only about 16 newtons. This is because the gravitational attraction on the moon is approximately one-sixth that on Earth. Although Earth still attracts the body on the moon, it's so far away that its force is negligible.

For Americans, there's often confusion when talking about mass because the United States still uses "pounds" as a measurement of weight. In the traditional system used in the United States, the unit of mass is called a *slug*. It's derived by dividing the weight in pounds by the acceleration of gravity (32 ft/s²); however, it's rarely used today. To avoid future problems, test takers should continue using SI units and *remember to express mass in kilograms and weight in Newtons*.

Another way to understand Newton's second law is to think of it as an object's change in momentum, which is defined as the product of the object's mass and its velocity:

$$Momentum = Mass \times Velocity$$

Which of the following has the greater momentum: a pitched baseball, a softball, or a bullet fired from a rifle?

A bullet with a mass of 5 grams (0.005 kilograms) is fired from a rifle with a muzzle velocity of 2,200 mph. Its momentum is calculated as:

$$\frac{2,200 \text{ miles}}{1 \text{ hour}} \times \frac{5,280 \text{ feet}}{1 \text{ mile}} \times \frac{1 \text{ m}}{3.28 \text{ feet}} \times \frac{1 \text{ hour}}{3,600 \text{ seconds}} \times 0.005 \text{kg} = 4.92 \text{ kg. m/seconds}$$

A softball has a mass between 177 grams and 198 grams and is thrown by a college pitcher at 50 miles per hour. Taking an average mass of 188 grams (0.188 kilograms), a softball's momentum is calculated as:

$$\frac{50 \text{ miles}}{1 \text{ hour}} \times \frac{5{,}280 \text{ feet}}{1 \text{ mile}} \times \frac{1 \text{ m}}{3.28 \text{ ft}} \times \frac{1 \text{ hour}}{3{,}600 \text{ seconds}} \times 0.188 \text{ kg} = 4.19 \text{ kg.m/seconds}$$

That's only slightly less than the momentum of the bullet. Although the speed of the softball is considerably less, its mass is much greater than the bullet's.

A professional baseball pitcher can throw a 145-gram baseball at 100 miles per hour. A similar calculation (try doing it!) shows that the pitched hardball has a momentum of about 6.48 kg.m/seconds. That's more momentum than a speeding bullet!

So why is the bullet more harmful than the hard ball? It's because the force that it applies acts on a much smaller area.

Instead of using acceleration, Newton's second law is expressed here as the change in momentum (with the delta symbol "Δ" meaning "change"):

$$Force = \frac{\Delta\, Momentum}{\Delta\, Time} = \frac{\Delta\, (Mass \times Velocity)}{\Delta\, Time} = Mass \times \frac{\Delta\, Velocity}{\Delta\, Time}$$

The rapid application of force is called *impulse*. Another way of stating Newton's second law is in terms of the impulse, which is the force multiplied by its time of application:

$$Impulse = Force \times \Delta\, Time = Mass \times \Delta\, Velocity$$

In the case of the rifle, the force created by the pressure of the charge's explosion in its shell pushes the bullet, accelerating it until it leaves the barrel of the gun with its *muzzle velocity* (the speed the bullet has when it leaves the muzzle). After leaving the gun, the bullet doesn't accelerate because the gas pressure is exhausted. The bullet travels with a constant velocity in the direction it's fired (ignoring the force exerted against the bullet by friction and drag).

Similarly, the pitcher applies a force to the ball by using their muscles when throwing. Once the ball leaves the pitcher's fingers, it doesn't accelerate and the ball travels toward the batter at a constant speed (again ignoring friction and drag). The speed is constant, but the velocity can change if the ball travels along a curve.

Projectile Motion

According to Newton's first law, if no additional forces act on the bullet or ball, it travels in a straight line. This is also true if the bullet is fired in outer space. However, here on Earth, the force of gravity continues to act so the motion of the bullet or ball is affected.

What happens when a bullet is fired from the top of a hill using a rifle held perfectly horizontal? Ignoring air resistance, its horizontal velocity remains constant at its muzzle velocity. Its vertical velocity (which is zero when it leaves the gun barrel) increases because of gravity's acceleration. Each passing second, the bullet traces out the same distance horizontally while increasing distance vertically (shown in the figure below). In the end, the projectile traces out a **parabolic curve**.

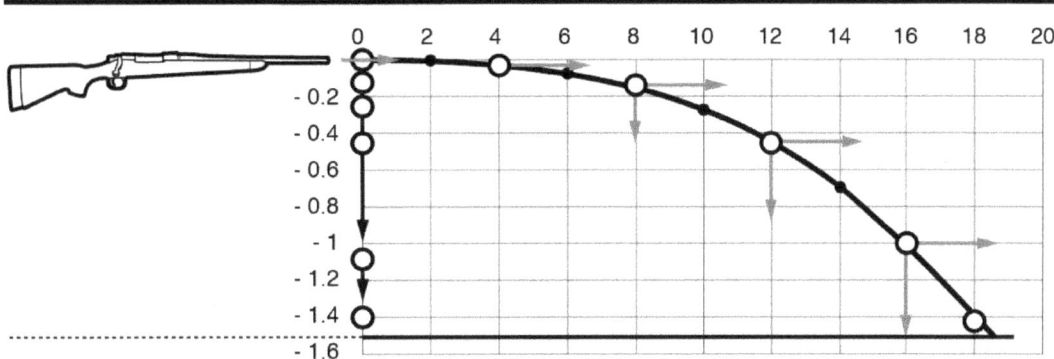

This vertical, downward acceleration is why a pitcher must put an arc on the ball when throwing across home plate. Otherwise, the ball will fall at the batter's feet.

It's also interesting to note that if an artillery crew simultaneously drops one cannonball and fires another one horizontally, the two cannonballs will hit the ground at the same time since both balls are accelerating at the same rate and experience the same changes in vertical velocity.

What if air resistance is taken into account? This is best answered by looking at the horizontal and vertical motions separately.

The horizontal velocity is no longer constant because the initial velocity of the projectile is continually reduced by the resistance of the air. This is a complex problem in fluid mechanics, but it's sufficient to note that that the projectile doesn't fly as far before landing as predicted from the simple theory.

The vertical velocity is also reduced by air resistance. However, unlike the horizontal motion where the propelling force is zero after the cannonball is fired, the downward force of gravity acts continuously. The downward velocity increases every second due to the acceleration of gravity. As the velocity increases, the resisting force (called **drag**) increases with the square of the velocity. If the projectile is fired or dropped from a sufficient height, it reaches a terminal velocity such that the upward drag force equals the downward force of gravity. When that occurs, the projectile falls at a constant rate.

This is the same principle that's used for a parachute. Its drag (caused by its shape that scoops up air) is sufficient enough to slow down the fall of the parachutist to a safe velocity, thus avoiding a fatal crash on the ground.

So, what's the bottom line? If the vertical height isn't too great, a real projectile will fall short of the theoretical point of impact. However, if the height of the fall is significant and the drag of the object results in a small terminal fall velocity, then the projectile can go further than the theoretical point of impact.

What if the projectile is launched from a moving platform? In this case, the platform's velocity is added to the projectile's velocity. That's why an object dropped from the mast of a moving ship lands at the base of the mast rather than behind it. However, to an observer on the shore, the object traces out a parabolic arc.

Angular Momentum

In the previous examples, all forces acted through the center of the mass, but what happens if the forces aren't applied through the same line of action, like in the figure below?

A Mass Acted on by Forces Out of Line with Each Other

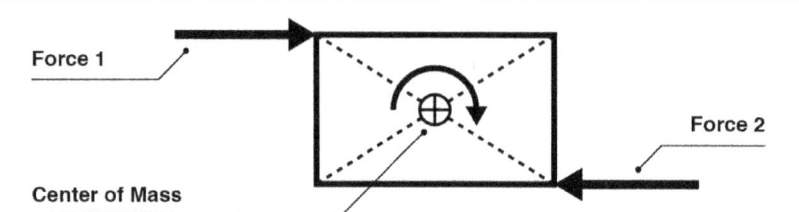

When this happens, the two forces create **torque** and the mass rotates around its center of gravity. In the figure above, the center of gravity is the center of the rectangle ("Center of Mass"), which is determined by the two, intersecting main diagonals. The center of an irregularly shaped object is found by hanging it from two different edges, and the center of gravity is at the intersection of the two "plumb lines."

Newton's second law still applies when the forces form a moment pair, but it must be expressed in terms of angular acceleration and the moment of inertia. The **moment of inertia** is a measure of the body's resistance to rotation, similar to the mass's resistance to linear acceleration. The more compact the body, the less the moment of inertia and the faster it rotates, much like how an ice skater spinning with outstretched arms will speed up as the arms are brought in close to the body.

The concept of torque is important in understanding the use of wrenches and is likely to be on the test. The concept of torque and moment/lever arm will be taken up again below, when the physics of simple machines is presented.

Conservation of Angular Momentum

An object moving in a circular motion also has momentum; for circular motion, it is called **angular momentum**. This is determined by rotational inertia and rotational velocity and the distance of the mass from the axis of rotation or center of rotation. When objects are exhibiting circular motion, they also demonstrate the conservation of angular momentum, meaning that the angular momentum of a system is always constant, regardless of the placement of the mass. Rotational inertia can be affected by how far the mass of the object is placed with respect to the center of rotation (axis of rotation). The larger the distance between the mass and the center of rotation, the slower the rotational velocity. Conversely, if the mass is closer to the center of rotation, the rotational velocity increases. A change in one affects the other, thus conserving the angular momentum. This holds true as long as no external forces act upon the system.

For example, an ice skater spinning on one ice skate extends their arms out for a slower rotational velocity. When the skater brings their arms in close to their body (or lessens the distance between the mass and the center of rotation), their rotational velocity increases, and they spin much faster. Some skaters extend their arms straight up above their head, which causes an extension of the axis of rotation, thus removing any distance between the mass and the center of rotation and maximizing their rotational velocity.

Another example is when a person selects a horse on a merry-go-round: the placement of their horse can affect their ride experience. All of the horses are traveling with the same rotational speed, but in order to travel along the same plane as the merry-go-round turns, a horse on the outside will have a greater linear speed, due to it being farther away from the axis of rotation. Another way to think of it is that an outside horse has to cover a lot more ground than a horse on the inside, in order to keep up with the rotational speed of the merry-go-round platform. Thrill seekers should always select an outer horse.

Science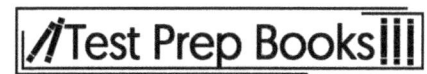

Principles of Light, Heat, Electricity, and Magnetism

The term **energy** typically refers to an object's ability to perform work. This can include a transfer of heat from one object to another, or from an object to its surroundings. Energy is usually measured in **Joules**. There are two main categories of energy: renewable and non-renewable.

- **Renewable**: energy produced from the exhaustion of a resource that can be replenished. Burning wood to produce heat, then replanting trees to replenish the resource is an example of using renewable energy.

- **Non-renewable**: energy produced from the exhaustion of a resource that cannot be replenished. Burning coal to produce heat would be an example of a non-renewable energy. Although coal is a natural resource that is mined or harvested from the earth, it cannot be regrown or replenished. Other examples include oil and natural gas (fossil fuels).

Temperature is measured in degrees Celsius (°C) or Kelvin (K). Temperature should not be confused with heat. **Heat** is a form of energy: a change in temperature or a transfer of heat can also be a measure of energy. The amount of energy measured by the change in temperature (or a transfer) is the measure of heat.

Heat energy (thermal energy) can be transferred through the following ways:

Conduction
Conduction is the heating of one object by another through the actual touching of molecules, in order to transfer heat across the objects involved. A spiral burner on an electric stovetop heats from one molecule touching another to transfer the heat via conduction.

Convection
Heat transfer due to the movement/flow of molecules from areas of high concentration to ones of low concentration. Warmer molecules tend to rise, while colder molecules tend to sink. The heat in a house will rise from the vents in the floor to the upper levels of the structure and circulate in that manner, rising and falling with the movement of the molecules. This molecular movement helps to heat or cool a house and is often called **convection current**.

Radiation
The sun warms the earth through **radiation** or radiant energy. Radiation does not need any medium for the heat to travel; therefore, the heat from the sun can radiate to the earth across space.

Greenhouse Effect
The sun transfers heat into the earth's atmosphere through radiation traveling in waves. The atmosphere helps protect the earth from extreme exposure to the sun, while reflecting some of the waves continuously within the atmosphere, creating habitable temperatures. The rest of the waves are meant to dissipate out through the atmosphere and back into space. However, humans have created pollutants and released an overabundance of certain gasses into the earth's atmosphere, causing a layer of blockage. So, the waves that should be leaving the atmosphere continue to bounce back upon the earth repeatedly, thus contributing to global warming. This is a negative effect from the extra re-radiation of the sun's energy and causes planetary overheating.

This additional warming is not something easily or quickly reversed. Because the rate of reflection within the atmosphere only multiplies the more a light wave is bounced around, it will take a concerted effort to undue past reflectance and stop future reflectance of the light waves in the earth's atmosphere. Once the re-reflectance occurs, it duplicates exponentially, along with the additional compounding of more waves. Each degree the atmospheric temperature increases has a profound effect on the delicate balance of our planet, including the melting of polar ice caps, the rise of tidal currents—which cause strong weather systems—and the depletion of specific ecosystems necessary to sustain certain species of animals or insects, to name a few.

Electrostatics

Electrostatics is the study of electric charges at rest. A charge comes from an atom having more or fewer electrons than protons. If an atom has more electrons than protons, it has a negative charge. If an atom has fewer electrons than protons, it has a positive charge. It is important to remember that opposite charges attract each other, while like charges repel each other. So, a negative attracts a positive, a negative repels a negative, and similarly, a positive repels a positive. Just as energy cannot be created or destroyed, neither can charge; charge is transferred. This transfer can be done through touch.

If a person wears socks and scuffs their feet across carpeting, they are transferring electrons to the carpeting through friction. If that person then goes to touch a light switch, they will receive a small shock, which is the electrons transferring from the switch to their hand. The person lost electrons to the carpet, which left them with a positive charge; therefore, the electrons from the switch attract to the person for the transfer. The shock is the electrons jumping from the switch to the person's finger.

Another method of charging an object is through induction. **Induction** is when a charged object is brought near, but not touched to, a neutral conducting object. The charged object will cause the electrons within the conductor to move. If the charged object is negative, the electrons will be induced away from the charged object and vice versa.

Yet another way to charge an object is through polarization. **Polarization** can be achieved by simply reconfiguring the electrons on an object. If a person were to rub a balloon on their hair, the balloon would then stick to a wall. This is because rubbing the balloon causes it to become negatively charged and when the balloon is held against a neutral wall, the negatively charged balloon repels all of the wall's electrons, causing a positively charged surface on the wall. This type of charge would be temporary, due to the massive size of the wall, and the charges would quickly redistribute.

Electric Current

Electrical current is the process by which electrons carry charge. In order to make the electrons move so that they can carry a charge, a change in voltage must be present. On a small scale, this is demonstrated through the electrons travelling from the light switch to a person's finger in the example where the person scuffed their socks on a carpet. The difference between the switch and the finger caused the electrons to move. On a larger and more sustained scale, this movement would need to be more controlled. This can be achieved through batteries/cells and generators. Batteries or cells have a chemical reaction that takes place inside, causing energy to be released and a charge to be able to move freely. Generators convert mechanical energy into electric energy.

If a wire is run from touching the end of a battery to the end of a light bulb, and then another is run from touching the base of the light bulb to the opposite end of the original battery, the light bulb will light up. This is due to a complete circuit being formed with the battery and the electrons being carried across the voltage drop (the two ends of the battery). The appearance of the light from the bulb is the visible heat caused by the friction of the electrons moving through the filament.

Electric Energy

Electric energy can be derived from a number of sources including coal, wind, sun, and nuclear reactions. Electricity has numerous applications, including being able to transfer into light, sound, heat, or magnetic forces.

Magnetic Forces

Magnetic forces can occur naturally in certain types of materials. If two straight rods are made from iron, they will naturally have a negative end (pole) and a positive end (pole). These charged poles react just like any charged item:

opposite charges attract and like charges repel. They will attract each other when set up positive to negative, but if one rod is turned around, the two rods will repel each other due to the alignment of negative to negative and positive to positive.

These types of forces can also be created and amplified by using an electric current.

The relationship between magnetic forces and electrical forces can be explored by sending an electric current through a stretch of wire, which creates an electromagnetic force around the wire from the charge of the current, as long as the flow of electricity is sustained. This magnetic force can also attract and repel other items with magnetic properties. Depending upon the strength of the current in the wire, a smaller or larger magnetic force can be generated around this wire. As soon as the current is cut off, the magnetic force also stops.

Magnetic Energy
Magnetic energy can be harnessed, or controlled, from natural sources or from a generated source (a wire carrying electric current). Magnetic forces are used in many modern applications, including the creation of super-speed transportation. Super-magnets are used in rail systems and supply a cleaner form of energy than coal or gasoline.

Sound/Acoustic Energy
Just like light, sound travels in waves and both are forms of energy. The transmittance of a sound wave produced when plucking a guitar string sends vibrations at a specific frequency through the air, resulting in one's ear hearing a specific note or sets of notes that form a chord. If the same guitar is plugged into an electric amplifier, the strength of the wave is increased, producing what is perceived as a "louder" note. If a glass of water is set on the amplifier, the production of the sound wave can also be visually observed in the vibrations in the water. If the guitar were being plucked loudly enough and in great succession, the force created by the vibrations of the sound waves could even knock the glass off of the amplifier.

Waves can travel through different mediums. When they reach a different material (i.e., light traveling from air to water), they can bend around and through the new material. This is called **refraction**.

If one observes a straw in half a glass of water from above, the straw appears to be bent at the height of the water. The straw is still straight, but the observation of light passing from air to water (different materials) makes the straw seem as though it bends at the water line. This illusion occurs because the human eye can perceive the light travels differently through the two materials. The light might slow down in one material, or refract or reflect off of the material, causing differences in an object's appearance.

In another example, imagine a car driving straight along a paved road. If one or two of the tires hit the gravel along the side of the road, the entire car will pull in that direction, due to the tires in the gravel now traveling slower than the tires on the paved road. This is what happens when light travels from one medium to another: its path becomes warped, like the path of the car, rather than traveling in a straight line. This is why a straw appears to be bent when the light travels from water to air; the path is warped.

When waves encounter a barrier, like a closed door, parts of the wave may travel through tiny openings. Once a wave has moved through a narrow opening, the wave begins to spread out and may cause interference. This process is called diffraction.

Principles of Matter and Atomic Structure

Elements, Compounds, and Mixtures
Everything that takes up space and has mass is composed of **matter**. Understanding the basic characteristics and properties of matter helps with classification and identification.

An **element** is a substance that cannot be chemically decomposed to a simpler substance, while still retaining the properties of the element.

Compounds are composed of two or more elements that are chemically combined. The constituent elements in the compound are in constant proportions by mass.

When a material can be separated by physicals means (such as sifting it through a colander), it is called a **mixture**. Mixtures are categorized into two types: **heterogeneous** and **homogeneous**. Heterogeneous mixtures have physically distinct parts, which retain their different properties. A mix of salt and sugar is an example of a heterogeneous mixture. With heterogenous mixtures, it is possible that different samples from the same parent mixture may have different proportions of each component in the mixture. For example, in the sugar and salt mixture, there may be uneven mixing of the two, causing one random tablespoon sample to be mostly salt, while a different tablespoon sample may be mostly sugar.

A homogeneous mixture, also called a **solution,** has uniform properties throughout a given sample. An example of a homogeneous solution is salt fully dissolved in warm water. In this case, any number of samples taken from the parent solution would be identical.

Atoms, Molecules, and Ions

The basic building blocks of matter are **atoms,** which are extremely small particles that retain their identity during chemical reactions. Atoms can be singular or grouped to form elements. Elements are composed of one type of atom with the same properties.

Molecules are a group of atoms—either the same or different types—that are chemically bonded together by attractive forces. For example, hydrogen and oxygen are both atoms but, when bonded together, form water.

Ions are electrically-charged particles that are formed from an atom or a group of atoms via the loss or gain of electrons.

Basic Properties of Solids, Liquids, and Gases

Matter exists in certain **states**, or physical forms, under different conditions. These states are called **solid**, **liquid**, or **gas**.

A solid has a rigid, or set, form and occupies a fixed shape and volume. Solids generally maintain their shape when exposed to outside forces.

Liquids and gases are considered fluids, which have no set shape. Liquids are fluid, yet are distinguished from gases by their incompressibility (incapable of being compressed) and set volume. Liquids can be transferred from one container to another, but cannot be forced to fill containers of different volumes via compression without causing damage to the container. For example, if one attempts to force a given volume or number of particles of a liquid, such as water, into a fixed container, such as a small water bottle, the container would likely explode from the extra water.

A gas can easily be compressed into a confined space, such as a tire or an air mattress. Gases have no fixed shape or volume. They can also be subjected to outside forces, and the number of gas molecules that can fill a certain volume vary with changes in temperature and pressure.

Atomic Models

Theories of the atomic model have developed over the centuries. The most commonly referenced model of an atom was proposed by Niels Bohr. Bohr studied the models of J.J. Thomson and Ernest Rutherford and adapted his own theories from these existing models. Bohr compared the structure of the atom to that of the Solar System, where there is a center, or nucleus, with various sized orbitals circulating around this nucleus. This is a simplified version of what scientists have discovered about atoms, including the structures and placements of any orbitals. Modern science has made further adaptations to the model, including the fact that orbitals are actually made of electron "clouds."

Atomic Structure: Nucleus, Electrons, Protons, and Neutrons

Following the Bohr model of the atom, the nucleus, or core, is made up of positively charged **protons** and neutrally charged **neutrons**. The neutrons are theorized to be in the nucleus with the protons to provide greater "balance" at the center of the atom. The nucleus of the atom makes up the majority (more than 99%) of the mass of an atom, while the orbitals surrounding the nucleus contain negatively charged **electrons**. The entire structure of an atom is incredibly small.

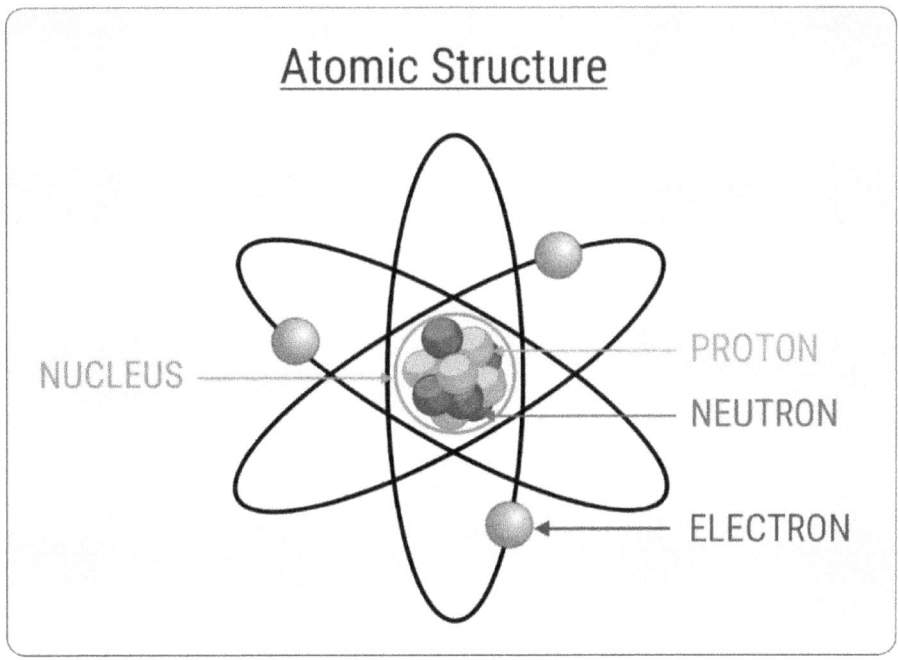

Atomic Number, Atomic Mass, and Isotopes

The **atomic number** of an atom is determined by the number of protons within the nucleus. When a substance is composed of atoms that all have the same atomic number, it is called an **element**. Elements are arranged by atomic number and grouped by properties in the **periodic table**.

An atom's **mass number** is determined by the sum of the total number of protons and neutrons in the atom. Most nuclei have a net neutral charge, and all atoms of one type have the same atomic number. However, there are some atoms of the same type that have a different mass number, due to an imbalance of neutrons. These are called **isotopes**. In isotopes, the atomic number, which is determined by the number of protons, is the same, but the mass number, which is determined by adding the protons and neutrons, is different due to the irregular number of neutrons.

Electron Arrangements

Electrons are most easily organized into distributions of subshells called **electron configurations**. Subshells fill from the inside (closest to the nucleus) to the outside. Therefore, once a subshell is filled, the next shell farther from the nucleus begins to fill, and so on. Atoms with electrons on the outside of a noble gas core (an atom with an electron inner shell that corresponds to the configuration of one of the noble gases, such as Neon) and pseudo-noble gas core (an atom with an electron inner shell that is similar to that of a noble gas core along with (n -1) d^{10} electrons),

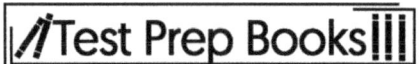

are called **valence electrons**. Valence electrons are primarily the electrons involved in chemical reactions. The similarities in their configurations account for similarities in properties of groups of elements. Essentially, the groups (vertical columns) on the periodic table all have similar characteristics, such as solubility and reactivity, due to their similar electron configurations.

Chemical Reactions

Types of Chemical Reactions

Chemical reactions are characterized by a chemical change in which the starting substances, or reactants, differ from the substances formed, or products. Chemical reactions may involve a change in color, the production of gas, the formation of a precipitate, or changes in heat content.

The following are the basic types of chemical reactions:

Reaction Type	Definition	Example
Decomposition	A compound is broken down into two or more smaller elements or compounds.	$2H_2O \rightarrow 2H_2 + O_2$
Synthesis	Two or more elements or compounds are joined together.	$2H_2 + O_2 \rightarrow 2H_2O$
Single Displacement	A single element or ion takes the place of another in a compound. Also known as a substitution reaction.	$Zn + 2HCl \rightarrow ZnCl_2 + H_2$
Double Displacement	Two elements or ions exchange a single atom each to form two different compounds, resulting in different combinations of cations and anions in the final compounds. Also known as a metathesis reaction.	$H_2SO_4 + 2NaOH \rightarrow Na_2SO_4 + 2H_2O$
Oxidation-Reduction	Elements undergo a change in oxidation number. Also known as a redox reaction.	$2S_2O_3^{2-}(aq) + I_2(aq) \rightarrow S_4O_6^{2-}(aq) + 2I^-(aq)$
Acid-Base	Involves a reaction between an acid and a base, which usually produces a salt and water	$HBr + NaOH \rightarrow NaBr + H_2O$
Combustion	A hydrocarbon (a compound composed of only hydrogen and carbon) reacts with oxygen to form carbon dioxide and water.	$CH_4 + 2O_2 \rightarrow CO_2 + 2H_2O$

Balancing Chemical Reactions

Chemical reactions are expressed using chemical equations. Chemical equations must be balanced with equivalent numbers of atoms for each type of element on each side of the equation. **Antoine Lavoisier**, a French chemist, was the first to propose the Law of Conservation of Mass for the purpose of balancing a chemical equation. The law states, "Matter is neither created nor destroyed during a chemical reaction."

The reactants are located on the left side of the arrow, while the products are located on the right side of the arrow. Coefficients are the numbers in front of the chemical formulas. Subscripts are the numbers to the lower right of chemical symbols in a formula. To tally atoms, one should multiply the formula's coefficient by the subscript of each chemical symbol. For example, the chemical equation $2H_2 + O_2 \rightarrow 2H_2O$ is balanced. For H, the coefficient of 2 multiplied by the subscript 2 = 4 hydrogen atoms. For O, the coefficient of 1 multiplied by the subscript 2 = 2 oxygen atoms. Coefficients and subscripts of 1 are understood and never written. When known, the form of the substance is noted with (g)=gas, (s)=solid, (l)=liquid, or (aq)=aqueous.

Catalysts

Catalysts are substances that accelerate the speed of a chemical reaction. A catalyst remains unchanged throughout the course of a chemical reaction. In most cases, only small amounts of a catalyst are needed. Catalysts increase the rate of a chemical reaction by providing an alternate path requiring less activation energy. **Activation energy** refers to the amount of energy required for the initiation of a chemical reaction.

Catalysts can be homogeneous or heterogeneous. Catalysts in the same phase of matter as its reactants are **homogeneous**, while catalysts in a different phase than reactants are **heterogeneous**. It is important to remember catalysts are selective. They don't accelerate the speed of all chemical reactions, but catalysts do accelerate specific chemical reactions.

Enzymes

Enzymes are a class of catalysts instrumental in biochemical reactions, and in most, if not all, examples are proteins. Like all catalysts, enzymes increase the rate of a chemical reaction by providing an alternate path requiring less activation energy. Enzymes catalyze thousands of chemical reactions in the human body. Enzymes are proteins and possess an active site, which is the part of the molecule that binds the reacting molecule, or substrate. The "lock and key" analogy is used to describe the substrate key fitting precisely into the active site of the enzyme lock to form an enzyme-substrate complex.

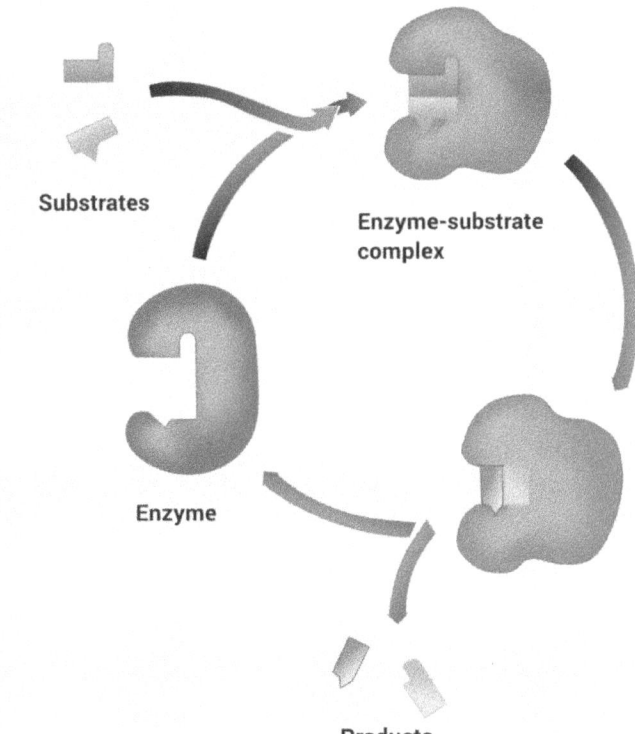

Many enzymes work in tandem with cofactors or coenzymes to catalyze chemical reactions. **Cofactors** can be either inorganic (not containing carbon) or organic (containing carbon). **Organic cofactors** can be either coenzymes or prosthetic groups tightly bound to an enzyme. **Coenzymes** transport chemical groups from one enzyme to another. Within a cell, coenzymes are continuously regenerating and their concentrations are held at a steady state.

Several factors including temperature, pH, and concentrations of the enzyme and substrate can affect the catalytic activity of an enzyme. For humans, the optimal temperature for peak enzyme activity is approximately body temperature at 98.6 °F, while the optimal pH for peak enzyme activity is approximately 7 to 8. Increasing the concentrations of either the enzyme or substrate will also increase the rate of reaction, up to a certain point.

The activity of enzymes can be regulated. A common form of metabolic control is **feedback inhibition**, where the pathway is controlled by inhibitory binding of the product to an enzyme earlier in the pathway.

pH, Acids, and Bases

pH refers to the power or potential of hydrogen atoms and is used as a scale for a substance's acidity. In chemistry, pH represents the hydrogen ion concentration (written as $[H^+]$) in an aqueous, or watery, solution. The hydrogen ion concentration, $[H^+]$, is measured in moles of H^+ per liter of solution.

The **pH scale** is a logarithmic scale used to quantify how acidic or basic a substance is. pH is the negative logarithm of the hydrogen ion concentration: $pH = -\log[H^+]$. A one-unit change in pH correlates with a ten-fold change in hydrogen ion concentration. The pH scale typically ranges from zero to 14, although it is possible to have pHs outside of this range. Pure water has a pH of 7, which is considered neutral. pH values less than 7 are considered acidic, while pH values greater than 7 are considered basic, or alkaline.

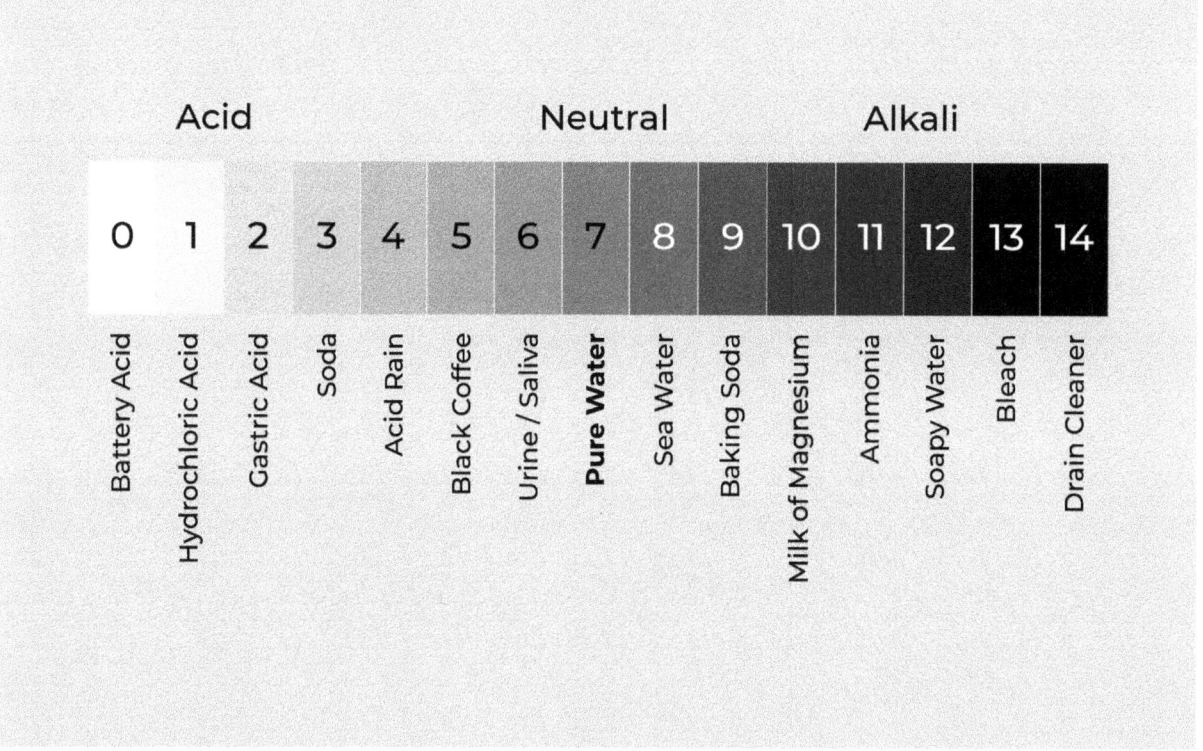

Generally speaking, an acid is a substance capable of donating hydrogen ions, while a base is a substance capable of accepting hydrogen ions. A **buffer** is a molecule that can act as either a hydrogen ion donor or acceptor. Buffers are crucial in the blood and body fluids, and prevent the body's pH from fluctuating into dangerous territory. pH can be measured using a pH meter, test paper, or indicator sticks.

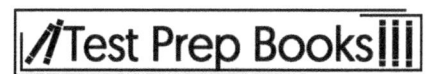

Earth Science

Properties of Earth Materials

Geology is the study of the nature and composition of the rocks and materials that make up the Earth, how they were formed, and the physical and chemical processes that have changed Earth over time.

Earth can be imagined as a giant construction of billions of Lego blocks, and that these blocks represent different minerals. A **mineral** is a naturally occurring inorganic solid composed of certain chemical elements (or atoms) in a defined crystalline structure. When minerals are aggregated together with other minerals, organic compounds (carbon-containing remains of decomposed plant or animal matter), and/or mineraloids (minerals that lack a defined crystalline structure), rocks are formed. Rock types are classified based on their mechanism of formation and the materials of their compositions.

The three fundamental classifications of rocks include:

- Sedimentary
- Igneous
- Metamorphic

Sedimentary rocks form at the Earth's surface (on land and in bodies of water) through deposition and cementation of fragments of other rocks, organic matter, and minerals. These materials, called **sediment**, are deposited and accumulate in layers called **strata**, which get pressed into a solid over time when more sediment settles on top. Sedimentary rocks are further classified as either clastic/detrital, biochemical, chemical, or other. **Clastic** or **detrital rocks** are composed of other inorganic rocks or organic particles, respectively. **Biochemical rocks** have an organic component (like coal, which is composed of decayed plant matter). **Chemical rocks** form from a solution containing dissolved materials that became supersaturated, and minerals precipitate out of solution. Halite, or rock salt, is an example of a chemical sedimentary rock. Sedimentary rocks that do not fit into these types are categorized as "other." These rocks are formed from fragments formed by asteroid or comet impacts or from fragments of volcanic lava.

Igneous rocks are composed of molten material beneath the Earth's surface called **magma** and are classified based on where the magma cooled and solidified; they can be intrusive/plutonic, extrusive/volcanic, or hypabyssal. **Intrusive** or **plutonic rocks**, such as granite, form when magma cools slowly within or beneath the Earth's surface. Because they solidify slowly, these rocks tend to have a coarse grain, larger crystalline structure of their mineral constituents, and rough appearance. By contrast, *unbold the word "or"* form from rapid cooling as magma escapes the Earth's surface as lava and have a smooth or fine-grained appearance, with tiny crystals or ones that are too small to see. A common example of an extrusive igneous rock is glassy obsidian. **Hypabyssal rocks** are formed at levels between intrusive and extrusive (just below the surface); they aren't nearly as common.

Metamorphic rocks form from the transformation of other rocks via a process called **metamorphism**. This transformation happens when existing rocks—sedimentary, igneous, or other metamorphic rocks—are subjected to significant heat and pressure, which causes physical and/or chemical changes. Based on their appearance, metamorphic rocks are classified as either foliated or non-foliated. **Foliated rocks** are layered or folded, which means they form from compression in one direction and result in visible layers or banding within the rock. Examples include gneiss or slate. **Non-foliated rocks**, such as marble, receive equal pressure from all directions and thus have a homogenous appearance.

It should be noted that classification is not always completely clear and some rocks don't quite fit the criteria for one of these three categories, so they are sometimes lumped together in a category called "**other rocks**." A classic example is a fossil. A **fossil** is a rock formed from the remains or impression of dead plants or animals, but it doesn't fit into any biochemical class of rocks because fossils themselves are wholly composed of organic material and only formed under strict conditions, although they are commonly found within sedimentary rock.

Earth's Systems, Processes, Geologic Structures, and Time

Earth's Layers

Earth has three major layers: a thin solid outer surface or **crust**, a dense **core**, and a **mantle** between them that contains most of the Earth's matter. This layout resembles an egg, where the eggshell is the crust, the mantle is the egg white, and the core is the yolk. The outer crust of the Earth consists of igneous or sedimentary rocks over metamorphic rocks. Together with the upper portion of the mantle, it forms the **lithosphere**, which is broken into tectonic plates.

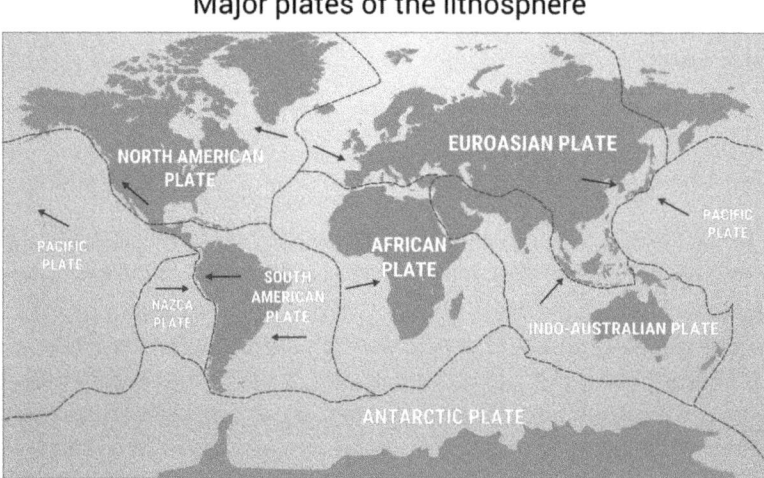

The mantle can be divided into three zones. The **upper mantle** is adjacent to the crust and composed of solid rock. Below the upper mantle is the **transition zone**. The **lower mantle** below the transition zone is a layer of completely solid rock. Underneath the mantle is the molten **outer core** followed by the compact, solid **inner core**. The inner and outer cores contain the densest elements, consisting of mostly iron and nickel.

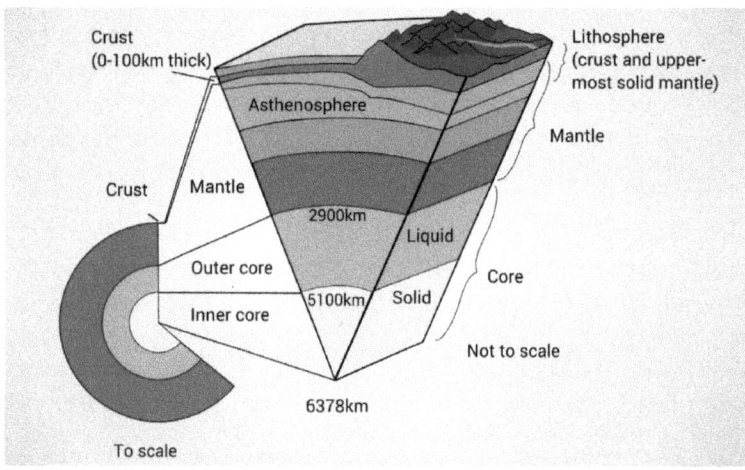

Science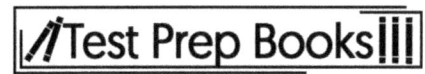

Shape and Size of the Earth

The Earth isn't a perfect sphere; it's slightly elliptical. From center to surface, its radius is almost 4,000 miles, and its circumference around the equator is about 24,902 miles. In comparison, the Sun's radius is 432,288 miles—over 1,000 times larger than the Earth's—and the Moon's radius is about 1,000 miles.

Geographical Features

The Earth's surface is dynamic and consists of various landforms. As tectonic plates are pushed together, **mountains** are formed. **Canyons** are deep trenches that are usually created by plates moving apart but can also be created by constant weathering and erosion from rivers and runoff. **Deltas** are flat, triangular stretches of land formed by rivers that deposit sediment and water into the ocean. **Sand dunes** are mountains of sand located in desert areas or the bottom of the ocean. They are formed by wind and water movement when there's an absence of plants or other features that would otherwise hold the sand in place.

The Earth's Magnetic Field

The Earth's **magnetic field** is created by the magnetic forces that extend from the Earth's interior to outer space. It can be modeled as a magnetic dipole tilted about 10 degrees from the Earth's rotational axis, as if a bar magnet was placed at an angle inside the Earth's core. The **geomagnetic pole** located near Greenland in the northern hemisphere is actually the south pole of the Earth's magnetic field, and vice versa for the southern geomagnetic pole. The **magnetosphere** is the Earth's magnetic field, which extends tens of thousands of kilometers into space and protects the Earth and the atmosphere from damaging solar wind and cosmic rays.

Plate Tectonics Theory and Evidence

The theory of **plate tectonics** hypothesizes that the continents weren't always separated like they are today but were once joined and slowly drifted apart. Evidence for this theory is based upon the fossil record. Fossils of one species were found in regions of the world now separated by an ocean. It's unlikely that a single species could have travelled across the ocean or that two separate species evolved into a single species.

Folding and Faulting

The exact number of tectonic plates is debatable, but scientists estimate there are around nine to fifteen major plates and almost 40 minor plates. The line where two plates meet is called a **fault.** The San Andreas Fault is where the Pacific and North American plates meet. Faults or boundaries are classified depending on the interaction between plates. Two plates collide at **convergent boundaries. Divergent boundaries** occur when two plates move away from each other. Tectonic plates can move vertically and horizontally.

Continental Drift, Seafloor Spreading, Magnetic Reversals

The movement of tectonic plates is similar to pieces of wood floating in a pool of water. They can bob up and down as well as bump, slide, and move away from each other. These different interactions create the Earth's landscape. The collision of plates can create mountain ranges, while their separation can create canyons or underwater chasms. One plate can also slide atop another and push it down into the Earth's hot mantle, creating magma and volcanoes, in a process called **subduction**.

Unlike a regular magnet, the Earth's magnetic field changes over time because it's generated by the motion of molten iron alloys in the outer core. Although the magnetic poles can wander geographically, they do so at such a slow rate that they don't affect the use of compasses in navigation. However, at irregular intervals that are several hundred thousand years long, the fields can reverse, with the north and south magnetic poles switching places.

Characteristics of Volcanoes

Volcanoes are mountainous structures that act as vents to release pressure and magma from the Earth's crust. During an **eruption**, the pressure and magma are released, and volcanoes smoke, rumble, and throw ash and **lava**, or molten rock, into the air. **Hot spots** are volcanic regions of the mantle that are hotter than surrounding regions.

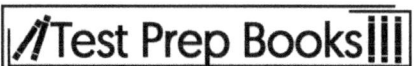

Characteristics of Earthquakes

Earthquakes occur when tectonic plates slide or collide as a result of the crust suddenly releasing energy. Stress in the Earth's outer layer pushes together two faults. The motion of the planes of the fault continues until something makes them stop. The **epicenter** of an earthquake is the point on the surface directly above where the fault is slipping. If the epicenter is located under a body of water, the earthquake may cause a **tsunami**, a series of large, forceful waves.

Seismic waves and Triangulation

Earthquakes cause **seismic waves**, which travel through the Earth's layers and give out low-frequency acoustic energy. Triangulation of seismic waves helps scientists determine the origin of an earthquake.

The Water Cycle
Evaporation and Condensation

The **water cycle** is the cycling of water between its three physical states: solid, liquid, and gas. The Sun's thermal energy heats surface water so it evaporates. As water vapor collects in the atmosphere from evaporation, it eventually reaches a saturation level where it condenses and forms clouds heavy with water droplets.

Precipitation

When the droplets condense as clouds get heavy, they fall as different forms of precipitation, such as rain, snow, hail, fog, and sleet. **Advection** is the process of evaporated water moving from the ocean and falling over land as precipitation.

Runoff and Infiltration

Runoff and infiltration are important parts of the water cycle because they provide water on the surface available for evaporation. **Runoff** can add water to oceans and aid in the advection process. **Infiltration** provides water to plants and aids in the transpiration process.

Transpiration

Transpiration is an evaporation-like process that occurs in plants and soil. Water from the stomata of plants and from pores in soil evaporates into water vapor and enters the atmosphere.

Historical Geology
Principle of Uniformitarianism

Uniformitarianism is the assumption that natural laws and processes haven't changed and apply everywhere in the universe. In geology, uniformitarianism includes the **gradualist model**, which states that "the present is the key to the past" and claims that natural laws functioned at the same rates as observed today.

Basic Principles of Relative Age Dating

Relative age dating is the determination of the relative order of past events without determining absolute age. The Law of Superposition states that older geological layers are deeper than more recent layers. Rocks and fossils can be used to compare one stratigraphic column with another. A **stratigraphic column** is a drawing that describes the vertical location of rocks in a cliff wall or underground. Correlating these columns from different geographic areas allows scientists to understand the relationships between different areas and strata. Before the discovery of radiometric dating, geologists used this technique to determine the ages of different materials. Relative dating can only determine the sequential order of events, not the exact time they occurred. The **Law of Fossil Succession**

states that when the same kinds of fossils are found in rocks from different locations, the rocks are likely the same age.

Absolute (Radiometric) Dating

Absolute or **radiometric dating** is the process of determining age on a specified chronology in archaeology and geology. It attempts to provide a numerical age by measuring the radioactive decay of elements (such as carbon-14) trapped in rocks or minerals and using the known rate of decay to determine how much time has passed.

Characteristics and Processes of the Earth's Oceans and Other Bodies of Water
Distribution and Location of the Earth's Water

A **body of water** is any accumulation of water on the Earth's surface. It usually refers to oceans, seas, and lakes, but also includes ponds, wetlands, and puddles. Rivers, streams, and canals are bodies of water that involve the movement of water.

Most bodies of water are naturally occurring geographical features, but they can also be artificially created like lakes created by dams. Saltwater oceans make up 96% of the water on the Earth's surface. Freshwater makes up 2.5% of the remaining water.

Seawater Composition

Seawater is water from a sea or ocean. On average, seawater has a salinity of about 3.5%, meaning every kilogram of seawater has approximately 35 grams of dissolved sodium chloride salt. The average density of saltwater at the surface is 1.025 kg/L, making it denser than pure or freshwater, which has a density of 1.00 kg/L. Because of the dissolved salts, the freezing point of saltwater is also lower than that of pure water; salt water freezes at −2 °C (28 °F). As the concentration of salt increases, the freezing point decreases. Thus, it's more difficult to freeze water from the Dead Sea—a saltwater lake known to have water with such high salinity that swimmers cannot sink.

Coastline Topography and the Topography of Ocean Floor

Topography is the study of natural and artificial features comprising the surface of an area. **Coastlines** are an intermediate area between dry land and the ocean floor. The ground progressively slopes from the dry coastal area to the deepest depth of the ocean floor. At the continental shelf, there's a steep descent of the ocean floor. Although it's often believed that the ocean floor is flat and sandy like a beach, its topography includes mountains, plateaus, and valleys.

Tides, Waves, and Currents

Tides are caused by the pull of the Moon and the Sun. When the Moon is closer in its orbit to the Earth, its gravity pulls the oceans away from the shore. When the distance between the Moon and the Earth is greater, the pull is weaker, and the water on Earth can spread across more land. This relationship creates low and high tides. Waves are influenced by changes in tides as well as the wind. The energy transferred from wind to the top of large bodies of water creates *crests* on the water's surface and waves below. Circular movements in the ocean are called

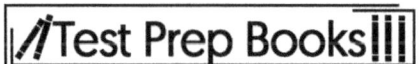

currents. They result from the **Coriolis Effect**, which is caused by the Earth's rotation. Currents spin in a clockwise direction above the equator and counterclockwise below the equator.

Estuaries and Barrier Islands
An **estuary** is an area of water located on a coast where a river or stream meets the sea. It's a transitional area that's partially enclosed, has a mix of salty and fresh water, and has calmer water than the open sea. **Barrier islands** are coastal landforms created by waves and tidal action parallel to the mainland coast. They usually occur in chains, and they protect the coastlines and create areas of protected waters where wetlands may flourish.

Islands, Reefs, and Atolls
Islands are land that is completely surrounded by water. **Reefs** are bars of rocky, sandy, or coral material that sit below the surface of water. They may form from sand deposits or erosion of underwater rocks. An **atoll** is a coral reef in the shape of a ring (but not necessarily circular) that encircles a lagoon. In order for an atoll to exist, the rate of its erosion must be slower than the regrowth of the coral that composes the atoll.

Polar Ice, Icebergs, Glaciers
Polar ice is the term for the sheets of ice that cover the poles of a planet. **Icebergs** are large pieces of freshwater ice that break off from glaciers and float in the water. A **glacier** is a persistent body of dense ice that constantly moves because of its own weight. Glaciers form when snow accumulates at a faster rate than it melts over centuries. They form only on land, in contrast to **ice caps**, which can form from sheets of ice in the ocean. When glaciers deform and move due to stresses created by their own weight, they can create **crevasses** and other large distinguishing land features.

Lakes, Ponds, and Wetlands
Lakes and **ponds** are bodies of water that are surrounded by land. They aren't part of the ocean and don't contain flowing water. Lakes are larger than ponds, but otherwise the two bodies don't have a scientific distinction. **Wetlands** are areas of land saturated by water. They have a unique soil composition and provide a nutrient-dense area for vegetation and aquatic plant growth. They also play a role in water purification and flood control.

Streams, Rivers, and River Deltas
A **river** is a natural flowing waterway usually consisting of freshwater that flows toward an ocean, sea, lake, or another river. Some rivers flow into the ground and become dry instead of reaching another body of water. Small rivers are usually called **streams** or **creeks**. River **deltas** are areas of land formed from the sediment carried by a river and deposited before it enters another body of water. As the river reaches its end, the flow of water slows, and the river loses the power to transport the sediment so it falls out of suspension.

Geysers and Springs
A **spring** is a natural occurrence where water flows from an aquifer to the Earth's surface. A **geyser** is a spring that intermittently and turbulently discharges water. Geysers form only in certain hydrogeological conditions. They require proximity to a volcanic area or magma to provide enough heat to boil or vaporize the water. As hot water and steam accumulate, pressure grows and creates the spraying geyser effect.

Properties of Water that Affect Earth Systems
Water is a chemical compound composed of two hydrogen atoms and one oxygen atom (H_2O) and has many unique properties. In its solid state, water is less dense than its liquid form; therefore, ice floats in water. Water also has a very high **heat capacity**, allowing it to absorb a high amount of the Sun's energy without getting too hot or evaporating. Its chemical structure makes it a polar compound, meaning one side has a negative charge while the

other is positive. This characteristic—along with its ability to form strong intermolecular hydrogen bonds with itself and other molecules—make water an effective solvent for other chemicals.

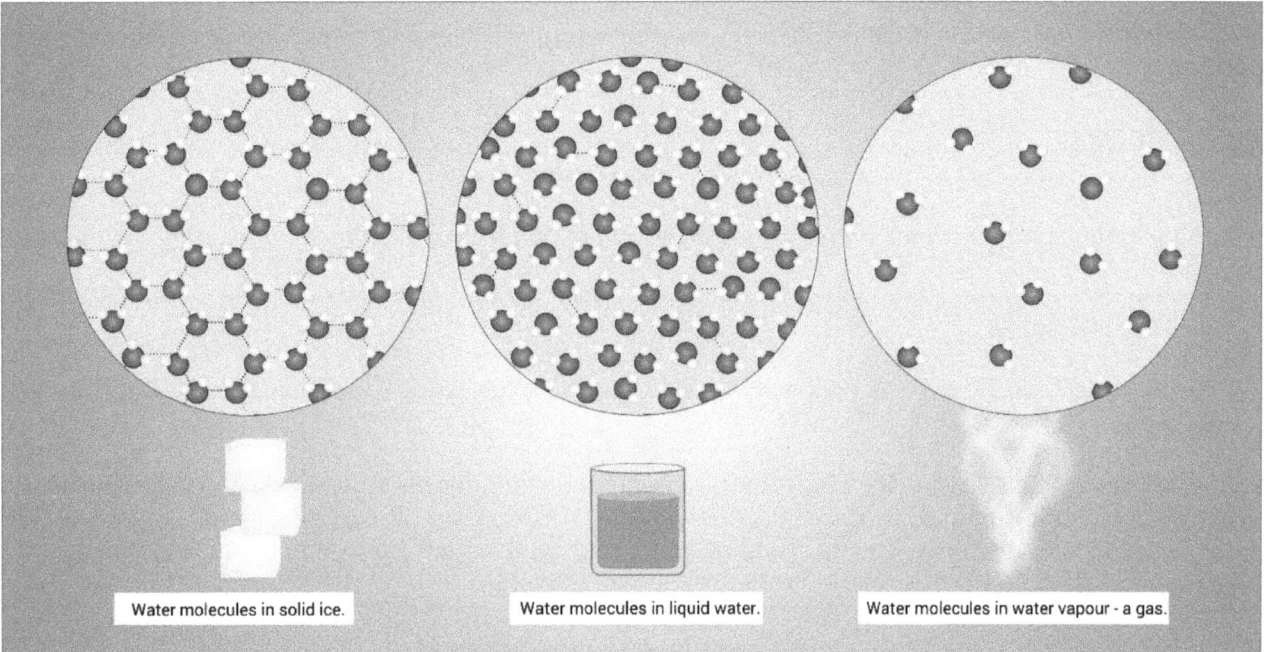

Water molecules in solid ice. | Water molecules in liquid water. | Water molecules in water vapour - a gas.

Basic Structure and Composition of the Earth's Atmosphere

Layers

The Earth's atmospheric layers are determined by their temperatures but are reported by their distance above sea level. Listed from closest to sea level on upward, the levels are:

- **Troposphere:** sea level to 11 miles above sea level
- **Stratosphere:** 11 miles to 31 miles above sea level
- **Mesosphere:** 31 miles to 50 miles above sea level
- **Ionosphere:** 50 miles to 400 miles above sea level
- **Exosphere**: 400 miles to 800 miles above sea level

The ionosphere and exosphere are together considered the **thermosphere**. The ozone layer is in the stratosphere and weather experienced on Earth's surface is a product of factors in the troposphere.

Composition of the Atmosphere

The Earth's atmosphere is composed of gas particles: 78% nitrogen, 21% oxygen, 1% other gases such as argon, and 0.039% carbon dioxide. The atmospheric layers are created by the number of particles in the air and gravity's pull upon them.

Atmospheric Pressure and Temperature

The lower atmospheric levels have higher atmospheric pressures due to the mass of the gas particles located above. The air is less dense (it contains fewer particles per given volume) at higher altitudes. The temperature changes from the bottom to top of each atmospheric layer. The tops of the troposphere and mesosphere are colder than their bottoms, but the reverse is true for the stratosphere and thermosphere. Some of the warmest temperatures are actually found in the thermosphere because of a type of radiation that enters that layer.

Earth's Movements and Position in the Solar System

Structure of the Solar System
The **solar system** is an elliptical planetary system with a large sun in the center that provides gravitational pull on the planets.

Laws of Motion
Planetary motion is governed by three scientific laws called **Kepler's laws**:

1. The orbit of a planet is elliptical in shape, with the Sun as one focus.

2. An imaginary line joining the center of a planet and the center of the Sun sweeps out equal areas during equal intervals of time.

3. For all planets, the ratio of the square of the orbital period is the same as the cube of the average distance from the Sun.

The most relevant of these laws is the first. Planets move in elliptical paths because of gravity; when a planet is closer to the Sun, it moves faster because it has built up gravitational speed. As illustrated in the diagram below, the second law states that it takes planet 1 the same time to travel along the A1 segment as the A2 segment, even though the A2 segment is shorter.

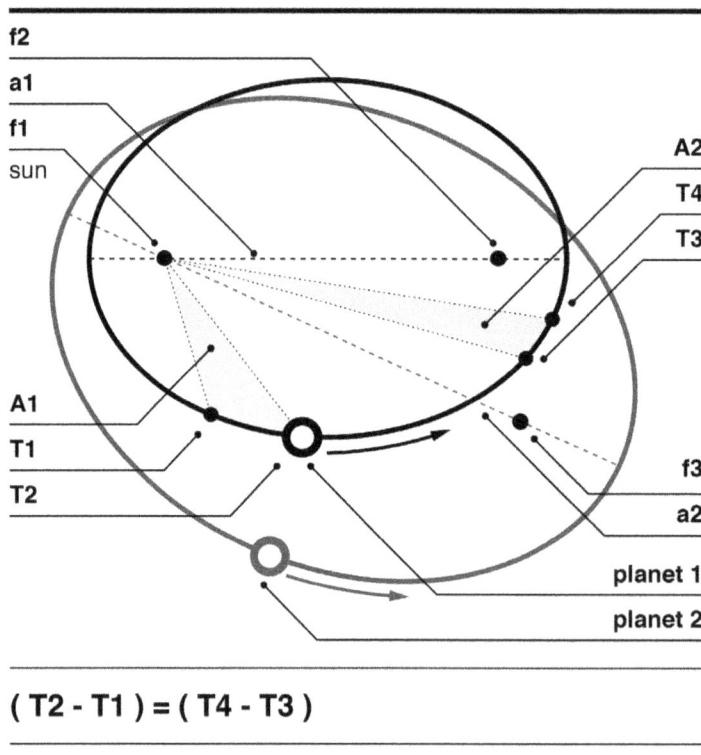

Characteristics of the Sun, Moon, and Planets
The Sun is comprised mainly of hydrogen and helium. Metals make up only about 2% of its total mass. The Sun is 1.3 million kilometers wide, weighs 1.989×10^{30} kilograms, and has temperatures of 5,800 Kelvin (9980 °F) on the

surface and 15,600,000 Kelvin (28 million °F) at the core. The Sun's enormous size and gravity give it the ability to provide sunlight. The gravity of the Sun compresses hydrogen and helium atoms together through nuclear fusion and releases energy and light.

The Moon has a distinct core, mantle, and crust. It has elevations and craters created by impacts with large objects in the solar system. The Moon makes a complete orbit around the Earth every 27.3 days. It's relatively large compared to other moons in the Solar System, with a diameter one-quarter of the Earth and a mass 1/81 of the Earth.

The eight planets of the Solar System are divided into four inner (or **terrestrial**) planets and four outer (or **Jovian**) planets. In general, terrestrial planets are small, and Jovian planets are large and gaseous. The planets in the Solar System are listed below from nearest to farthest from the Sun:

- Mercury: The smallest planet in the system and the one that is closest to the Sun. Because it's so close, it only takes about 88 days for Mercury to completely orbit the Sun It has a large iron core and the surface has craters like Earth's moon. There's no atmosphere, and it doesn't have any orbiting moons/satellites. From Earth, Mercury looks bright.

- Venus: The second planet is bright and has about the same size, composition, and gravity as Earth. It orbits the Sun every 225 days Its atmosphere creates clouds of sulfuric acid, and there's even thunder and lightning.

- Earth: The third planet orbits the Sun every year (about 365 days). Scientists believe it's the only planet in this system that's capable of supporting life.

- Mars: The Red Planet looks red because there's iron oxide on the surface. It also takes around 687 days to complete its orbit around the Sun. Interestingly, a day on Mars (one rotation about its axis), is very similar to the 24-hour day on Earth. Mars has a thin atmosphere as well as the largest mountain, canyon, and crater that astronomers have ever been able to see. Volcanoes, valleys, deserts, and polar ice caps like those on Earth have also been seen on its surface.

- Jupiter: The largest planet in the solar system is comprised mainly of hydrogen and helium (helium makes up 25% of its mass). The atmosphere on Jupiter has band-like clouds made of ammonia crystals that create tremendous storms and turbulence on the surface. Winds blow at around 100 meters per second, or over 220 miles per hour!

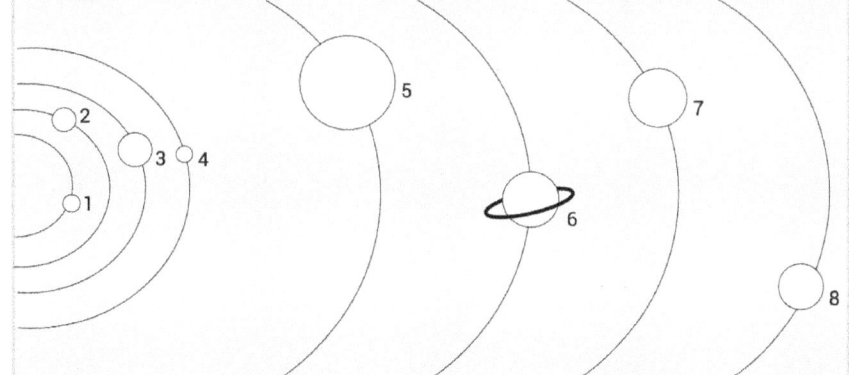

- Saturn: The second-largest planet is comprised mainly of hydrogen and helium along with other trace elements. The core is believed to be rock and ice. Saturn has a layer of metallic hydrogen. Winds are even stronger than those on Jupiter, reaching up to 1,100 miles per hour. Saturn has 61 moons, but the planet is most famous for its beautiful rings. There's no definitive explanation for how the rings formed, but two popular theories say they could be remnants from when Saturn itself formed, or they were moons that were destroyed in the past.

- Uranus: This planet has the coldest atmosphere of any in the Solar System, with a temperature that reaches −224.2°C (−371.56°F). It's also mainly made of hydrogen and helium, but it has water, ammonia, methane, and even some hydrocarbons (the material humans are made of). A solid surface has yet to be observed through the thick layer of gas covering the planet. Uranus has 27 known moons.

- Neptune: The furthest planet is the third-largest by mass, and the second-coldest. It has 12 orbiting moons, an atmosphere like Uranus', a Great Dark Spot, and the strongest recorded winds of any planet in the system (reaching speeds of 2,100 kilometers per hour).

Asteroids, Meteoroids, Comets, and Dwarf/Minor Planets

Several other bodies travel through the universe. **Asteroids** are orbiting bodies composed of minerals and rock. They're also known as **minor planets**—a term given to any astronomical object in orbit around the Sun that doesn't resemble a planet or a comet. **Meteoroids** are mini-asteroids with no specific orbiting pattern. **Meteors** are meteoroids that have entered the Earth's atmosphere and started melting from contact with greenhouse gases. **Meteorites** are meteors that have landed on Earth. **Comets** are composed of dust and ice and look like a comma with a tail from the melting ice as they streak across the sky.

Theories of Origin of the Solar System

One theory of the origins of the Solar System is the **nebular hypothesis**, which posits that the Solar System was formed by clouds of extremely hot gas called a **nebula**. As the nebula gases cooled, they became smaller and started rotating. Rings of the nebula left behind during rotation eventually condensed into planets and their satellites. The remaining nebula formed the Sun.

Another theory of the Solar System's development is the **planetesimal hypothesis**. This theory proposes that planets formed from cosmic dust grains that collided and stuck together to form larger and larger bodies. The larger bodies attracted each other, growing into moon-sized protoplanets and eventually planets.

Interactions of the Earth-Moon-Sun System

The Earth's Rotation and Orbital Revolution Around the Sun

Besides revolving around the Sun, the Earth also spins like a top. It takes one day for the Earth to complete a full spin, or rotation. The same is true for other planets, except that their "days" may be shorter or longer. One Earth day is about 24 hours, while one Jupiter day is only about nine Earth hours, and a Venus day is about 241 Earth days. Night occurs in areas that face away from the Sun, so one side of the planet experiences daylight and the other experiences night. This phenomenon is the reason that the Earth is divided into time zones. The concept of time zones was created to provide people around the world with a uniform standard time, so the Sun would rise around 7:00 AM, regardless of location.

Effect on Seasons

The Earth's tilted axis creates the seasons. When Earth is tilted toward the Sun, the Northern Hemisphere experiences summer while the Southern Hemisphere has winter—and vice versa. As the Earth rotates, the distribution of direct sunlight slowly changes, explaining how the seasons gradually change.

Phases of the Moon

The Moon goes through two phases as it revolves around Earth: waxing and waning. Each phase lasts about two weeks:

- **Waxing**: the right side of the Moon is illuminated
    - **New moon** (dark): the Moon rises and sets with the Sun
    - **Crescent**: a tiny sliver of illumination on the right
    - First quarter: the right half of the Moon is illuminated
    - **Gibbous**: more than half of the Moon is illuminated
    - **Full moon**: the Moon rises at sunset and sets at sunrise
- **Waning**: the left side of the Moon is illuminated
    - **Gibbous**: more than half is illuminated, only here it is the left side that is illuminated
    - **Last quarter**: the left half of the Moon is illuminated
    - **Crescent**: a tiny sliver of illumination on the left
- **New moon** (dark): the Moon rises and sets with the Sun

Effect on Tides

Although the Earth is much larger, the Moon still has a significant gravitational force that pulls on Earth's oceans. At its closest to Earth, the Moon's gravitation pull is greatest and creates high tide. The opposite is true when the Moon is farthest from the Earth: less pull creates low tide.

Solar and Lunar Eclipses

Eclipses occur when the Earth, the Sun, and the Moon are all in line. If the three bodies are perfectly aligned, a total eclipse occurs; otherwise, it's only a partial eclipse. A **solar eclipse** occurs when the Moon is between the Earth and the Sun, blocking sunlight from reaching the Earth. A **lunar eclipse** occurs when the Earth interferes with the Sun's light reflecting off the full moon. The Earth casts a shadow on the Moon, but the particles of the Earth's atmosphere refract the light, so some light reaches the Moon, causing it to look yellow, brown, or red.

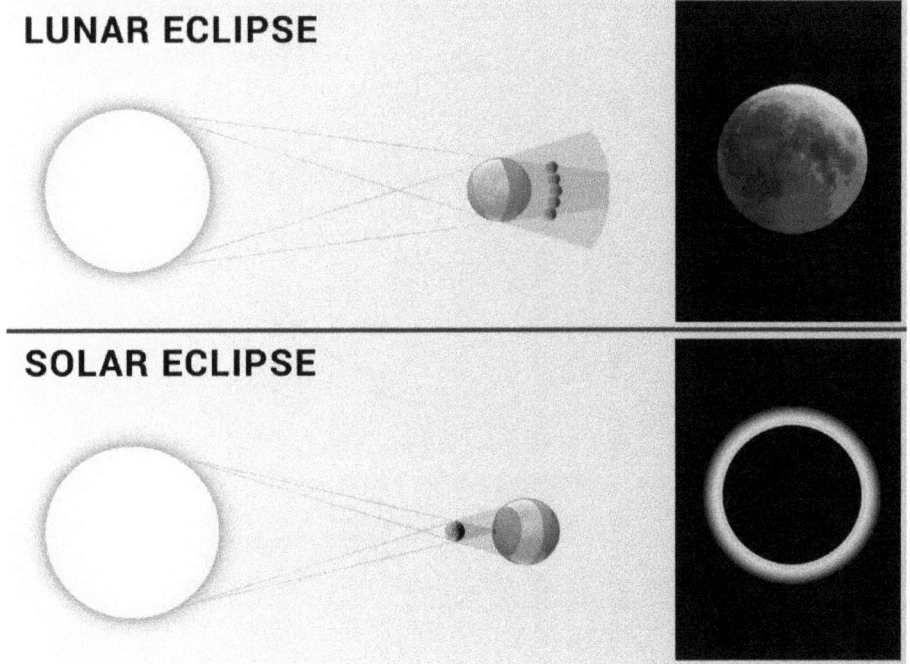

Time Zones

Longitudinal, or vertical, lines determine how far east or west different regions are from each other. These lines, also known as **meridians**, are the basis for time zones, which allocate different times to regions depending on their position eastward and westward of the prime meridian.

The Sun, Other Stars, and the Solar System

Structure of the Solar System

The **solar system** is an elliptical planetary system with a large sun in the center that provides gravitational pull on the planets.

Laws of Planetary Motion

Planetary motion is governed by three scientific laws called Kepler's laws:

1. The orbit of a planet is elliptical in shape, with the Sun as one focus.

2. An imaginary line joining the center of a planet and the center of the Sun sweeps out equal areas during equal intervals of time.

3. For all planets, the ratio of the square of the orbital period is the same as the cube of the average distance from the Sun.

The most relevant of these laws is the first. Planets move in elliptical paths because of gravity; when a planet is closer to the Sun, it moves faster because it has built up gravitational speed. As illustrated in the diagram below, the second law states that it takes planet 1 the same time to travel along the A1 segment as the A2 segment, even though the A2 segment is shorter.

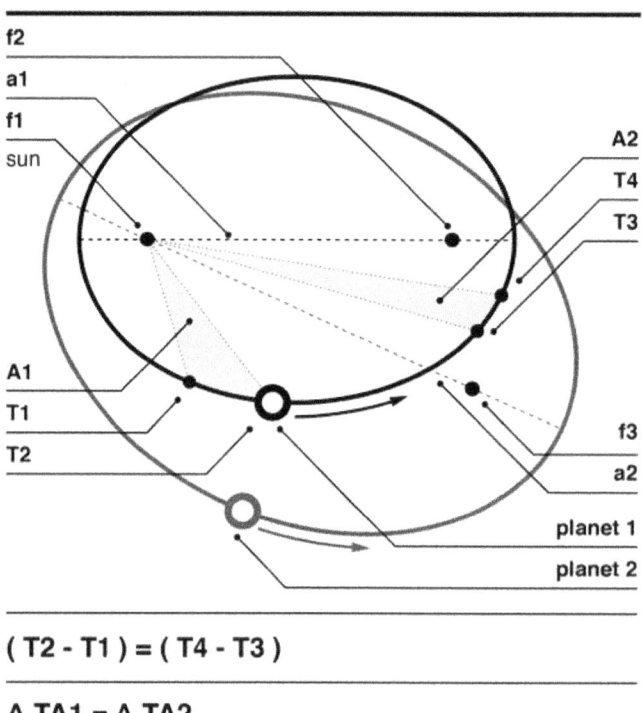

Kepler's Laws of Planetary Motion

$(T2 - T1) = (T4 - T3)$

$\Delta TA1 = \Delta TA2$

Science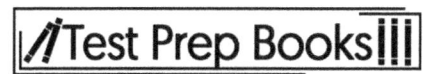

Characteristics of the Sun, Moon, and Planets

The Sun is comprised mainly of hydrogen and helium. Metals make up only about 2% of its total mass. The Sun is 1.3 million kilometers wide, weighs 1.989×10^{30} kilograms, and has temperatures of 5,800 Kelvin (9980 °F) on the surface and 15,600,000 Kelvin (28 million °F) at the core. The Sun's enormous size and gravity give it the ability to provide sunlight. The gravity of the Sun compresses hydrogen and helium atoms together through nuclear fusion and releases energy and light.

The Moon has a distinct core, mantle, and crust. It has elevations and craters created by impacts with large objects in the solar system. The Moon makes a complete orbit around the Earth every 27.3 days. It's relatively large compared to other moons in the Solar System, with a diameter one-quarter of the Earth and a mass 1/81 of the Earth.

The eight planets of the Solar System are divided into four inner (or terrestrial) planets and four outer (or Jovian) planets. In general, terrestrial planets are small, and Jovian planets are large and gaseous. The planets in the Solar System are listed below from nearest to farthest from the Sun:

- Mercury: the smallest planet in the Solar System; it only takes about 88 days to completely orbit the Sun
- Venus: around the same size, composition, and gravity as Earth and orbits the Sun every 225 days
- Earth: the only known planet with life
- Mars: called the Red Planet due to iron oxide on the surface; takes around 687 days to complete its orbit
- Jupiter: the largest planet in the system; made up of mainly hydrogen and helium
- Saturn: mainly composed of hydrogen and helium along with other trace elements; has 61 moons; has beautiful rings, which may be remnants of destroyed moons
- Uranus: the coldest planet in the system, with temperatures as low as -224.2 °C (-371.56 °F)
- Neptune: the last and third-largest planet; also, the second-coldest planet

Asteroids, Meteoroids, Comets, and Dwarf/Minor Planets

Several other bodies travel through the universe. **Asteroids** are orbiting bodies composed of minerals and rock. They're also known as **minor planets**—a term given to any astronomical object in orbit around the Sun that doesn't resemble a planet or a comet. **Meteoroids** are mini-asteroids with no specific orbiting pattern. **Meteors** are meteoroids that have entered the Earth's atmosphere and started melting from contact with greenhouse gases. **Meteorites** are meteors that have landed on Earth. **Comets** are composed of dust and ice and look like a comma with a tail from the melting ice as they streak across the sky.

Theories of Origin of the Solar System

One theory of the origins of the Solar System is the **nebular hypothesis**, which posits that the Solar System was formed by clouds of extremely hot gas called a **nebula**. As the nebula gases cooled, they became smaller and started rotating. Rings of the nebula left behind during rotation eventually condensed into planets and their satellites. The remaining nebula formed the Sun.

Another theory of the Solar System's development is the **planetesimal hypothesis**. This theory proposes that planets formed from cosmic dust grains that collided and stuck together to form larger and larger bodies. The larger bodies attracted each other, growing into moon-sized protoplanets and eventually planets.

The Earth's Rotation and Orbital Revolution Around the Sun

Besides revolving around the Sun, the Earth also spins like a top. It takes one day for the Earth to complete a full spin, or rotation. The same is true for other planets, except that their "days" may be shorter or longer. One Earth day is about 24 hours, while one Jupiter day is only about nine Earth hours, and a Venus day is about 241 Earth days. Night occurs in areas that face away from the Sun, so one side of the planet experiences daylight and the other experiences night. This phenomenon is the reason that the Earth is divided into time zones. The concept of time zones was created to provide people around the world with a uniform standard time, so the Sun would rise around 7:00 AM, regardless of location.

Effect on Seasons

The Earth's tilted axis creates the seasons. When Earth is tilted toward the Sun, the Northern Hemisphere experiences summer while the Southern Hemisphere has winter—and vice versa. As the Earth rotates, the distribution of direct sunlight slowly changes, explaining how the seasons gradually change.

Phases of the Moon

The Moon goes through two phases as it revolves around Earth: waxing and waning. Each phase lasts about two weeks:

- Waxing: the right side of the Moon is illuminated
- New moon (dark): the Moon rises and sets with the Sun
- Crescent: a tiny sliver of illumination on the right
- First quarter: the right half of the Moon is illuminated
- Gibbous: more than half of the Moon is illuminated
- Full moon: the Moon rises at sunset and sets at sunrise
- Waning: the left side of the Moon is illuminated
- Gibbous: more than half is illuminated, only here it is the left side that is illuminated
- Last quarter: the left half of the Moon is illuminated
- Crescent: a tiny sliver of illumination on the left
- New moon (dark): the Moon rises and sets with the Sun

Effect on Tides

Although the Earth is much larger, the Moon still has a significant gravitational force that pulls on Earth's oceans. At its closest to Earth, the Moon's gravitation pull is greatest and creates high tide. The opposite is true when the Moon is farthest from the Earth: less pull creates low tide.

Solar and Lunar Eclipses

Eclipses occur when the Earth, the Sun, and the Moon are all in line. If the three bodies are perfectly aligned, a total eclipse occurs; otherwise, it's only a partial eclipse. A **solar eclipse** occurs when the Moon is between the Earth and the Sun, blocking sunlight from reaching the Earth. A **lunar eclipse** occurs when the Earth interferes with the Sun's light reflecting off the full moon. The Earth casts a shadow on the Moon, but the particles of the Earth's atmosphere refract the light, so some light reaches the Moon, causing it to look yellow, brown, or red.

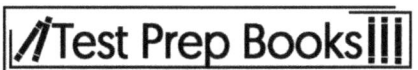

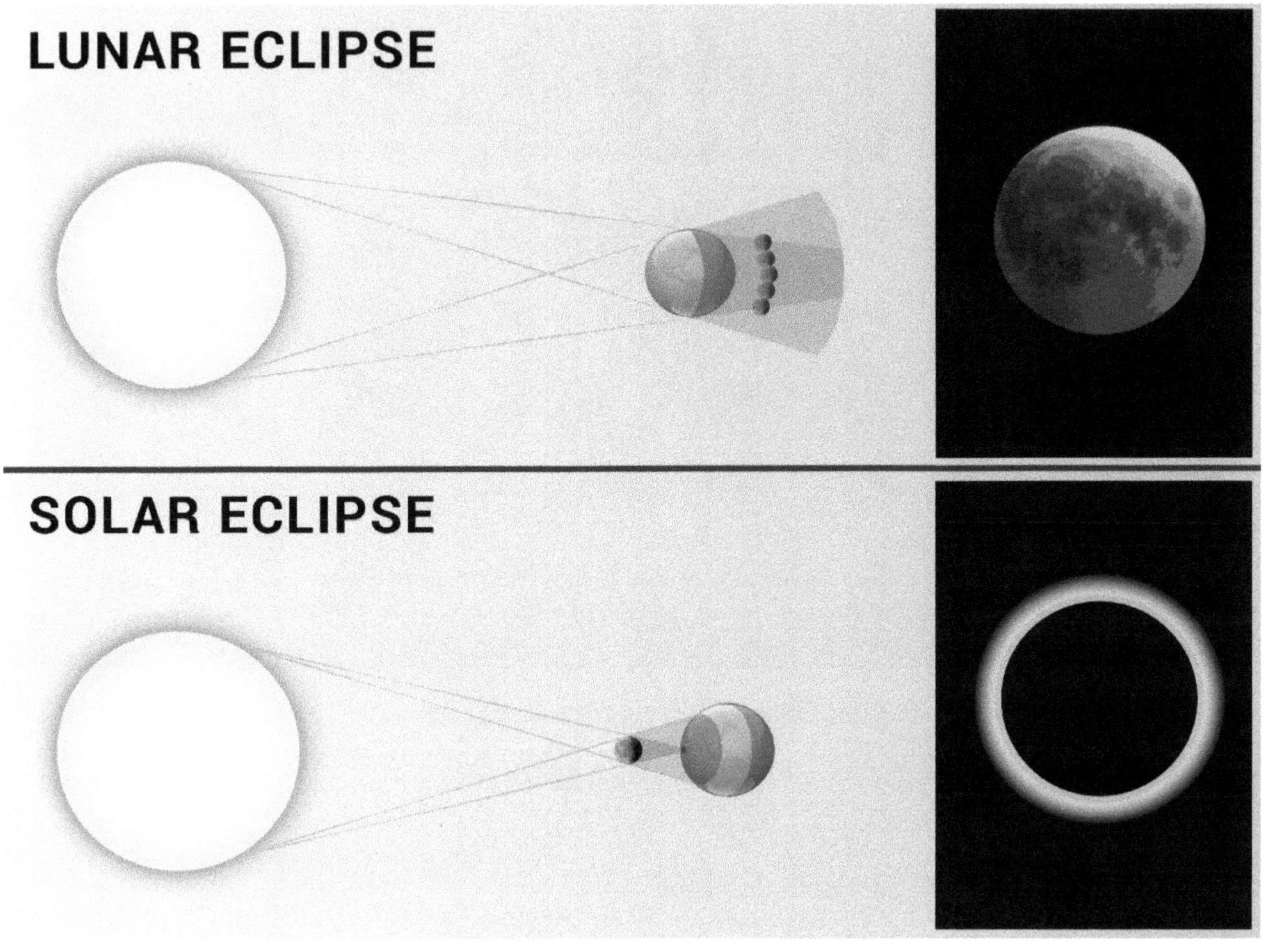

Time Zones
Longitudinal, or vertical, lines determine how far east or west different regions are from each other. These lines, also known as **meridians,** are the basis for time zones, which allocate different times to regions depending on their position eastward and westward of the prime meridian.

Effect of Solar Wind on the Earth
Solar winds are streams of charged particles emitted by the Sun, consisting of mostly electrons, protons, and alpha particles. The Earth is largely protected from solar winds by its magnetic field. However, the winds can still be observed, as they create phenomena like the beautiful Northern Lights (or Aurora Borealis).

Galaxies
Galaxies are clusters of stars, rocks, ice, and space dust. Like everything else in space, the exact number of galaxies is unknown, but there could be as many as a hundred billion. There are three types of galaxies: spiral, elliptical, and irregular. Most galaxies are **spiral galaxies**; they have a large, central galactic bulge made up of a cluster of older stars. They look like a disk with spinning arms. **Elliptical galaxies** are groups of stars with no pattern of rotation.

They can be spherical or extremely elongated, and they don't have arms. **Irregular galaxies** vary significantly in size and shape.

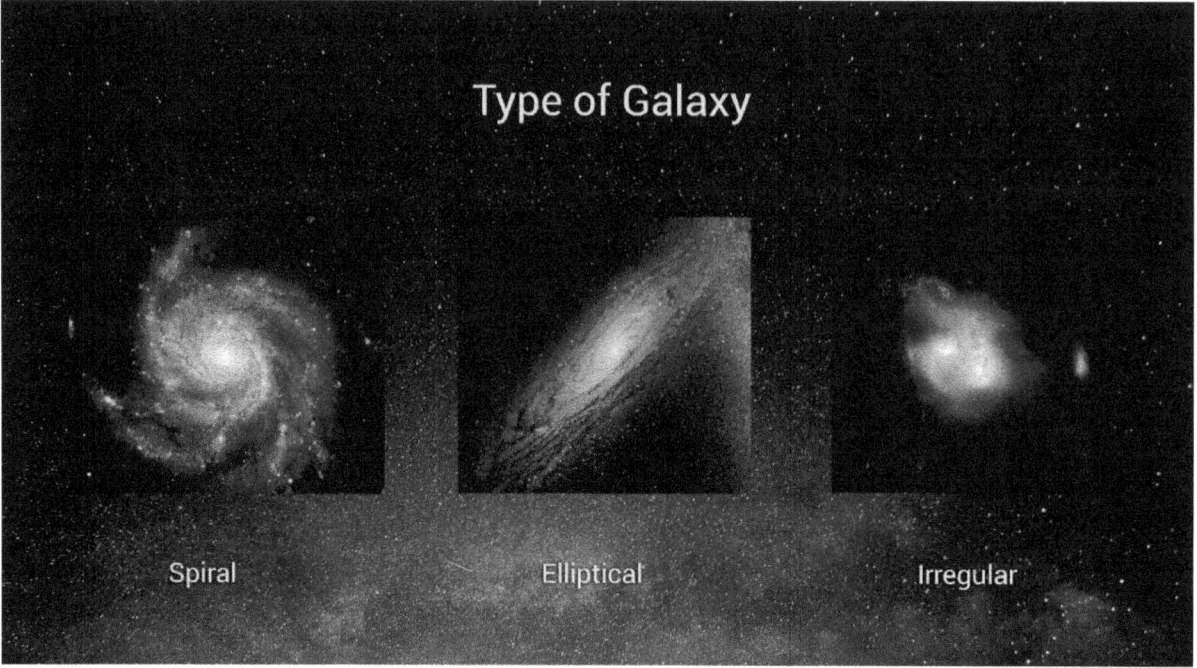

To say that galaxies are large is an understatement. Most galaxies are 1,000 to 100,000 parsecs in diameter, with one **parsec** equal to about 19 trillion miles. The Milky Way is the galaxy that contains Earth's Solar System. It's one of the smaller galaxies that has been studied. The diameter of the Milky Way is estimated to be between 31,000 to 55,000 parsecs.

Characteristics of Stars and Their Life Cycles
Life Cycle of Stars
All stars are formed from nebulae. Depending on their mass, stars take different pathways during their evolution. Low- and medium-mass stars start as nebulae and then become red giants and white dwarfs. High-mass stars become red supergiants, supernovas, and then either neutron stars or black holes. Official stars are born as red dwarfs because they have plentiful amounts of gas—mainly hydrogen—to undergo nuclear fusion. Red dwarfs mature into white dwarfs before expending their hydrogen fuel source. When the fuel is spent, it creates a burst of energy that expands the star into a red giant. Red giants eventually condense to form white dwarfs, which is the final stage of a star's life.

Stars that undergo nuclear fusion and energy expenditure extremely quickly can burst in violent explosions called **supernovas**. These bursts can release as much energy in a few seconds as the Sun can release in its entire lifetime. The particles from the explosion then condense into the smallest type of star—a neutron star—and eventually form a **black hole**, which has such a high amount of gravity that not even light energy can escape. The Sun is currently a red dwarf, early in its life cycle.

Color, Temperature, Apparent Brightness, Absolute Brightness, and Luminosity
The color of a star depends on its surface temperature. Stars with cooler surfaces emit red light, while the hottest stars give off blue light. Stars with temperatures between these extremes, such as the Sun, emit white light. The **apparent brightness** of a star is a measure of how bright a star appears to an observer on the Earth. The **absolute brightness** is a measure of the intrinsic brightness of a star and is measured at a distance of exactly 10 parsecs away. The **luminosity** of a star is the amount of light emitted from its surface.

Science Process

Interpreting and Applying

The skills needed to think critically, scientifically, and to follow the scientific method are referred to as **process skills**. These skills are the soil from which scientific knowledge is nurtured and grown. There are six fundamental process skills:

- **Observation**—using the senses to gather information
- **Communication**—using words, drawings, graphs, charts, or videos to effectively present observations
- **Classification**—grouping or categorizing objects or events based on certain attributes or criteria, i.e., sorting subjects into height and weight, grouping plants by species, etc.
- **Measurement**—using tools and instruments to describe dimensional variations in an object or event, such as measuring tape, graduated cylinders, clocks, etc.
- **Inference**—drawing conclusions from observations based on prior knowledge or education, i.e., "the grass is wet; it must have rained last night."
- **Prediction**—anticipating the outcome of an event based on prior knowledge or experiences, i.e., "there are many clouds in the sky; it's going to rain tonight." Prediction is the essential skill in forming a solid hypothesis.

In addition to the basic process skills, there are other skills needed in scientific experiments. One essential skill is **generalization**—a type of inference deduced by broad observations of large groups of people or objects that is used frequently in quantitative research. Because of the near-impossibility of sampling a whole population, generalizations are applied to represent a whole population as accurately as possible.

The final step of the scientific method is to make inferences from observed data, which is also known as forming a **conclusion**. Conclusions are placed at the end of scientific papers and wrap up the experimental procedure with its respective inferences. For example, if the experimental data from the plant growth experiment showed that plants with more light grew 2cm more than plants with minimal light in a given period of time, the conclusion may be that certain components of light stimulate plant growth, so the more light that a plant receives, the taller it will grow.

Nature of Scientific Knowledge
Subject to Change

The nature of science is to continuously gather knowledge in order to develop an understanding of the universe. Because of its experimental nature, there's no such thing as "absolute truth" in science. Even the oldest theories are constantly tested in order to improve our understanding or disregard those that no longer apply in light of new observations and interpretations.

Consistent with Evidence

Science is subject to change because of evidence presented in light of new findings. Science is dependent upon the inferences made from evidence obtained through observation. Introductions, expansions, and revisions of scientific theories must present evidence to ascertain that they're still true.

Based on Reproducible Evidence

Before scientific knowledge is established as true, it must be reproducible—that is, the entire experiment must be able to be duplicated by either the same scientist or a different one to ensure its validity.

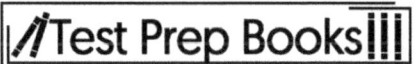

Includes Unifying Concepts and Processes

Scientific knowledge must be unified, meaning there are central ideas common to all sciences from which new and improved information can grow. There are standards for unifying concepts and processes that students are required to learn in grades K-12, which include:

- Systems, Order, and Organization
  - Observing the universe in distinct parts and understanding all elements that compose these parts to form the whole—i.e., organisms, galaxies, cells, numbers, government, the entire known universe, etc.

- Evidence, Models, and Explanation
  - Scientific theories are based on collected evidence, which provides explanations and the basis for models that enhance understanding and enable scientists to make predictions.

- Change, Consistency, and Measurement
  - The natural world is consistently changing, yet many patterns are repeated over time—i.e., change of seasons, tidal phases, moon phases, etc.

- Evolution and Equilibrium
  - Organisms are genetically diverse, and traits that are advantageous for survival are passed on through the generations. Natural systems all trend towards equilibrium—a state of balance between opposing processes.

- Form and Function
  - There is a relationship between an object's structure and its function—i.e., tooth shape, cell shape, leaf thickness, etc.

Analyzing

Identifying Problems Based on Observations

Human beings are, by nature, very curious. Since long before the scientific method was established, people have been making observations and predicting outcomes, manipulating the physical world to create extraordinary things—from the first man-made fire in 6000 B.C.E. to the satellite that orbited Pluto in 2016. Although the history of the scientific method is sporadic and attributed to many different people, it remains the most reliable way to obtain and utilize knowledge about the observable universe. The scientific method consists of the following steps:

- Make an observation
- Create a question
- Form a hypothesis
- Conduct an experiment
- Collect and analyze data
- Form a conclusion

The first step is to identify a problem based on an observation—the who, what, when, where, why, and how. An **observation** is the analysis of information using basic human senses: sight, sound, touch, taste, and smell. Observations can be two different types—qualitative or quantitative. A **qualitative observation** describes what is being observed, such as the color of a house or the smell of a flower. **Quantitative observations** measure what is being observed, such as the number of windows on a house or the intensity of a flower's smell on a scale of 1-5.

Observations lead to the identification of a problem, also called an **inference**. For example, if a fire truck is barreling down a busy street, the inferences could be:

- There's a fire.
- Someone is hurt.
- Some kid pulled the fire alarm at a local school.

Inferences are logical predictions based on experience or education that lead to the formation of a hypothesis.

Forming and Testing a Hypothesis

A **hypothesis** is a testable explanation of an observed scenario and is presented in the form of a statement. It's an attempt to answer a question based on an observation, and it allows a scientist to predict an outcome. A hypothesis makes assumptions on the relationship between two different variables, and answers the question: "If I do this, what happens to that?"

In order to form a hypothesis, there must be an independent variable and a dependent variable that can be measured. The **independent variable** is the variable that is manipulated, and the **dependent variable** is the result of the change.

For example, suppose a student wants to know how light affects plant growth. Based upon what he or she already knows, the student proposes (hypothesizes) that the more light to which a plant is exposed, the faster it will grow.

- Observation: Plants exposed to lots of light seem to grow taller.
- Question: Will plants grow faster if there's more light available?
- Hypothesis: The more light the plant has, the faster it will grow.
- Independent variable: The amount of time exposed to light (able to be manipulated)
- Dependent variable: Plant growth (the result of the manipulation)

Once a hypothesis has been formed, it must be tested to determine whether it's true or false. (How to test a hypothesis is described in a subsequent section.) After it has been tested and validated as true over and over, then a hypothesis can develop into a theory, model, or law.

Development of Theories, Models, and Laws

Theories, models, and laws have one thing in common: *they develop on the basis of scientific evidence that has been tested and verified by multiple researchers on many different occasions*. Listed below are their exact definitions:

- **Theory**: An explanation of natural patterns or occurrences—i.e., the theory of relativity, the kinetic theory of gases, etc.

- **Model**: A representation of a natural pattern or occurrence that's difficult or impossible to experience directly, usually in the form of a picture or 3-D representation—i.e., Bohr's atomic model, the double-helix model of DNA, etc.

- **Law**: A mathematical or concise description of a pattern or occurrence in the observable universe—i.e., Newton's law of gravity, the laws of thermodynamics, etc.

The terms *theory, model,* and *law* are often used interchangeably in the sciences, although there's an essential difference: theories and models are used to explain *how and why* something happens, while laws describe exactly *what* happens. A common misconception is that theories develop into laws. But theories and models never become laws because they inherently describe different things.

Type	Function	Examples
Theory	To explain how and why something happens	Einstein's Theory of Special Relativity The Big Bang Theory
Model	To represent how and why something happens	A graphical model or drawing of an atom
Laws	To describe exactly what happens	$E = mc^2$ $F = ma$ $PV = nRT$

In order to ensure that scientific theories are consistent, scientists continually gather information and evidence on existing theories to improve their accuracy.

Experimental Design

To test a hypothesis, one must conduct a carefully designed experiment. There are four basic requirements that must be present for an experiment to be valid:

1. A control
2. Variables
3. A constant
4. Repeated and collected data

The **control** is a standard to which the resultant findings are compared. It's the baseline measurement that allows for scientists to determine whether the results are positive or negative. For the example of light affecting plant growth, the control may be a plant that receives no light at all.

The **independent variable** is manipulated (a good way to remember this is *I* manipulate the *I*ndependent variable), and the **dependent variable** is the result of changes to the independent variable. In the plant example, the independent variable is the amount of time exposed to light, and the dependent variable is the resulting growth (or lack thereof) of the plant. For this experiment, there may be three plants—one that receives a minimal amount of light, the control, and one that receives a lot of light.

Finally, there must be constants in an experiment. A **constant** is an element of the experiment that remains unchanged. Constants are extremely important in minimizing inconsistencies within the experiment that may lead to results outside the parameters of the hypothesis. For example, some constants in the above case are that all plants receive the same amount of water, all plants are potted in the same kind of soil, the species of the plant used in each condition is the same, and the plants are stored at the same temperature. If, for instance, the plants received different amounts of water as well as light, it would be impossible to tell whether the plants responded to changes in water or light.

Once the experiment begins, a disciplined scientist must always record the observations in meticulous detail, usually in a journal. A good journal includes dates, times, and exact values of both variables and constants. Upon reading this journal, a different scientist should be able to clearly understand the experiment and recreate it exactly. The journal includes all **collected data**, or any observed changes. In this case, the data is rates of plant growth, as well as any other phenomena that occurred as a result of the experiment. A well-designed experiment also includes repetition in order to get the most accurate possible readings and to account for any errors, so several trials may be conducted.

Even in the presence of diligent constants, there are an infinite number of reasons that an experiment can (and will) go wrong, known as **sources of error**. All experimental results are inherently accepted as imperfect, if ever so slightly, because experiments are conducted by human beings, and no instrument can measure anything perfectly. The goal of scientists is to minimize those errors to the best of their ability. (Determining sources of error will be discussed in a subsequent section.)

Evaluating and Generalizing

Trends in Data

The ability to recognize trends in data allows scientists to make predictions, not only about the present or near future (such as in a hypothesis), but also about the distant future and even the past. The practice of collecting data and spotting patterns is referred to as **trend analysis**.

Graphs, charts, and tables are helpful in interpreting quantitative data because they provide a visual representation that can be easily analyzed. Graphs are typically created from the tables and charts in which the data were collected. The line graph on plant growth, for example, was created from the data table of observations. The methods in which data are presented (graphs, charts, etc.) are simply ways for scientists to determine trends by recognizing relationships between variables.

Relationships Between Variables

The most common relationship examined in an experiment is between two variables (independent and dependent), most often referred to as x and y. The independent variable (x) is displayed on the horizontal axis of a coordinate plane, and the dependent variable (y) is displayed on the vertical axis.

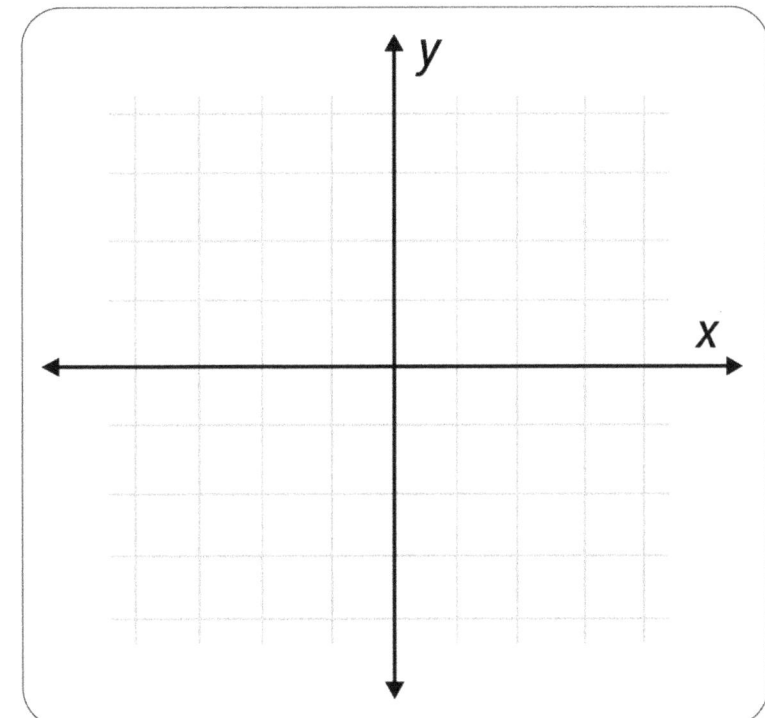

The placement of the variables in this way provides a visual representation of what happens to y when x is manipulated. In analyzing trends, x is used to predict y, and since y is the result of x, then x comes before y in time. For example, in the experiment on plant growth, the hours the plant was exposed to light had to happen before growth could occur.

When analyzing the relationship between the variables, scientists will consider the following questions:

- Does y increase or decrease with x, or does it do both?
- If it increases or decreases, how fast does it change?
- Does y stay steady through certain values of x, or does it jump dramatically from one value to the other?
- Is there a strong relationship? If given a value of x, can one predict what will happen to y?

If, in general, y increases as x increases, or y decreases and x decreases, it is known as a **positive correlation**. The data from the plant experiment show a positive correlation—as time exposed to light (x) increases, plant growth (y) increases. If the variables trend in the opposite direction of each other—that is, if y increases as x decreases, or vice versa—it is called a **negative correlation**. If there doesn't seem to be any visible pattern to the relationship, it is referred to as *no* or **zero correlation**.

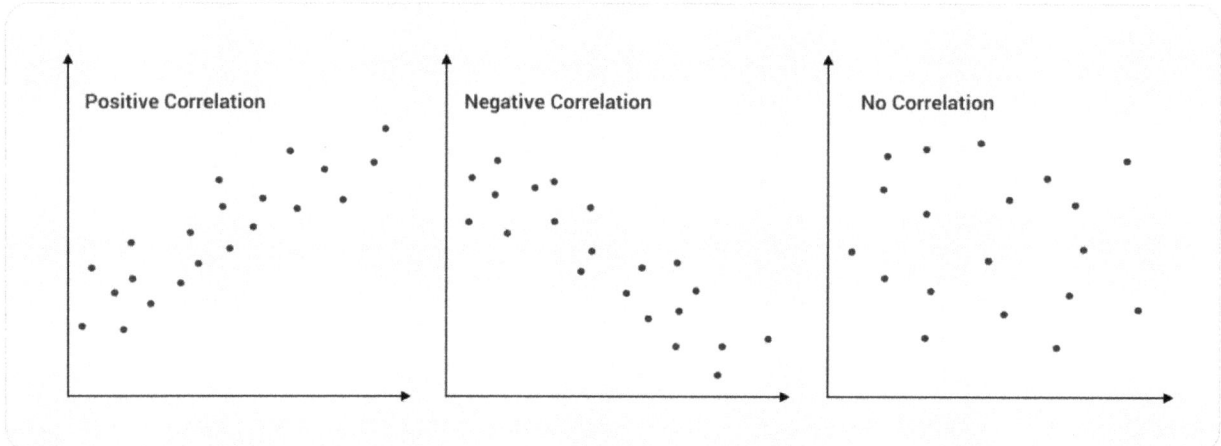

Experiments that show positive or negative correlation within their data indicate that the variables are related. This allows scientists to make predictions based on the data.

Predictions Based on Data

Science is amazing in that it actually allows people to predict the future and see into the past with a certain degree of accuracy. Using numerical correlations created from quantitative data, one can see in a general way what will happen to y when something happens to x.

The best way to get a useful overview of quantitative data to facilitate predictions is to use a scatter plot, which plots each data point individually. As shown above, there may be slight fluctuations from the correlation line, so one may not be able to predict what happens with *every* change, but he or she will be able to have a general idea of what is going to happen to *y* with a change in *x*. To demonstrate, the graph with a line of best fit created from the plant growth experiment is below.

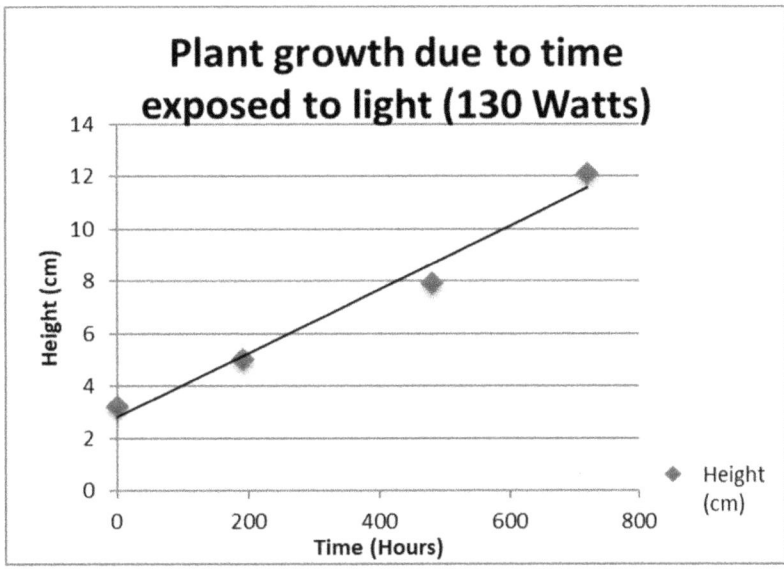

Using the trend line within the data, one can estimate what will happen to plant growth at a given length of time exposed to light. For example, it can be estimated that with 700 hours of time, the plant is expected to grow to a height of about 11 cm. The plant may not grow to exactly 11 cm, but it will likely grow to about that height based on previous data. This process allows scientists to draw conclusions based on data.

Drawing Valid Conclusions Based on Data

Drawing conclusions is the process of analyzing patterns in data and determining whether the relationship is **causal**, meaning that one variable is the cause of the change in the other. There are many correlations that aren't casual, such as a city where alcohol sales increase as crime increases. Although there's a positive correlation between the two, crime may not be the factor that causes an increase in alcohol sales. There could be other factors, such as an increase in unemployment, which increases both alcohol sales and crime rates. Although crime and alcohol sales are positively correlated, they aren't causally correlated.

For this reason, it's important for scientists to carefully design their experiments with all the appropriate constants to ensure that the relationships are causal. If a relationship is determined to be causal by isolating the variables from all other factors, only then can conclusions be drawn based on data. In the plant growth experiment, the conclusion is that light affects plant growth because the data shows they are causally correlated since the two variables were entirely isolated.

Practice Quiz

1. Which of the following structures is unique to eukaryotic cells?
    a. Cell walls
    b. Nuclei
    c. Cell membranes
    d. Organelles

2. Which cellular organelle is used for digestion to recycle materials?
    a. The Golgi apparatus
    b. The lysosome
    c. The centrioles
    d. The mitochondria

3. The fact that the Earth is tilted as it revolves around the Sun creates which phenomenon?
    a. Life
    b. Plate tectonics
    c. Wind
    d. Seasonality

4. Which of the following scientists contributed the theory of gravitation, the theory of color, and the major laws of motion?
    a. Charles Darwin
    b. Albert Einstein
    c. Max Planck
    d. Isaac Newton

5. "This flower is dead; someone must have forgotten to water it." This statement is an example of which of the following?
    a. A classification
    b. An observation
    c. An inference
    d. A collection

See answers on the next page.

Answer Explanations

1. B: The structure exclusively found in eukaryotic cells is the nucleus. Animal, plant, fungi, and protist cells are all eukaryotic. DNA is contained within the nucleus of eukaryotic cells, and they also have membrane-bound organelles that perform complex intracellular metabolic activities. Prokaryotic cells (archaea and bacteria) do not have a nucleus or other membrane-bound organelles and are less complex than eukaryotic cells.

2. B: The cell structure responsible for cellular storage, digestion, and waste removal is the lysosome. Lysosomes are like recycle bins. They are filled with digestive enzymes that facilitate catabolic reactions to regenerate monomers. The Golgi apparatus is designed to tag, package, and ship out proteins destined for other cells or locations. The centrioles typically play a large role only in cell division when they ratchet the chromosomes from the mitotic plate to the poles of the cell. The mitochondria are involved in energy production and are the powerhouses of the cell.

3. D: This is the only answer choice created by Earth's tilt. The Earth rotates around the Sun at an axis of 23.5 degrees, which causes different latitudes to receive varying amounts of direct sunlight throughout the year.

4. D: Isaac Newton is most famous for his contributions to science through the theory of gravitation, the theory of color, and laws of motion, which makes Choice *D* the correct answer. Charles Darwin is responsible for the theory of evolution by natural selection, so Choice *A* is incorrect. Albert Einstein is most famous for his theory of mass-energy equivalence and theories of relativity, so Choice *B* isn't the correct answer. Finally, Max Planck was the originator of quantum theory and the processes that occur at the subatomic level; thus, Choice *C* is also incorrect.

5. C: An inference is a logical prediction of a why an event occurred based on previous experiences or education. The person in this example knows that plants need water to survive; therefore, the prediction that someone forgot to water the plant is a reasonable inference, hence Choice *C* is correct. A classification is the grouping of events or objects into categories, so Choice *A* is incorrect. An observation analyzes situations using human senses, so Choice *B* is incorrect. Choice *D* is incorrect because collecting is the act of gathering data for analysis.

Social Studies

History

Analyzing Historical Sources and Recognizing Perspectives

Primary and Secondary Sources

Traditionally, historical documents have been separated into two major categories: primary sources and secondary sources. Understanding the features of each is crucial for building historical inquiry skills. Students must learn how to deconstruct primary and secondary sources to gain a better understanding of historical context and personal perspective.

Primary sources contain firsthand documentation of a historical event or era. Primary sources are provided by people who have experienced an historical era or event. Primary sources capture a specific moment, context, or era in history. They are valued as eyewitness accounts and personal perspectives. Examples include diaries, memoirs, journals, letters, interviews, photographs, context-specific artwork, government documents, constitutions, newspapers, personal items, libraries, and archives. Another example of a primary source is the Declaration of Independence. This historical document captures the revolutionary sentiment of an era in American history.

Authors of secondary sources write about events, contexts, and eras in history with a relative amount of experiential, geographic, or temporal distance. Normally, secondary source authors aren't firsthand witnesses. In some cases, they may have experienced an event, but they are offering secondhand, retrospective accounts of their experience. All scholars and historians produce secondary sources—they gather primary source information and synthesize it for a new generation of students. Monographs, biographies, magazine articles, scholarly journals, theses, dissertations, textbooks, and encyclopedias are all secondary sources. In some rare instances, secondary sources become so enmeshed in their era of inquiry that they later become primary sources for future scholars and analysts.

Validity of Social Studies Information

Relevant information is that which is pertinent to the topic at hand. Particularly when doing research online, it is easy to get overwhelmed with the wealth of information available. Before conducting research, then, students need to begin with a clear idea of the question they want to answer.

For example, a student may be interested in learning more about marriage practices in Jane Austen's England. If that student types "marriage" into a search engine, he or she will have to sift through thousands of unrelated sites before finding anything related to that topic. Narrowing down search parameters, then, can aid in locating relevant information.

When using a book, students can consult the table of contents, glossary, or index to discover whether the book contains relevant information before using it as a resource. If the student finds a hefty volume on Jane Austen, he or she can flip to the index in the back, look for the word *marriage* and find out how many page references are listed in the book. If there are few or no references to the subject, it is probably not a relevant or useful source.

In evaluating research articles, students may also consult the title, abstract, and keywords before reading the article in its entirety. Referring to the date of publication will also determine whether the research contains up-to-date discoveries, theories, and ideas about the subject or is outdated.

Social Studies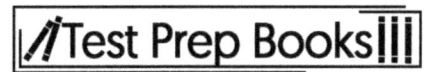

There are several additional criteria that need to be examined before using a source for a research topic.

The following questions will help determine whether a source is credible:

Author

- Who is he or she?
- Does he or she have the appropriate credentials—e.g., M.D, PhD?
- Is this person authorized to write on the matter through their job or personal experiences?
- Is he or she affiliated with any known credible individuals or organizations?
- Has he or she written anything else?

Publisher

- Who published/produced the work? Is it a well-known journal, like National Geographic, or a tabloid, like The National Enquirer?
- Is the publisher from a scholarly, commercial, or government association?
- Do they publish works related to specific fields?
- Have they published other works?
- If a digital source, what kind of website hosts the text? Does it end in .edu, .org, or .com?

Bias

- Is the writing objective? Does it contain any loaded or emotional language?
- Does the publisher/producer have a known bias, such as Fox News or CNN?
- Does the work include diverse opinions or perspectives?
- Does the author have any known bias—e.g., Michael Moore, Bill O'Reilly, or the Pope? Is he or she affiliated with any organizations or individuals that may have a known bias—e.g., Citizens United or the National Rifle Association?
- Does the magazine, book, journal, or website contain any advertising?

References

- Are there any references?
- Are the references credible? Do they follow the same criteria as stated above?
- Are the references from a related field?

Accuracy/Reliability

- Has the article, book, or digital source been peer reviewed?
- Are all of the conclusions, supporting details, or ideas backed with published evidence?
- If a digital source, is it free of grammatical errors, poor spelling, and improper English?
- Do other published individuals have similar findings?

Coverage

- Are the topic and related material both successfully addressed?
- Does the work add new information or theories to those of their sources?
- Is the target audience appropriate for the intended purpose?

Multiple Points of View and Frames of Reference

Many people want to rise above their historical contexts, but it is an impossibility. Whether one likes it or not, the ideas of humanity are always influenced by the forces of history. The individual and collective consciousness of

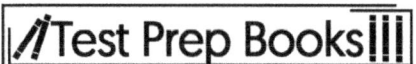

humanity is often dictated by historical events and situations. A Jew writing in Germany during World War II would inevitably be affected in some capacity by the anti-Semitic tendencies of Nazism. A Texas-based Mexican national writing during the Mexican-American War of the 1840s would inevitably be influenced by American expansionism. A college student writing and liking posts on Facebook during the Great Recession of 2008 would inevitably be exposed to the effects of the stock market's decline. Even if the author does not comment on these events, they still shape the author's point of view. When analyzing a history text or a historical cartoon, test takers should first ask key questions: When, where, and why was this documented created? Often the answers to these questions provide test takers with the evidence they need to properly analyze the documents and answer multiple choice questions.

In some cases, the author of a document explicitly comments on history. The author may refer to historical persons, events, or dates. Test takers should take note of these persons, events, and dates because they offer evidence for answering questions or prompts. For instance, a primary source such as Anne Frank's diary directly refers to the events of World War II and the aggressions of Germans. In other cases, it is up to the test taker to decode the implicit messages embedded in a text in order to gain a better understanding of historical influences. A good place to start with this decoding process is the date the document was created. If test takers know the date of a document, they can begin to illuminate historical correlations. For instance, a historian writing in the 1960s might not explicitly discuss the historical opinions of the New Left (a political movement of the 1960s), but a test taker may be able to decode the implicit messages embedded in the text and infer that the historian may have been influenced by that era of political thought.

Evaluating Whether the Author's Evidence is Factual, Relevant, and Sufficient

It's important to read any piece of writing critically. The goal is to discover the point and purpose of what the author is writing about through analysis. It's also crucial to establish the point or stance the author has taken on the topic of the piece. After determining the author's perspective, readers can then more effectively develop their own viewpoints on the subject.

If the argument is that wind energy is the best solution, the author will use facts that support this idea. That same author may leave out relevant facts on solar energy. The way the author uses facts can influence the reader, so it's important to consider the facts being used, how those facts are being presented, and what information might be left out.

Making Judgments About How Different Ideas Impact the Author's Argument

To reach supportable judgments and conclusions in social studies, students must be prepared to categorize and synthesize a variety of primary and secondary sources, paying close attention to which sources are legitimate sources of fact or opinion. Students must also be able to justifiably quote information from these sources to establish historical generalizations, or general statements that identify themes that unite or separate source materials. Often, a generalization identifies key features, relationships, or differences found throughout multiple sources.

Identifying Bias

Bias exists in all forms of written and visual documentation. In social studies, it is especially important to look out for bias, in both primary and secondary sources. Bias can stem from various sources, including: historical context, cultural background, personal beliefs, political affiliation, and religious values. All these things shape the way an individual sees and writes about history and society. For example, a conservative author writing in the late 1980s may have been likely to support the political initiative known as the War on Drugs. This likelihood is due to political affiliation and historical context. The 1980s was a conservative era in American politics, thanks to the rise of President Ronald Reagan. It was also a historical era that responded accordingly to the crack epidemic and gained conservative support for expanded police enforcement. Additionally, a communist political cartoonist in the Soviet Union during the Cold War may be likely to paint a picture of the United States as an aggressor. That era of history

Social Studies

pitted the Soviet Union against the United States on a global level. Biases even emerge in secondary sources; people analyzing history are influenced by their own cultural-historical contexts.

Outlines, Reports, Databases, Narratives, Literature, and Visuals

Students should not only be able to analyze maps and other infographics, but they should also be able to create graphs, charts, tables, documents, maps, timelines, and other visual materials to represent geographic, political, historical, economic, and cultural features. Students should be made aware of the different options they have to present data. They should understand that maps visually display geographic features, and they can be used to illustrate key relationships in human geography and natural geography. Maps can indicate themes in history, politics, economics, culture, social relationships, demographic distributions, and climate change. Students can also choose to display data or information in a variety of graphs: Bar graphs compare two or more things with parallel bars; line graphs show change over time with strategic points placed carefully between vertical and horizontal axes; and pie graphs divide wholes into percentages or parts. Likewise, students can choose to use timelines or tables to present data/information. Timelines arrange events or ideas into chronological order, and tables arrange words or numbers into columns or rows. Outlines can be used by students to organize data into topics and subtopics. Narratives and reports can be used to present findings and thoughts in a cohesive written format. These are just some of the visual tools students can use to help visually convey their historical questions or ideas.

Maps and Other Graphics

Geographers utilize a variety of maps in their study of the spatial world. Projections are maps that represent the spherical globe on a flat surface. Conformal projections attempt to preserve shape but distort size and area. For example, the most well-known projection, the Mercator projection, drastically distorts the size of land areas at the poles. In this particular map, Antarctica, one of the smallest continents, appears massive, while the areas closer to the equator are depicted more accurately. Other projections attempt to lessen the amount of distortion; the equal-area projection, for example, attempts to accurately represent the size of landforms. However, equal-area projections alter the shapes and angles of landforms regardless of their positioning on the map. Other projections are hybrids of the two primary models. For example, the Robinson projection tries to balance form and area in order to create a more visually accurate representation of the spatial world. Despite the efforts to maintain consistency with shapes, projections cannot provide accurate representations of the Earth's surface due to their flat, two-dimensional nature. In this sense, projections are useful symbols of space, but they do not always provide the most accurate portrayal of reality.

Unlike projections, topographic maps display contour lines, which represent the relative elevation of a particular place and are very useful for surveyors, engineers, and/or travelers. For example, hikers may refer to topographic maps to calculate their daily climbs.

Similar to topographic maps, **isoline maps** are also useful for calculating data and differentiating between the characteristics of two places. These maps use symbols to represent values and lines to connect points with the same value. For example, an isoline map could display average temperatures of a given area. The sections which share the same average temperature would be grouped together by lines. Additionally, isoline maps can help geographers study the world by generating questions. For example, is elevation the only reason for differences in temperature? If not, what other factors could cause the disparity between the values?

Thematic maps are also quite useful because they display the geographical distribution of complex political, physical, social, cultural, economic, or historical themes. For example, a thematic map could indicate an area's election results using a different color for each candidate. There are several different kinds of thematic maps, including dot-density maps and flow-line maps. A *dot-density map* uses dots to illustrate volume and density; these dots could represent a certain population, or the number of specific events that have taken place in an area. Flow-line maps utilize lines of varying thicknesses to illustrate the movement of goods, people, or even animals between

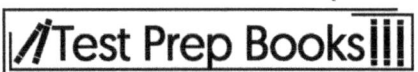

two places. Thicker lines represent a greater number of moving elements, and thinner lines represent a smaller number.

Interconnections Among the Past, Present, and Future

Analyzing Cause-and-Effect Relationships

Every time someone studies history, it is very much a collision of past, present, and future. Historians are concerned for the past, rooted in the present, and thinking about the future. Historical analysis is, therefore, a process infusing the present in the past in hopes of predicting (or deterring) certain social interactions in the future.

When examining the historical narratives of events, it is important to understand the relationship between causes and effects. A cause can be defined as something, whether an event, social change, or other factor, that contributes to the occurrence of certain events; the results of causes are called effects. Those terms may seem simple enough, but they have drastic implications on how one explores history. Events such as the American Revolution or the Civil Rights Movement may appear to occur spontaneously, but a closer examination will reveal that these events depended on earlier phenomena and patterns that influenced the course of history.

There can be multiple causes and effects for any situation. The existence of multiple causes can be seen through the settling of the American West. Many historians have emphasized the role of Manifest Destiny—the national vision of expanding across the continent—as a driving force behind the growth of the United States. Yet there were many different influences behind the expansion westward. Northern abolitionists and southern planters saw the frontier as a way to either extend or limit slavery. Economic opportunities in the West also encouraged travel westward, as did the gradual pacification, relocation, or eradication of Native American tribes. In fact, Manifest Destiny as well as economic and political reasons played significant roles in justifying the pacification, relocation, or eradication of the Native American tribal nations.

Even an individual cause can be subdivided into smaller factors or stretched out in a gradual process. Although there were numerous issues that led to the Civil War, slavery was the primary cause. However, that topic stretched back to the very founding of the nation, and the existence of slavery was a controversial topic during the creation of the Declaration of Independence and the Constitution. The abolition movement as a whole did not start until the 1830s, but nevertheless, slavery is a cause that gradually grew more important over the following decades. In addition, opponents of slavery were divided by different motivations—some believed that it stifled the economy, while others focused on moral issues.

On the other end of the spectrum, a single event can have numerous results. The rise of the telegraph, for example, had several effects on American history. The telegraph allowed news to travel much quicker and turned events into immediate national news, such as the sinking of the USS Maine, which sparked the Spanish-American War. In addition, the telegraph helped make railroads run more efficiently by improving the links between stations. The faster speed of both travel and communications led to a shift in time itself, and localized times were replaced by standardized time zones across the nation.

By looking at different examples of cause and effect closely, it becomes clear that no event occurs without one—if not multiple—causes behind it, and that each historical event can have a variety of direct and indirect consequences.

One of the most critical elements of cause-and-effect relationships is how they are relevant not only in studying history but also in contemporary events. People must realize that events and developments today will likely have a number of consequences later on. Therefore, the study of cause and effect remains vital in understanding the past, the present, and the future.

Describing the Connections Between People, Places, Environments, Processes, and Events

The primary role of social studies is to illuminate connections between people, places, environments, processes, and events. Therefore, test takers must be prepared to examine correlations and causations in social studies. Correlations are connections that do not necessarily show any signs of causation. Two things are correlated when they happen to the same people, or in the same circumstances, or at the same time. For example, the increased popularity of apocalyptic literature in 2008 and 2009 can be **correlated** with the Great Recession that occurred around that time. However, these two events might not be **causally related**. A relationship is causal when one thing causes another to happen. In other words, the rise in apocalyptic literature may be caused by other cultural changes, such as an increasing disenchantment with humanity, a disenchantment caused by an increase in global wars and genocide.

Other connections can be discovered by analyzing causation. For instance, the mass immigration of Irish workers to the United States in the 19th century can likely be understood as a cause and effect scenario spawned by the great potato famine of that era—immigrants had to flee Ireland because their families were going to starve to death. In this instance, one thing caused another. Students of social studies must constantly be on the search for these connections. They must study the ways in which geography (for example, the Rio Grande River) affects immigration patterns (for example, undocumented immigration from Mexico to America in the 20th and 21st centuries). They must even be aware of the ways in which people (for example, Adolf Hitler) influence events (the rise of Nazi Germany in the 1930s and 1940s).

Connections are discussed in passages, political cartoons, and test questions. Test takers must be able to contextualize, historicize, and analyze connections. Too often the field of social studies is taught as a linear timeline. But, in reality, the field of social studies is more like a complex web of ideas, characters, events, eras, movements, counter-movements, and belief systems. Additionally, views of historical events change throughout history. Today we may analyze slavery differently than the era in which slavery was legal in the United States. Therefore, students of social studies must also be aware of their own connections to history and all the variables that form its foundations. Below is one example of a cognitive map showing the connections between people, places, environments, processes, and events in social studies.

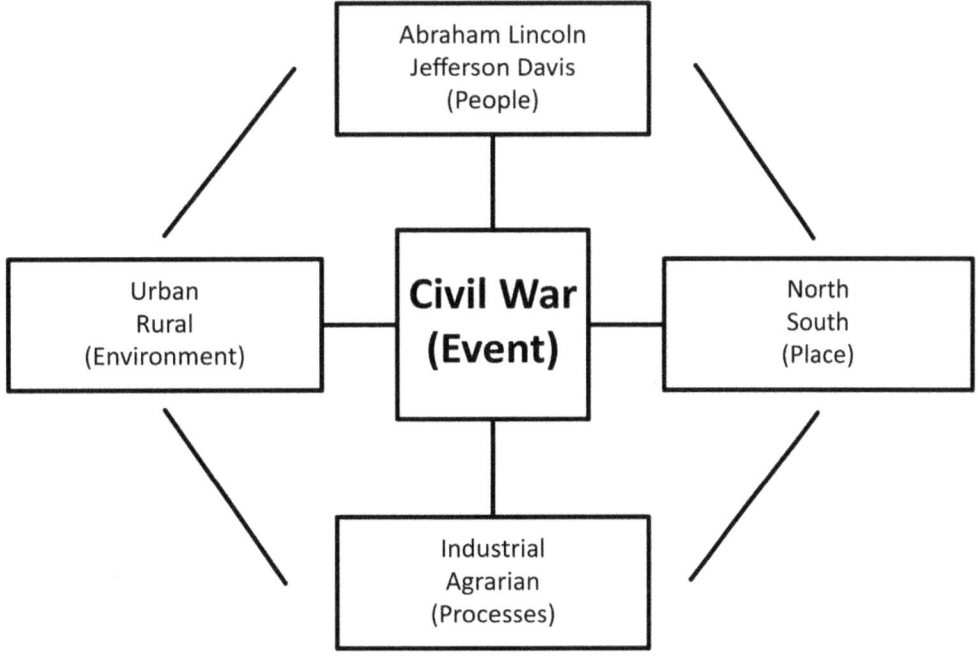

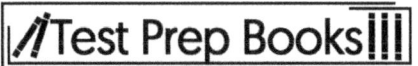

Putting Events in Order and Understanding the Steps in a Process

Social studies students must understand how to determine the timeline/chronology of events through a process called sequencing. Sequencing allows students to gain a better understanding of change over time in history. Social studies exams often employ test questions that force students to recall the correct chronology, or time order, of important historical events.

Along with sequencing, social studies students should be able to carry out a process known as categorizing. Categorizing is the process by which historical themes, events, agents, persons, movements, or ideas are placed in designated categories that help students understand their historical significance. Categorization is usually most effective when certain words or phrases are organized by themes or concepts. For instance, the categorical concept of "economic depression" could help students better understand such historical events as the Panic of 1819, the Great Depression, and the Great Recession. Categorization allows students to link unrelated events in history.

Identifying associations and cause-and-effect relationships strengthens a student's ability to sequence events in history. All U.S. history is a series of associated events leading to still other events. A cause is what made something happen. An effect is what happens because of something. Understanding cause-and-effect helps students to understand the proverbial *why* of history; it helps them breathe more meaning into history.

Comparing and contrasting is another strategy that will make students more historically informed. In history, we often compare two or more things to understand their similarities and differences better. Part of the historical process is understanding what historical characteristics are unique or utterly common. Students might, for instance, compare and contrast the American Revolution to the Texas Revolution to gain a better understanding of the ways in which such variables as time, geographic location, and contributing persons affect history.

Summarizing is a strategy that is also used often throughout the historical process in a social studies classroom. Students will not only have to summarize the meaning of historical events or eras, but they will also need to know how to summarize the important points of primary and secondary sources. Summaries allow students to convey their knowledge in a short, concise, digestible fashion. Part of summarizing requires that students find the main idea of a particular article, source, or paragraph. Main ideas help students make their summaries even more concise and effective. Summarizing sometimes requires students to make generalizations or draw inferences/conclusions. Often there are "gaps of information" in the sources provided to students. Students will have to use background knowledge and critical-thinking skills to fill in these gaps with generalizations (broad, sweeping statements) or inferences/conclusions (educated guesses, predictions, or assumptions).

Analyzing the Relationship of Events, Processes, and/or Ideas

Events, processes, and ideas can be related in different ways. Earlier events don't necessarily *cause* later ones; in many cases, they simply occurred prior to the later event. For example, although the battles at Concord and Lexington may seem to be instantaneous eruptions of violence during the American Revolution, they stemmed from a variety of factors. The most obvious influences behind those two battles were the assortment of taxes and policies imposed on the Thirteen Colonies following the French and Indian War from 1754 to 1763. Taxation without direct representation, combined with the deployment of British soldiers to enforce these policies, greatly increased American resistance. Earlier events, such as the Boston Massacre and the Boston Tea Party, similarly stemmed from conflicts between British soldiers and local colonists over perceived tyranny and rebelliousness. Therefore, the start of the American Revolution progressed from earlier developments.

Specific Eras in World and U.S. History

Classical Civilizations

There were a number of powerful civilizations during the classical period. Mesopotamia was home to one of the earliest civilizations between the Euphrates and the Tigris rivers in the Near East. The rivers provided water and

Social Studies

vegetation for early humans, but they were surrounded by desert. This led to the beginning of irrigation efforts to expand water and agriculture across the region, which resulted in the area being known as the Fertile Crescent.

The organization necessary to initiate canals and other projects led to the formation of cities and hierarchies, which would have considerable influence on the structure of later civilizations. For example, the new hierarchies established different classes within the societies, such as kings, priests, artisans, and workers. Over time, these city-states expanded to encompass outside territories, and the city of Akkad became the world's first empire in 2350 B.C. In addition, Mesopotamian scribes developed systemized drawings called pictograms, which were the first system of writing in the world; furthermore, the creation of wedge-shaped cuneiform tablets preserved written records for multiple generations.

Later, Mesopotamian kingdoms made further advancements. For example, Babylon established a sophisticated mathematical system based on numbers from one to sixty; this not only influenced modern concepts, such as the number of minutes in each hour, but also created the framework for math equations and theories. In addition, the Babylonian king Hammurabi established a complex set of laws, known as the Code of Hammurabi, which would set a precedent for future legal systems.

Meanwhile, another major civilization began to form around the Nile River in Africa. The Nile's relatively predictable nature allowed farmers to use the river's water and the silt from floods to grow many crops along its banks, which led to further advancements in irrigation. Egyptian rulers mobilized the kingdom's population for incredible construction projects, including the famous pyramids. Egyptians also improved pictographic writing with their more complex system of hieroglyphs, which allowed for more diverse styles of writing. The advancements in writing can be seen through the Egyptians' complex system of religion, with documents such as the *Book of the Dead* outlining not only systems of worship and pantheons of deities but also a deeper, more philosophical concept of the afterlife.

While civilizations in Egypt and Mesopotamia helped to establish class systems and empires, other forms of government emerged in Greece. Despite common ties between different cities, such as the Olympic Games, each settlement, known as a polis, had its own unique culture. Many of the cities were oligarchies, in which a council of distinguished leaders monopolized the government; others were dictatorships ruled by tyrants. Athens was a notable exception by practicing an early form of democracy in which free, landholding men could participate, but it offered more freedom of thought than other systems.

Taking advantage of their proximity to the Mediterranean Sea, Greek cities sent expeditions to establish colonies abroad that developed their own local traditions. In the process, Greek merchants interacted with Phoenician traders, who had developed an alphabetic writing system built on sounds instead of pictures. This diverse network of exchanges made Greece a vibrant center of art, science, and philosophy. For example, the Greek doctor Hippocrates established a system of ethics for doctors called the Hippocratic Oath, which continues to guide the modern medical profession. Complex forms of literature were created, including the epic poem "The Iliad," and theatrical productions were also developed. Athens in particular sought to spread its vision of democratic freedom throughout the world, which led to the devastating Peloponnesian War between allies of Athens and those of oligarchic Sparta from 431 to 404 B.C.

Alexander the Great helped disseminate Greek culture to new regions. Alexander was in fact an heir to the throne of Macedon, which was a warrior kingdom to the north of Greece. After finishing his father's work of unifying Greece under Macedonian control, Alexander successfully conquered Mesopotamia, which had been part of the Persian Empire. The spread of Greek institutions throughout the Mediterranean and Near East led to a period of Hellenization, during which various civilizations assimilated Greek culture; this allowed Greek traditions, such as architecture and philosophy, to endure into the present day.

Greek ideas were later assimilated, along with many other concepts, into the Roman Empire. Located west of Greece on the Italian peninsula, Rome greatly expanded its territories and grew to be a powerful empire through the conquering of its neighboring civilizations; by 44 B.C., Rome had conquered much of Western Europe, northern Africa, and the Near East. Romans were very creative, and they adapted new ideas and innovated new technologies to strengthen their power. For example, Romans built on the engineering knowledge of Greeks to create arched pathways, known as aqueducts, to transport water for long distances and devise advanced plumbing systems.

One of Rome's greatest legacies was its system of government. Early Rome was a republic, a democratic system in which leaders are elected by the people. Although the process still heavily favored wealthy elites, the republican system was a key inspiration for later institutions such as the United States. Octavian "Augustus" Caesar later made Rome into an empire, and the senate had only a symbolic role in the government. The new imperial system built on the examples of earlier empires to establish a vibrant dynasty that used a sophisticated legal code and a well-trained military to enforce order across vast regions. Even after Rome itself fell to barbarian invaders in fifth century A.D., the eastern half of the empire survived as the Byzantine Empire until 1453 A.D. Furthermore, the Roman Empire's institutions continued to influence and inspire later medieval kingdoms, including the Holy Roman Empire; even rulers in the twentieth century called themselves Kaiser and Tsar, titles which stem from the word "Caesar."

In addition, the Roman Empire was host to the spread of new religious ideas. In the region of Israel, the religion of Judaism presented a new approach to worship via monotheism, which is the belief in the existence of a single deity. An offshoot of Judaism called Christianity spread across the Roman Empire and gained popularity. While Rome initially suppressed the religion, it later backed Christianity and allowed the religious system to endure as a powerful force in medieval times.

Twentieth-Century Development and Transformations in World History

At the turn of the twentieth century, imperialism had led to powers, such as France, the United States, and Japan, to establish spheres of influence throughout the world. The combination of imperial competition and military rivalries led to the outbreak of World War I when Archduke Ferdinand of Austria was assassinated in 1914. The war pitted the Allies, including England, France, and Russia, against the Central Powers of Austria-Hungary, Germany, and the Ottoman Empire—a large Islamic realm that encompassed Turkey, Palestine, Saudi Arabia, and Iraq. The rapid advances in military technology turned the war into a prolonged bloodbath that took its toll on all sides. By the end of the war in 1918, the Ottoman Empire had collapsed, the Austrian-Hungarian Empire was split into multiple countries, and Russia had descended into a civil war that would lead to the rise of the Soviet Union and Communism.

The Treaty of Versailles ended the war, but the triumphant Allies also levied heavy fines on Germany, which led to resentment that would be accentuated by the Great Depression of the 1930s. The Great Depression destabilized the global economy and led to the rise of fascism, a militarized and dictatorial system of government, in nations such as Germany and Italy. The rapid expansion of the Axis Powers of Germany, Italy, and Japan led to the outbreak of World War II. The war was even more global than the previous conflicts, with battles occurring in Europe, Africa, and Asia. World War II encouraged the development of new technologies, such as advanced radar and nuclear weapons, that would continue to influence the course of future wars.

In the aftermath of World War II, the United Nations was formed as a step toward promoting international cooperation. Based on the preceding League of Nations, the United Nations included countries from around the world and gave them a voice in world policies. The formation of the United Nations coincided with the independence of formerly colonized states in Africa and Asia, and those countries joined the world body. A primary goal of the United Nations was to limit the extent of future wars and prevent a third world war; while the United Nations could not prevent the outbreak of wars, it nevertheless tried to peacefully resolve them. In addition to promoting world peace, the United Nations also helped protect human rights.

Even so, the primary leadership in the early United Nations was held by the United States and its allies, which contributed to tensions with the Soviet Union. The United States and the Soviet Union, while never declaring war on each other, fueled a number of proxy wars and coups across the world in what would be known as the Cold War.

Cold War divisions were especially noticeable in Europe, where communist regimes ruled the eastern region and democratic governments controlled the western portion. These indirect struggles often involved interference with foreign politics, and sometimes local people began to resent Soviet or American attempts to influence their countries. For example, American and Soviet interventions in Iran and Afghanistan contributed to fundamentalist Islamic movements. The Cold War ended when the Soviet Union collapsed in 1991, but the conflict affected nations across the globe and continues to influence current issues.

Another key development during the twentieth century, as noted earlier with the United Nations, was that most colonized nations broke free from imperial control and asserted their independence. Although these nations achieved autonomy and recognition in the United Nations, they still suffered from the legacies of imperialism. The borders of many countries in Africa and Asia were arbitrarily determined by colonists with little regard to the arrangement of native populations. Therefore, many former colonies have suffered conflicts between different ethnic groups; this was also the case with the British colony in India, which became independent in 1947. Violence occurred when it split into India and Pakistan because the borders were largely based on religious differences. In addition, former colonial powers continue to assert economic control that inhibits the growth of native economies. On the other hand, the end of direct imperialism has helped a number of nations, such as India and Iran, rise as world powers that have significant influence on the world as a whole.

Additionally, there were considerable environmental reforms worldwide during the twentieth century. In reaction to the growing effects of industrialization, organizations around the world protested policies that damaged the environment. Many of these movements were locally based, but others expanded to address various environmental threats across the globe. The United Nations helped carry these environmental reforms forward by making them part of international policies. For example, in 1997, many members of the United Nations signed a treaty, known as the *Kyoto Protocol*, that tried to reduce global carbon dioxide emissions.

Most significantly, the twentieth century marked increasing globalization. The process had already been under way in the nineteenth century as technological improvements and imperial expansions connected different parts of the world, but the late twentieth century brought globalization to a new level. Trade became international, and local customs from different lands also gained prominence worldwide. Cultural exchanges occur on a frequent basis, and many people have begun to ponder the consequences of such rapid exchanges. One example of globalization was the 1993 establishment of the European Union—an economic and political alliance between several European nations.

European Exploration and Colonization in the U.S.

When examining how Europeans explored what would become the United States of America, one must first examine why Europeans came to explore the New World as a whole. In the fifteenth century, tensions increased between the Eastern and Mediterranean nations of Europe and the expanding Ottoman Empire to the east. As war and piracy spread across the Mediterranean, the once-prosperous trade routes across Asia's Silk Road began to decline, and nations across Europe began to explore alternative routes for trade.

Italian explorer Christopher Columbus proposed a westward route. Contrary to popular lore, the main challenge that Columbus faced in finding backers was not proving that the world was round. Much of Europe's educated elite knew that the world was round; the real issue was that they rightly believed that a westward route to Asia, assuming a lack of obstacles, would be too long to be practical. Nevertheless, Columbus set sail in 1492 after obtaining support from Spain and arrived in the West Indies three months later.

Spain launched further expeditions to the new continents and established *New Spain*. The colony consisted not only of Central America and Mexico, but also the American Southwest and Florida. France claimed much of what would become Canada, along with the Mississippi River region and the Midwest. In addition, the Dutch established colonies that covered New Jersey, New York, and Connecticut. Each nation managed its colonies differently, and thus influenced how they would assimilate into the United States. For example, Spain strove to establish a system of

Christian missions throughout its territory, while France focused on trading networks and had limited infrastructure in regions such as the Midwest.

Even in cases of limited colonial growth, the land of America was hardly vacant, because a diverse array of Native American nations and groups were already present. Throughout much of colonial history, European settlers commonly misperceived native peoples as a singular, static entity. In reality, Native Americans had a variety of traditions depending on their history and environment, and their culture continued to change throughout the course of their interactions with European settlers. For example, tribes such as the Cheyenne and Comanche used horses, which were introduced by white settlers, to become powerful warrior nations. However, a few generalizations can be made: many, but not all, tribes were matrilineal, which gave women a fair degree of power, and land was commonly seen as belonging to everyone. These differences, particularly European settlers' continual focus on land ownership, contributed to increasing prejudice and violence.

Situated on the Atlantic Coast, the Thirteen Colonies that would become the United States of America constituted only a small portion of North America. Even those colonies had significant differences that stemmed from their different origins. For example, the Virginia colony under John Smith in 1607 started with male bachelors seeking gold, whereas families of Puritans settled Massachusetts. As a result, the Thirteen Colonies—Virginia, Massachusetts, Connecticut, Maryland, New York, New Jersey, Pennsylvania, Delaware, Rhode Island, New Hampshire, Georgia, North Carolina, and South Carolina—had different structures and customs that would each influence the United States.

Competition among several imperial powers in eastern areas of North America led to conflicts that would later bring about the independence of the United States. The French and Indian War from 1754 to 1763, which was a subsidiary war of the Seven Years' War, ended with Great Britain claiming France's Canadian territories as well as the Ohio Valley. The war was costly for all the powers involved, which led to increased taxes on the Thirteen Colonies. In addition, the new lands to the west of the colonies attracted new settlers, and they came into conflict with Native Americans and British troops that were trying to maintain the boundaries laid out by treaties between Great Britain and the Native American tribes. These growing tensions with Great Britain, as well as other issues, eventually led to the American Revolution, which ended with Britain relinquishing its control of the colonies.

Britain continued to hold onto its other colonies, such as Canada and the West Indies, which reflects the continued power of multiple nations across North America, even as the United States began to expand across the continent. Many Americans advocated expansion regardless of the land's current inhabitants, but the results were often mixed. Still, events both abroad and within North America contributed to the growth of the United States. For example, the French Revolution and rise of Napoleon led to the Louisiana Purchase in 1803, when France sold a large chunk of land consisting of Louisiana and much of the Midwest to the United States. Meanwhile, as Spanish power declined, Mexico claimed independence in 1821, but the new nation became increasingly vulnerable to foreign pressure. In the Mexican-American War (1846-1848), Mexico surrendered territory to the United States that eventually became California, Nevada, Utah, and New Mexico, as well as parts of Arizona, Colorado, and Wyoming.

Even as the United States sought new inland territory, American interests were also expanding overseas via trade. As early as 1784, the ship *Empress of China* traveled to China to establish trading connections. American interests had international dimensions throughout the nation's history. For example, during the presidency of Andrew Jackson, the *Potomac* was dispatched to Sumatra in 1832 to avenge the deaths of American sailors. This incident exemplifies how U.S. foreign trade connected with imperial expansion.

This combination of continental and seaward growth adds a deeper layer to American development, because it was not purely focused on western expansion. For example, take the 1849 Gold Rush; a large number of Americans and other immigrants traveled to California by ship and settled western territories before more eastern areas, such as Nevada and Idaho. Therefore, the United States' early history of colonization and expansion is a complex network of diverse cultures.

Social Studies

The American Revolution and the Founding of the Nation in United States History

The American Revolution largely occurred as a result of changing values in the Thirteen Colonies that broke from their traditional relationship with England. Early on in the colonization of North America, the colonial social structure tried to mirror the stratified order of Great Britain. In England, the landed elites were seen as intellectually and morally superior to the common man, which led to a paternalistic relationship. This style of governance was similarly applied to the colonial system; government was left to the property-owning upper class, and the colonies as a whole could be seen as a child dutifully serving "Mother England."

However, the colonies' distance from England meant that actual, hereditary aristocrats from Britain only formed a small percentage of the overall population and did not even fill all the positions of power. By the mid-eighteenth century, much of the American upper class consisted of local families who acquired status through business rather than lineage. Despite this, representatives from Britain were appointed to govern the colonies. As a result, a rift began to form between the colonists and British officials.

Tensions began to rise in the aftermath of the French and Indian War of 1754 to 1763. To recover the financial costs of the long conflict, Great Britain drew upon its colonies to provide the desired resources. Since the American colonists did not fully subscribe to the paternal connection, taxation to increase British revenue, such as the Stamp Act of 1765, was met with increasing resistance. Britain sent soldiers to the colonies and enacted the 1765 Quartering Act to require colonists to house the troops. In 1773, the Tea Act, which legitimized Britain's taxing of the colonies, led disgruntled colonists to raid ships importing tea and destroy their contents in an act known as the Boston Tea Party.

Uncertain about whether they should remain loyal to Britain, representatives from twelve colonies formed the First Continental Congress in 1774 to discuss what they should do next. When Patriot militiamen at Lexington and Concord fought British soldiers in April 1775, the Revolutionary War began. While the rebel forces worked to present the struggle as a united, patriotic effort, the colonies remained divided throughout the war. Thousands of colonists, known as Loyalists or Tories, supported Britain. Even the revolutionaries proved to be significantly fragmented, and many militias only served in their home states. The Continental Congress was also divided over whether to reconcile with Britain or push for full separation. These issues hindered the ability of the revolutionary armies to resist the British, who had superior training and resources at their disposal.

Even so, the Continental Army, under General George Washington, gradually built up a force that utilized Prussian military training and backwoods guerrilla tactics to make up for their limited resources. Although the British forces continued to win significant battles, the Continental Army gradually reduced Britain's will to fight as the years passed. Furthermore, Americans appealed to the rivalry that other European nations had with the British Empire. The support was initially limited to indirect assistance, but aid gradually increased. After the American victory at the Battle of Saratoga in 1777, France and other nations began to actively support the American cause by providing much-needed troops and equipment.

In 1781, the primary British army under General Cornwallis was defeated by an American and French coalition at Yorktown, Virginia, which paved the way for peace negotiations. The Treaty of Paris in 1783 ended the war, recognized the former colonies' independence from Great Britain, and gave America control over territory between the Appalachian Mountains and Mississippi River. However, the state of the new nation was still uncertain. The new nation's government initially stemmed from the state-based structure of the Continental Congress and was incorporated into the Articles of Confederation in 1777.

The Articles of Confederation emphasized the ideals of the American Revolution, particularly the concept of freedom from unjust government. Unfortunately, the resulting limitations on the national government left most policies—even ones with national ramifications—up to individual states. For example, states sometimes simply decided to not pay taxes. Many representatives did not see much value in the National Congress and simply did not attend the meetings. Some progress was still made during the period, such as the Northwest Ordinance of 1787, which organized the western territories into new states; nevertheless, the disjointed links in the state-oriented government inhibited significant progress.

Although many citizens felt satisfied with this decentralized system of government, key intellectuals and leaders in America became increasingly disturbed by the lack of unity. An especially potent fear among them was the potential that, despite achieving official independence, other powers could threaten America's autonomy. In 1786, poor farmers in Massachusetts launched an insurrection, known as Shays' Rebellion, which sparked fears of additional uprisings and led to the creation of the **Constitutional Convention** in 1787.

While the convention initially intended to correct issues within the Articles of Confederation, speakers, such as James Madison, compellingly argued for the delegates to devise a new system of government that was more centralized than its predecessor. The Constitution was not fully supported by all citizens, and there was much debate about whether or not to support the new government. Even so, in 1788, the Constitution was ratified. Later additions, such as the Bill of Rights, would help protect individual liberty by giving specific rights to citizens. In 1789, George Washington became the first president of the newly created executive branch of the government, and America entered a new stage of history.

Major Events and Developments in U.S. History from Founding to Present

One early development was the growth of political parties—something that Washington tried and failed to stop from forming. Federalists, such as Alexander Hamilton, wanted to expand the national government's power, while Democratic-Republicans, such as Thomas Jefferson, favored states' rights. The United States suffered multiple defeats by Britain in the War of 1812, but individual American victories, such as the Battle of New Orleans, still strengthened nationalistic pride.

In the aftermath of the war, the Federalists were absorbed into the Democratic-Republicans, which began the Era of Good Feelings. However, two new parties eventually emerged. The Democrats, whose leader Andrew Jackson became president in 1828, favored "Jacksonian" democracy, which emphasized mass participation in elections. However, Jackson's policies largely favored white male landowners and suppressed opposing views. The Whigs supported Federalist policies but also drew on democratic principles, particularly with marginalized groups such as African Americans and women.

At the same time, settlers continued to expand west in search of new land and fortune. The Louisiana Purchase of 1803 opened up large amounts of land west of the Mississippi River, and adventurers pushed past even those boundaries toward the western coast. The vision of westward growth into the frontier is a key part of American popular culture, but the expansion was often erratic and depended on a combination of incentives and assurances of relative security. Hence, some areas, such as California and Oregon, were settled more quickly than other areas to the east. Some historians have pointed to the growth of the frontier as a means through which American democracy expanded.

However, the matter of western lands became an increasingly volatile issue as the controversy over slavery heightened. Not all northerners supported abolition, but many saw the practice as outdated and did not want it to expand. Abolitionists formed the Republican Party, and their candidate, Abraham Lincoln, was elected as president in 1860. In response, southern states seceded and formed the Confederate States of America. The ensuing Civil War lasted from 1861 to 1865 and had significant consequences. Slavery was abolished in the United States, and the power of individual states was drastically curtailed. After being reunified, southern states worked to retain control over freed slaves, and the Reconstruction period was followed by Jim Crow segregation. As a result, blacks were barred from public education, unable to vote, and forced to accept their status as second-class citizens.

After the Civil War, the United States increasingly industrialized and became part of the larger Industrial Revolution, which took place throughout the western world. Steps toward industrialization had already begun as early as Jackson's presidency, but the full development of American industry took place in the second half of the nineteenth

Social Studies

century. Railroads helped link cities like Chicago to locations across the West, which allowed for rapid transfer of materials. New technologies, such as electricity, allowed leisure time for those with enough wealth. Even so, the Gilded Age was also a period of disparities, and wealthy entrepreneurs rose while impoverished workers struggled to make their voices heard.

The late nineteenth and early twentieth century not only marked U.S. expansion within North America but also internationally. For example, after the Spanish-American War in 1898, the United States claimed control over Guam, Puerto Rico, and the Philippines. Rivalries in Europe culminated in World War I, in which great powers ranging from France to Russia vied for control in a bloody struggle. Americans did not enter the war until 1917, but we had a critical role in the final phase of the war. During the peace treaty process, President Woodrow Wilson sought to establish a League of Nations in order to promote global harmony, but his efforts only achieved limited success.

After World War I, the United States largely stayed out of international politics for the next two decades. Still, American businesses continued overseas ventures and strengthened the economy in the 1920s. However, massive speculation in the stock market in 1929 triggered the Great Depression—a financial crisis that spread worldwide as nations withdrew from the global economy. The crisis shepherded in the presidency of Franklin D. Roosevelt, who reformed the Democratic Party and implemented new federal programs known as the New Deal.

The Great Depression had ramifications worldwide and encouraged the rise of fascist governments in Italy and Germany. Highly dictatorial, fascism emphasized nationalism and militarism. World War II began when the Axis powers of Germany, Italy, and Japan built up their military forces and launched invasions against neighboring nations in 1939. As part of the Allies, which also included Britain, France, and the Soviet Union, America defeated the Axis powers in 1945 and asserted itself as a global force.

The Union of Soviet Socialist Republics had emerged through the Bolshevik Revolution in 1917 in Russia and militantly supported Communism—a socialist system of government that called for the overthrow of capitalism. Although the Soviet Union formed an alliance with the United States during World War II, relations chilled, and the Cold War began in 1947. Although no true war was declared between the two nations, both the Union of Soviet Socialist Republics and the United States engaged in indirect conflict by supporting and overthrowing foreign governments.

Meanwhile, the Civil Rights Movement began to grow as marginalized groups objected to racial segregation and abuse by whites across the nation. Civil rights leaders, such as Martin Luther King Jr., argued for nonviolent resistance, but others, such as Malcolm X, advocated more radical approaches. Civil rights groups became increasingly discontented during the Vietnam War because they felt they were being drafted for a foreign war that ignored domestic problems. Even so, significant reforms, such as the Voting Rights Act of 1965, opened up new opportunities for freedom and equality in America.

In 1991, the Soviet Union collapsed, leaving the United States as the dominant global power. However, as the United States struggled to fill the void left by the Soviet Union, questions arose about America's role in the world. Terrorist acts, such as the 9/11 attack on the World Trade Center in 2001, have shed doubt on the United States' ability to enforce its authority on an international scale.

Twentieth-Century Developments and Transformations in the United States

Although the United States began industrializing in the second half of the nineteenth century, American technology continued to develop in new directions throughout the course of the twentieth century. A key example was the invention of the modern assembly line. Assembly lines and conveyor belts had already become a prominent part of industrial work, but Henry Ford combined conveyor belts with the system of assembly workers in 1913 in order to produce Model T automobiles. This streamlined production system, in which multiple parts were assembled by different teams along the conveyors, allowed industries in the United States to grow ever larger.

Ford's assembly lines also promoted the growth of the automobile as a means of transportation. Early cars were an expensive and impractical novelty and were primarily the toys of the rich. The Model T, on the other hand, was relatively affordable, which made the car available to a wider array of consumers. Many of the automobiles' early issues, such as radiator leaks and fragile tires, were gradually corrected, and this made the car more appealing than horses. With the support of President Eisenhower, the Federal Aid Highway Act of 1956 paved the way for a network of interstates and highways across the nation.

At the same time, a revolutionary approach to transportation was emerging: flight. Blimps and balloons were already gaining popularity by the turn of the twentieth century, but aviators struggled to create an airplane. The first critical success was by the Wright Brothers in 1903, and they demonstrated that aircrafts did not need to be lighter than air. In time, airplanes surpassed the popularity of balloons and blimps, which tended to be more volatile. Aircraft also added a new dimension to warfare, and aircraft carriers became an integral piece of the American navy during World War II.

Furthermore, by demonstrating that heavier-than-air vehicles could actually carry passengers upward, the stage was set for the space race in the second half of the twentieth century. In 1958, the U.S. government created the National Aeronautics and Space Administration (NASA) to head the budding initiative to extend American power into space. After the Soviet Union successfully launched the Sputnik satellite into Earth's orbit in 1957 and sent the first human in space in 1961, the United States intensified its own space program through the Apollo missions. Apollo 11 successfully landed on the moon in 1969 with Buzz Aldrin and Neil Armstrong. Later ventures into space would focus on space shuttles and satellites, and the latter significantly enhanced communications worldwide.

Indeed, the twentieth century also made considerable advancements in communications and media. Inventions such as the radio greatly boosted communication across the nation and world, such that news could be reported immediately rather than take days. Furthermore, motion pictures evolved from black-and-white movies at theaters to full-color television sets in households. From animation to live films, television matured into a compelling art form in popular culture. Live-action footage gave a new layer to news broadcasts and proved instrumental in the public's reaction to events, such as the Civil Rights Movement and the Vietnam War. With the success of the space program, satellites became a fundamental piece of Earth's communications network by transmitting signals across the planet instantaneously.

Further communications advancements resulted from the development of computer technology. The early computers in the twentieth century were enormous behemoths that were too bulky and expensive for anything but government institutions. However, computers gradually became smaller while still storing large amounts of data. A turning point came with the 1976 release of the Apple computer by entrepreneurs Steve Wozniak and Steve Jobs. The computer had a simplistic design that made it marketable for a mass consumer audience, and computers eventually became household items. Similarly, the networks that would become the Internet originated as government systems, but in time they were extended to commercial avenues that became a vibrant element of modern communications.

However, other advancements in American science during the twentieth century were aimed toward more lethal purposes. In response to the multiple wars throughout the century, the United States built up a powerful military force, and new technologies were devised for that purpose. One of the deadliest creations was the atomic bomb, which split molecular atoms to produce powerful explosions; in addition to the sheer force of the bombs, the aftereffects included toxic radiation and electronic shutdowns. Developed and used in the last days of World War II, the nuclear bomb was the United States' most powerful weapon during the Cold War.

On the other hand, the twentieth century also marked new approaches to the natural environments in America. In reaction to the depletion of natural habitats by industrialization and overhunting, President Theodore Roosevelt helped preserve areas for what would become the National Parks in 1916. Laws, such as the Clean Water Act of

Social Studies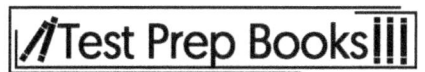

1972, helped improve the health of ecosystems, which benefitted not only wildlife but people across the nation. This also led to the development of alternative energy sources such as wind and solar power.

America continues to change and grow into the twenty-first century by building on preexisting ideas but also pioneering new concepts. As globalization becomes an increasingly prominent phenomenon, American businesses strive to adapt their products to consumers worldwide while also funneling in new ideas from other nations. Yet many of the current developments in American enterprises stem in part from earlier events in American history. For example, the environmental movement has expanded to address new issues such as global warming. NASA continues its space exploration endeavors, but entrepreneurs hope one day to travel to Mars. Therefore, the history of technology within the United States remains an engaging and relevant subject in the present.

Civics/Government

The Role of the Citizen in a Democratic Society

Citizens express their political beliefs and public opinion through participation in politics. The conventional ways citizens can participate in politics in a democratic state include:

- Obeying laws
- Voting in elections
- Running for public office
- Staying interested in and informed of current events
- Learning U.S. history
- Attending public hearings to be informed and to express opinions on issues, especially on the local level
- Forming interest groups to promote common goals
- Forming political action committees (PACs) that raise money to influence policy decisions
- Petitioning government to create awareness of issues
- Campaigning for a candidate
- Contributing to campaigns
- Using mass media to express political ideas, opinions, and grievances

Obeying Laws

Citizens living in a democracy have several rights and responsibilities to uphold. The first duty is that they uphold the established laws of the government. In a democracy, a system of nationwide laws is necessary to ensure that there is some degree of order. Therefore, citizens must obey the laws and also help enforce them because a law that is inadequately enforced is almost useless. Optimally, a democratic society's laws will be accepted and followed by the community as a whole.

However, conflict can occur when an unjust law is passed. For example, much of the civil rights movement centered around Jim Crow laws in the South that supported segregation between black and whites. Yet these practices were encoded in state laws, which created a dilemma for African Americans who wanted equality but also wanted to respect the law. Fortunately, a democracy offers a system in which government leaders and policies are constantly open to change in accordance with the will of citizens. Citizens can influence the laws that are passed by voting for and electing members of the legislative and executive branches to represent them at the local, state, and national levels.

Voting

In a democratic state, the most common way to participate in politics is by voting for candidates in an election. **Voting** allows the citizens of a state to influence policy by selecting the candidates who share their views and make

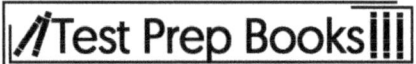

policy decisions that best suit their interests, or candidates who they believe are most capable of leading the country. In Canada, all citizens over 18—regardless of gender, race, or religion—are allowed to vote.

Since the Progressive movement and the increased social activism of the 1890s to the 1920s that sought to eliminate corruption in government, direct participation in politics through voting has increased. Citizens can participate by voting in the following types of elections:

- **Direct primaries**: Citizens can nominate candidates for public office.
- **National, state, and municipal elections**: Citizens elect their representatives in government.
- **Recall elections**: Citizens can petition the government to vote an official out of office before their term ends.
- **Referendums**: Citizens can vote directly on proposed laws or amendments to the state constitution.
- **Voter initiatives**: Citizens can petition their local or state government to propose laws that will be approved or rejected by voters.

Running for Public Office

Citizens also have the ability to run for elected office. By becoming leaders in the government, citizens can demonstrate their engagement and help determine government policy. Citizen involvement in the selection of leaders is vital in a democracy because it helps to prevent the formation of an elite group that does not answer to the public. Without the engagement of citizens who run for office, voters are limited in their ability to select candidates that appeal to them. In this case, voting options would become stagnant, inhibiting the nation's ability to grow and change over time. As long as citizens are willing to take a stand for their vision of Canada, the government will remain dynamic and diverse.

Citizen Interest

These features of a democracy give it the potential to reshape itself continually in response to new developments in society. In order for a democracy to function, it is of the utmost importance that citizens care about the course of politics and be aware of current issues. Apathy among citizens is a constant problem that threatens the endurance of democracies. Citizens should have a desire to take part in the political process, lest they simply accept the status quo and fail to fulfill their civic role. Moreover, they must have acute knowledge of the political processes and the issues that they can address as citizens.

A fear among the Founding Fathers was the prevalence of mob rule, in which the common people did not take interest in politics except to vote for their patrons; this was the usual course of politics in the colonial era, as the common people left the decisions to the established elites. Without understanding the world around them, citizens may not fully grasp the significance of political actions and thereby fail to make wise decisions in that regard. Therefore, citizens must stay informed about current affairs, ranging from local to global matters, so that they can properly address them as voters or elected leaders.

Historical Knowledge

Furthermore, knowledge of the nation's history is essential for healthy citizenship. History continues to have an influence on present political decisions. For example, Supreme Court rulings often take into account previous legal precedents and verdicts, so it is important to know about those past events and how they affect the current processes. It is especially critical that citizens are aware of the context in which laws were established because it helps clarify the purpose of those laws. For example, an understanding of the problems with the Articles of Confederation allows people to comprehend some of the reasons behind the framework of the Constitution. In addition, history as a whole shapes the course of societies and the world; therefore, citizens should draw on this knowledge of the past to realize the full consequences of current actions. Issues such as climate change, conflict in

Social Studies

the Middle East, and civil rights struggles are rooted in events and cultural developments that reach back centuries and should be addressed.

Therefore, education is a high priority in democracies because it has the potential to instill younger generations of citizens with the right mindset and knowledge required to do their part in shaping the nation. Optimally, education should cover a variety of different subjects, ranging from mathematics to biology, so that individuals can explore whatever paths they wish to take in life. Even so, social studies are especially important because students should understand how democracies function and understand the history of the nation and world. Historical studies should cover national and local events as well because they help provide the basis for the understanding of contemporary politics. Social studies courses should also address the histories of foreign nations because contemporary politics has global consequences. In addition, history lessons should remain open to multiple perspectives, even those that might criticize a nation's past actions, because citizens should be exposed to diverse perspectives that they can apply as voters and leaders.

The Structure and Functions of Different Levels of Government in the United States

A **political institution** is an organization created by the government to enact and enforce laws, act as a mediator during conflict, create economic policy, establish social systems, and carry out some power. These institutions maintain a rigid structure of internal rules and oversight, especially if the power is delegated, like agencies under the executive branch.

The Constitution established a federal government divided into three branches: legislative, executive, and judicial.

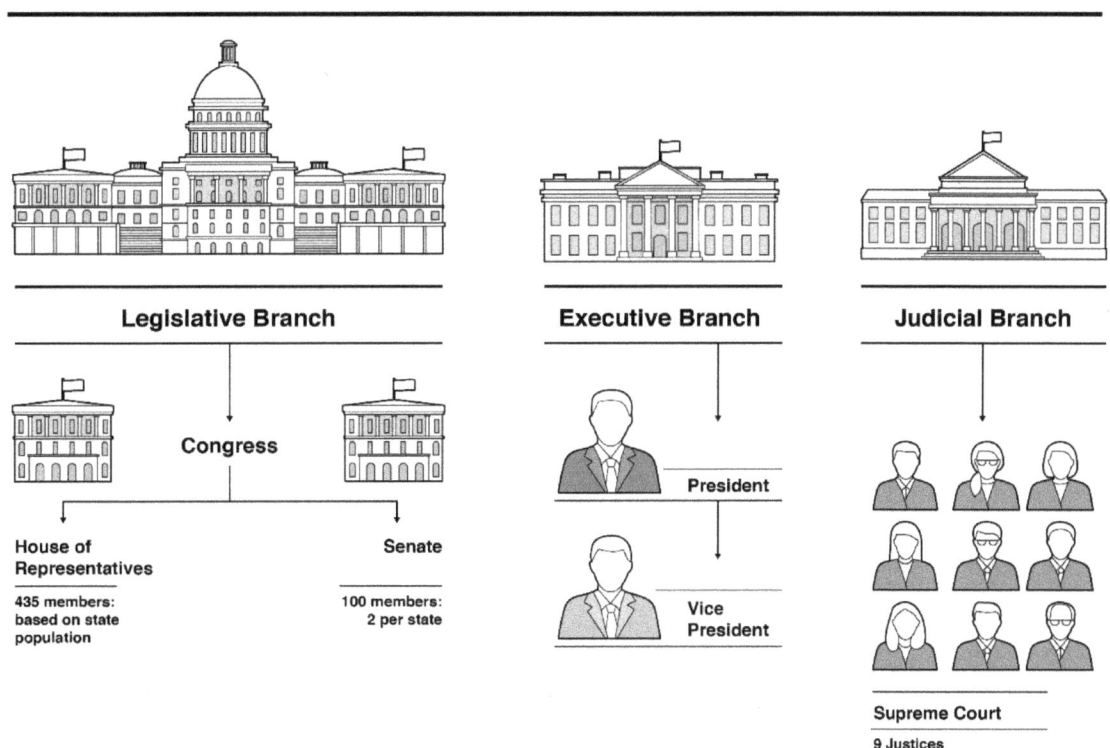

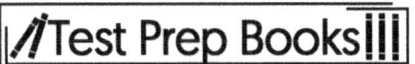

Executive Branch

The **executive branch** is responsible for enforcing the laws. The executive branch consists of the president, the vice president, the president's cabinet, and federal agencies created by Congress to execute some delegated task or authority.

The president of the United States:

- Serves a four-year term and is limited to two terms in office
- Is the chief executive officer of the United States and commander-in-chief of the armed forces
- Is elected by the Electoral College
- Appoints cabinet members, federal judges, and the heads of federal agencies
- Vetoes or signs bills into law
- Handles foreign affairs, including appointing diplomats and negotiating treaties
- Must be at least thirty-five years old, a natural-born U.S. citizen, and have lived in the United States for at least fourteen years

The vice president:

- Serves four-year terms alongside and at the will of the president
- Acts as president of the Senate
- Assumes the presidency if the president is incapacitated
- Assumes any additional duties assigned by the president

The cabinet members:

- Are appointed by the president
- Act as heads for the fifteen executive departments
- Advise the president in matters relating to their departments and carry out delegated power

Note that the president can only sign and veto laws and cannot initiate them himself. As head of the executive branch, it is the responsibility of the president to execute and enforce the laws passed by the legislative branch.

Although Congress delegates their legislative authority to agencies in an enabling statute, they are located in the executive branch because they are tasked with executing their delegated authority. The president enjoys the power of appointment and removal over all federal agency workers, except those tasked with quasi-legislative or quasi-judicial powers.

Legislative Branch

The **legislative branch** is responsible for enacting federal laws. This branch possesses the power to declare war, regulate interstate commerce, approve or reject presidential appointments, and investigate the other branches. The legislative branch is **bicameral**, meaning it consists of two houses: the lower house, called the House of Representatives, and the upper house, known as the Senate. Both houses are elected by popular vote.

Members of both houses are intended to represent the interests of the constituents in their home states and to bring their concerns to a national level while also being consistent with the interests of the nation as a whole. Drafts of laws, called bills, are proposed in one chamber and then are voted upon according to that chamber's rules; should the bill pass the vote in the first house of Congress, the other legislative chamber must approve it before it can be sent to the president.

The two houses (or chambers) are similar though they differ on some procedures such as how debates on bills take place.

House of Representatives

The **House of Representatives** is responsible for enacting bills relating to revenue; impeaching federal officers, including the president and Supreme Court justices; and electing the president in the case of no candidate reaching a majority in the Electoral College.

In the House of Representatives:

- Each state's representation in the House of Representatives is determined proportionally by population, with the total number of voting seats limited to 435.
- There are six nonvoting members in the House, one each from Washington, D.C.; Puerto Rico; American Samoa; Guam; the Northern Mariana Islands; and the U.S. Virgin Islands.
- The Speaker of the House is elected by the other representatives and is responsible for presiding over the House. In the event that the president and vice president are unable to fulfill their duties, the Speaker of the House will succeed to the presidency.
- The representatives of the House serve two-year terms.
- The requirements for eligibility in the House include:
    - Must be twenty-five years of age
    - Must have been a U.S. citizen for at least seven years
    - Must be a resident of the state they are representing by the time of the election

Senate

The **Senate** has the exclusive powers to confirm or reject all presidential appointments, ratify treaties, and try impeachment cases initiated by the House of Representatives.

In the Senate:

- The number of representatives is one hundred, with two representatives from each state.
- The vice president presides over the Senate and breaks a tied vote, if necessary.
- The representatives serve six-year terms.
- The requirements for eligibility in the Senate include:
    - Must be thirty years of age
    - Must have been a U.S. citizen for the past nine years
    - Must be a resident of the state they are representing at the time of their election

Legislative Process

Although all members of the houses vote on whether or not bills should become laws, the senators and representatives also serve on committees and subcommittees dedicated to specific areas of policy. These committees are responsible for debating the merit of bills, revising bills, and passing or killing bills that are assigned to their committee. If it passes, they then present the bill to the entire Senate or House of Representatives (depending on which they are a part of). In most cases, a bill can be introduced in either the Senate or the House, but a majority vote of both houses is required to approve a new bill before the President may sign the bill into law.

Judicial Branch

The **judicial branch**, though it cannot pass laws itself, is tasked with interpreting the law and ensuring citizens receive due process under the law. The judicial branch consists of the **Supreme Court**, the highest court in the country, overseeing all federal and state courts. Lower **federal courts** are the district courts and the courts of appeals.

In the Supreme Court:

- Judges are appointed by the president and confirmed by the Senate.
- Judges serve until retirement, death, or impeachment.
- Judges possess sole power to judge the constitutionality of a law.
- Judges set precedents for lower courts based on their decisions.
- Judges try appeals that have proceeded from the lower courts.

Checks and Balances

Notice that a system of checks and balances between the branches exists. This is to ensure that no branch oversteps its authority. They include:

- Checks on the Legislative Branch:
    - The president can veto bills passed by Congress.
    - The president can call special sessions of Congress.
    - The judicial branch can rule legislation unconstitutional.
- Checks on the Executive Branch:
    - Congress has the power to override presidential vetoes by a two-thirds majority vote.
    - Congress can impeach or remove a president, and the chief justice of the Supreme Court presides over impeachment proceedings.
    - Congress can refuse to approve presidential appointments or ratify treaties.
- Checks on the Judicial Branch:
    - The president appoints justices to the Supreme Court, as well as district courts and courts of appeals.
    - The president can pardon federal prisoners.
    - The executive branch can refuse to enforce court decisions.
    - Congress can create federal courts below the Supreme Court.
    - Congress can determine the number of Supreme Court justices.
    - Congress can set the salaries of federal judges.
    - Congress can refuse to approve presidential appointments of judges.
    - Congress can impeach and convict federal judges.

Social Studies

The three branches of government operate separately, but they must rely on each other to create, enforce, and interpret the laws of the United States.

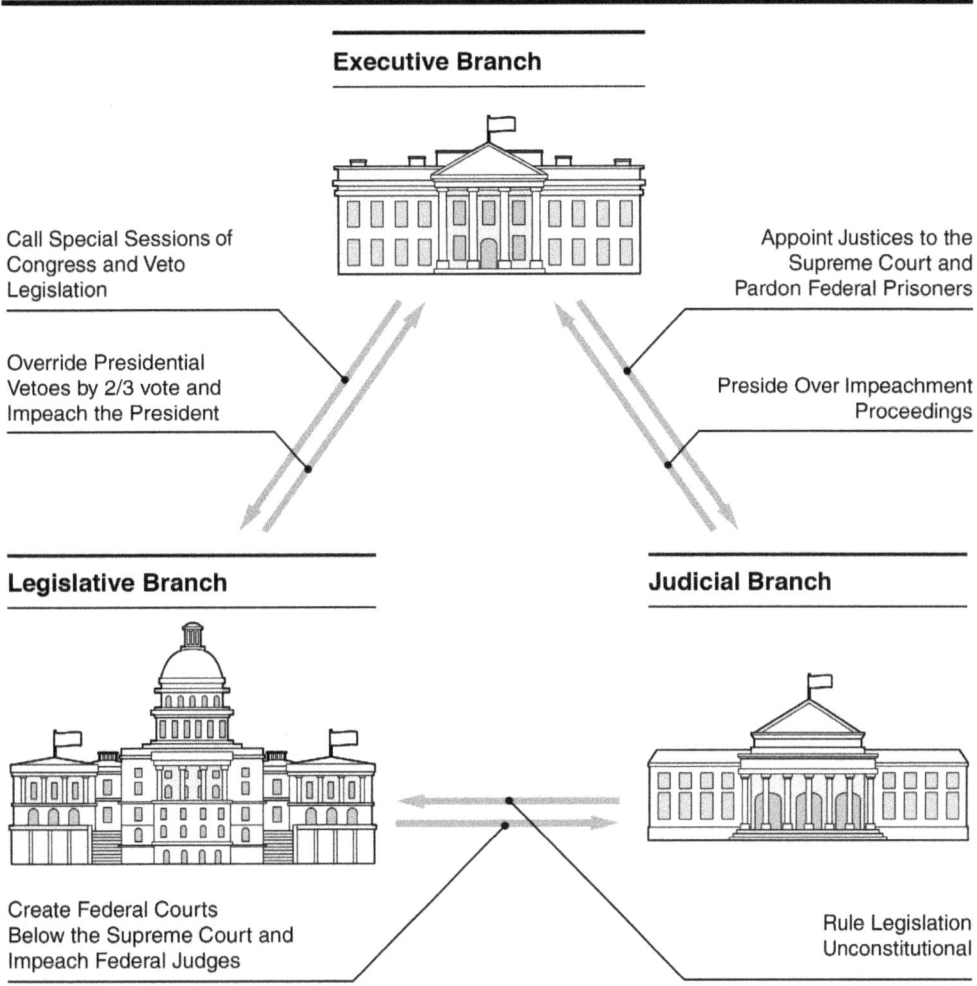

How Laws are Enacted and Enforced
To enact a new law:

- The bill is introduced to Congress.
- The bill is sent to the appropriate committee for review and revision.
- The approved bill is sent to the Speaker of the House and the majority party leader of the Senate, who places the bill on the calendar for review.

- The houses debate the merits of the bill and recommend amendments.
    - In the House of Representatives, those who wish to debate about a bill are allowed only a few minutes to speak, and amendments to the bill are limited.
    - In the Senate, debates and amendments are unlimited, and those who wish to postpone a vote may do so by filibuster, refusing to stop speaking.
- The approved bill is revised in both houses to ensure identical wording in both bills.
- The revised bill is returned to both houses for final approval.
- The bill is sent to the president, who may
    - Sign the bill into law
    - Veto the bill
    - Take no action, resulting in the bill becoming law if Congress remains in session for ten days or dying if Congress adjourns before ten days have passed

The Role of State Government

While the federal government manages the nation as a whole, state governments address issues pertaining to their specific territory. In the past, states claimed the right, known as **nullification**, to refuse to enforce federal laws that they considered unconstitutional. However, conflicts between state and federal authority, particularly in the South in regard to first, slavery, and later, discrimination, have led to increased federal power, and states cannot defy federal laws. Even so, the **Tenth Amendment** limits federal power to those powers specifically granted in the Constitution, and the rest of the powers are retained by the states and citizens. Therefore, individual state governments are left in charge of decisions with immediate effects on their citizens, such as state laws and taxes.

In this way, the powers of government are separated both horizontally between the three branches of government (executive, legislative, and judicial) and vertically between the levels of government (federal, state, and local).

Like the federal government, state governments consist of executive, judicial, and legislative branches, but the exact configuration of those branches varies between states. For example, while most states follow the bicameral structure of Congress, Nebraska has only a single legislative chamber. Additionally, requirements to run for office, length of terms, and other details vary from state to state. State governments have considerable authority within their states, but they cannot impose their power on other states.

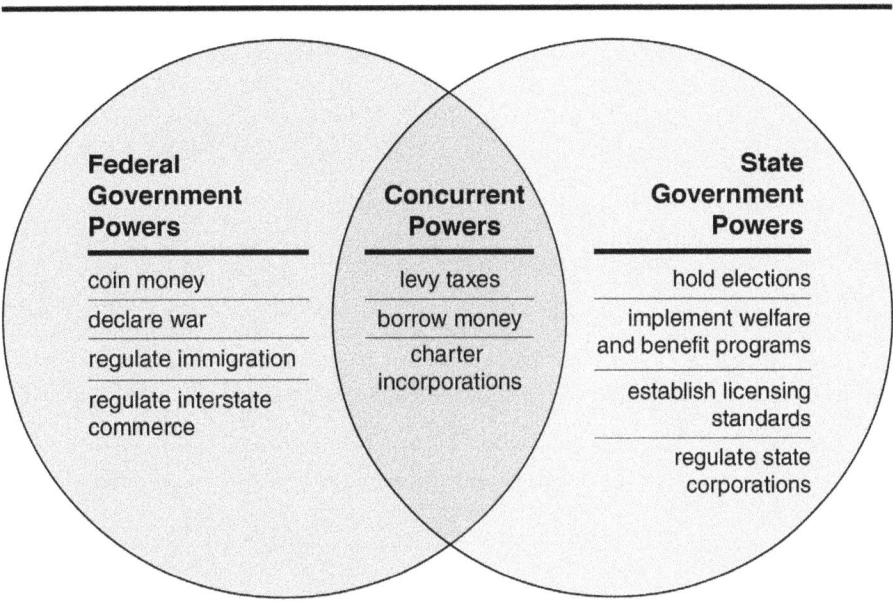

The Role of Local Government
Local governments, which include town governments, county boards, library districts, and other agencies, are especially variable in their composition. They often reflect the overall views of their state governments but also have their own values, rules, and structures. Generally, local governments function in a democratic fashion, although the exact form of government depends on its role. Depending on the location within the state, local government may have considerable or minimal authority based on the population and prosperity of the area; some counties may have strong influence in the state, while others may have a limited impact.

Native American Tribes
Native American tribes are treated as dependent nations that answer to the federal government but may be immune to state jurisdiction. As with local governments, the exact form of governance is left up to the tribes, which ranges from small councils to complex systems of government. Other U.S. territories, including the District of Columbia (site of Washington, D.C.) and acquired islands, such as Guam and Puerto Rico, have representation within Congress, but their legislators cannot vote on bills.

Election System
As members of a Constitutional Republic with certain aspects of a **democracy**, U.S. citizens are empowered to elect most government leaders, but the process varies between branch and level of government. Presidential elections at the national level use the **Electoral College system**. Rather than electing the president directly, citizens cast their ballots to select **electors** that represent each state in the college.

Legislative branches at the federal and state level are also determined by elections. In some areas, judges are elected, but in other states judges are appointed by elected officials. The U.S. has a **two-party system**, meaning that most government control is under two major parties: the Republican Party and the Democratic Party. It should be noted that the two-party system was not designed by the Constitution but gradually emerged over time.

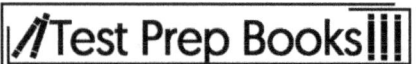

Electoral Process

During the **electoral process**, the citizens of a state decide who will represent them at the local, state, and federal level. Different political officials that citizens elect through popular vote include but are not limited to:

- City mayor
- City council members
- State representative
- State governor
- State senator
- House member
- U.S. Senator
- President

The Constitution grants the states the power to hold their own elections, and the voting process often varies from city to city and state to state.

While a popular vote decides nearly all local and state elections, the president of the United States is elected by the *Electoral College*, rather than by popular vote. Presidential elections occur every four years on the first Tuesday after the first Monday in November.

The electoral process for the president of the United States includes:

Primary Elections and Caucuses

In a presidential election, *nominees* from the two major parties, as well as some third parties, run against each other. To determine who will win the nomination from each party, the states hold **primary elections** or **caucuses**.

During the primary elections, the states vote for who they want to win their party's nomination. In some states, primary elections are closed, meaning voters may only vote for candidates from their registered party, but other states hold *open primaries* in which voters may vote in either party's primary.

Some states hold *caucuses* in which the members of a political party meet in small groups, and the decisions of those groups determine the party's candidate.

Each state holds a number of delegates proportional to its population, and the candidate with the most delegate votes receives the nomination. Some states give all of their delegates (*winner-take-all*) to the primary or caucus winner, while some others split the votes more proportionally.

Conventions

The two major parties hold national conventions to determine who will be the nominee to run for president from each party. The **delegates** each candidate won in the primary elections or caucuses are the voters who represent their states at the national conventions. The candidate who wins the most delegate votes is given the nomination. Political parties establish their own internal requirements and procedures for how a nominee is nominated.

Conventions are typically spread across several days, and leaders of the party give speeches, culminating with the candidate accepting the nomination at the end.

Social Studies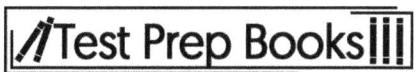

Campaigning

Once the nominees are selected from each party, they continue campaigning into the national election. Prior to the mid-1800s, candidates did not actively campaign for themselves, considering it dishonorable to the office, but campaigning is now rampant. Modern campaigning includes, but is not limited to:

- Raising money
- Meeting with citizens and public officials around the country
- Giving speeches
- Issuing policy proposals
- Running internal polls to determine strategy
- Organizing strategic voter outreach in important districts
- Participating in debates organized by a third-party private debate commission
- Advertising on television, through mail, or on the Internet

General Election

On the first Tuesday after the first Monday in November of an election year, every four years, the people cast their votes by secret ballot for president in a **general election**. Voters may vote for any candidate, regardless of their party affiliation. The outcome of the popular vote does not decide the election; instead, the winner is determined by the Electoral College.

Electoral College

When the people cast their votes for president in the general election, they are casting their votes for the *electors* from the *Electoral College* who will elect the president. In order to win the presidential election, a nominee must win 270 of the 538 electoral votes. The number of electors is equal to the total number of senators and representatives from each state plus three electoral votes for Washington D.C. which does not have any voting members in the legislative branch.

The electors typically vote based on the popular vote from their states. Although the Constitution does not require electors to vote for the popular vote winner of their state, no elector voting against the popular vote of their state has ever changed the outcome of an election. Due to the Electoral College, a nominee may win the popular vote and still lose the election.

For example, let's imagine that there are only two states — Wyoming and New Mexico — in a presidential election. Wyoming has three electoral votes and awards them all to the winner of the election by majority vote. New Mexico has five electoral votes and also awards them all to the winner of the election by majority vote. If 500,000 people in Wyoming vote and the Republican candidate wins by a vote of 300,000 to 200,000, the Republican candidate will win the three electoral votes for the state. If the same number of people vote in New Mexico, but the Republican candidate loses the state by a vote of 249,000 to 251,000, the Democratic candidate wins the five electoral votes from that state. This means the Republican candidate will have received 549,000 popular votes but only three electoral votes, while the Democratic candidate will have received 451,000 popular votes but will have won five electoral votes. Thus, the Republican won the popular vote by a considerable margin, but the Democratic candidate will have been awarded more electoral votes, which are the only ones that matter.

	Wyoming	New Mexico	Total # of Votes
Republican Votes	300,000	249,000	**549,000**
Democratic Votes	200,000	251,000	**451,000**
Republican Electoral Votes	3	0	**3**
Democratic Electoral Votes	0	5	**5**

If no one wins the majority of electoral votes in the presidential election, the House of Representatives decides the presidency, as required by the Twelfth Amendment. They may only vote for the top three candidates, and each state delegation votes as a single bloc. Twenty-six votes, a simple majority, are required to elect the president. The House has only elected the president twice, in 1801 and 1825.

Here how many electoral votes each state and the District of Columbia have:

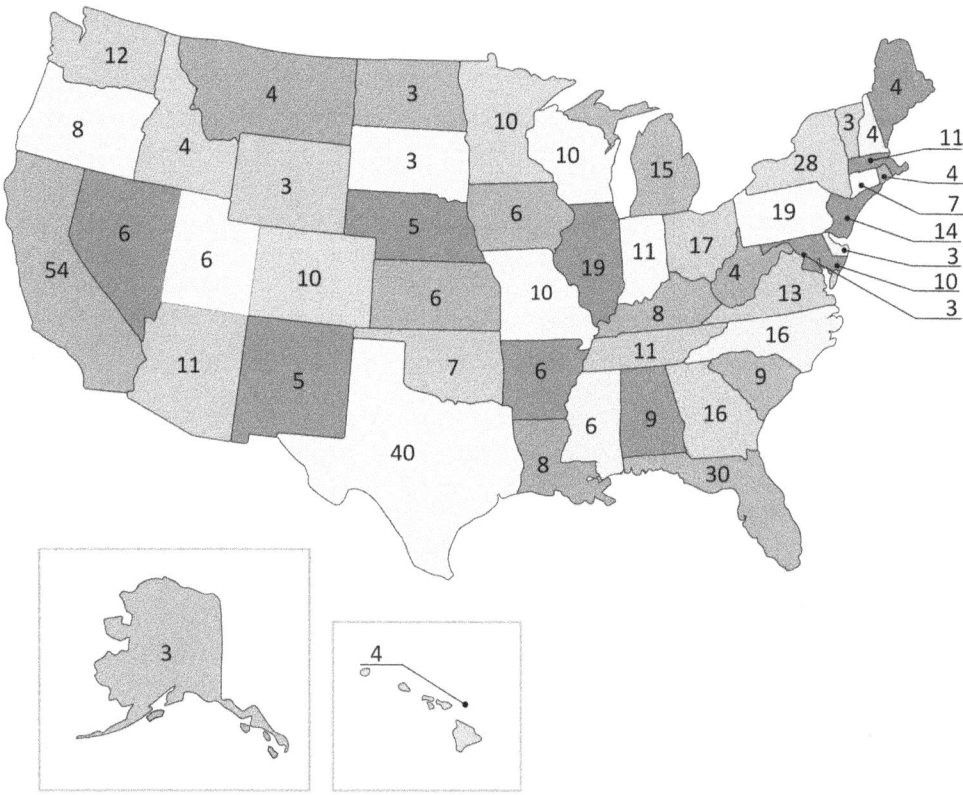

Purposes and Characteristics of Various Governance Systems

Government is the physical manifestation of the political entity or ruling body of a state. It includes the formal institutions that manage and maintain a society. The form of government does not determine the state's **economic system**, though these concepts are often closely tied. Many forms of government are based on a society's economic system. However, while the form of government refers to the methods by which a society is managed, the term **economy** refers to the management of resources in a society. Many forms of government exist, often as hybrids of two or more forms of government or economic systems. Forms of government can be distinguished based on

Social Studies

protection of civil liberties, protection of rights, distribution of power, power of government, and principles of Federalism.

Regime is the term used to describe the ruling body and corresponding political conditions under which citizens live. A regime is defined by the amount of power the government possesses and the number of people who comprise the ruling body. It is closely related to the form of government because the form of government largely creates the political conditions. Regimes are governmental bodies that control both the form and the limit of term of their office. For example, authoritarianism is an example of a form of government and type of regime. A regime is considered to be ongoing until the culture, priorities, and values of the government are altered, either through a peaceful transition of power or a violent overthrow of the current regime.

The forms of government operated by regimes include:

Aristocracy

An **aristocracy** is a form of government composed of a small group of wealthy rulers, either holding hereditary titles of nobility or membership in a higher class. Variations of aristocratic governments include:

- **Oligarchy**: form of government where political power is consolidated in the hands of a small group of people
- **Plutocracy**: type of oligarchy where a wealthy, elite class dominates the state and society

Though no aristocratic governments exist today, it was the dominant form of government during ancient times, including the:

- Vassals and lords during the Middle Ages, especially in relation to feudalism
- City-state of Sparta in ancient Greece

Authoritarian

An **authoritarian state** is one in which a single party rules indefinitely. The ruling body operates with unrivaled control and complete power to make policy decisions, including the restriction of denying civil liberties such as freedom of speech, press, religion, and protest. Forms of authoritarian governments include autocracy, dictatorship, and totalitarianism.

- The Soviet Union, Nazi Germany, and modern-day North Korea are all examples of states with authoritarian governments.

Democracy

Democracy is a form of government in which the people act as the ruling body by electing representatives to voice their views. Forms of democratic governments include:

- **Direct democracy**: democratic government in which the people make direct decisions on specific policies by majority vote of all eligible voters, like in ancient Athens
- **Representative democracy**: democratic government in which the people elect representatives to vote in a legislative body. This form of government is also known as a representative republic or indirect democracy. Representative democracy is currently the most popular form of government in the world.

The presidential and parliamentary systems are the most common forms of representative democracy. In the **presidential system**, the executive operates in its own branch distinct from the legislature. In addition, the president is typically both the head of state and head of government. Examples of presidential systems include Brazil, Nigeria, and the United States.

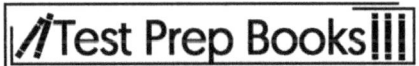

In the **parliamentary system**, the prime minister serves as the head of government. The legislative branch, typically a parliament, elects the prime minister and also has the authority to replace the prime minister with a vote of no confidence. This practically means that the parliament has considerable influence over the office of prime minister. Parliamentary systems often include a president as the head of state, but the office is mostly ceremonial, functioning like a figurehead. Examples of parliamentary systems include Germany, Australia, and Pakistan.

The presidential system is better designed to distribute power between separate branches of government, which theoretically provides more stability. Presidents serve for a limited number of years, while prime ministers serve until death, resignation, or dismissal.

In the parliamentary system, the interconnectedness between parliament and the prime minister facilitates efficient governance, capable of adjusting to developing situations. In contrast, the presidential system is more prone to political gridlock because there is no direct connection between the legislative and executive branches. The legislature in a presidential system cannot replace the executive, like in the parliamentary system. The separation of powers in a presidential system can lead to disagreement between the executive and legislature, causing gridlock and other delays in governance.

Federalism is a set of principles that divides power between a central government and regional governments. Sovereign states often combine into a federation, and in doing so, they cede some degree of sovereignty to a functional central government that handles broad national policies. The United States and Canada are examples of governments with a Federalist structure.

Monarchy

Monarchy is a form of government in which the state is ruled by a sovereign leader. This leader is called a **monarch** and is typically a hereditary ruler. Monarchs have often justified their power due to some divine right to rule. Types of monarchies include:

- **Absolute monarchy**: a monarchy in which the monarch has complete power over the people and the state
- **Constitutional monarchy**: a type of monarchy in which the citizens of the state are protected by a constitution. A separate branch, typically a parliament, makes legislative decisions, and the monarch and legislature share power.
- **Crowned republic**: a type of monarchy in which the monarch holds only a ceremonial position and the people hold sovereignty over the state. It is defined by the monarch's lack of executive power.

Examples of monarchies:

- Kingdom of Saudi Arabia is an absolute monarchy.
- Australia is a crowned republic.

Economics

Fundamental Economic Concepts

Economics is the study of human behavior in response to the production, consumption, and distribution of assets or wealth. Economics can help individuals or societies make decisions for themselves dependent upon their needs, wants, and resources. Economics is divided into two subgroups: microeconomics and macroeconomics.

Microeconomics is the study of individual or small group behaviors and patterns related to markets of goods and services. It specifically looks at single factors that could affect these behaviors and decisions. For example, the use of coupons in a grocery store could affect an individual's product choice, quantity purchased, and overall savings that

Social Studies

could be directed to a different purchase. **Microeconomics** encompasses the study of many things, including scarcity, choice, opportunity costs, economics systems, factors of production, supply and demand, market efficiency, the role of government, distribution of income, and product markets.

Macroeconomics examines a much larger scale of the economy. It focuses on how aggregate factors such as demand, output, and spending habits affect the people in a society or nation. For example, if a national company moves its production overseas to save on costs, how will production, labor, and capital be affected? Macroeconomics explores any and all criterion and microeconomic elements that have an effect on the economy. Since macroeconomics concerns large-scale economic elements, it is used by governments and businesses to create economic policies and procedures.

Microeconomics
Scarcity
People have different needs and wants, and the question arises, are the resources available to supply those needs and wants? Limited resources and high demand create **scarcity**. When a product is scarce, there is a short supply of it. For example, when the newest version of a cellphone is released, people line up to buy the phone or put their name on a wait list if the phone is not immediately available. The new cellphone may become a scarce commodity. In turn, the phone company may raise their prices, knowing that people may be willing to pay more for an item in such high demand. If a competing company lowers the cost of the phone but has contingencies, such as extended contracts or hidden fees, the buyer will still have the opportunity to purchase the scarce product. Limited resources and extremely high demand create scarcity and, in turn, cause companies to acquire opportunity costs.

Factors of Production
There are four factors of production:

- Land: both renewable and nonrenewable resources
- Labor: effort put forth by people to produce goods and services
- Capital: the tools used to create goods and services
- Entrepreneurs: persons who combine land, labor, and capital to create new goods and services

The four factors of production are used to create goods and services to make economic profit. All four factors strongly impact one another.

Supply and Demand
Supply and demand are the most important concepts of economics in a market economy. **Supply** is the amount of a product that a market can offer. **Demand** is the quantity of a product needed or desired by buyers. The price of a product is directly related to supply and demand. The price of a product and the demand for that product go hand in hand in a market economy. For example, when there are a variety of treats at a bakery, certain treats are in higher demand than others. The bakery can raise the cost of the more demanded items as supplies get limited. Conversely, the bakery can sell the less desirable treats by lowering the cost of those items as an incentive for buyers to purchase them.

Product Markets
Product markets are where goods and services are bought and sold. Product markets provide a place for sellers to offer goods and services and for consumers to purchase them. The annual value of goods and services exchanged throughout the year is measured by the **Gross Domestic Product (GDP)**, a monetary measure of goods and services made either quarterly or annually. Department stores, gas stations, grocery stores, and other retail stores are all examples of product markets. However, product markets do not include any raw or unfinished materials.

Theory of the Firm

The behavior of firms is composed of several theories varying between short- and long-term goals. There are four basic firm behaviors: perfect competition, profit maximization, short run, and long run. Each firm follows a pattern, depending on its desired outcome. Theory of the Firm posits that firms, after conducting market research, make decisions that will maximize their profits.

- Perfect competition:
- In perfect competition, several businesses are selling the same product simultaneously.
- There are so many businesses and consumers that none will directly impact the market.
- Each business and consumer is aware of the competing businesses and markets.
- Profit maximization:
- Firms decide the quantity of a product that needs to be produced in order to receive maximum profit gains. Profit is the total amount of revenue made after subtracting costs.
- Short run:
- A short amount of time where fixed prices cannot be adjusted
- The quantity of the product depends on the varying amount of labor. Less labor means less product.
- Long run:
- An amount of time where fixed prices can be adjusted
- Firms try to maximize production while minimizing labor costs.

Overall, microeconomics operates on a small scale, focusing on how individuals or small groups use and assign resources.

Macroeconomics

Macroeconomics analyzes the economy as a whole. It studies unemployment, interest rates, price levels, and national income, which are all factors that can affect the nation as a whole, and not just individual households. Macroeconomics studies all large factors to determine how, or if, they will affect future trend patterns of production, consumption, and economic growth.

Measures of Economic Performance

Measurements of economic performance determine if an economy is growing, stagnant, or deteriorating. To measure the growth and sustainability of an economy, several indicators can be used. Economic indicators provide data that economists can use to determine if there are faulty processes or if some form of intervention is needed.

One of the main indicators of a country's economic performance is the **Gross Domestic Product (GDP)**. GDP growth provides important information that can be used to determine fiscal or financial policies. The GDP does not measure income distribution, quality of life, or losses due to natural disasters. For example, if a community lost everything to a hurricane, it would take a long time to rebuild the community and stabilize its economy. That is why there is a need to take into account more balanced performance measures when factoring overall economic performance.

Other indicators used to measure economic performance are unemployment or employment rates, inflation, savings, investments, surpluses and deficits, debt, labor, trade terms, the HDI (Human Development Index), and the HPI (Human Poverty Index).

Unemployment

Unemployment occurs when an individual does not have a job, is actively trying to find employment, and is not getting paid. Official unemployment rates do not factor in the number of people who have stopped looking for work, but true unemployment rates do.

Social Studies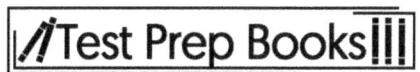

There are three types of unemployment: cyclical, frictional, and structural.

Cyclical
Comes as a result of the regular economic cycle and variations in supply and demand; This usually occurs during a recession.
Frictional
When workers voluntarily leave their jobs; An example would be a person changing careers.
Structural
When companies' needs change and a person no longer possesses the skills needed.

Given the nature of a market economy and the fluctuations of the labor market, a 100 percent employment rate is impossible to reach.

Inflation

Inflation is when the value of money decreases and the cost of goods and services increases over time. Supply, demand, and money reserves all affect inflation. Generally, inflation is measured by the **Consumer Price Index (CPI)**, a tool that tracks price changes of goods and services. The CPI measures goods and services such as gasoline, cars, clothing, and food. When the cost of goods and services increase, manufacturers may reduce the quantity they produce due to lower demand. This decreases the purchasing power of the consumer. Basically, as more money is printed, it holds less and less value in purchasing power. When inflation occurs, consumers spend and save less because their currency is worth less. However, if inflation occurs steadily over time, the people can better plan and prepare for future necessities.

Inflation can vary from year to year, usually never fluctuating more than 2 percent. Central banks try to prevent drastic increases or decreases of inflation to prohibit prices from rising or falling too far. Inflation can also vary based on different monetary currencies. Although rare, any country's economy may experience hyperinflation (when inflation rates increase to over 50 percent), while other economies may experience deflation (when the cost of goods and services decrease over time). Deflation occurs when the inflation rate drops below zero percent.

Business Cycle

A **business cycle** is when the Gross Domestic Product (GDP) moves downward and upward over a long-term growth trend. These cycles help determine where the economy currently stands, as well as where it could be heading. Business cycles usually occur almost every six years and have four phases: expansion, peak, contraction, and trough. Here are some characteristics of each phase:

- Expansion:
- Increased employment rates and economic growth
- Production and sales increase
- On a graph, expansion is where the lines climb.
- Peak:
- Employment rates are at or above full employment and the economy is at maximum productivity.
- On a graph, the peak is the top of the hill, where expansion has reached its maximum.
- Contraction:
- When growth starts slowing
- Unemployment is on the rise.
- On a graph, contraction is where the graph begins to slide back down or contract.
- Trough:
- The cycle has hit bottom and is waiting for the next cycle to start again.
- On a graph, the trough is the bottom of the contraction prior to when it starts to climb back up.

When the economy is expanding or "booming," the business cycle is going from a trough to a peak. When the economy is headed down and toward a recession, the business cycle is going from a peak to a trough.

Four phases of a business cycle:

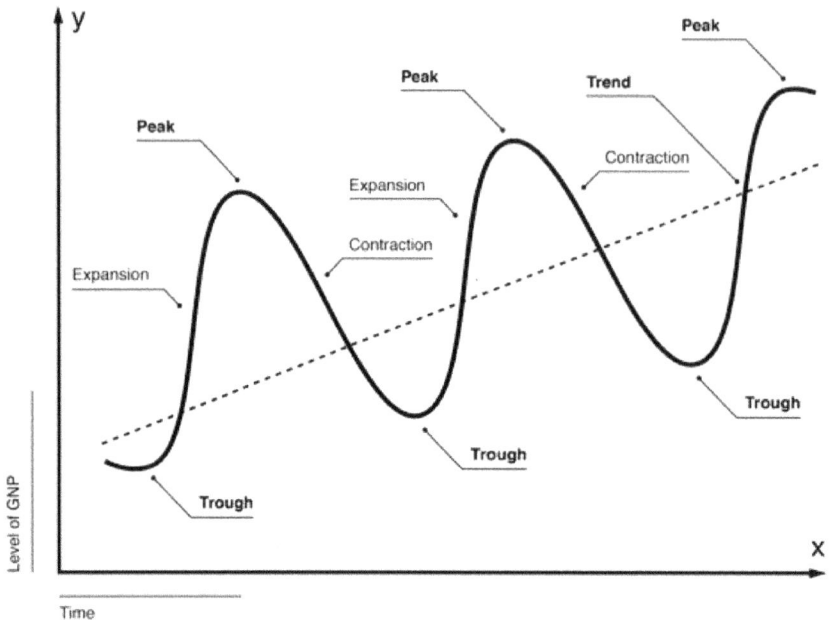

Economic Growth

The most common tool for measuring economic growth is the **Gross Domestic Product (GDP)**. The increase of goods and services over time indicates positive movement in economic growth. The quantity of goods and services produced is not always an indicator of economic growth, however; the value of the goods and services produced matters more than the quantity.

There are many causes of economic growth, which can be short- or long-term. In the short term, if aggregate demand (the total demand for goods and services produced at a given time) increases, then the overall GDP increases as well. As the GDP increases, interest rates may decrease, which may encourage greater spending and investing. Real estate prices may also rise, and there may be lower income taxes. All of these short-term factors can stimulate economic growth.

In the long term, if aggregate supply (the total supply of goods or services in a given time period) increases, then there is potential for an increase in capital as well. With more working capital, more infrastructure and jobs can be created. With more jobs, there is an increased employment rate, and education and training for jobs will improve. New technologies will be developed, and new raw materials may be discovered. All of these long-term factors can also stimulate economic growth.

Other causes of economic growth include low inflation and stability. Lower inflation rates encourage more investing as opposed to higher inflation rates that cause market instability. Stability encourages businesses to continue investing. If the market is unstable, investors may question the volatility of the market.

Potential Costs of Economic Growth:

- Inflation: When economic growth occurs, inflation tends to be high. If supply cannot keep up with demand, then the inflation rate may be unmanageable.

Social Studies

- Economic booms and recessions: The economy goes through cycles of booms and recessions. This causes inflation to fluctuate over time, which puts the economy into a continuous cycle of rising and falling.
- Account inefficiencies: When the economy grows, consumers and businesses increase their import spending. The increase of import spending affects the current account and causes a shortage.
- Environmental costs: When the economy is growing, there is an abundance of output, which may result in more pollutants and a reduction in quality of life.
- Inequalities: Growth occurs differently among members of society. While the wealthy may be getting richer, those living in poverty may just be getting on their feet. So, while economic growth is happening, it may happen at very different rates.

While these potential costs could affect economic growth, if the growth is consistent and stable, then it can occur without severe inflation swings. As technology improves, new ways of production can reduce negative environmental factors as well.

Government Involvement in the Economy

Market Efficiency and the Role of Government (Taxes, Subsidies, and Price Controls)

Market efficiency is directly affected by supply and demand. The government can help the market stay efficient by either stepping in when the market is inefficient and/or providing the means necessary for markets to run properly. For example, society needs two types of infrastructure: physical (bridges, roads, etc.) and institutional (courts, laws, etc.). The government may impose taxes, subsidies, and price controls to increase revenue, lower prices of goods and services, ensure product availability for the government, and maintain fair prices for goods and services.

The Purpose of Taxes, Subsidies, and Price Controls

Taxes	Subsidies	Price Controls
-Generate government revenue -Discourage purchase or use of bad products such as alcohol or cigarettes	-Lower the price of goods and services -Reassure the supply of goods and services -Allow opportunities to compete with overseas vendors	-Act as emergency measures when government intervention is necessary -Set a minimum or maximum price for goods and services

Fiscal Policy

Fiscal policy refers to how the government adjusts spending and tax rates to influence the functions of the economy. Fiscal policies can either increase or decrease tax rates and spending. These policies represent a tricky balancing act, because if the government increases taxes too much, consumer spending and monetary value will decrease. Conversely, if the government lowers taxes, consumers will have more money in their pockets to buy more goods and services, which increases demand and the need for companies to supply those goods and services. Due to the higher demand, suppliers can add jobs to fulfill that demand. While increases in supply, demand, and jobs are positive for the overall economy, they may result in a devaluation of the dollar and less purchasing power.

Money and Banking

Money is a means of exchange that provides a convenient way for sellers and consumers to understand the value of their goods and services. As opposed to bartering (when sellers and consumers exchange goods or services as equal trades), money is convenient for both buyers and sellers.

There are three main forms of money: commodity, fiat, and bank. Here are characteristics of each form:

- Commodity money: a valuable good, such as precious metals or tobacco, used as money

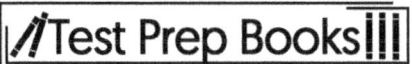

- Fiat money: currency that has no intrinsic value but is recognized by the government as valuable for trade, such as paper money
- Bank money: Money that is credited by a bank to those who deposit it into bank accounts, such as checking and savings accounts or credit

While price levels within the economy set the demand for money, most countries have central banks that supply the actual money. Essentially, banks buy and sell money. Borrowers can take loans and pay back the bank, with interest, providing the bank with extra capital.

A central bank has control over the printing and distribution of money. Central banks serve three main purposes: manage monetary growth to help steer the direction of the economy, be a backup to commercial banks that are suffering, and provide options and alternatives to government taxation.

The Federal Reserve is the central bank of the United States. The Federal Reserve controls banking systems and determines the value of money in the United States. Basically, the Federal Reserve is the bank for banks.

All Western economies have to keep a minimum amount of protected cash called required reserve. Once banks meet those minimums, they can then lend or loan the excess to consumers. The required reserves are used within a fractional reserve banking system (fractional because a small portion is kept separate and safe). Not only do banks reserve, manage, and loan money, but they also help form monetary policies.

Monetary Policy

The central bank and other government committees control the amount of money that is made and distributed. The money supply determines monetary policy. Three main features sustain monetary policy:

1. Assuring the minimum amount held within banks (bank reserves): when banks are required to hold more money in reserve funds, they are less willing to lend money to help control inflation.

2. Adjusting interest rates: raising interest rates makes borrowing more costly, which can slow down unsustainable growth and lower inflation. Lowering interest rates encourages borrowing and can stimulate struggling economies.

3. Purchasing and selling bonds (open market operations): Controlling the money supply by buying bonds to increase it and selling bonds to reduce it.

In the United States, the Federal Reserve maintains monetary policy. There are two main types of monetary policy: expansionary and contractionary.

- Expansionary monetary policy:
    - Increases the money supply
    - Lowers unemployment
    - Increases consumer spending
    - Increases private sector borrowing
    - Possibly decreases interest rates to very low levels, even near zero
    - Decreases reserve requirements and federal funds
- Contractionary monetary policy:
    - Decreases the money supply
    - Helps control inflation
    - Possibly increases unemployment due to slowdowns in economic growth
    - Decreases consumer spending
    - Decreases loans and/or borrowing

The Federal Reserve uses monetary policy to try to achieve maximum employment and secure inflation rates. Because the Federal Reserve is the bank of banks, it truly strives to be the last-resort option for distressed banks. This is because once these kinds of institutions begin to rely on the Federal Reserve for help, all parts of the banking industry—such as those dealing with loans, bonds, interest rates, and mortgages—are affected.

Government Policies and International Trade

Governments' involvement in their domestic economies varied throughout the Cold War, depending on the countries' history and ideology. European countries were capitalist, meaning that considerable economic freedom was granted to private corporations and individuals. However, European countries continued Keynesian style economic policies, so the government continued to play a role in regulating economic activity as well as heavily investing in social programs and infrastructure. In contrast, the Soviet Union and China continued to exercise centralized control over the economy through Five-Year plans that directed economic activity and controlled the supply of goods. Many African, Middle Eastern, South American, and Southeast Asian countries had considerable government involvement in their domestic economies. Land reform, nationalization of industries, and robust social service programs were common in those regions as countries sought to spur development. However, these developing countries often lacked capital to fund development projects, forcing them to cede some economic control to multinational corporations or the **International Monetary Fund (IMF).**

Along with the World Bank, the IMF was a global association that developed after World War II. These global associations provided loans to governments for the purpose of development. The loans often had extensive conditions that reduced the recipient state's control over the economy. For example, loans from the IMF regularly forced states to privatize state-owned companies, cut social programs, and reduce government subsidies. In addition to global financial associations, some countries entered into free trade agreements. These agreements successfully increased trade, but they also reduced the countries' flexibility in economic policy. For example, free trade agreements limited the signatories' ability to impose tariffs on foreign goods or provide subsidies to certain domestic industries. Examples of twentieth century free trade agreements include the: **General Agreement on Tariffs and Trade** (1947), **European Coal and Steel Community** (1951), **North American Free Trade Agreement** (1994), and the **World Trade Organization** (1995).

Consumer Economics

Consumer economics is a term used to describe the ways in which consumers make decisions about their roles in a capitalist economy. The factors that consumers consider when buying goods and services include satisfaction and utility. Most consumers want to obtain as much satisfaction and/or utility from their purchase as possible; in colloquial terms, they want the biggest bang for the buck. Consumers also have to consider the quantity of goods and services they are able to purchase at any given time, in accordance with the current price. This phenomenon is known as demand. When individual demand combines with aggregate demand, it is called market demand. Individual demands and market demands are also factors that consumers must consider when making decisions. These demands—individual and aggregate—drive consumer tastes. Most consumers do not demand goods that do not provide them with utility or satisfaction.

Consumers must also consider supply and scarcity. Consumers do not always have enough time or money to make their purchases, and this is known as scarcity. Scarcity basically means that consumers have to make choices: they cannot always have all the goods they want and participate in all their preferred activities. Likewise, all consumers—individuals, households, businesses, and governments—are bound to the supply chains of goods. At times, the actual goods or services might become scarce, meaning there are not enough products or services to meet consumer demand. As a result, consumers might have to consider alternative options for utility or satisfaction.

When an individual decides between possibilities, that individual is making a choice. Choices allow people to compare opportunity costs. *Opportunity costs* are benefits that a person could have received, but gave up, in choosing another course of action. What is an individual willing to trade or give up for a different choice? For

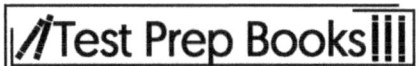

example, if an individual pays someone to mow the lawn because he or she would rather spend that time doing something else, then the opportunity cost of paying someone to mow the lawn is worth the time gained from not doing the job himself or herself.

Individuals earn an income by trading their labor—both mental and physical—for pay. They then budget their money through spending or saving it. As consumers, every choice has an opportunity cost since they must choose which goods and services they want to buy with a limited income. By purchasing one good or service, they give up the chance to purchase another.

Additionally, consumers have the choice to save money when they don't have enough money to purchase what they want, or when they want to utilize a savings account to use during emergencies or periods of economic difficulty. People also choose to save for retirement, a time when they will no longer be working and drawing a salary. Saving money by putting it in a bank is considered low-risk—the bank will pay the saver a low interest rate to keep it safe, but it will not increase much in value. A riskier path is investing money through the purchase of valuable items (or assets) in the hopes that they will increase in worth over time and yield returns (or profits). Assets can include shares in companies, real estate or land investments, or capital such as money, equipment, and structures used to create wealth.

Geography

Concepts and Terminology of Physical and Human Geography

Physical Region

The Earth's surface, like many other things in the broader universe, does not remain the same for long; in fact, it changes daily. The Earth's surface is subject to a variety of physical processes that continue to shape its appearance. Water, wind, temperature, or sunlight play a role in continually altering the Earth's surface.

Erosion involves the movement of soil from one place to another and can be caused by a variety of stimuli including ice, snow, water, wind, and ocean waves. Wind erosion occurs in generally flat, dry areas with loose topsoil. Over time, the persistent winds can dislodge significant amounts of soil into the air, reshaping the land and wreaking havoc on those who depend on agriculture for their livelihoods. Water can also cause erosion. For example, erosion caused by the Colorado River helped to form the Grand Canyon. Over time, the river moved millions of tons of soil, cutting a huge gorge in the Earth along the way. In water erosion, material carried by the water is referred to as sediment. With time, some sediment can collect at the mouths of rivers, forming deltas, which become small islands of fertile soil. This process of detaching loose soils and transporting them to a different location where they remain for an extended period of time is referred to as **deposition**, which is the end result of the erosion process.

In contrast to erosion, weathering does not involve the movement of any outside stimuli. Instead, the surface of the Earth is broken down physically or chemically. Physical weathering involves the effects of atmospheric conditions such as water, ice, heat, or pressure. For example, when ice forms in the cracks of large rocks or pavement, it can break down or split open the material. Chemical weathering generally occurs in warmer climates and involves organic material that breaks down rocks, minerals, or soil. Scientists believe this process led to the creation of fossil fuels such as oil, coal, and natural gas.

Climate

Weather is the condition of the Earth's atmosphere at a particular time. Climate is different; instead of focusing on one particular day, climate is the relative pattern of weather in a place for an extended period of time. For example, the city of Atlanta, Georgia generally has a humid subtropical climate; however, it also occasionally experiences snowstorms in the winter months. Over time, geographers, meteorologists, and other Earth scientists have determined these patterns that are indicative to north Georgia. Almost all parts of the world have predictable climate patterns, which are influenced by the surrounding geography.

The Central Coast of California is an example of a place with a predictable climate pattern. Santa Barbara, California, one of the region's larger cities, has almost the same temperature for most of the year, with only minimal fluctuation during the winter months. The temperatures there, which average between 75° and 65° Fahrenheit regardless of the time of year, are influenced by a variety of different climatological factors including elevation, location relative to the mountains and ocean, and ocean currents.

Other factors affecting climate include elevation, prevailing winds, vegetation, and latitudinal position on the globe.

Earth-Sun Relationships

Other major lines of latitude and longitude exist to divide the world into regions relative to the direct rays of the sun. These lines correspond with the Earth's tilt, and are responsible for the seasons. For example, the northern hemisphere is tilted directly toward the sun from June 22 to September 23, which creates the summer season in that part of the world. Conversely, the southern hemisphere is tilted away from the direct rays of the sun and experiences winter during those same months.

The area between the **Tropic of Cancer** and the **Tropic of Capricorn** (called the tropics) has more direct exposure to the sun, tends to be warmer year-round, and experiences fewer variations in seasonal temperatures. Most of the Earth's population lives in the area between the Tropic of Cancer and the Arctic Circle (66.5 degrees north), which is one of the middle latitudes. In the Southern Hemisphere, the middle latitudes exist between the Tropic of Capricorn and the Antarctic Circle (66.5 degrees south). In both of these places, indirect rays of the sun strike the Earth. Therefore, seasons are more pronounced, and milder temperatures generally prevail. The final region, known as the high latitudes, is found north of the Arctic Circle and south of the Antarctic Circle. These regions generally tend to be cold all year, and experience nearly twenty-four hours of sunlight during their respective summer solstice and twenty-four hours of darkness during the winter solstice.

Seasons in the Southern Hemispheres are opposite of those in the Northern Hemisphere due to the position of the Earth as it rotates around the sun. An **equinox** occurs when the sun's rays are directly over the Equator, and day and night are of almost equal length throughout the world. Equinoxes occur twice a year; the autumnal equinox occurs around September 22nd, while the spring equinox occurs around March 20th. Since the Northern and Southern hemispheres experience opposite seasons, the season names vary based on location (i.e. when the Northern Hemisphere is experiencing summer, the Southern Hemisphere is in winter).

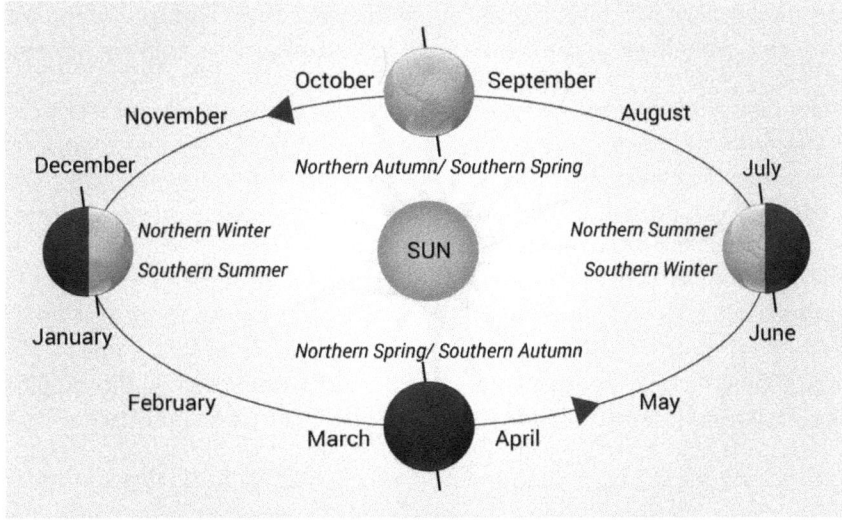

Climate, Vegetation, Soil, and Geology

Climate inevitably affects the vegetation, soil, and geology/geomorphology of particular regions around the globe. In terms of vegetation, the world can be divided into four major biomes: forest, savannah, grassland, and desert. These biomes produce different types of land vegetation. In a forest biome, trees form a continuous canopy. In a savannah biome, trees are with various grasses. In a grassland biome, the entire environment is covered in grass. In a desert biome, there is little to no land vegetation. Vegetation is both a product of the soil and a contributor to the soil. Erosion of the soil, for instance, can be minimized through planting crops and conserving the environment. The earth's geology/geomorphology is also fundamentally tied to vegetation and the soil. Different elevations and climates, for instance, produce different vegetation and soil. Likewise, the nutrients present in vegetation and the soil may affect the geological components of the earth.

Climate zones are created by the Earth's tilt as it travels around the Sun. These zones are delineated by the equator and four other special latitudinal lines: the Tropic of Cancer or Northern Tropic at 23.5° North; the Tropic of Capricorn or Southern Tropic at 23.5° South; the Arctic Circle at 66.5° North; and the Antarctic Circle at 66.5° South. The areas between these lines of latitude represent different climate zones. Tropical climates are hot and wet, like rainforests, and tend to have abundant plant and animal life, while polar climates are cold and usually have little plant and animal life. Temperate zones can vary and experience the four seasons.

Major Landforms, Climates, and Ecosystems

Earth is an incredibly large place filled with a variety of land and water ecosystems. Marine ecosystems cover over 75 percent of the Earth's surface and contain over 95 percent of the Earth's water. Marine ecosystems can be broken down into two primary subgroups: freshwater ecosystems, which only encompass around 2 percent of the earth's surface; and ocean ecosystems, which make up over 70 percent. Terrestrial ecosystems vary based on latitudinal distance from the equator, elevation, and proximity to mountains or bodies of water. For example, in the high latitudinal regions north of the Arctic Circle and south of the Antarctic Circle, frozen tundra dominates. Tundra, which is characterized by low temperatures, short growing seasons, and minimal vegetation, is only found in regions that are far away from the direct rays of the sun.

In contrast, deserts can be found throughout the globe and are created by different ecological factors. For example, the world's largest desert, the Sahara, is almost entirely within the tropics; however, other deserts like the Gobi in China, the Mojave in the United States, and the Atacama in Chile, are close to mountain ranges such as the Himalayas, the Sierra Nevada, and the Andes, respectively. In the United States, temperate deciduous forests dominate the southeastern region. The midwestern states such as Nebraska, Kansas, and the Dakotas, are primarily grasslands. The states of the Rocky Mountains can have decidedly different climates relative to elevation. Denver, Colorado, will often see snowfalls well into April or May due to colder temperatures, whereas cities in the eastern part of the state, with much lower elevations, may see their last significant snowfall in March.

The tropics generally experience warmer temperatures due to their position on the Earth in relation to the sun. However, like most of the world, the tropics also experience a variety of climatological regions. In Brazil, Southeast Asia, Central America, and even Northern Australia, tropical rainforests are common. These forests, which are known for abundant vegetation, daily rainfall, and a wide variety of animal life, are essential to the health of the world's ecosystems. For example, the Amazon Rain Forest's billions of trees produce substantial amounts of oxygen and absorb an equivalent amount of carbon dioxide—the substance that many climatologists assert is causing climate change or global warming. Unlike temperate deciduous forests whose trees lose their leaves during the fall and winter months, tropical rain forests are always lush, green, and warm. In fact, some rainforests are so dense with vegetation that a few indigenous tribes have managed to exist within them without being influenced by any sort of modern technology, virtually maintaining their ancient way of life in the modern era.

The world's largest land ecosystem, the taiga, is found primarily in high latitudinal areas, which receive very little direct sunlight. These forests are generally made up of coniferous trees, which do not lose their leaves at any point during the year as deciduous trees do. Taigas are cold-climate regions that make up almost 30 percent of the world's land area. These forests dominate the northern regions of Canada, Scandinavia, and Russia, and provide the vast majority of the world's lumber.

Climates are influenced by five major factors: elevation, latitude, proximity to mountains, ocean currents, and wind patterns. For example, the cold currents off the coast of California provide the West Coast of the United States with pleasant year-round temperatures. Conversely, Western Europe, which is at the nearly the same latitude as most of Canada, is influenced by the warm waters of the Gulf Stream, an ocean current that acts as a conveyor belt, moving warm tropical waters to the icy north.

In fact, the Gulf Stream's influence is so profound that it even keeps Iceland—an island nation in the far North Atlantic—relatively warm.

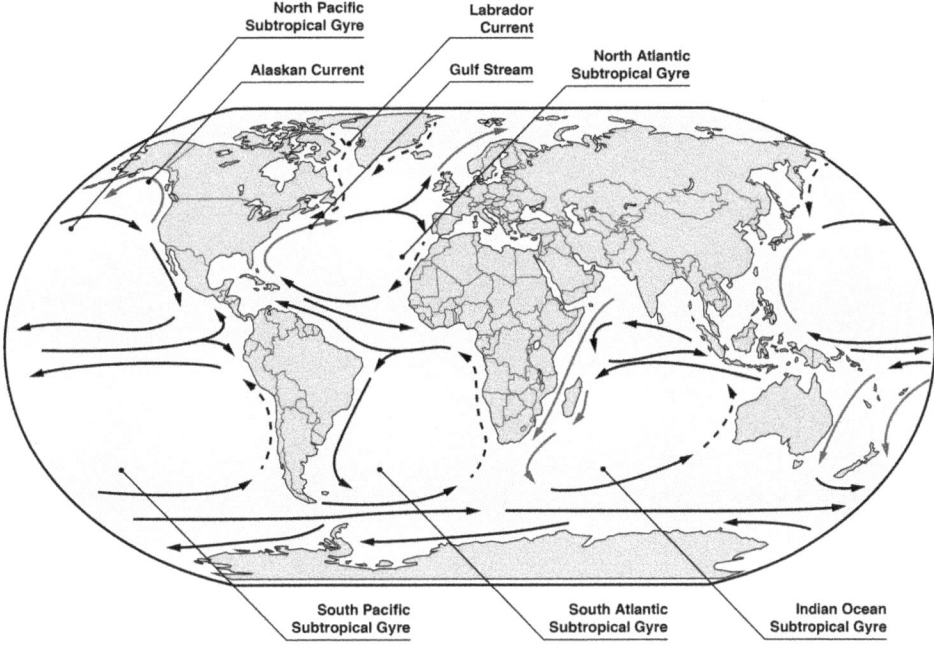

There are seven or eight major plates in the lithosphere and several minor plates. These tectonic plates explain the changing topography, or shape, of earth.

There are three types of boundaries between plates: divergent, convergent, and transform. All boundaries can be sites of volcanic activity. A divergent boundary occurs when plates separate. Lava fills in the space the plates create and hardens into rock, which creates oceanic crust. In a convergent boundary, if one of the plates is in the ocean, that plate is denser due to the weight of water. The dense ocean plate will slip under the land plate, causing a subduction zone where the plate moves underneath. Where plates converge on land, the continental crusts are both lighter with a similar density, and as a result they will buckle together and create mountains.

In transform boundaries, adjacent plates sliding past each other create friction and pressure that destroy the edges of the boundary and cause earthquakes. Transform boundaries don't produce magma, as they involve lateral movement.

Just as plates pushing together cause mountains, canyons are deep trenches caused by plates moving apart. Weather and erosion from rivers and precipitation run-off also create canyons. Deltas form when rivers dump their sediments and water into oceans. They are triangular flat stretches of land that are kind of like a triangular spatula; the handle represents the river, and the triangle represents the mouth of a delta.

Sand dunes are another landform caused by wind or waves in combination with the absence of plants to hold sand in place. These are found in sandy areas like the desert or the ocean.

Using Geographic Concepts to Analyze Spatial Phenomena

Regions

Geographers divide the world into regions in order to more fully understand differences inherent with the world, its people, and its environment. Lines of latitude such as the Equator, the Tropics, and the Arctic and Antarctic Circles already divide the Earth into solar regions relative to the amount of either direct or indirect sunlight that they receive. Although not the same throughout, the middle latitudes generally have a milder climate than areas found within the tropics. Furthermore, tropical locations are usually warmer than places in the middle latitudes, but that is not always the case. For example, the lowest place in the United States—Death Valley, California—is also home to the nation's highest-ever recorded temperature. Likewise, the Andes Mountains in Peru and Ecuador, although found near the Equator, are also home to heavy snow, low temperatures, and dry conditions, due to their elevation.

Formal regions are spatially defined areas that have overarching similarities or some level of homogeneity or uniformity. Although not exactly alike, a formal region generally has at least one characteristic that is consistent throughout the entire area. For example, the United States could be classified as one massive formal region because English is the primary language spoken in all fifty states. Even more specifically, the United States is a linguistic region—a place where everyone generally speaks the same language.

Functional regions are areas that also have similar characteristics but do not have clear boundaries. Large cities and their metropolitan areas form functional regions, as people from outside the official city limit must travel into the city regularly for work, entertainment, restaurants, etc. Other determining factors of a functional region could be a sports team, a school district, or a shopping center. For example, New York City has two professional baseball, basketball, and football teams. As a result, its citizens may have affinities for different teams even though they live in the same city. Conversely, a citizen in rural Idaho may cheer for the Seattle Seahawks, even though they live over 500 miles from Seattle.

Linguistics

Linguistics, or the study of language, groups certain languages together according to their commonalities. For example, the Romance languages—French, Spanish, Italian, Romanian, and Portuguese—all share language traits from Latin. These languages, also known as vernaculars, or more commonly spoken dialects, evolved over centuries of physical isolation on the European continent. The Spanish form of Latin emerged into today's Spanish language. Similarly, the Bantu people of Africa travelled extensively and spread their language, now called Swahili, which became the first Pan-African language. Since thousands of languages exist, it is important to have a widespread means of communication that can interconnect people from different parts of the world. One way to do this is through a lingua franca, or a common language used for business, diplomacy, and other cross-national relationships. English is a primary lingua franca around the world, but there are many others in use as well.

Religion

Religion has played a tremendous role in creating the world's cultures. Devout Christians crossed the Atlantic in hopes of finding religious freedom in New England, Muslim missionaries and traders travelled to the Spice Islands of the East Indies to teach about the Koran, and Buddhist monks traversed the Himalayan Mountains into Tibet to spread their faith. In some countries, religion helps to shape legal systems. These nations, termed theocracies, have

Social Studies

no separation of church and state and are more common in Islamic nations such as Saudi Arabia, Iran, and Qatar. In contrast, even though religion has played a tremendous role in the history of the United States, its government remains secular, or nonreligious, due to the influence of European Enlightenment philosophy at the time of its inception. Like ethnicity and language, religion is a primary way that individuals and people groups self-identify. As a result, religious influences can shape a region's laws, architecture, literature, and music. For example, when the Ottoman Turks, who are Muslim, conquered Constantinople, which was once the home of the Eastern Orthodox Christian Church, they replaced Christian places of worship with mosques. Additionally, they replaced different forms of Roman architecture with those influenced by Arabic traditions.

Economics

Economic activity also has a spatial component. Nations with few natural resources generally tend to import what they need from nations willing to export raw materials to them. Furthermore, areas that are home to certain raw materials generally tend to alter their environment in order to maintain production of those materials. In the San Joaquin Valley of California, an area known for extreme heat and desert-like conditions, local residents have engineered elaborate drip irrigation systems to adequately water lemon, lime, olive, and orange trees, utilizing the warm temperatures to constantly produce citrus fruits. Additionally, other nations with abundant petroleum reserves build elaborate infrastructures in order to pump, house, refine, and transport their materials to nations who require gasoline, diesel, or natural gas. Essentially, inhabitants of different spatial regions on Earth create jobs, infrastructure, and transportation systems to ensure the continued flow of goods, raw materials, and resources out of their location so long as financial resources keep flowing into the area.

Political System

The terms nation and state are often used interchangeably, but in political theory, they are two very distinct concepts. Nation refers to a people's cultural identity, while state refers to a territory's political organization and government.

Unlike states, there are no definitive requirements to be a nation; the nation just needs to include a group that is bound together by some shared defining characteristics such as the following:

- Language
- Culture and traditions
- Beliefs and religion
- Homeland
- Ethnicity
- History
- Mythology

The term state is commonly used to reference a nation-state, especially in regard to their government. There are four requirements for a political entity to be recognized as a state:

- Territory: a clearly defined geographic area with distinct borders

- Population: citizens and noncitizens living within the borders of the territory with some degree of permanence

- Legitimacy: legal authority to rule that is recognized by the citizens of the state and by other states

- Sovereignty: a political entity's right and power to self-govern without interference from external forces

Nation-state is the term used to describe a political entity with both a clearly defined nation and state. In a nation-state, the majority population of the state is a nation that identifies the territory as their homeland and shares a common history and culture. It is also possible to have several nations in the same nation-state. For example, there

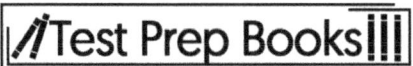

are Canadians in Canada and nations of Aboriginal peoples. The presence of multiple nations raises issues related to sovereignty.

> Example of a nation: Sikhs in India

> Example of a state: Vatican City

> Example of a nation-state: Germany

Innovation and Diffusion

Technological innovation in the earliest hearths of domestication, allowed the regions to become centers for trade, government, art, science, language acquisition, writing systems, and specialized economic activities. Additionally, these agricultural hearths became epicenters for economic inequality and social stratification, as increases in the wealth of certain farmers and merchants inevitably led to financial strata in each hearth.

As the varying cultures residing in each of the earliest hearths of domestication developed and evolved via spontaneous ideological adaptations, inventive technological advancements, and self-perpetuating cycles of population growth, elaborate continental trading systems emerged. A larger process of cultural diffusion allowed disparate ideas, traditions, and practices to be outwardly spread and exchanged between groups. This transfer of culture and knowledge impacted the daily interactions of previously isolated groups, thrusting them into a new, broader world of complex, multilateral social exchange.

Major World Regions

East Asia is the easternmost region of Asia, and it includes the countries of China, Japan, Mongolia, North Korea, South Korea, and Taiwan. Hong Kong and Macau are also in East Asia. The climate of East Asia is relatively temperate and predictable because of the East Asian monsoon flow, which produces cold, dry winters and extremely rainy summers. As the oldest and largest country in East Asia, China has a disproportionate impact on East Asian culture, particularly in terms of philosophy, language, and religion. Aside from Japan, East Asian countries continue to follow some aspects of the traditional Chinese calendar and celebrate the Lunar New Year.

Sub-Saharan Africa refers to the region of Africa that is south of the Sahara, encompassing forty-six out of the fifty-four countries in Africa. Sub-Saharan Africa has some of the most diverse climate zones in the world, ranging from tropical rainforests in Central Africa to hot deserts in the Horn of Africa. The culture of sub-Saharan Africa is similarly diverse, with more than 1,000 languages spoken in the region. Traditional African belief systems and traditions have remained intact in sub-Saharan Africa, and cultural practices often vary from village to village. Sub-Saharan African countries also have a shared history with European colonization, which is why Christianity is the most popular regional religion. Colonization and imperialism left a brutal legacy in the region, heavily contributing to its endemic poverty and sectarian conflicts.

Latin America refers to a region in North and South America that was colonized by Spain, France, and Portugal. The precise definition of Latin America varies, but the most common grouping includes Mexico, the Caribbean, Central America, and South America. The climate and geography of Latin America differs by region, and examples of this climatic diversity include Caribbean tropics, Brazilian and Colombian rainforests, the hot deserts of Mexico, and the cold deserts of Argentina. European colonization had a lasting impact on contemporary Latin American culture. The region is overwhelmingly Catholic, nearly all countries predominantly speak the Romance language of their colonizers, and most countries have a syncretic culture that blends European, African, and indigenous traditions.

Europe is in the western half of the Eurasian continental area with its western edge bordering Atlantic Ocean to the west, its southern edge bordering North Africa to the south, and its southeastern edge bordering Turkey. Russia and Turkey are transcontinental countries with European territory, and their inclusion in Europe is a matter of perspective. Western Europe has a mild oceanic climate, Southern Europe has a Mediterranean climate, Northern

Europe (Scandinavia) has a cold climate, and Eastern Europe has a temperate continental climate. European culture is heavily influenced by the Roman Empire, and Europeans overwhelmingly practice Christianity.

Southwest Asia comprises the bulk of the Middle East, and it consists of countries in Mesopotamia and the Arabian Peninsula. Southwest Asia's climate is generally hot and arid with the notable exception of the Tigris and Euphrates watersheds in Mesopotamia, which forms part of the Fertile Crescent. Additionally, Southwest Asia has a significant amount of coastal areas due to its borders with the Mediterranean Sea, Red Sea, Persian Gulf, and Caspian Sea. Southwest Asian culture is closely tied to Islam, and the five most spoken languages are Arabic, Hebrew, Kurdish, Persian (Farsi), and Turkish. Southwest Asian culture is generally more traditionally patriarchal than other regions, and sectarian violence is widespread due to the region's colonial borders, religious conflicts, and resource disputes.

North Africa refers to the northernmost region of Africa, and its eastern region is commonly included as part of the Middle East. Aside from the northern coast's Mediterranean climate and Nile River Valley, the rest of North Africa has a hot and arid desert climate. North Africa has strong ethnic, cultural, and linguistic ties to Southwest Asia, which date back to the Muslim conquest of the region between 600 and 1000 C.E. Coptic Christians are the largest minority group, with significant populations in Algeria, Egypt, Morocco, and Tunisia. In addition, nomadic tribe-based societies continue to operate in the Western Sahara.

The United States has numerous regions. The Atlantic seaboard and the West Coast are commonly grouped together due to their similarities, including extensive coastlines, concentration of wealth, high population density, and metropolitan culture. The Northeast and Pacific Northwest have some of the densest forests in the United States. The Upper Midwest has extreme variations between its summer and winter temperatures, while the Lower Midwest is part of the Great Plains, which lies between the Mississippi River and Rocky Mountains. The South has a subtropical climate, and it has the most conservative and traditional culture in the United States by a significant margin. The Southwest is home to vast hot deserts, and, given its shared history and proximity to Mexico, Hispanic Americans strongly influence Southwestern culture.

Texas is in the Northern Hemisphere, the northern half of the Earth between the equator and the North Pole. Texas is located on the North American continent, a landmass in the Western Hemisphere that encompasses half of the Earth to the west of the prime meridian. Texas is part of the United States of America, and it's usually considered part of the Southwestern or Sunbelt regions. Texas is bordered by the states of Louisiana to the east, Oklahoma to the north, Arkansas to the northeast, and New Mexico to the west. Texas is also bordered by Mexico to the south and the Gulf of Mexico to the southeast. The Gulf of Mexico is a large body of saltwater that serves as a major port for international trade, making Texas a leader in the American shipping industry. The state of Texas, from Port Arthur (coastal east) to El Paso (mountainous west), spans nearly 773 miles.

Economic, Political, and Social Factors

How the Components of Culture Affect the Way People Live

Humans both adapt themselves to their environment and adapt their environment to suit their needs. Humans create social systems with the goal of providing people with access to what they need to live more productive, fulfilling, and meaningful lives. Sometimes, humans create destructive systems, but generally speaking, humans tend to leverage their environments to make their lives easier. For example, in warmer climates, people tend to wear lighter clothing such as shorts, linen shirts, and hats. In the excessively sun-drenched nations of the Middle East, both men and women wear flowing white clothing complete with both a head and neck covering in order to prevent the blistering effects of exposure to the sun. Likewise, the native Inuit peoples of northern Canada and Alaska use the thick furs from the animals they kill to insulate their bodies against the bitter cold.

Humans must also manipulate their environments to ensure that they have sufficient access to food and water. In locations where water is not readily available, humans have had to invent ways to redirect water for drinking or agriculture. For example, the city of Los Angeles, America's second most populous city, did not have adequate

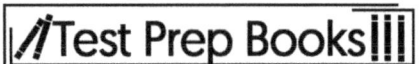

freshwater resources to sustain its population. However, city and state officials realized that abundant water resources existed approximately three hundred miles to the east. Rather than relocating some of its population to areas with more abundant water resources, the State of California undertook one of the largest construction projects in the history of the world, the Los Angeles Aqueduct, which is a massive water transportation system that connects water-rich areas with the thirsty citizens of Los Angeles.

Farming is another way in which humans use the environment for their advantage. The very first permanent British Colony in North America, Jamestown, VA, was characterized by a hot and humid climate with fertile soil. Consequently, its inhabitants engaged in agriculture for both food and profit. Twelve years after Jamestown's founding in 1607, it was producing millions of dollars of tobacco each year. In order to sustain this booming industry, millions of African slaves and indentured servants from Europe were imported to provide labor. Conversely, poor soil in the New England colonies did not allow for widespread cash crop production, and the settlers there generally only grew enough food for themselves on small subsistence farms. Due in part to this environmental difference, slavery failed to take a strong foothold in these states, thus creating distinct cultures within the same country.

Systems of education have a powerful impact on people's way of life as well as regional characteristics. Most countries require universal attendance in primary school; however, there is tremendous variety in secondary school and higher education.

Advanced industrial countries in North America, Europe, East Asia, and Australia commonly use standardized test results to sort secondary school students into special education, vocational, general education, and rigorous academic programs. This stratification shapes the socioeconomic roles students will later adopt in capitalist economies. Furthermore, students' professional and social trajectories are differentiated based on their participation in higher education systems.

Countries with emerging economies, such as China and India, place a premium on education due to the close relationship between education and economic development. As a result, many families tailor daily life around educational achievement, mirroring or exceeding the focus on it in advanced industrial countries. Many students in emerging economies also seek higher education opportunities in advanced industrial countries.

Less developed regions in Africa, Latin America, and the Middle East generally have weak secondary education programs and limited higher education opportunities. Additionally, female students tend to receive fewer educational opportunities, which reinforces traditional gender norms. Overall, the lack of universal education systems undermines development.

World Populations and Globalization

Two primary realms exist within the study of geography. The first, **physical geography**, essentially correlates with the land, water, and foliage of the Earth. The second, **human geography**, is the study of the Earth's people and how they interact with their environment. Several geographical factors impact the human condition, such as access to natural resources. For example, human populations tend to be higher around more reliable sources of fresh water. The metropolitan area of New York City, which has abundant freshwater resources, is home to over 18 million people. Australia, on the other hand, an entire country and continent, has much less accessibility to fresh water and houses only 7 million more people. Although water is not the only factor in this disparity, it certainly plays a role in population density—the total number of people in a particular place divided by the total land area, usually in square miles or square kilometers. Australia's population density is about 7 people per square mile, while the most densely populated nation on Earth, Bangladesh, is home to 2,889 people per square mile.

Population density can have a devastating impact on both the physical environment/ecosystem and the humans who live within the environment/ecosystem of a particular place. For example, Delhi, one of India's most populated cities, is home to nearly five million gasoline-powered vehicles. Each day, those vehicles emit an enormous amount

Social Studies

of carbon monoxide into the atmosphere, which directly affects the Delhi citizens' quality of life. In fact, the smog and pollution problems have gotten so severe that many drivers cannot see fifty feet in front of them. Additionally, densely populated areas within third-world nations, or developing nations, struggle significantly in their quest to balance the demands of the modern economy with their nation's lack of infrastructure. For example, nearly as many automobiles operate every day in major American cities like New York and Los Angeles as they do in Delhi, but they create significantly less pollution due to cleaner burning engines, better fuels, and governmental emission regulations.

One of the most significant demographic trends in world history is the increase in populations, which began to increase exponentially in the twentieth century. Before the 1800s, it took thousands of years to reach 1 billion people in the world. However, by 1999, the world population had increased to more than 6 billion people. As of 2016, the world population is 7.4 billion, and it is estimated that the population will increase to more than 11 billion by 2100. This is largely a result of a lower child mortality rate and higher life expectancy due to scientific progress. The effects of having a larger population are most visible in Africa and Asia, especially in India and China. Although larger populations provide for a larger workforce, they also put strain on the economy because more young people require employment.

Migration is governed by two primary causes: push factors that cause someone to leave an area, and pull factors that lure someone to a particular place. These two factors often work in concert with one another. For example, the United States of America has experienced significant internal migration from the industrial states in the Northeast (such as New York, New Jersey, Connecticut) to the Southern and Western states. This massive migration, which continues into the present-day, is due to high rents in the northeast, dreadfully cold winters, and lack of adequate retirement housing, all of which are push factors. These push factors lead to migration to the Sunbelt, a term geographers use to describe states with warm climates and less intense winters.

International migration also takes place between countries, continents, and other regions. The United States has long been the world's leading nation in regard to immigration, the process by which people permanently relocate to a new nation. Conversely, developing nations that suffer from high levels of poverty, pollution, warfare, and other violence all have significant push factors, which cause people to leave and move elsewhere. This process, known as emigration, is when people in a particular area leave in order to seek a better life in a different—usually better—location.

Immigration has changed the demographics of countries and can have positive and negative effects. Migration and immigration have occurred due to famine, warfare, and lack of economic prospects. Immigration can aid countries struggling to maintain a workforce, and it can also bring in needed medical professionals, scientists, and others with special training. However, immigration also puts strain on developed economies to support migrants who arrive without the necessary education and training to thrive in the advanced economies. Until recently, immigrants were encouraged, or in some cases, forced to assimilate and take on the customs and culture of their new country. For example, in the United States, legislation was passed to force German immigrants to learn English. More recently, developed countries have struggled to assimilate new arrivals to their countries, such as the recent surge of refugees into Europe. Unfortunately, the failure to adequately assimilate immigrants has created greater inequality and prevalence of radical behavior.

Due to improvements in transportation and communication, the world has become figuratively smaller. For example, university students now compete directly with others all over the world to obtain the skills that employers desire. Additionally, many corporations in developed nations have begun to outsource labor to nations with high levels of educational achievement but lower wage expectations. **Globalization**, the process of opening the marketplace to all nations throughout the world, has only just started to take hold in the modern economy. As industrial sites shift to the developing world, more opportunities become available for those nation's citizens as well. However, due to the massive amounts of pollution produced by factories, the process of globalization also has had significant ecological impacts. The most widely known impact, climate change, which most climatologists assert is caused by an increase of carbon dioxide in the atmosphere, remains a serious problem that has posed challenges for developing nations, who need industries in order to raise their standard of living, and developed nations, whose citizens use a tremendous amount of fossil fuels to run their cars, heat their homes, and maintain their ways of life.

Cultural Patterns and Characteristics in Various Regions

Although it is a significant factor, population density is not the only source of strain on a place's resources. Historical forces such as civil war, religious conflict, genocide, and government corruption can also profoundly alter the lives of a nation's citizens. For example, the war-torn nation of Somalia has not had a functioning government for nearly three decades. As a result, the nation's citizens have virtually no access to hospital care, vaccinations, or proper facilities for childbirth. Due to these and other factors, the nation's infant mortality rate, or the total number of child deaths per 1,000 live births, stands at a whopping 98.39/1000. When compared to Iceland's 1.82/1000, it's quite evident that Somalia struggles to provide basic services in the realm of childbirth and there is a dire need for humanitarian assistance.

Literacy rates, like infant mortality rates, are also excellent indicators of the relative level of development in a particular place. Many developing nations have both economic and social factors that hinder their ability to educate their own citizens. Due to radical religious factions within some nations like Afghanistan and Pakistan, girls are often denied the ability to attend school, which further reduces the nation's overall literacy rate. For example, girls in Afghanistan have a 24.2 percent literacy rate, one of the lowest rates of any record-keeping nation on Earth. Although literacy rates are useful in determining a nation's development level, high literacy rates do exist within developing nations. For example, Suriname, which has a significantly lower GDP (Gross Domestic Product) than Afghanistan, enjoys a 94 percent literacy rate among both sexes. Utilizing this and other data, geographers can form questions and conduct further research about such phenomena. Demographic data, such as population density, the infant mortality rate, and the literacy rate all provide insight into the characteristics of a particular place and help geographers better understand the spatial world.

The demographic transition model is a concept that explains the pattern of population change by examining two key statistics of a country: birth rate and death rate. This model suggests that as a country becomes more developed, the birth and death rates move through a predictable cycle.

Interpreting Maps

Geographical concepts are visually conveyed through maps. The map below illustrates some key points about geography.

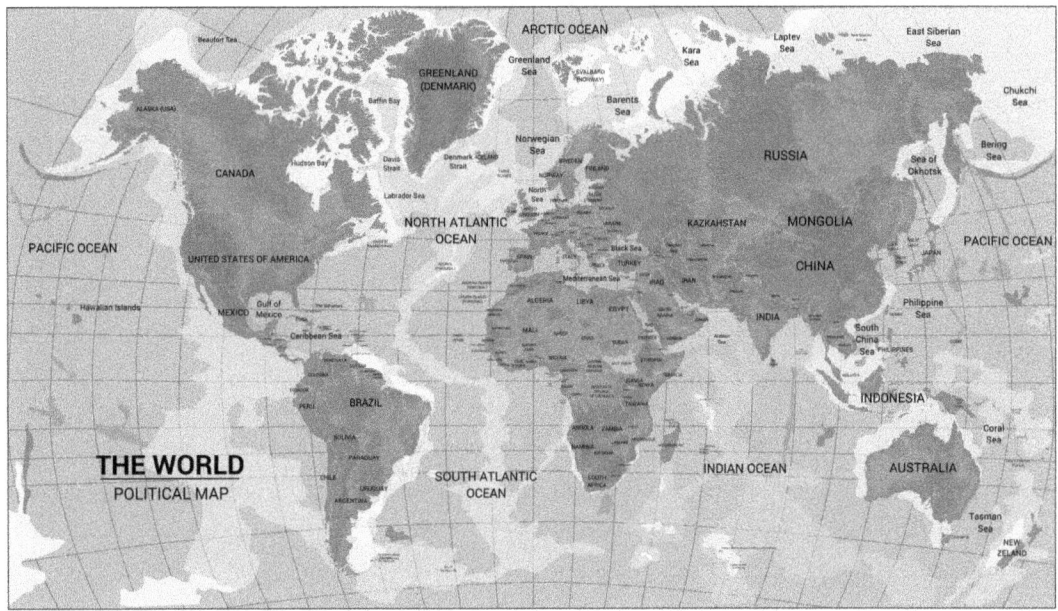

This is a traditional map of the world that displays all countries and six of the seven continents. Countries are the most common regional identifiers, and they can be identified on this map by their labels. The continents are not identified on this map, with the exception of Australia, but they are larger landmasses that encompass most of the countries in their respective areas; the other five visible continents are North America, South America, Europe, Africa, and Asia. The seventh continent, Antarctica, is found at the South Pole and has been omitted from the map.

The absence of Antarctica leads into the issues of distortion, in which geographical features are altered on a map. Some degree of distortion is to be expected with a two-dimensional flat map of the world because the earth is a sphere. A map projection transforms a spherical map of the world into a flattened perspective, but the process generally alters the spatial appearance of landmasses. For instance, Greenland often appears, such as in the map above, larger than it really is.

Furthermore, Antarctica's exclusion from the map is, in fact, a different sort of distortion—that of the mapmakers' biases. Mapmakers determine which features are included on the map and which ones are not. Antarctica, for example, is often missing from maps because, unlike the other continents, it has a limited human population. Moreover, a study of the world reveals that many of the distinctions on maps are human constructions.

Maps reveal key features about the world. Some maps display variations in topography, or the differences in elevation of the terrain. A section of a topographical map can be viewed below. Where the lines are closer together, the terrain is steeper, and when the lines are more spread out, the terrain is flatter.

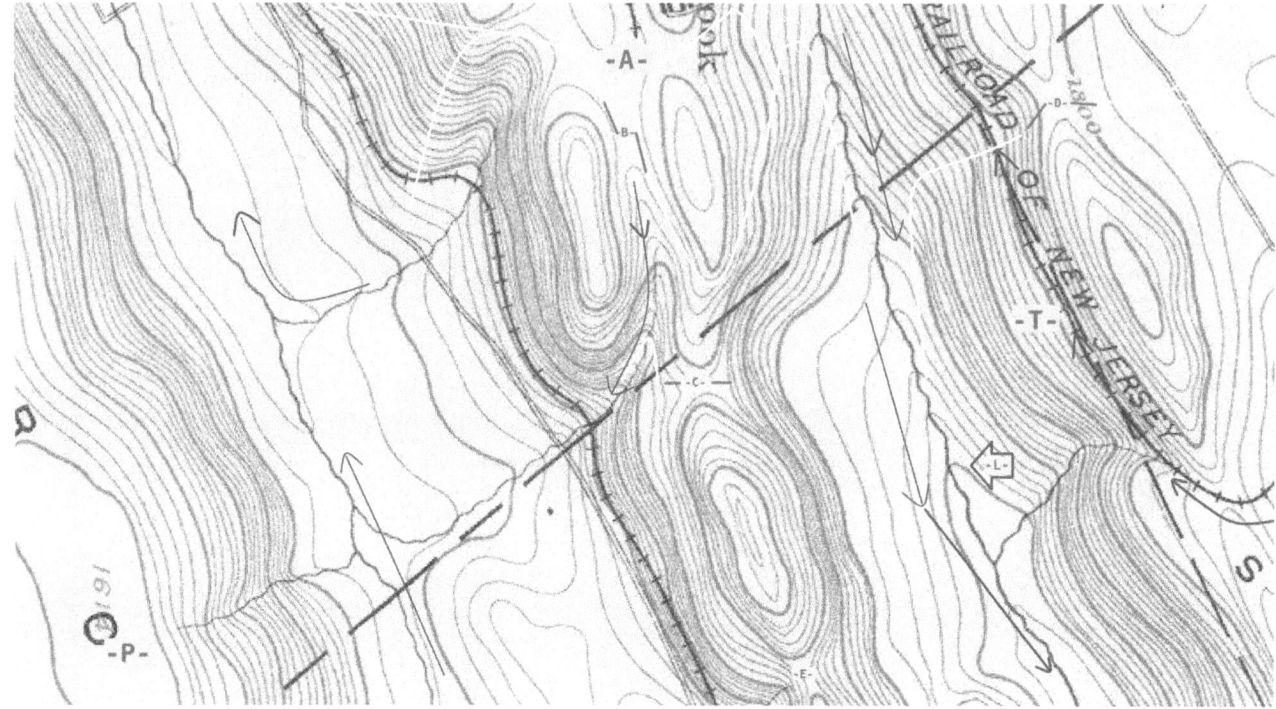

On some colored maps, the oceans, represented in blue between the continents, vary in coloration depending on depth. The differences demonstrate **bathymetry**, which is the study of the ocean floor's depth. Paler areas represent less depth, while darker spots reflect greater depth.

Maps may also display horizonal and vertical lines representing latitude and longitude. The horizontal lines, known as parallels, mark the calculated latitude of those locations and reveal how far north or south these areas are from the equator, which bisects the map horizontally.

Longitude, as signified by the vertical lines, determines how far east or west different regions are from each other. The lines of longitude, known as meridians, are also the basis for time zones, which determine the time for different regions. As one travels west between time zones, the given time moves backward accordingly. Conversely, if one travels east, the time moves forward.

There are two particularly significant longitudinal lines. First, the **Prime [Greenwich] Meridian** marks zero degrees in longitude, and thus determines the other lines. The line circles the globe and divides it into the Eastern and Western hemispheres. Second, **the International Date Line** represents the change between calendar days. By traveling westward across the International Date Line, a traveler would essentially leap forward a day. For example, a person departing from the United States on Sunday would arrive in Japan on Monday. By traveling eastward across the line, a traveler would go backward a day. For example, a person departing from China on Monday would arrive in Canada on Sunday.

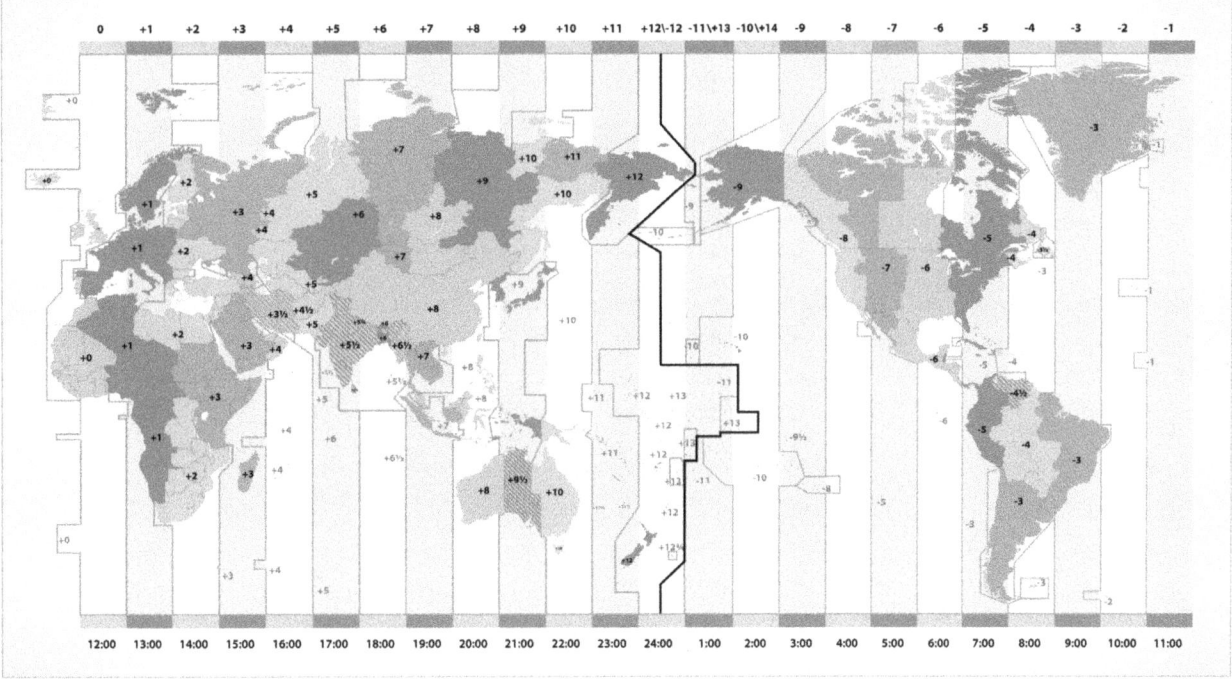

Although world maps are useful in showing the overall arrangement of continents and nations, it is also important at times to look more closely at individual countries because they have unique features that are only visible on more detailed maps.

For example, take the following map of the United States of America. The country is split into multiple states that have their own cultures and localized governments. Other countries are often split into various divisions, such as provinces, and while these features are ignored for the sake of clarity on larger maps, they are important when studying specific nations. Individual states can be further subdivided into counties and townships, and they may have their own maps that can be examined for closer analysis.

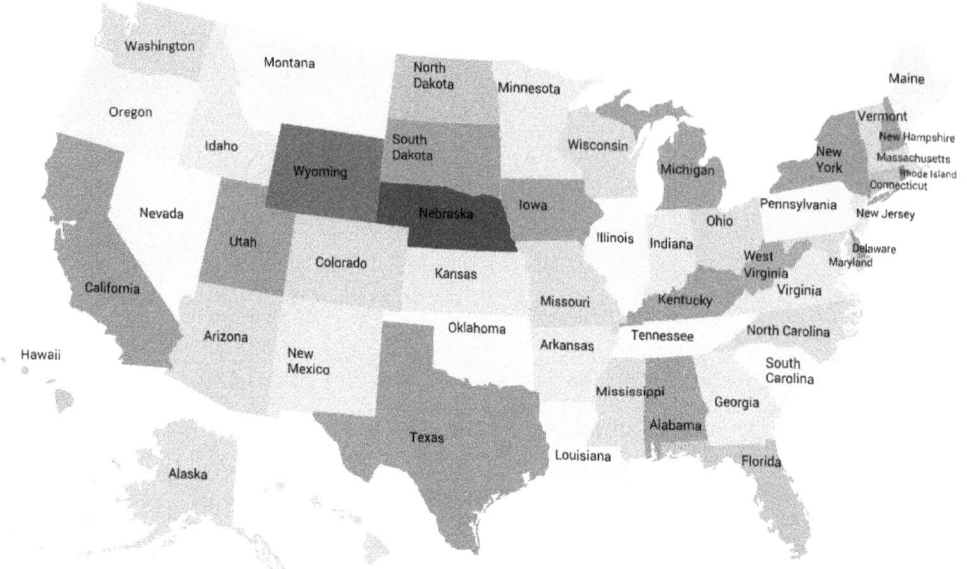

Finally, one of the first steps in examining any map should be to locate its key or legend, which will explain what different symbols represent on the map. As these symbols can be arbitrary depending on the maker, a key will help to clarify the different meanings.

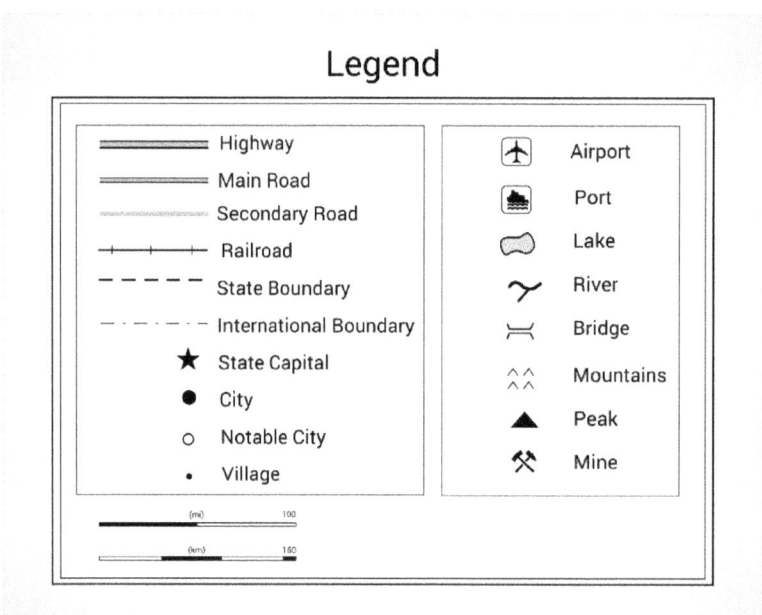

Practice Quiz

1. Which document established the first system of government in the United States?
   a. Declaration of Independence
   b. Constitution
   c. Articles of Confederation
   d. Bill of Rights

2. What are the two main parts of the federal legislative branch?
   a. President and vice president
   b. Federal and state
   c. District court and court of appeals
   d. Senate and House of Representatives

3. First-hand accounts of an event, subject matter, time period, or an individual are referred to as what type of source?
   a. Primary sources
   b. Secondary sources
   c. Direct sources
   d. Indirect sources

4. All but which of the following are true of the Tropics?
   a. They are consistently hit with direct rays of the sun.
   b. They fall between the Tropics of Cancer and Capricorn.
   c. They are nearer the Equator than the Middle Latitudes.
   d. They are always warmer than other parts of the Globe.

Question 5 is based on the following map:

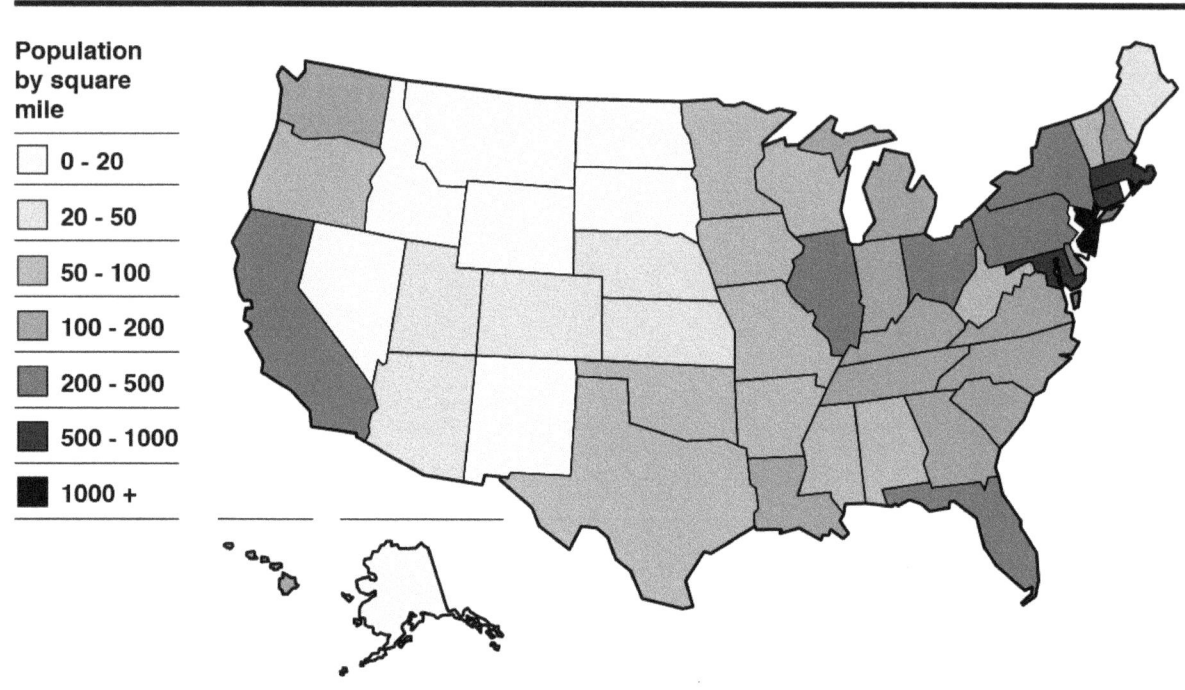

5. According to the map, what area of the United States has the highest population density?
   a. Northwest
   b. Northeast
   c. Southwest
   d. Southeast

See answers on the next page.

Answer Explanations

1. C: Issued in 1776, the Declaration of Independence, Choice A, explained why the colonists decided to break away from England but did not establish a government. That was left to the Articles of Confederation, which were adopted in 1781. The Articles of Confederation, Choice C, established a very weak central government that was replaced by the Constitution, Choice B, in 1789. It established a stronger executive branch. In 1791, the Bill of Rights, Choice D, amended the Constitution by guaranteeing individual rights.

2. D: The president and vice president are part of the executive branch, not the legislative branch. The question focuses specifically on the federal level, so state government should be excluded from consideration. As for the district court and the court of appeals, they are part of the judicial branch. The legislative branch is made up of Congress, which consists of the House of Representatives and the Senate.

3. A: Firsthand accounts are given by primary sources—individuals who provide personal or expert accounts of an event, subject matter, time period, or of an individual. They are viewed more as objective accounts than subjective. Secondary sources are accounts given by an individual or group of individuals who were not physically present at the event or who did not have firsthand knowledge of an individual or time period. Secondary sources are sources that have used research in order to create a written work. Direct and indirect sources are not terms used in literary circles.

4. D: Although nearest the direct rays of the sun, the Tropics are not always warm. In fact, the nations of Ecuador and Peru, which are entirely within the Tropics, are home to the Andes Mountains, which remain snowcapped the entire year. This climatological anomaly is also due to cooler ocean currents and the orographic effect. Choices A, B, and C are all true of the Tropics.

5. B: Choice B is correct. The map is a density map illustrating population density by state in the United States. Accordingly, the darker areas have higher population density. The darkest area of the map is the Northeast, so Choice B is correct. Choices A, C, and D show less population density than the Northeast.

HiSET Practice Test #1

Language Arts: Reading

The poem below, "The Human Seasons," was written by John Keats. Read it and answer questions 1–7.

> Four Seasons fill the measure of the year;
> There are four seasons in the mind of man:
> He has his lusty Spring, when fancy clear
> Takes in all beauty with an easy span:
> 5   He has his Summer, when luxuriously
> Spring's honied cud of youthful thought he loves
> To ruminate, and by such dreaming high
> Is nearest unto heaven: quiet coves
> His soul has in its Autumn, when his wings
> 10 He furleth close; contented so to look
> On mists in idleness—to let fair things
> Pass by unheeded as a threshold brook.
> He has his Winter too of pale misfeature,
> Or else he would forego his mortal nature.

1. What literary device does Keats primarily use in this poem?
   a. Simile
   b. Soliloquy
   c. Hyperbole
   d. Extended metaphor

2. The meaning of the word "ruminate" in line 7 is closest to:
   a. Ponder
   b. Unwind
   c. Respond
   d. Incorporate

3. According to the poem, how does a man change between Spring and Autumn?
   a. He starts preparing for his future.
   b. He feels more deeply connected to nature.
   c. He spends less time thinking about beautiful things.
   d. He becomes more sensible about how he spends his time.

4. Why does Keats end the poem with Winter?
   a. Winter represents the end of man's life.
   b. The narrator's least favorite season is winter.
   c. Winter is the final season of the calendar year.
   d. The poem is organized from the hottest season to the coldest.

5. Which statement would the narrator probably agree with?
   a. People are most content when they are young.
   b. People should appreciate the beauty of everyday life more.
   c. People change as they move through different stages of life.
   d. People spend too much time on daydreaming instead of being active.

6. What does "he would forego his mortal nature" mean in the final line?
    a. He would take a break.
    b. He would postpone or avoid death.
    c. He would give up nature for technology.
    d. He would move away from the countryside.

7. Which of the following is an example of alliteration in this poem?
    a. "in the mind of man"
    b. "On mists of idleness"
    c. "his wings / He furleth closed"
    d. "unheeded as a threshold brook"

Read the following excerpt and answer questions 8-14.

As long ago as 1860 it was the proper thing to be born at home. At present, so I am told, the high gods of medicine have decreed that the first cries of the young shall be uttered upon the anesthetic air of a hospital, preferably a fashionable one. So young Mr. and Mrs. Roger Button were fifty years ahead of style when they decided, one day in the summer of 1860, that their first baby should be born in a hospital. Whether this anachronism had any bearing upon the astonishing history I am about to set down will never be known.

I shall tell you what occurred, and let you judge for yourself.

The Roger Buttons held an enviable position, both social and financial, in ante-bellum Baltimore. They were related to the This Family and the That Family, which, as every Southerner knew, entitled them to membership in that enormous peerage which largely populated the Confederacy. This was their first experience with the charming old custom of having babies—Mr. Button was naturally nervous. He hoped it would be a boy so that he could be sent to Yale College in Connecticut, at which institution Mr. Button himself had been known for four years by the somewhat obvious nickname of "Cuff."

On the September morning consecrated to the enormous event he arose nervously at six o'clock, dressed himself, adjusted an impeccable stock, and hurried forth through the streets of Baltimore to the hospital, to determine whether the darkness of the night had borne in new life upon its bosom.

When he was approximately a hundred yards from the Maryland Private Hospital for Ladies and Gentlemen he saw Doctor Keene, the family physician, descending the front steps, rubbing his hands together with a washing movement—as all doctors are required to do by the unwritten ethics of their profession.

Mr. Roger Button, the president of Roger Button & Co., Wholesale Hardware, began to run toward Doctor Keene with much less dignity than was expected from a Southern gentleman of that picturesque period. "Doctor Keene!" he called. "Oh, Doctor Keene!"

The doctor heard him, faced around, and stood waiting, a curious expression settling on his harsh, medicinal face as Mr. Button drew near.

"What happened?" demanded Mr. Button, as he came up in a gasping rush. "What was it? How is she? A boy? Who is it? What—"

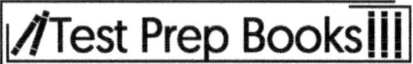

"Talk sense!" said Doctor Keene sharply. He appeared somewhat irritated.

"Is the child born?" begged Mr. Button.

Doctor Keene frowned. "Why, yes, I suppose so—after a fashion." Again he threw a curious glance at Mr. Button.

From "The Curious Case of Benjamin Button" by F.S. Fitzgerald, 1922.

8. According to the passage, what major event is about to happen in this story?
    a. Mr. Button is about to go to a funeral.
    b. Mr. Button's wife is about to have a baby.
    c. Mr. Button is getting ready to go to the doctor's office.
    d. Mr. Button is about to go shopping for new clothes.

9. What kind of tone does the above passage have?
    a. Nervous and excited
    b. Sad and angry
    c. Shameful and confused
    d. Grateful and joyous

10. As it is used in the fourth paragraph, the word *consecrated* most nearly means:
    a. Numbed
    b. Chained
    c. Dedicated
    d. Moved

11. What does the author mean to do by adding the following statement?

    "rubbing his hands together with a washing movement—as all doctors are required to do by the unwritten ethics of their profession."

    a. Suggest that Mr. Button is tired of the doctor.
    b. Try to explain the detail of the doctor's profession.
    c. Hint to readers that the doctor is an unethical man.
    d. Give readers a visual picture of what the doctor is doing.

12. Which of the following best describes the development of this passage?
    a. It starts in the middle of a narrative in order to transition smoothly to a conclusion.
    b. It is a chronological narrative from beginning to end.
    c. The sequence of events is backwards—we go from future events to past events.
    d. It introduces the setting of the story and its characters.

13. Which of the following is an example of an imperative sentence?
    a. "Oh, Doctor Keene!"
    b. "Talk sense!"
    c. "Is the child born?"
    d. "Why, yes, I suppose so—"

14. This passage can best be described as what type of text?
    a. Expository
    b. Descriptive
    c. Narrative
    d. Persuasive

Read this article about NASA technology and answer questions 15–20.

When researchers and engineers undertake a large-scale scientific project, they may end up making discoveries and developing technologies that have far wider uses than originally intended. This is especially true at NASA, one of the most influential and innovative scientific organizations in America. NASA *spinoff technology* refers to innovations originally developed for NASA space projects that are now used in a wide range of different commercial fields. Many consumers are unaware that products they are buying are based on NASA research! Spinoff technology proves that it's worthwhile to invest in science research because it could enrich people's lives in unexpected ways.

The first spinoff technology worth mentioning is baby food. In space, where astronauts have limited access to fresh food and fewer options about their daily meals, malnutrition is a serious concern. Consequently, NASA researchers were looking for ways to enhance the nutritional value of astronauts' food. Scientists found that a certain type of algae could be added to food to improve the food's neurological benefits. When experts in the commercial food industry learned of this algae's potential to boost brain health, they were quick to begin their own research. The nutritional substance from algae then developed into a product called life's DHA, which can be found in over 90 percent of infant food sold in America.

Another intriguing example of a spinoff technology can be found in fashion. People who are always dropping their sunglasses may have invested in a pair of sunglasses with scratch-resistant lenses, which are made of glass that is impossible to scratch, even when dropped on an abrasive surface. This innovation is incredibly advantageous for people who are clumsy, but most shoppers don't know that this technology was originally developed by NASA. Scientists first created scratch-resistant glass to help protect costly and crucial equipment from getting scratched in space, especially the helmet visors in space suits. However, sunglasses companies later realized that this technology could be profitable for their products, and they licensed the technology from NASA.

15. What is the main purpose of this article?
    a. To advise consumers to do more research before making a purchase
    b. To persuade readers to support NASA's research
    c. To tell a narrative about the history of space technology
    d. To define and describe examples of spinoff technology

16. What is the organizational structure of this article?
    a. A general definition followed by more specific examples
    b. A general opinion followed by supporting evidence
    c. An important moment in history followed by chronological details
    d. A popular misconception followed by counterevidence

17. Why did NASA scientists research algae?
    a. They already knew algae was healthy for babies.
    b. They were interested in how to grow food in space.
    c. They were looking for ways to add health benefits to food.
    d. They hoped to use it to protect expensive research equipment.

18. What does the word *neurological* mean in the second paragraph?
    a. Related to the body
    b. Related to the brain
    c. Related to vitamins
    d. Related to technology

19. Why does the author mention space suit helmets?
    a. To give an example of astronaut fashion
    b. To explain where sunglasses got their shape from
    c. To explain how astronauts protect their eyes
    d. To give an example of valuable space equipment

Read the following excerpt and answer questions 20-26.

Insects as a whole are preeminently creatures of the land and the air. This is shown not only by the possession of wings by a vast majority of the class, but by the mode of breathing to which reference has already been made, a system of branching air-tubes carrying atmospheric air with its combustion-supporting oxygen to all the insect's tissues. The air gains access to these tubes through a number of paired air-holes or spiracles, arranged segmentally in series.

It is of great interest to find that, nevertheless, a number of insects spend much of their time under water. This is true of not a few in the perfect winged state, as for example aquatic beetles and water-bugs ('boatmen' and 'scorpions') which have some way of protecting their spiracles when submerged, and, possessing usually the power of flight, can pass on occasion from pond or stream to upper air. But it is advisable in connection with our present subject to dwell especially on some insects that remain continually under water till they are ready to undergo their final molt and attain the winged state, which they pass entirely in the air. The preparatory instars of such insects are aquatic; the adult instar is aerial. All mayflies, dragonflies, and caddisflies, many beetles and two-winged flies, and a few moths thus divide their life-story between the water and the air. For the present we confine attention to the stoneflies, the mayflies, and the dragonflies, three well-known orders of insects respectively called by systematists the Plecoptera, the Ephemeroptera, and the Odonata.

In the case of many insects that have aquatic larvae, the latter are provided with some arrangement for enabling them to reach atmospheric air through the surface-film of the water. But the larva of a stonefly, a dragonfly, or a mayfly is adapted more completely than these for aquatic life; it can, by means of gills of some kind, breathe the air dissolved in water.

Excerpt from *The Life-Story of Insects* by Geo H. Carpenter

20. Which statement best details the central idea in this passage?
    a. It introduces certain insects that transition from water to air.
    b. It delves into entomology, especially where gills are concerned.
    c. It defines what constitutes insects' breathing.
    d. It invites readers to have a hand in the preservation of insects.

HiSET Practice Test #1

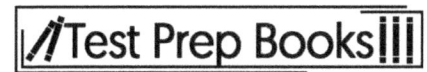

21. Which definition most closely relates to the usage of the word *molt* in the passage?
    a. An adventure of sorts, especially underwater
    b. Mating act between two insects
    c. The act of shedding part or all of the outer shell
    d. Death of an organism that ends in a revival of life

22. What is the purpose of the first paragraph in relation to the second paragraph?
    a. The first paragraph serves as a cause, and the second paragraph serves as an effect.
    b. The first paragraph serves as a contrast to the second.
    c. The first paragraph is a description for the argument in the second paragraph.
    d. The first and second paragraphs are merely presented in a sequence.

23. What does the following sentence most nearly mean?

    The preparatory instars of such insects are aquatic; the adult instar is aerial.

    a. The volume of water is necessary to prep the insect for transition rather than the volume of the air.
    b. The abdomen of the insect is designed like a star in the water as well as the air.
    c. The early stages in between periods of molting are acted out in the water, while the last stage is in the air.
    d. These insects breathe first in the water through gills yet continue to use the same organs to breathe in the air.

24. Which of the statements reflects information that one could reasonably infer based on the author's tone?
    a. The author's tone is persuasive and attempts to call the audience to action.
    b. The author's tone is passionate due to excitement over the subject and personal narrative.
    c. The author's tone is informative and exhibits interest in the subject of the study.
    d. The author's tone is somber, depicting some anger at the state of insect larvae.

25. Which statement best describes stoneflies, mayflies, and dragonflies?
    a. They are creatures of the land and the air.
    b. They have a way of protecting their spiracles when submerged.
    c. Their larvae can breathe the air dissolved in water through gills of some kind.
    d. The preparatory instars of these insects are aerial.

26. According to the passage, what is true of "boatmen" and "scorpions"?
    a. They have no way of protecting their spiracles when submerged.
    b. They have some way of protecting their spiracles when submerged.
    c. They usually do not possess the power of flight.
    d. They remain continually under water till they are ready to undergo their final molt.

This article discusses the famous poet and playwright William Shakespeare. Read it and answer questions 27–34.

People who argue that William Shakespeare isn't responsible for the plays attributed to his name are known as anti-Stratfordians (from the name of Shakespeare's birthplace, Stratford-upon-Avon). The most common anti-Stratfordian claim is that William Shakespeare simply was not educated enough or from a high enough social class to have written plays overflowing with references to such a wide range of subjects like history, the classics, religion, and international culture. William Shakespeare was the son of a glove-maker, he only had a basic grade-school education, and he never set foot outside of England—so how could he have produced plays of such sophistication and imagination? How could he have written in such detail about historical figures and events, or about different cultures and locations around Europe? According to anti-Stratfordians, the depth of knowledge contained in Shakespeare's plays suggests a well-traveled writer from a wealthy

251

background with a university education, not a countryside writer like Shakespeare. But in fact, there isn't much substance to such speculation, and most anti-Stratfordian arguments can be refuted with a little background about Shakespeare's time and upbringing.

First of all, those who doubt Shakespeare's authorship often point to his common birth and brief education as stumbling blocks to his writerly genius. Although it's true that Shakespeare did not come from a noble class, his father was a very *successful* glove-maker and his mother was from a very wealthy land-owning family—so while Shakespeare may have had a country upbringing, he was certainly from a well-off family and would have been educated accordingly. Also, even though he did not attend university, grade-school education in Shakespeare's time was actually quite rigorous and exposed students to classic drama through writers like Seneca and Ovid. It's not unreasonable to believe that Shakespeare received a very solid foundation in poetry and literature from his early schooling.

Next, anti-Stratfordians tend to question how Shakespeare could write so extensively about countries and cultures he had never visited before (for example, several of his most famous works like *Romeo and Juliet* and *The Merchant of Venice* were set in Italy, on the opposite side of Europe). But again, this criticism doesn't hold up under scrutiny. For one thing, Shakespeare was living in London, a bustling metropolis of international trade, the most populous city in England, and a political and cultural hub of Europe. In the daily crowds of people, Shakespeare would certainly have been able to meet travelers from other countries and hear firsthand accounts of life in their home country. And, in addition to the influx of information from world travelers, this was also the age of the printing press. This jump in technology made it possible to print and circulate books much more easily than in the past. This also allowed for a freer flow of information across different countries, allowing people to read about life and ideas throughout Europe. One needn't travel the continent in order to learn and write about its different cultures.

27. The main purpose of this article is to:
    a. Explain two sides of an argument and allow readers to choose which side they agree with
    b. Encourage readers to be skeptical about the authorship of famous poems and plays
    c. Give historical background about an important literary figure
    d. Criticize a theory by presenting counterevidence

28. Which sentence contains the author's thesis?
    a. "People who argue that William Shakespeare isn't responsible for the plays attributed to his name are known as anti-Stratfordians."
    b. "But in fact, there isn't much substance to such speculation, and most anti-Stratfordian arguments can be refuted with a little background about Shakespeare's time and upbringing."
    c. "It's not unreasonable to believe that Shakespeare received a very solid foundation in poetry and literature from his early schooling."
    d. "Next, anti-Stratfordians tend to question how Shakespeare could write so extensively about countries and cultures he had never visited before."

29. In the first paragraph, "How could he have written in such detail about historical figures and events, or about different cultures and locations around Europe?" is an example of which of the following?
    a. Hyperbole
    b. Onomatopoeia
    c. Rhetorical question
    d. Appeal to authority

30. How does the author respond to the claim that Shakespeare was not well-educated because he didn't attend university?
    a. By insisting upon Shakespeare's natural genius
    b. By explaining grade-school curriculum in Shakespeare's time
    c. By comparing Shakespeare with other uneducated writers of his time
    d. By pointing out that Shakespeare's wealthy parents probably paid for private tutors

31. The word *bustling* in the third paragraph most nearly means:
    a. Busy
    b. Foreign
    c. Expensive
    d. Undeveloped

32. What can be inferred from the article?
    a. Shakespeare's peers were jealous of his success and wanted to attack his reputation.
    b. Until recently, classical drama was only taught in universities.
    c. International travel was extremely rare in Shakespeare's time.
    d. In Shakespeare's time, glove-makers weren't part of the upper class.

33. Why does the author mention *Romeo and Juliet*?
    a. It's Shakespeare's most famous play.
    b. It was inspired by Shakespeare's trip to Italy.
    c. It's an example of a play set outside of England.
    d. It was unpopular when Shakespeare first wrote it.

34. Which statement would the author probably agree with?
    a. It's possible to learn things from reading rather than firsthand experience.
    b. If you want to be truly cultured, you need to travel the world.
    c. People never become successful without a university education.
    d. All of the world's great art comes from Italy.

A traveler prepares for a journey in this excerpt from a novel. Read it and answer questions 35–40.

When I got on the coach the driver had not taken his seat, and I saw him talking with the landlady. They were evidently talking of me, for every now and then they looked at me. Some of the people who were sitting on the bench outside the door came and listened, and then looked at me, most of them pityingly. I could hear a lot of words often repeated, queer words, for there were many nationalities in the crowd; so I quietly got my polyglot dictionary from my bag and looked them out. I must say they weren't cheering to me, for amongst them were "Ordog"—Satan, "pokol"—hell, "stregoica"—witch, "vrolok" and "vlkoslak"—both of which mean the same thing, one being Slovak and the other Servian for something that is either were-wolf or vampire.

When we started, the crowd round the inn door, which had by this time swelled to a considerable size, all made the sign of the cross and pointed two fingers towards me. With some difficulty I got a fellow-passenger to tell me what they meant; he wouldn't answer at first, but on learning that I was English, he explained that it was a charm or guard against the evil eye. This was not very pleasant for me, just starting for an unknown place to meet an unknown man; but everyone seemed so kind-hearted, and so sorrowful, and so sympathetic that I couldn't help but be touched. I shall never forget the last glimpse which I had of the inn-yard and its crowd of picturesque figures, all crossing themselves, as they stood round the wide archway, with its background of rich foliage

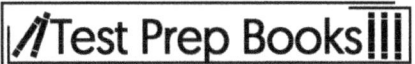

of oleander and orange trees in green tubs clustered in the centre of the yard. Then our driver cracked his big whip over his four small horses, which ran abreast, and we set off on our journey.

I soon lost sight and recollection of ghostly fears in the beauty of the scene as we drove along, although had I known the language, or rather languages, which my fellow-passengers were speaking, I might not have been able to throw them off so easily. Before us lay a green sloping land full of forests and woods, with here and there steep hills, crowned with clumps of trees or with farmhouses, the blank gable end to the road. There was everywhere a bewildering mass of fruit blossoms—apple, plum, pear, cherry; and as we drove by, I could see the green grass under the trees spangled with the fallen petals. In and out amongst these green hills of what they call here the "Mittel Land" ran the road, losing itself as it swept round the grassy curve, or was shut out by the straggling ends of pine woods, which here and there ran down the hillsides like tongues of flame. The road was rugged, but still we seemed to fly over it with a feverish haste. I couldn't understand then what the haste meant, but the driver was evidently bent on losing no time in reaching Borgo Prund.

35. What type of narrator is found in this passage?
    a. First person
    b. Second person
    c. Third-person limited
    d. Third-person omniscient

36. Which of the following is true of the traveler?
    a. He wishes the driver would go faster.
    b. He's returning to the country of his birth.
    c. He has some familiarity with the local customs.
    d. He doesn't understand all of the languages being used.

37. How does the traveler's mood change between the second and third paragraphs?
    a. From relaxed to rushed
    b. From fearful to charmed
    c. From confused to enlightened
    d. From comfortable to exhausted

38. Who is the traveler going to meet?
    a. A kind landlady
    b. A distant relative
    c. A friendly villager
    d. A complete stranger

39. Based on the details in this passage, what can readers probably expect to happen in the story?
    a. The traveler will become a farmer.
    b. The traveler will arrive late at his destination.
    c. The traveler will soon encounter danger or evil.
    d. The traveler will have a pleasant journey and make many new friends.

40. Which sentence from the passage provides a clue for question 39?
    a. "I must say they weren't cheering to me, for amongst them were "Ordog"—Satan, "pokol"—hell, "stregoica"—witch, "vrolok" and "vlkoslak"—both of which mean the same thing, one being Slovak and the other Servian for something that is either were-wolf or vampire."
    b. "When I got on the coach the driver had not taken his seat, and I saw him talking with the landlady."
    c. "Then our driver cracked his big whip over his four small horses, which ran abreast, and we set off on our journey."
    d. "There was everywhere a bewildering mass of fruit blossoms—apple, plum, pear, cherry; and as we drove by, I could see the green grass under the trees spangled with the fallen petals."

41. Which phrase below best defines *inference*?
    a. Reading between the lines
    b. Skimming a text for context clues
    c. Writing notes or questions that need answers during the reading experience
    d. Summarizing the text

42. Which phrase best defines *connotation*?
    a. An author's use of footnotes in their informational text
    b. An author's use of words or phrases to mean exactly what they say
    c. An author's use of allusion
    d. An author's use of words or phrases to evoke meaning beyond their literal definitions

Questions 43–50 are based on the following passages:

Passage I

Lethal force, or deadly force, is defined as the physical means to cause death or serious harm to another individual. The law holds that lethal force is only acceptable when you or another person are in immediate and unavoidable danger of death or severe bodily harm. For example, a person could be beating someone in such a way that the victim is suffering severe trauma that could result in death or serious harm. This would be an instance where lethal force would be acceptable and possibly the only way to save the victim from irrevocable damage.

Another example of when to use lethal force would be when someone enters your home with a deadly weapon. The intruder's presence and possession of the weapon indicate malicious intent and the ability to inflict death or severe injury upon you and your loved ones. Again, lethal force can be used in this situation. Lethal force can also be applied to prevent the harm of another individual. If a woman is being brutally assaulted and is unable to fend off an attacker, lethal force can be used to defend her as a last-ditch effort. If she is in immediate jeopardy of rape, harm, and/or death, lethal force could be the only response that could effectively deter the assailant.

The key to understanding the concept of lethal force is the term *last resort*. Deadly force cannot be taken back; it should be used only to prevent severe harm or death. The law does distinguish whether the means of one's self-defense is fully warranted or if the individual goes out of control in the process. If you continually attack the assailant after they are rendered incapacitated, this would be causing unnecessary harm, and the law can bring charges against you. Likewise, if you kill an attacker unnecessarily after defending yourself, you can be charged with murder. This would move lethal force beyond necessary defense, making it no longer a last resort but rather a use of excessive force.

Passage II

Assault is the unlawful and intentional act that causes reasonable apprehension in another individual either by an imminent threat or by initiating offensive contact. Assaults can vary, encompassing physical strikes, threatening body language, and even provocative language. In the case of the latter, even if a hand has not been laid, it is still considered an assault because of its threatening nature.

Let's look at an example. A homeowner is angered because his neighbor blows fallen leaves onto his freshly mowed lawn. Irate, the homeowner gestures a fist to his neighbor and threatens to bash his head in for littering on his lawn. The homeowner's physical motions and verbal threats herald a physical threat against the other neighbor. These factors classify the homeowner's reaction as an assault. If the angry neighbor hits the threatening homeowner in retaliation, that would constitute an assault as well because he physically hit the homeowner.

Assault also centers on the involvement of weapons in a conflict. If someone fires a gun at another person, this could be interpreted as an assault unless the shooter acted in self-defense. If an individual drew a gun or a knife on someone with the intent to harm them, that would be considered assault. However, it's also considered an assault if someone simply aims a weapon, loaded or not, at another person in a threatening manner.

43. What is the purpose of the second passage?
    a. To inform the reader about what assault is and how it is committed
    b. To inform the reader about how assault is a minor example of lethal force
    c. To disprove the previous passage concerning lethal force
    d. To recount an incident in which the author was assaulted

44. According to the passages, using lethal force would be legal in which of the following situations?
    a. A disgruntled cashier yells obscenities at a customer.
    b. A thief is seen running away with stolen cash.
    c. A man is attacked in an alley by another man with a knife.
    d. A woman punches another woman in a bar.

45. Given the information in the passages, which of the following must be true about assault?
    a. Assault charges are more severe than unnecessary use of force charges.
    b. There are various forms of assault.
    c. Smaller, weaker people cannot commit assaults.
    d. Assault is justified only as a last resort.

46. Which of the following, if true, would most seriously undermine the explanation proposed by the author of Passage I in the third paragraph?
    a. An instance of lethal force in self-defense is not absolutely absolved from blame. The law considers the necessary use of force at the time it is committed.
    b. An individual who uses lethal force under necessary defense is in direct compliance of the law under most circumstances.
    c. Lethal force in self-defense should be forgiven in all cases for the peace of mind of the primary victim.
    d. The use of lethal force is not evaluated on the intent of the user but rather the severity of the primary attack that warranted self-defense.

47. Based on the passages, what can be inferred about the relationship between assault and lethal force?
    a. An act of lethal force always leads to a type of assault.
    b. An assault will result in someone using lethal force.
    c. An assault with deadly intent can lead to an individual using lethal force to preserve their well-being.
    d. If someone uses self-defense in a conflict, it is called deadly force; if actions or threats are intended, it is called assault.

48. Which of the following best describes the way the passages are structured?
    a. Both passages open by defining a legal concept and then continue to describe situations that further explain the concept.
    b. Both passages begin with situations, introduce accepted definitions, and then cite legal ramifications.
    c. Passage I presents a long definition, while Passage II begins by showing an example of assault.
    d. Both cite specific legal doctrines and proceed to explain the rulings.

49. What can be inferred about the role of intent in lethal force and assault?
    a. Intent is irrelevant. The law does not take intent into account.
    b. Intent is vital for determining the lawfulness of using lethal force but not for assault.
    c. Intent is very important for determining both lethal force and assault; intent is examined in both parties and helps determine the severity of the issue.
    d. The intent of the assailant is the main focus for determining legal ramifications; it is used to determine if the defender was justified in using force to respond.

50. The author uses the example in the second paragraph of Passage II in order to do what?
    a. To demonstrate two different types of assault by showing how each specifically relates to the other
    b. To demonstrate a single example of two different types of assault, then adding in the third type of assault in the example's conclusion
    c. To prove that the definition of lethal force is altered when the victim in question is a homeowner and his property is threatened
    d. To suggest that verbal assault can be an exaggerated crime by the law and does not necessarily lead to physical violence

Language Arts: Writing

Read the selection about traveling in an RV and answer Questions 1–7.

I have to admit that when my father bought a recreational vehicle (RV), I thought he was making a huge mistake. I didn't really know anything about RVs, but I knew that my dad was as big a "city slicker" as there was. (1) <u>In fact, I even thought he might have gone a little bit crazy.</u> On trips to the beach, he preferred to swim at the pool, and whenever he went hiking, he avoided touching any plants for fear that they might be poison ivy. Why would this man, with an almost irrational fear of the outdoors, want a 40-foot camping behemoth?

(2) <u>The RV</u> was a great purchase for our family and brought us all closer together. Every morning (3) <u>we would wake up, eat breakfast, and broke camp.</u> We laughed at our own comical attempts to back The Beast into spaces that seemed impossibly small. (4) <u>We rejoiced as "hackers."</u> When things inevitably went wrong and we couldn't solve the problems on our own, we discovered the incredible helpfulness and friendliness of the RV community. (5) <u>We even made some new friends in the process.</u>

(6) <u>Above all, it allowed us to share adventures. While traveling across America,</u> which we could not have experienced in cars and hotels. Enjoying a campfire on a chilly summer evening with the

mountains of Glacier National Park in the background, or waking up early in the morning to see the sun rising over the distant spires of Arches National Park are memories that will always stay with me and our entire family. (7) Those are also memories that my siblings and me have now shared with our own children.

1. Which of the following would be the best choice for this sentence?

    In fact, I even thought he might have gone a little bit crazy.

    a. (No change; best as written.)
    b. Move the sentence so that it comes before the preceding sentence.
    c. Move the sentence to the end of the first paragraph.
    d. Omit the sentence.

2. Choose the best replacement for the underlined text (reproduced below).

    The RV was a great purchase for our family and brought us all closer together.

    a. (No change)
    b. Not surprisingly, the RV
    c. Furthermore, the RV
    d. As it turns out, the RV

3. Which is the best version of the underlined portion of this sentence (reproduced below)?

    Every morning we would wake up, eat breakfast, and broke camp.

    a. (No change)
    b. we would wake up, eat breakfast, and break camp.
    c. would we wake up, eat breakfast, and break camp?
    d. we are waking up, eating breakfast, and breaking camp.

4. Which is the best version of the underlined portion of this sentence (reproduced below)?

    We rejoiced as "hackers."

    a. (No change)
    b. To a nagging problem of technology, we rejoiced as "hackers."
    c. We rejoiced when we figured out how to "hack" a solution during a difficult situation.
    d. To "hack" our way to a solution, we had to rejoice.

5. Which is the best version of the underlined portion of this sentence (reproduced below)?

    We even made some new friends in the process.

    a. (No change)
    b. In the process was the friends we were making.
    c. We are even making some new friends in the process.
    d. We will make new friends in the process.

6. Which is the best version of the underlined portion of these sentences (reproduced below)?

   <u>Above all, it allowed us to share adventures. While traveling across America</u>, which we could not have experienced in cars and hotels.

   a. (No change)
   b. Above all, it allowed us to share adventures while traveling across America
   c. Above all, it allowed us to share adventures; while traveling across America
   d. Above all, it allowed us to share adventures—while traveling across America

7. Which is the best version of the underlined portion of this sentence (reproduced below)?

   <u>Those are also memories that my siblings and me</u> have now shared with our own children.

   a. (No change)
   b. Those are also memories that me and my siblings
   c. Those are also memories that my siblings and I
   d. Those are also memories that I and my siblings

Read the following section about Fred Hampton and answer Questions 8–20.

Fred Hampton desired to see lasting social change for African American people through nonviolent means and community recognition. (8) <u>In the meantime,</u> he became an African American activist during the American Civil Rights Movement and led the Chicago chapter of the Black Panther Party.

Hampton's Education

Hampton was born and raised (9) <u>in the Maywood neighborhood of Chicago, Illinois in 1948.</u> Gifted academically and a natural athlete, he became a stellar baseball player in high school. (10) <u>After graduating from Proviso East High School in 1966, he later went on to study law at Triton Junior College. While studying at Triton, Hampton joined and became a leader of the National Association for the Advancement of Colored People (NAACP). As a result of his leadership, the NAACP gained more than 500 members.</u> Hampton worked relentlessly to establish recreational facilities in the Maywood neighborhood and improve the educational resources provided to the impoverished black community.

The Black Panthers

The Black Panther Party (BPP) (11) <u>was another that</u> formed around the same time as and was similar in function to the NAACP. Hampton was quickly attracted to the (12) <u>Black Panther Party's approach</u> to the fight for equal rights for African Americans. Hampton eventually joined the chapter and relocated to downtown Chicago to be closer to its headquarters.

His charismatic personality, organizational abilities, sheer determination, and rhetorical skills (13) <u>enable him to quickly rise</u> through the chapter's ranks. Hampton soon became the leader of the Chicago chapter of the BPP where he organized rallies, taught political education classes, and established a free medical clinic. (14) <u>He also took part in the community police supervision project. He played an instrumental role</u> in the BPP breakfast program for impoverished African American children.

Hampton's (15) <u>greatest acheivment</u> as the <u>leader</u> of the BPP may have been his fight against street gang violence in Chicago. In 1969, (16) <u>Hampton was held by a press conference</u> where he made the gangs agree to a nonaggression pact known as the Rainbow Coalition. As a result of the pact, a multiracial alliance between blacks, Puerto Ricans, and poor youth was developed.

Assassination

(17) As the Black Panther Party's popularity and influence grew, the Federal Bureau of Investigation (FBI) placed the group under constant surveillance. In an attempt to neutralize the party, the FBI launched several harassment campaigns against the BPP, raided its headquarters in Chicago three times, and arrested over 100 of the group's members. Hampton was shot during such a raid that occurred on the morning of December 4th, 1969.

(18) In 1976; seven years after the event, it was revealed that William O'Neal, Hampton's trusted bodyguard, was an undercover FBI agent. (19) O'Neal will provide the FBI with detailed floor plans of the BPP's headquarters, identifying the exact location of Hampton's bed. It was because of these floor plans that the police were able to target and kill Hampton.

The assassination of Hampton fueled outrage amongst the African American community. It was not until years after the assassination that the police admitted wrongdoing. (20) The Chicago City Council now are commemorating December 4th as Fred Hampton Day.

8. Choose the best replacement for the underlined text (reproduced below).

    In the meantime, he became an African American activist during the American Civil Rights Movement and led the Chicago chapter of the Black Panther Party.

    a. (No change)
    b. Unfortunately,
    c. Finally,
    d. As a result,

9. Which is the best version of the underlined portion of this sentence (reproduced below)?

    Hampton was born and raised in the Maywood neighborhood of Chicago, Illinois in 1948.

    a. (No change)
    b. in the Maywood neighborhood, of Chicago, Illinois in 1948.
    c. in the Maywood neighborhood of Chicago, Illinois, in 1948.
    d. in Chicago, Illinois of Maywood neighborhood in 1948.

10. Which of the following sentences, if any, should begin a new paragraph?

    After graduating from Proviso East High School in 1966, he later went on to study law at Triton Junior College. While studying at Triton, Hampton joined and became a leader of the National Association for the Advancement of Colored People (NAACP). As a result of his leadership, the NAACP gained more than 500 members.

    a. (No change; best as written.)
    b. After graduating from Proviso East High School in 1966, he later went on to study law at Triton Junior College.
    c. While studying at Triton, Hampton joined and became a leader of the National Association for the Advancement of Colored People (NAACP).
    d. As a result of his leadership, the NAACP gained more than 500 members.

11. Choose the best replacement for the underlined text (reproduced below).

    The Black Panther Party (BPP) was another that formed around the same time as and was similar in function to the NAACP.

    a. (No change; best as written.)
    b. was another activist group that
    c. had a lot of members that
    d. was another school that

12. Which is the best version of the underlined portion of this sentence (reproduced below)?

    Hampton was quickly attracted to the Black Panther Party's approach to the fight for equal rights for African Americans.

    a. (No change)
    b. Black Panther Parties approach
    c. Black Panther Partys' approach
    d. Black Panther Parties' approach

13. Which is the best version of the underlined portion of this sentence (reproduced below)?

    His charismatic personality, organizational abilities, sheer determination, and rhetorical skills enable him to quickly rise through the chapter's ranks.

    a. (No change)
    b. are enabling him to quickly rise
    c. enabled him to quickly rise
    d. will enable him to quickly rise

14. Which is the best version of the underlined portion of this sentence (reproduced below)?

    He also took part in the community police supervision project. He played an instrumental role in the BPP breakfast program for impoverished African American children.

    a. (No change)
    b. He also took part in the community police supervision project but played an instrumental role
    c. He also took part in the community police supervision project, he played an instrumental role
    d. He also took part in the community police supervision project and played an instrumental role

15. Which word, if any, is misspelled?

    Hampton's greatest acheivement as the leader of the BPP may have been his fight against street gang violence in Chicago.

    a. (No change; best as written.)
    b. greatest
    c. acheivement
    d. leader

16. Which is the best version of the underlined portion of this sentence (reproduced below)?

> In 1969, <u>Hampton was held by a press conference</u> where he made the gangs agree to a nonaggression pact known as the Rainbow Coalition.

a. (No change)
b. Hampton held a press conference
c. Hampton, holding a press conference
d. Hampton to hold a press conference

17. Which is the best version of the underlined portion of this sentence (reproduced below)?

> <u>As the Black Panther Party's popularity and influence grew, the Federal Bureau of Investigation (FBI) placed the group under constant surveillance.</u>

a. (No change)
b. The Federal Bureau of Investigation (FBI) placed the group under constant surveillance as the Black Panther Party's popularity and influence grew.
c. Placing the group under constant surveillance, the Black Panther Party's popularity and influence grew.
d. As their influence and popularity grew, the FBI placed the group under constant surveillance.

18. Which is the best version of the underlined portion of this sentence (reproduced below)?

> <u>In 1976; seven years after the event,</u> it was revealed that William O'Neal, Hampton's trusted bodyguard, was an undercover FBI agent.

a. (No change)
b. In 1976, seven years after the event,
c. In 1976 seven years after the event,
d. In 1976. Seven years after the event,

19. Which is the best version of the underlined portion of this sentence (reproduced below)?

> <u>O'Neal will provide</u> the FBI with detailed floor plans of the BPP's headquarters, identifying the exact location of Hampton's bed.

a. (No change)
b. O'Neal provides
c. O'Neal provided
d. O'Neal, providing

20. Which is the best version of the underlined portion of this sentence (reproduced below)?

> <u>The Chicago City Council now are commemorating December 4th as Fred Hampton Day.</u>

a. (No change)
b. Fred Hampton Day by the Chicago City Council, December 4, is now commemorated.
c. Now commemorated December 4th is Fred Hampton Day.
d. The Chicago City Council now commemorates December 4th as Fred Hampton Day.

Read the essay entitled "Education is Essential to Civilization" and answer Questions 21–35.

Early in my career, (21) a master's teacher shared this thought with me "Education is the last bastion of civility." While I did not completely understand the scope of those words at the time, I have since come to realize the depth, breadth, truth, and significance of what he said. (22) Education provides society with a vehicle for (23) raising it's children to be civil, decent human beings with something valuable to contribute to the world. It is really what makes us human and what (24) distinguishes us as civelized creatures.

Being "civilized" humans means being "whole" humans. Education must address the minds, bodies, and souls of students. (25) It would be detrimental to society, only meeting the needs of the mind, if our schools were myopic in their focus. As humans, we are multidimensional, multifaceted beings who need more than head knowledge to survive. (26) The human heart and psyche have to be fed in order for the mind to develop properly, and the body must be maintained and exercised to help fuel brain functioning. Education is a basic human right, and it allows us to sustain a democratic society in which participation is fundamental to its success. It should inspire students to seek better solutions to world problems and to dream of a more equitable society. Education should never discriminate on any basis, and it should create individuals who are self-sufficient, patriotic, and tolerant of (27) others' ideas.

(28) All children can learn. Although not all children learn in the same manner. All children learn best, however, when their basic physical needs are met and they feel safe, secure, and loved. Students are much more responsive to a teacher who values them and shows them respect as individual people. Teachers must model at all times the way they expect students to treat them and their peers. If teachers set high expectations for (29) there students, the students will rise to that high level. Teachers must make the well-being of students their primary focus and must not be afraid to let students learn from their own mistakes.

In the modern age of technology, a teacher's focus is no longer the "what" of the content, (30) but more importantly, the 'why.' Students are bombarded with information and have access to any information they need right at their fingertips. Teachers have to work harder than ever before to help students identify salient information (31) so to think critically about the information they encounter. Students have to (32) read between the lines, identify bias, and determine who they can trust in the milieu of ads, data, and texts presented to them.

Schools must work in concert with families in this important mission. While children spend most of their time in school, they are dramatically and indelibly shaped (33) with the influences of their family and culture. Teachers must not only respect this fact, (34) but must strive to include parents in the education of their children and must work to keep parents informed of progress and problems. Communication between the classroom and home is essential for a child's success.

Humans have always aspired to be more, to do more, and to better ourselves and our communities. This is where education lies, right at the heart of humanity's desire to be all that we can be. Education helps us strive for higher goals and better treatment of ourselves and others. I shudder to think what would become of us if education ceased to be the "last bastion of civility." (35) We must be unapologetic about expecting excellence from our students? Our very existence depends upon it.

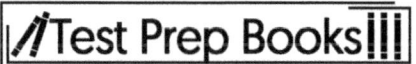

21. Which is the best version of the underlined portion of this sentence (reproduced below)?

    Early in my career, a master's teacher shared this thought with me "Education is the last bastion of civility."

    a. (No change)
    b. a master's teacher shared this thought with me: "Education is the last bastion of civility."
    c. a master's teacher shared this thought with me: "Education is the last bastion of civility".
    d. a master's teacher shared this thought with me. "Education is the last bastion of civility."

22. Which is the best version of the underlined portion of this sentence (reproduced below)?

    Education provides society with a vehicle

    a. (No change)
    b. Education provide
    c. Education will provide
    d. Education providing

23. Which is the best version of the underlined portion of this sentence (reproduced below)?

    for raising it's children to be civil, decent human beings with something valuable to contribute to the world.

    a. (No change)
    b. raises its children to be
    c. raising its' children to be
    d. raising its children to be

24. Which of these, if any, is misspelled?

    It is really what makes us human and what distinguishes us as civelized creatures.

    a. None of the underlined words are misspelled.
    b. distinguishes
    c. civelized
    d. creatures

25. Which is the best version of the underlined portion of this sentence (reproduced below)?

    It would be detrimental to society, only meeting the needs of the mind, if our schools were myopic in their focus.

    a. (No change)
    b. It would be detrimental to society if our schools were myopic in their focus, only meeting the needs of the mind.
    c. Only meeting the needs of our mind, our schools were myopic in their focus, detrimental to society.
    d. Myopic is the focus of our schools, being detrimental to society for only meeting the needs of the mind.

26. Which of these sentences, if any, should begin a new paragraph?

    The human heart and psyche have to be fed in order for the mind to develop properly, and the body must be maintained and exercised to help fuel brain functioning. Education is a basic human right, and it allows us to sustain a democratic society in which participation is fundamental to its success. It should inspire students to seek better solutions to world problems and to dream of a more equitable society.

   a. (No change; best as written.)
   b. The human heart and psyche have to be fed in order for the mind to develop properly, and the body must be maintained and exercised to help fuel the working of the brain.
   c. Education is a basic human right, and it allows us to sustain a democratic society in which participation is fundamental to its success.
   d. It should inspire students to seek better solutions to world problems and to dream of a more equitable society.

27. Which is the best version of the underlined portion of this sentence (reproduced below)?

    Education should never discriminate on any basis, and it should create individuals who are self-sufficient, patriotic, and tolerant of <u>others' ideas.</u>

   a. (No change)
   b. other's ideas
   c. others ideas
   d. others's ideas

28. Which is the best version of the underlined portion of this sentence (reproduced below)?

    <u>All children can learn. Although not all children learn in the same manner.</u>

   a. (No change)
   b. All children can learn although not all children learn in the same manner.
   c. All children can learn although, not all children learn in the same manner.
   d. All children can learn, although not all children learn in the same manner.

29. Which is the best version of the underlined portion of this sentence (reproduced below)?

    If teachers set high expectations for <u>there students</u>, the students will rise to that high level.

   a. (No change)
   b. they're students
   c. their students
   d. thare students

30. Which is the best version of the underlined portion of this sentence (reproduced below)?

    In the modern age of technology, a teacher's focus is no longer the "what" of the content, <u>but more importantly, the 'why.'</u>

   a. (No change)
   b. but more importantly, the "why."
   c. but more importantly, the 'why'.
   d. but more importantly, the "why".

31. Which is the best version of the underlined portion of this sentence (reproduced below)?

   Teachers have to work harder than ever before to help students identify salient information <u>so to think critically</u> about the information they encounter.

   a. (No change)
   b. and to think critically
   c. but to think critically
   d. nor to think critically

32. Which is the best version of the underlined portion of this sentence (reproduced below)?

   Students have to <u>read between the lines, identify bias, and determine</u> who they can trust in the milieu of ads, data, and texts presented to them.

   a. (No change)
   b. read between the lines, identify bias, and determining
   c. read between the lines, identifying bias, and determining
   d. reads between the lines, identifies bias, and determines

33. Which is the best version of the underlined portion of this sentence (reproduced below)?

   While children spend most of their time in school, they are dramatically and indelibly shaped <u>with the influences</u> of their family and culture.

   a. (No change)
   b. for the influences
   c. to the influences
   d. by the influences

34. Which is the best version of the underlined portion of this sentence (reproduced below)?

   Teachers must not only respect this fact, <u>but must strive</u> to include parents in the education of their children and must work to keep parents informed of progress and problems.

   a. (No change)
   b. but to strive
   c. but striving
   d. but strived

35. Which is the best version of the underlined portion of this sentence (reproduced below)?

   <u>We must be unapologetic about expecting excellence from our students? Our very existence depends upon it.</u>

   a. (No change)
   b. We must be unapologetic about expecting excellence from our students, our very existence depends upon it.
   c. We must be unapologetic about expecting excellence from our students—our very existence depends upon it.
   d. We must be unapologetic about expecting excellence from our students our very existence depends upon it.

Read the following passage and answer Questions 36–40.

Although many Missourians know that Harry S. Truman and Walt Disney hailed from their great state, probably far fewer know that it was also home to the remarkable George Washington Carver. (36) <u>As a child, George was driven to learn, and he loved painting.</u> At the end of the Civil War, Moses Carver, the slave owner who owned George's parents, decided to keep George and his brother and raise them on his farm.

He even went on to study art while in college but was encouraged to pursue botany instead. He spent much of his life helping others (37) <u>by showing them better ways to farm, his ideas improved agricultural productivity</u> in many countries. One of his most notable contributions to the newly emerging class of Black farmers was to teach them the negative effects of agricultural monoculture, i.e. (38) <u>growing the same crops in the same fields year after year, depleting the soil of much needed nutrients and results in a lesser yielding crop.</u>

Carver was an innovator, always thinking of new and better ways to do things, and is most famous for his over three hundred uses for the peanut. Toward the end of his career, (39) <u>Carver returns</u> to his first love of art. Through his artwork, he hoped to inspire people to see the beauty around them and to do great things themselves. (40) <u>Because Carver died,</u> he left his money to help fund ongoing agricultural research. Today, people still visit and study at the George Washington Carver Foundation at Tuskegee Institute.

36. Which of the following would be the best choice for this sentence (reproduced below)?

    As a child, George was driven to learn, and he loved painting.

    a. (No change)
    b. Move to the end of the first paragraph.
    c. Move to the beginning of the first paragraph.
    d. Move to the end of the second paragraph.

37. Which is the best version of the underlined portion of this sentence (reproduced below)?

    He spent much of his life helping others <u>by showing them better ways to farm, his ideas improved agricultural productivity</u> in many countries.

    a. (No change)
    b. by showing them better ways to farm his ideas improved agricultural productivity
    c. by showing them better ways to farm ... his ideas improved agricultural productivity
    d. by showing them better ways to farm; his ideas improved agricultural productivity

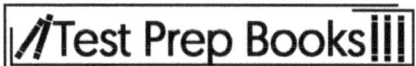

38. Which is the best version of the underlined portion of this sentence (reproduced below)?

   One of his most notable contributions to the newly emerging class of Black farmers was to teach them the negative effects of agricultural monoculture, i.e. growing the same crops in the same fields year after year, depleting the soil of much needed nutrients and results in a lesser yielding crop.

   a. (No change)
   b. growing the same crops in the same fields year after year, depleting the soil of much needed nutrients and resulting in a lesser yielding crop.
   c. growing the same crops in the same fields year after year, depletes the soil of much needed nutrients and resulting in a lesser yielding crop.
   d. grows the same crops in the same fields year after year, depletes the soil of much needed nutrients and resulting in a lesser yielding crop.

39. Which is the best version of the underlined portion of this sentence (reproduced below)?

   Toward the end of his career, Carver returns to his first love of art.

   a. (No change)
   b. Carver is returning
   c. Carver returned
   d. Carver was returning

40. Which is the best version of the underlined portion of this sentence (reproduced below)?

   Because Carver died, he left his money to help fund ongoing agricultural research.

   a. (No change)
   b. Although Carver died,
   c. When Carver died,
   d. Finally Carver died,

Read the following passage and answer Questions 41–50.

   (41) Christopher Columbus is often credited for discovering America. This is incorrect. First, it is impossible to "discover" something where people already live; however, Christopher Columbus did explore places in the New World that were previously untouched by Europe, (42) so the ships set sail from Palos, Spain. Another correction must be made, as well: Christopher Columbus was not the first European explorer to reach the Americas! (43) Nevertheless, it was Leif Erikson who first came to the New World and contacted the natives nearly 500 years before Christopher Columbus.

   Leif Erikson, the son of Erik the Red (a famous Viking outlaw and explorer in his own right), was born in either (44) 970 or 980. Depending on which historian you read. (45) His own family, though, did not raise Leif, which was a Viking tradition. Instead, one of Erik's prisoners taught Leif reading and writing, languages, sailing, and weaponry. At age 12, Leif was considered a man and returned to his family. He killed a man during a dispute shortly after his return, and the council banished the Erikson clan to Greenland.

   In 999, Leif left Greenland and traveled to Norway, where he would serve as a guard to King Olaf Tryggvason. It was there that he became a convert to Christianity. (46) Later trying to return home, Leif with the intention of taking supplies and spreading Christianity to Greenland, but his ship was blown off course and he arrived in a strange new land: present-day Newfoundland, Canada.

When he finally returned to his adopted homeland, Greenland, (47) Leif consults with a merchant who had also seen the shores of this previously unknown land we now know as Canada. The son of the legendary Viking explorer then gathered a crew of 35 men and set sail. Leif became the first European to set foot in the New World as he explored present-day Baffin Island and Labrador, Canada. His crew called the land Vinland since it was plentiful with grapes.

During their time in present-day Newfoundland, Leif's expedition made contact with the natives, whom they referred to as Skraelings (48) (which translates to 'wretched ones' in Norse). There are several secondhand accounts of their meetings. Some contemporaries described trade between the peoples. (49) Other accounts describes clashes where the Skraelings defeated the Viking explorers with long spears, while still others claim the Vikings dominated the natives. Regardless of the circumstances, it seems that the Vikings made contact of some kind. This happened around 1000, nearly 500 years before Columbus famously sailed the ocean blue.

Eventually, in 1003, Leif set sail for home and arrived at Greenland with a ship full of timber. (50) In 1020, 17 years later. The legendary Viking died. Many believe that Leif Erikson should receive more credit for his contributions in exploring the New World.

41. Which is the best version of the underlined portion of this sentence (reproduced below)?

    Christopher Columbus is often credited for discovering America. This is incorrect.

    a. (No change)
    b. Christopher Columbus is often credited for discovering America this is incorrect.
    c. Christopher Columbus is often credited for discovering America, this is incorrect.
    d. Christopher Columbus is often credited for discovering America: this is incorrect.

42. Which of the following facts would be the most relevant to include here?

    however, Christopher Columbus did explore places in the New World that were previously untouched by Europe, so the ships set sail from Palos, Spain.

    a. (No change; best as written.)
    b. so Columbus discovered Watling Island in the Bahamas.
    c. so the ships were named them the Santa María, the Pinta, and the Niña.
    d. so the term "explorer" would be more accurate.

43. Which is the best version of the underlined portion of this sentence (reproduced below)?

    Nevertheless, it was Leif Erikson who first came to the New World and contacted the natives nearly 500 years before Christopher Columbus.

    a. (No change)
    b. Rather,
    c. Finally,
    d. Suddenly,

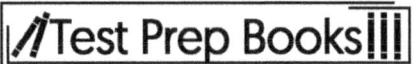

44. Which is the best version of the underlined portion of this sentence (reproduced below)?

   Leif Erikson, the son of Erik the Red (a famous Viking outlaw and explorer in his own right), was born in either 970 or 980. Depending on which historian you read.

   a. (No change)
   b. 970 or 980! depending on which historian you read.
   c. 970 or 980, depending on which historian you read.
   d. 970 or 980; depending on which historian you read.

45. Which of the following would be the best choice for this sentence?

   His own family, though, did not raise Leif, which was a Viking tradition.

   a. (No change; best as written.)
   b. Move to the end of the second paragraph.
   c. Move to the beginning of the second paragraph.
   d. Switch with the following sentence.

46. Which is the best version of the underlined portion of this sentence (reproduced below)?

   Later trying to return home, Leif with the intention of taking supplies and spreading Christianity to Greenland, but his ship was blown off course and he arrived in a strange new land: present-day Newfoundland, Canada.

   a. (No change)
   b. To return home later, Leif
   c. Leif later tried to return home
   d. Leif to return home tried later

47. Which is the best version of the underlined portion of this sentence (reproduced below)?

   When he finally returned to his adopted homeland, Greenland, Leif consults with a merchant who had also seen the shores of this previously unknown land we now know as Canada.

   a. (No change)
   b. Leif consulted
   c. Leif consulting
   d. Leif was consulted

48. Which is the best version of the underlined portion of this sentence (reproduced below)?

   During their time in present-day Newfoundland, Leif's expedition made contact with the natives whom they referred to as Skraelings (which translates to 'wretched ones' in Norse).

   a. (No change)
   b. (which translates to "wretched ones" in Norse.)
   c. (which translates to 'wretched ones' in Norse.)
   d. (which translates to "wretched ones" in Norse).

49. Which is the best version of the underlined portion of this sentence (reproduced below)?

   Other accounts describes clashes where the Skraelings defeated the Viking explorers with long spears, while still others claim the Vikings dominated the natives.

   a. (No change)
   b. Other account's describe
   c. Other accounts describe
   d. Others account's describes

50. Which is the best version of the underlined portion of this sentence (reproduced below)?

   In 1020, 17 years later. The legendary Viking died

   a. (No change)
   b. In 1020, 17 years later; the legendary Viking died.
   c. In 1020 17 years later the legendary Viking died.
   d. In 1020, 17 years later, the legendary Viking died.

51. What is the structure of the following sentence?

   The restaurant is unconventional because it serves both Chicago style pizza and New York style pizza.

   a. Simple
   b. Compound
   c. Complex
   d. Compound-complex

52. The following sentence contains what kind of error?

   This summer, I'm planning to travel to Italy, take a Mediterranean cruise, going to Pompeii, and eat a lot of Italian food.

   a. Parallelism
   b. Sentence fragment
   c. Misplaced modifier
   d. Subject-verb agreement

53. The following sentence contains what kind of error?

   Forgetting that he was supposed to meet his girlfriend for dinner, Anita was mad when Fred showed up late.

   a. Parallelism
   b. Run-on sentence
   c. Misplaced modifier
   d. Subject-verb agreement

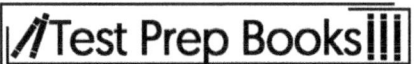

54. The following sentence contains what kind of error?

    Some workers use all their sick leave, other workers cash out their leave.

    a. Parallelism
    b. Comma splice
    c. Sentence fragment
    d. Subject-verb agreement

55. A student writes the following in an essay:

    Protestors filled the streets of the city. Because they were dissatisfied with the government's leadership.

    Which of the following is an appropriately punctuated correction for this sentence?
    a. Protestors filled the streets of the city, because they were dissatisfied with the government's leadership.
    b. Protesters, filled the streets of the city, because they were dissatisfied with the government's leadership.
    c. Because they were dissatisfied with the government's leadership protestors filled the streets of the city.
    d. Protestors filled the streets of the city because they were dissatisfied with the government's leadership.

56. While studying vocabulary, a student notices that the words *circumference*, *circumnavigate*, and *circumstance* all begin with the prefix *circum–*. The student uses her knowledge of affixes to infer that all of these words share what related meaning?
    a. Around, surrounding
    b. Travel, transport
    c. Size, measurement
    d. Area, location

57. A local newspaper is looking for writers for a student column. A student would like to submit his article to the newspaper, but he isn't sure how to format his article according to journalistic standards. What resource should he use?
    a. A thesaurus
    b. A dictionary
    c. A style guide
    d. A grammar book

58. A student encounters the word *aficionado* and wants to learn more about it. It doesn't sound like other English words he knows, so the student is curious to identify the word's origin. What resource should he consult?
    a. A thesaurus
    b. A dictionary
    c. A style guide
    d. A grammar book

59. Which of the following refers to what an author wants to express about a given subject?
    a. Primary purpose
    b. Plot
    c. Main idea
    d. Characterization

60. Which organizational style is used in the following passage?

    There are several reasons why the new student café has not been as successful as expected. One factor is that prices are higher than originally advertised, so many students cannot afford to buy food and beverages

there. Also, the café closes rather early; as a result, students go out into town to other late-night gathering places rather than meeting friends at the café on campus.

a. Cause-and-effect order
b. Compare-and-contrast order
c. Spatial order
d. Time order

Essay Prompt

Directions: The HiSET writing portion of the exam will allow you 45 minutes to write an essay. This essay is a test of your writing skills. Please do the following in your essay:

- Develop a position through explaining the supporting reasons and examples from the two passages and from personal experience.

- Organize ideas clearly, using an introduction, conclusion, body paragraphs, and effective transitions.

- Use appropriate word choice, different sentence construction, and a consistent style.

- Use proper grammar and writing conventions.

The two passages below are written to disagree with one another on the same issue of importance. Please read both passages carefully and determine the strengths and weaknesses of each argument. Then write an essay explaining your own opinion on the issue.

A school administration has asked the teachers to research cell phone use in the classroom. Then it asked them to state their opinions in an essay. The excerpts below were taken from two different papers.

Passage 1

In the modern classroom, cell phones have become indispensable. Cell phones, which are essentially handheld computers, allow students to take notes, connect to the web, perform complex computations, teleconference, and participate in surveys.

Additionally, due to their mobility and excellent reception, cell phones are necessary in emergencies. According to a 2005 study conducted by Dr. Havish and Dr. Braum, 85% of students said that they felt safer having access to their cell phones in class. For them, it was about having contact to the "outside world" if anything were to happen inside the classroom. Also, they were able to have direct communication with their families if one of them became sick or injured in some way.

Unlike tablets, laptops, or computers, cell phones are a readily available and free resource. Most school district budgets are already strained to begin with. According to University of Texas' technological journal *Bot*, since today's student is already strongly rooted in technology, "when teachers incorporate cell phones, they're 'speaking' the student's language," (Dr. Branson, 2010) which increases the chance of higher engagement.

Passage 2

As with most forms of technology, there is an appropriate time and place for the use of cell phones. Students are comfortable with cell phones, so it makes sense when teachers allow cell phone use at their discretion. Allowing cell phone use can prove advantageous if done correctly.

Unfortunately, if that's not the case—and often it isn't—then a sizable percentage of students pretend to pay attention while *surreptitiously* playing on their phones. It is a well-known fact that a large percentage of teachers across America disagree with the use of cell phones in the classroom, because students end up ignoring their lectures and instead play on their phones. With this information in mind, it can be said that cell phones are actually *hindering* our education as a country.

This type of disrespectful behavior is often justified by the argument that cell phones are not only a privilege but also a right (*Journal of Florida Technology*, 2012, p. 184). Under this logic, confiscating phones is akin to rummaging through students' backpacks. This is in stark contrast to several decades ago when teachers regulated where and when students accessed information.

Write an essay explaining your own position on the issue of whether or not to allow cell phone use in the classroom.

Make sure to use evidence from the passages provided along with reasons and examples from your own experience to support your position. Your essay should acknowledge opposing ideas. Please review your essay once you have finished for correct punctuation, grammar, and spelling.

Mathematics

1. What is the product of two irrational numbers?
   a. Irrational
   b. Irrational or rational
   c. Contradictory
   d. Complex and imaginary

2. You measure the width of your door to be 36 inches. The true width of the door is 35.75 inches. What is the relative error in your measurement?
   a. 0.7%
   b. 0.007%
   c. 0.99%
   d. 0.1%

3. The graph shows the position of a car over a 10-second time interval. Which of the following is the correct interpretation of the graph for the interval 1 to 3 seconds?

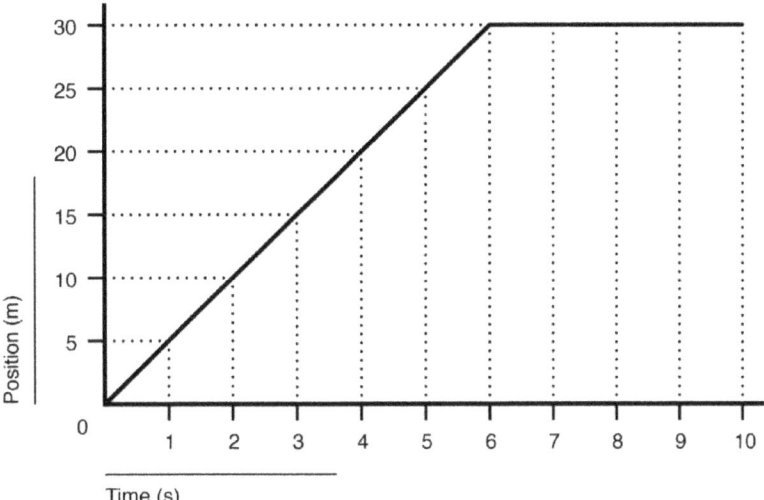

a. The car remains in the same position.
b. The car is traveling at a speed of 5 m/s.
c. The car is traveling up a hill.
d. The car is traveling at 5 mph.

4. Simplify:

$$\frac{4a^{-1}b^3}{a^4b^{-2}} \times \frac{3a}{b}$$

a. $12a^3b^5$
b. $12\frac{b^4}{a^4}$
c. $\frac{12}{a^4}$
d. $7\frac{b^4}{a}$

5. What are the zeros of the function: $f(x) = x^3 + 4x^2 + 4x$?
a. -2
b. $0, -2$
c. 2
d. $0, 2$

6. The number -4 can be classified as which of the following?
a. Real, rational, integer, whole, natural
b. Real, rational, integer, natural
c. Real, rational, integer
d. Real, irrational, complex

7. If $g(x) = x^3 - 3x^2 - 2x + 6$ and $f(x) = 2$, then what is $g(f(x))$?
a. -26
b. 6
c. $2x^3 - 6x^2 - 4x + 12$
d. -2

8. If the volume of a sphere is 288π cubic meters, what are the radius and surface area of the same sphere?
   a. Radius: 6 meters, surface area: 144π square meters
   b. Radius: 36 meters, surface area: 144π square meters
   c. Radius: 6 meters, surface area: 12π square meters
   d. Radius: 36 meters, surface area: 12π square meters

9. What is the solution to the following system of equations?

$$x^2 - 2x + y = 8$$

$$x - y = -2$$

   a. $(-2, 3)$
   b. There is no solution.
   c. $(-2, 0)\ (1, 3)$
   d. $(-2, 0)\ (3, 5)$

10. Mom's car drove 72 miles in 90 minutes. How fast did she drive in feet per second?
    a. 0.8 feet per second
    b. 48.9 feet per second
    c. 0.009 feet per second
    d. 70.4 feet per second

11. What is the simplified form of the expression: $(7n + 3n^3 + 3) + (8n + 5n^3 + 2n^4)$?
    a. $9n^4 + 15n - 2$
    b. $2n^4 + 5n^3 + 15n - 2$
    c. $9n^4 + 8n^3 + 15n$
    d. $2n^4 + 8n^3 + 15n + 3$

12. For the following similar triangles, what are the values of x and y (rounded to the nearest tenth)?

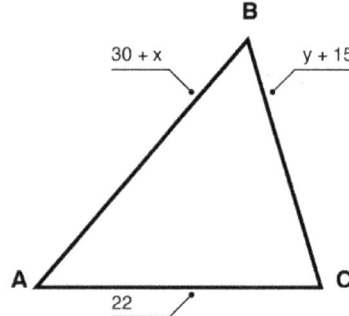
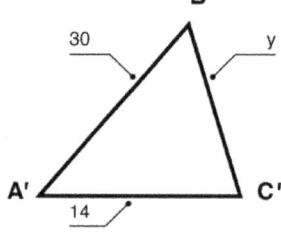

   a. $x = 16.5, y = 25.1$
   b. $x = 19.5, y = 24.1$
   c. $x = 17.1, y = 26.3$
   d. $x = 26.3, y = 17.1$

13. What is the product of the following expression?

$$(4x - 8)(5x^2 + x + 6)$$

  a. $20x^3 - 36x^2 + 16x - 48$
  b. $6x^3 - 41x^2 + 12x + 15$
  c. $20x^4 + 11x^2 - 37x - 12$
  d. $2x^3 - 11x^2 - 32x + 20$

14. How could the following equation be factored to find the zeros?

$$y = x^3 - 3x^2 - 4x$$

  a. $0 = x^2(x - 4), x = 0, 4$
  b. $0 = 3x(x + 1)(x + 4), x = 0, -1, -4$
  c. $0 = x(x + 1)(x - 4), x = 0, -1, 4$
  d. $0 = x^2(x - 1)(x - 4), x = 0, -1, 4$

15. A sample data set contains the following values: 1, 3, 5, 7. What is the standard deviation of the set?
  a. 2.58
  b. 4
  c. 6.23
  d. 1.1

16. If Sarah reads at an average rate of 21 pages in 4 nights, how long will it take her to read 140 pages?
  a. 26 nights
  b. 27 nights
  c. 8 nights
  d. 12 nights

17. What is the simplified quotient of $\frac{5x^3}{3x^2y} \div \frac{25}{3y^9}$?
  a. $\frac{125x}{9y^{10}}$
  b. $\frac{x}{5y^8}$
  c. $\frac{5}{xy^8}$
  d. $\frac{xy^8}{5}$

18. What are the center and radius of a circle with equation $4x^2 + 4y^2 - 16x - 24y + 51 = 0$?
  a. Center $(3, 2)$ and radius $\frac{1}{2}$
  b. Center $(2, 3)$ and radius $\frac{1}{2}$
  c. Center $(3, 2)$ and radius $\frac{1}{4}$
  d. Center $(2, 3)$ and radius $\frac{1}{4}$

19. 20 is 40% of what number?
  a. 500
  b. 8
  c. 200
  d. 50

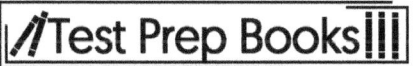

HiSET Practice Test #1

20. What is the solution for the following equation?

$$\frac{x^2 + x - 30}{x - 5} = 11$$

a. $x = -6$
b. There is no solution.
c. $x = 16$
d. $x = 5$

21. How do you solve $V = lwh$ for h?
a. $lwV = h$
b. $h = \frac{V}{lw}$
c. $h = \frac{Vl}{w}$
d. $h = \frac{Vw}{l}$

22. A ball is drawn at random from a ball pit containing 8 red balls, 7 yellow balls, 6 green balls, and 5 purple balls. What's the probability that the ball drawn is yellow?
a. $\frac{1}{26}$
b. $\frac{19}{26}$
c. $\frac{7}{26}$
d. 1

23. What is the domain for the function $y = \sqrt{x}$?
a. All real numbers
b. $x \geq 0$
c. $x > 0$
d. $y \geq 0$

24. An equilateral triangle has a perimeter of 18 feet. The sides of a square have the same length as the triangle's sides. What is the area of the square?
a. 6 square feet
b. 36 square feet
c. 256 square feet
d. 1,000 square feet

25. Simplify $(1.2 \times 10^{12} \div 3.0 \times 10^8)$ and write the result in scientific notation.
a. 0.4×10^4
b. 4.0×10^4
c. 4.0×10^3
d. 3.6×10^{20}

26. The phone bill is calculated each month using the equation $c = 50g + 75$. The cost of the phone bill per month is represented by c, and g represents the gigabytes of data used that month. What is the value and interpretation of the slope of this equation?
a. 75 dollars per day
b. 75 gigabytes per day
c. 50 dollars per day
d. 50 dollars per gigabyte

27. What are the zeros of $f(x) = x^2 + 4$?
   a. $x = -4$
   b. $x = \pm 2i$
   c. $x = \pm 2$
   d. $x = \pm 4i$

28. If the sides of a cube are 5 centimeters long, what is its volume?
   a. 10 cm³
   b. 15 cm³
   c. 50 cm³
   d. 125 cm³

29. What is the y-intercept for $y = x^2 + 3x - 4$?
   a. $y = 1$
   b. $y = -4$
   c. $y = 3$
   d. $y = 4$

30. Is the following function even, odd, neither, or both?

$$y = \frac{1}{2}x^4 + 2x^2 - 6$$

   a. Even
   b. Odd
   c. Neither
   d. Both

31. $x^4 - 16$ can be simplified to which of the following?
   a. $(x^2 - 4)(x^2 + 4)$
   b. $(x^2 + 4)(x^2 + 4)$
   c. $(x^2 - 4)(x^2 - 4)$
   d. $(x^2 - 2)(x^2 + 4)$

32. A shuffled deck of 52 cards contains 4 kings. One card is drawn and is not put back in the deck. Then, a second card is drawn. What's the probability that both cards are kings?
   a. $\frac{1}{169}$
   b. $\frac{1}{221}$
   c. $\frac{1}{13}$
   d. $\frac{4}{13}$

33. Which equation is NOT a function of x?
   a. $y = |x|$
   b. $y = x^2$
   c. $x = 3$
   d. $y = 4$

34. What's the probability of rolling a 6 at least once in two rolls of a die?
    a. $\frac{1}{3}$
    b. $\frac{1}{36}$
    c. $\frac{1}{6}$
    d. $\frac{5}{18}$

35. How could the following function be rewritten to identify the zeros?

$$y = 3x^3 + 3x^2 - 18x$$

   a. $y = 3x(x+3)(x-2)$
   b. $y = x(x-2)(x+3)$
   c. $y = 3x(x-3)(x+2)$
   d. $y = (x+3)(x-2)$

36. What is $4 \times 7 + (25 - 21)^2 \div 2$?
    a. 512
    b. 36
    c. 60.5
    d. 22

37. A pizzeria owner regularly creates jumbo pizzas, each with a radius of 9 inches. She is mathematically inclined and wants to know the area of the pizza to purchase the correct boxes and know how much she is feeding her customers. What is the area of the circle, in terms of π, with a radius of 9 inches?
    a. $3\pi \text{ in}^2$
    b. $18\pi \text{ in}^2$
    c. $81\pi \text{ in}^2$
    d. $9\pi \text{ in}^2$

38. For a group of 20 men, the median weight is 180 pounds, and the range is 30 pounds. If each man gains 10 pounds, which of the following would be true?
    a. The median weight will increase, and the range will remain the same.
    b. The median weight and range will both remain the same.
    c. The median weight will stay the same, and the range will increase.
    d. The median weight and range will both increase.

39. What is the type of function that is modeled by the values in the following table?

X	f(x)
1	2
2	4
3	8
4	16
5	32

   a. Linear
   b. Exponential
   c. Quadratic
   d. Cubic

40. Dwayne has received the following scores on his math tests: 78, 92, 83, and 97. What score must Dwayne get on his next math test to have an overall average of 90?
   a. 89
   b. 98
   c. 100
   d. 94

41. If the point $(-3, -4)$ is reflected over the x-axis, what new point does it make?
   a. $(-3, -4)$
   b. $(3, -4)$
   c. $(3, 4)$
   d. $(-3, 4)$

42. Johnny earns $2,334.50 from his job each month. He pays $1,437 for monthly expenses and saves the rest. Johnny is planning a vacation in 3 months that he estimates will cost $1,750 total. How much will Johnny have left over from 3 months of saving once he pays for his vacation?
   a. $948.50
   b. $584.50
   c. $852.50
   d. $942.50

43. The following graph compares the various test scores of the top three students in each of these teachers' classes. Based on the graph, which teacher's students had the smallest range of test scores?

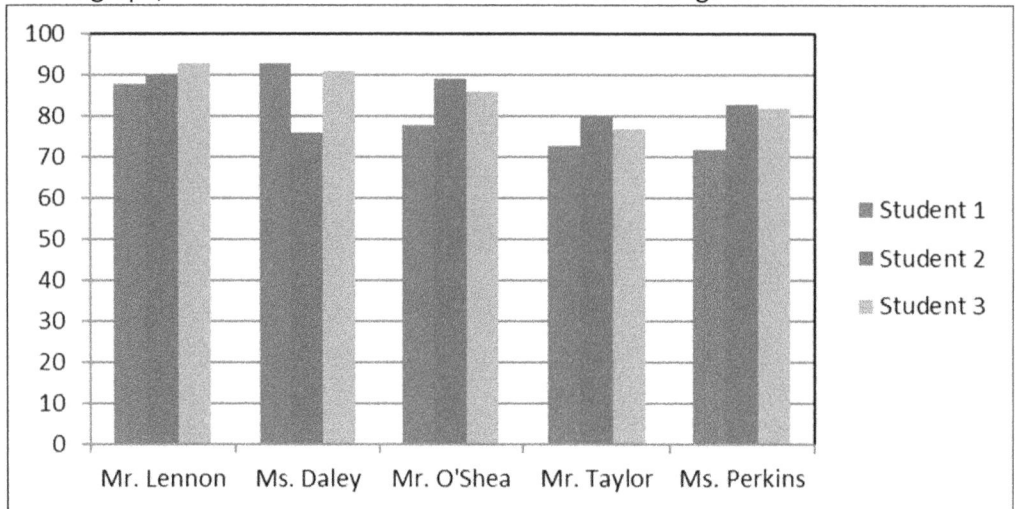

   a. Mr. Lennon
   b. Mr. O'Shea
   c. Mr. Taylor
   d. Ms. Daley

44. A line passes through the origin and through the point $(-3, 4)$. What is the slope of the line?
   a. $-\frac{4}{3}$
   b. $-\frac{3}{4}$
   c. $\frac{4}{3}$
   d. $\frac{3}{4}$

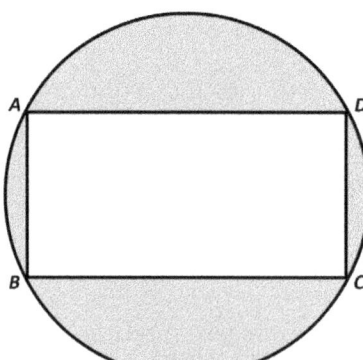

45. Rectangle $ABCD$ is inscribed in the circle above. The length of side AB is 9 inches and the length of side BC is 12 inches. What is the area of the shaded region?
   a. 64.4 sq. in.
   b. 68.6 sq. in.
   c. 62.8 sq. in.
   d. 61.3 sq. in.

46. On Monday, Robert mopped the floor in 4 hours. On Tuesday, he did it in 3 hours. If on Monday, his average rate of mopping was p sq. ft. per hour, what was his average rate on Tuesday?
   a. $\frac{4}{3}p$ sq. ft. per hour
   b. $\frac{3}{4}p$ sq. ft. per hour
   c. $\frac{5}{4}p$ sq. ft. per hour
   d. $p + 1$ sq. ft. per hour

47. What is the overall median of Dwayne's current scores: 78, 92, 83, 97?
   a. 80.5
   b. 85
   c. 90
   d. 87.5

48. Which of the following inequalities is equivalent to $3 - \frac{1}{2}x \geq 2$?
   a. $x \geq 2$
   b. $x \leq 2$
   c. $x \geq 1$
   d. $x \leq 1$

49. What is the length of the hypotenuse of a right triangle with one leg equal to 3 centimeters and the other leg equal to 4 centimeters?
   a. 7 cm
   b. 5 cm
   c. 25 cm
   d. 12 cm

50. Kimberley earns $10 an hour babysitting, and after 10 p.m., she earns $12 an hour. The time she works is rounded to the nearest hour for pay purposes. On her last job, she worked from 5:30 p.m. to 11:00 p.m. In total, how much did Kimberley earn on her last job?
   a. $45
   b. $57
   c. $62
   d. $42

51. This chart indicates how many sales of CDs, vinyl records, and MP3 downloads occurred over the last year. Approximately what percentage of the total sales was from CDs?

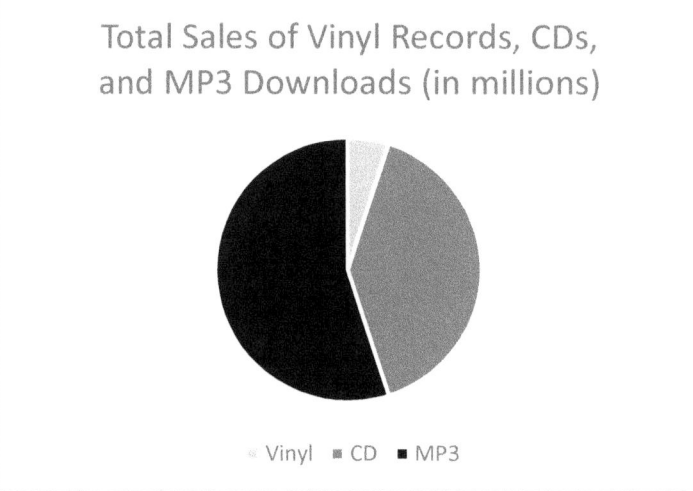

   a. 55%
   b. 25%
   c. 40%
   d. 5%

52. If $\sqrt{1+x} = 4$, what is x?
   a. 10
   b. 15
   c. 20
   d. 25

53. A line passes through the point $(1, 2)$ and crosses the y-axis at $y = 1$. Which of the following is an equation for this line?
   a. $y = 2x$
   b. $y = x + 1$
   c. $x + y = 1$
   d. $y = \frac{x}{2} - 2$

54. Which of the following equations best represents the problem below?

   The width of a rectangle is 2 centimeters less than the length. If the perimeter of the rectangle is 44 centimeters, then what are the dimensions of the rectangle?

   a. $2l + 2(l - 2) = 44$
   b. $(l + 2) + (l + 2) + l = 48$
   c. $l \times (l - 2) = 44$
   d. $(l + 2) + (l + 2) + l = 44$

55. What is the slope of this line?

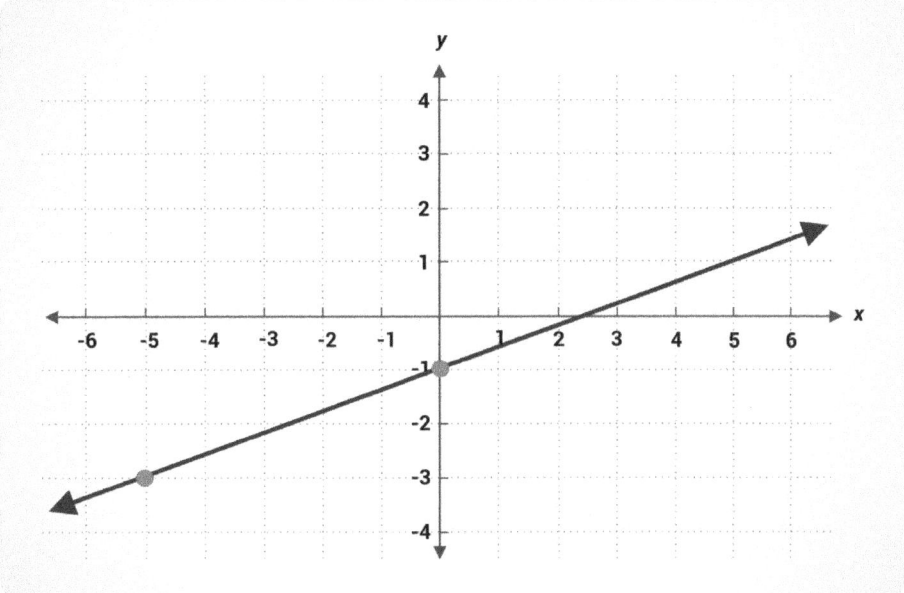

a. 2
b. $\frac{5}{2}$
c. $\frac{1}{2}$
d. $\frac{2}{5}$

Science

1. What is one feature that both prokaryotes and eukaryotes have in common?
    a. A plasma membrane
    b. A nucleus enclosed by a membrane
    c. Organelles
    d. A nucleoid

2. Which temperature scale is based on the phase changes of water?
    a. Fahrenheit
    b. Kelvin
    c. Rankine
    d. Celsius

3. What is the last phase of mitosis?
    a. Prophase
    b. Telophase
    c. Anaphase
    d. Metaphase

4. Pure gold is an example of which class of mineral?
   a. Carbonate
   b. Silicates
   c. Elements
   d. Oxides

5. Which of the following terms refers to stored energy of an object due to its position relative to others?
   a. Kinetic energy
   b. Potential energy
   c. Magnetic energy
   d. Nuclear energy

6. How many daughter cells are formed from one parent cell during meiosis?
   a. One
   b. Two
   c. Three
   d. Four

7. In which organelle do eukaryotes carry out aerobic respiration?
   a. Golgi apparatus
   b. Nucleus
   c. Mitochondrion
   d. Cytosol

8. Which of the following is most abundant in the Earth's atmosphere?
   a. Carbon dioxide
   b. Oxygen
   c. Nitrogen
   d. Water

9. Which portion of the electromagnetic spectrum has the longest wavelength?
   a. Radio waves
   b. Gamma rays
   c. X-rays
   d. Microwaves

10. What kind of energy do plants use in photosynthesis to create chemical energy?
    a. Light
    b. Electric
    c. Nuclear
    d. Cellular

11. Which of the following options would have the highest viscosity?
    a. Water
    b. Honey
    c. Alcohol
    d. Oxygen gas

12. Dew point is a measure of which of the following?
    I. Pressure
    II. Temperature at which water vapor condenses
    III. Temperature at which water evaporates

    a. Choices I and III
    b. Choices I and II
    c. Choices II and III
    d. All of the above

13. What type of biological molecule includes monosaccharides?
    a. Proteins
    b. Carbohydrates
    c. Nucleic acids
    d. Lipids

14. Which term describes a transfer of energy due to force being exerted on an object?
    a. Acceleration
    b. Synergy
    c. Work
    d. Pressure

15. Which level of protein structure is defined by the folds and coils of the protein's polypeptide backbone?
    a. Primary
    b. Secondary
    c. Tertiary
    d. Quaternary

16. Which base pairs with adenine in RNA?
    a. Thymine
    b. Guanine
    c. Cytosine
    d. Uracil

17. The Coriolis effect is created by which of the following?
    a. Wind
    b. Earth's rotation
    c. Earth's axis
    d. Mountains

18. The Big Bang theory helps explain which of the following?
    a. The expanding universe
    b. Dark matter
    c. Life
    d. Gravity

19. With which genotype would the recessive phenotype appear, if the dominant allele is marked with "A" and the recessive allele is marked with "a"?
    a. AA
    b. aa
    c. Aa
    d. aA

20. Dark storm clouds are usually located where?
    a. Between 5,000 and 13,000 meters above sea level
    b. Between 2,000 and 7,000 meters above sea level
    c. Less than 2,000 meters above sea level
    d. Outer space

21. The Sun transfers heat to the Earth through space via which mechanism?
    a. Convection
    b. Conduction
    c. Induction
    d. Radiation

22. What is one reason why speciation can occur?
    a. Geographic separation
    b. Seasons
    c. Daylight
    d. A virus

23. What is the broadest, or least specialized, classification of the Linnaean taxonomic system?
    a. Species
    b. Family
    c. Domain
    d. Phylum

24. According to Newton's three laws of motion, which of the following is true?
    a. Two objects cannot exert force on each other without touching.
    b. An object at rest has no inertia.
    c. The weight of an object is the same as the mass of the object.
    d. The weight of an object is equal to the mass of an object multiplied by the acceleration of gravity.

25. How are fungi similar to plants?
    a. They have a cell wall.
    b. They contain chloroplasts.
    c. They perform photosynthesis.
    d. They use carbon dioxide as a source of energy.

26. Kepler's laws help explain which of the following?
    a. How the Earth moves around the Sun
    b. How water moves around the Earth
    c. How sunlight moves through space
    d. How air moves around the Earth

27. What is the chemical reaction called when a compound is broken down into its basic components?
    a. A synthesis reaction
    b. A decomposition reaction
    c. An organic reaction
    d. An oxidation reaction

28. What important function are the roots of plants responsible for?
    a. Absorbing water from the surrounding environment
    b. Performing photosynthesis
    c. Conducting sugars downward through the leaves
    d. Supporting the plant body

29. Which of the following is a balanced chemical equation?
    a. $Na + Cl_2 \rightarrow NaCl$
    b. $2\,Na + Cl_2 \rightarrow NaCl$
    c. $2\,Na + Cl_2 \rightarrow 2\,NaCl$
    d. $2\,Na + 2\,Cl_2 \rightarrow 2\,NaCl$

30. Which of the following would occur in response to a change in water concentration?
    a. Phototropism
    b. Thermotropism
    c. Gravitropism
    d. Hydrotropism

31. What is the force that opposes motion?
    a. Reactive force
    b. Responsive force
    c. Friction
    d. Momentum

32. Which factor is NOT a consideration in population dynamics?
    a. Size and age of the population
    b. Immigration
    c. Hair color
    d. Number of births

33. Which of the following best describes this moon phase, as viewed from the northern hemisphere?

   a. Gibbous
   b. Waxing
   c. Waning
   d. Crescent

34. What is an isotope?
   a. For any given element, it is an atom with a different atomic number.
   b. For any given element, it is an atom with a different number of protons.
   c. For any given element, it is an atom with a different number of electrons.
   d. For any given element, it is an atom with a different mass number.

35. Which type of diagram describes the cycling of energy and nutrients in an ecosystem?
   a. Food web
   b. Phylogenetic tree
   c. Fossil record
   d. Pedigree chart

36. Viruses belong to which of the following classifications?
   a. Domain Archaea
   b. Kingdom Monera
   c. Kingdom Protista
   d. None of the above

37. What is the electrical charge of the nucleus?
   a. A nucleus always has a positive charge.
   b. A stable nucleus has a positive charge, but a radioactive nucleus may be neutral with no charge.
   c. A nucleus is always neutral with no charge.
   d. A stable nucleus is neutral with no charge, but a radioactive nucleus may have a charge.

38. In which phase of mitosis does DNA replication occur?
    a. Anaphase
    b. Metaphase
    c. Telophase
    d. None of the above

39. Currently, water can be found where?
    a. On the Earth
    b. Around Saturn
    c. On Jupiter's moons
    d. All of the above

40. Explain the law of conservation of mass as it applies to this reaction: $2\,H_2 + O_2 \rightarrow 2\,H_2O$.
    a. Electrons are lost.
    b. The hydrogen loses mass.
    c. New oxygen atoms are formed.
    d. There is no decrease or increase of matter.

41. Which apparatus would be best to use to look at a solar eclipse?
    a. A telescope facing the eclipse
    b. A pinhole camera facing away from the eclipse
    c. Sunglasses facing the eclipse
    d. Binoculars facing the eclipse

42. Which of the following is true regarding the middle of a cell membrane?
    a. It is hydrophilic.
    b. It is hydrophobic.
    c. It is made of phosphate.
    d. It is made of cellulose.

43. What object in the solar system becomes dim during a lunar eclipse?
    a. Sun
    b. Earth
    c. Moon
    d. Earth and Moon

44. Which of the following represents a Punnett square for a child with a father who is Gg and mother who is Gg? (G = green eyes; g = gray eyes)

a.

	Father g	Father g
Mother G	Gg	Gg
Mother G	Gg	Gg

b.

	Mother g	Father g
Mother G	Gg	Gg
Father G	Gg	Gg

c.

	Father G	Father g
Mother G	GG	Gg
Mother g	Gg	gg

d.

	Father G	Father g
Mother g	Gg	gg
Mother g	gg	gg

45. All single-celled eukaryotic organisms belong to which classification?
    a. Archaea
    b. Monera
    c. Protista
    d. Kingdom

46. Which statement is true regarding atomic structure?
    a. Protons orbit around a nucleus.
    b. Neutrons have a positive charge.
    c. Electrons are in the nucleus.
    d. Protons have a positive charge.

47. Which of the following is NOT a location where ATP is produced?
    a. Mitochondria
    b. Chloroplast
    c. Nucleus
    d. Cytosol

48. Which type of eclipse could you observe directly using a telescope?
    a. Neither solar nor lunar
    b. Lunar only
    c. Both solar and lunar
    d. Solar only

49. Which system of the body acts as a physical barrier against infections?
    a. Muscular system
    b. Endocrine system
    c. Integumentary system
    d. Lymphatic system

50. In which phase of mitosis do chromosomes separate and move to opposite sides of a cell?
    a. Prophase
    b. Anaphase
    c. Metaphase
    d. Telophase

51. Which type of eclipse is viewed during the daytime?
    a. Both solar and lunar
    b. Solar only
    c. Partial lunar
    d. Total lunar

52. Which of the following is a representation of a natural pattern or occurrence that's difficult or impossible to experience directly?
    a. A theory
    b. A model
    c. A law
    d. An observation

53. Which of the following best describes a diploid cell?
    a. A cell with two nuclei
    b. A cell with a phospholipid bilayer
    c. A cell with two sets of chromosomes
    d. A cell without a nucleus

54. Volcanic activity can occur in which of the following?
    a. Convergent boundaries
    b. Divergent boundaries
    c. The middle of a tectonic plate
    d. All of the above

55. Which round organelles are responsible for the production of proteins?
    a. Nucleolus
    b. Mitochondria
    c. Cytosol
    d. Ribosomes

56. What is the largest planet in our solar system and what is it mostly made of?
    a. Saturn, rocks
    b. Jupiter, ammonia
    c. Jupiter, hydrogen
    d. Saturn, helium

57. Which of the following structures is responsible for the exchange of gases between blood and air?
    a. Alveoli
    b. Capillaries
    c. Aorta
    d. Axon

58. Which of the following is a standard or series of standards to which the results from an experiment are compared?
    a. A control
    b. A variable
    c. A constant
    d. Collected data

59. A scientist is trying to determine the amount of poison that will kill a rat the fastest. Which of the following statements is an example of an appropriate hypothesis?
    a. Rats that are given lots of poison seem to die quickly.
    b. Does the amount of poison affect how quickly the rat dies?
    c. The more poison a rat is given, the quicker it will die.
    d. Poison is fatal to rats.

60. Which of the following correctly describes the independent and dependent variables in an experiment that tests how quickly a rat dies based on the amount of poison it eats?
    a. How quickly the rat dies is the independent variable; the amount of poison is the dependent variable.
    b. The amount of poison is the independent variable; how quickly the rat dies is the dependent variable.
    c. Whether the rat eats the poison is the independent variable; how quickly the rat dies is the dependent variable.
    d. The cage the rat is kept in is the independent variable; the amount of poison is the dependent variable.

Social Studies

1. The era following the Civil War is known as what?
   a. Antebellum Era
   b. Reconstruction
   c. Progressive Era
   d. Civil rights movement

2. Which of the following refers to the constitutional principle that power is divided between the federal and state governments?
   a. Republicanism
   b. Individual rights
   c. Separation of powers
   d. Federalism

3. Which of the following is the subgroup of economics that studies large-scale economic issues such as unemployment, interest rates, price levels, and national income?
   a. Microeconomics
   b. Macroeconomics
   c. Scarcity
   d. Supply and demand

4. What became the scholarly capital of the Hellenistic world during the reign of Alexander the Great?
   a. Jerusalem
   b. Athens
   c. Alexandria
   d. Constantinople

5. A homeowner hires a landscaping company to mow the grass because they would like to use that time to do something else. The trade-off of paying someone to do a job to make more valuable use of time is an example of what?
   a. Economic systems
   b. Supply and demand
   c. Opportunity cost
   d. Inflation

6. The president of the United States is the top official in the country. At the state level, the top official is the governor. What is the title for the top official at the city or local level?
   a. Councilman
   b. Mayor
   c. Chairman
   d. Ombudsman

7. What is the name of the policies developed by President Franklin Delano Roosevelt during the Great Depression?
   a. The Great Society
   b. The War Against Poverty
   c. Progressivism
   d. The New Deal

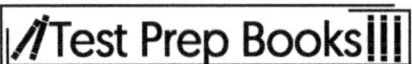

8. Which kind of market does NOT involve government interventions or monopolies while trades are made between suppliers and buyers?
   a. Free
   b. Command
   c. Gross
   d. Exchange

9. Renaissance scholars and artists were inspired by which classical civilization?
   a. Ancient Greece
   b. Ancient Egypt
   c. The Zhou Dynasty
   d. The Ottoman Empire

10. Which of the following types of government most closely resembles the structure of the US government?
    a. Democracy
    b. Direct democracy
    c. Representative democracy
    d. Socialist democracy

11. Which of the following consequences did NOT result from the discovery of the New World in 1492 AD?
    a. Proof that the world was round instead of flat
    b. The deaths of millions of Native Americans
    c. Biological exchange between Europe and the New World
    d. The creation of new syncretic religions

12. Which type of map illustrates the world's climatological regions?
    a. Topographic map
    b. Conformal projection
    c. Isoline map
    d. Thematic map

13. Which political concept describes a ruling body's ability to influence the actions, behaviors, or attitudes of a person or community?
    a. Authority
    b. Sovereignty
    c. Power
    d. Legitimacy

14. Which of the following was a consequence of World War II?
    a. The collapse of British and French empires in Asia and Africa
    b. A communist revolution in Russia
    c. The end of the Cold War
    d. The death of Franz Ferdinand, the Archduke of Austria

15. Which is NOT an indicator of economic growth?
    a. GDP (gross domestic product)
    b. Unemployment
    c. Inflation
    d. Theory of the firm

16. In which manner is absolute location expressed?
    a. The cardinal directions (north, south, east, and west)
    b. Through latitudinal and longitudinal coordinates
    c. Location nearest to a more well-known location
    d. Hemispherical position on the globe

17. Which of the following trends did NOT occur after the end of the Cold War in 1991?
    a. A decrease in nationalistic tension
    b. An increase in cultural and economic globalization
    c. An increase in religious fundamentalism
    d. An increase in environmentalism

18. Which feature differentiates a state from a nation?
    a. Shared history
    b. Common language
    c. Population
    d. Sovereignty

19. Which political theorist considered violence necessary in order for a ruler to maintain political power and stability?
    a. John Locke
    b. Jean-Jacques Rousseau
    c. Karl Marx
    d. Niccolo Machiavelli

20. Which of the following correctly lists the Thirteen Colonies?
    a. Connecticut, Delaware, Georgia, Maryland, Massachusetts, New Hampshire, New Jersey, New York, North Carolina, Pennsylvania, Rhode Island, South Carolina, Virginia
    b. Carolina, Connecticut, Delaware, Maryland, Massachusetts, New Hampshire, New Jersey, New York, Ohio, Pennsylvania, Rhode Island, Virginia, West Virginia
    c. Connecticut, Delaware, Georgia, Maine, Massachusetts, New Hampshire, New Jersey, New York, North Carolina, South Carolina, Pennsylvania, Vermont, Virginia
    d. Canada, Connecticut, Delaware, Georgia, Florida, Maryland, Massachusetts, New Hampshire, New York, North Carolina, Rhode Island, South Carolina, Virginia

21. What is the name of the central bank that controls the value of money in the United States?
    a. Commodity Reserve
    b. Central Reserve
    c. Federal Reserve
    d. Bank Reserve

22. Which of the following was NOT an issue contributing to the American Revolution?
    a. Increased taxes on the colonies
    b. Britain's defeat in the French and Indian War
    c. The stationing of British soldiers in colonists' homes
    d. Changes in class relations

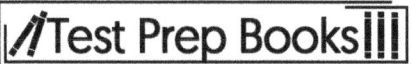

23. Which political theorist is considered the father of the social contract theory?
    a. John Stuart Mills
    b. Thomas Hobbes
    c. Aristotle
    d. Immanuel Kant

24. Which option does NOT sustain monetary policies?
    a. Closed market operations
    b. Open market operations
    c. Assuring bank reserves
    d. Adjusting interest rates

25. The election of a presidential candidate from which party led to the Civil War?
    a. Democrat
    b. Whig
    c. Republican
    d. Federalist

26. Which political orientation emphasizes maintaining traditions and stability over progress and change?
    a. Socialism
    b. Liberalism
    c. Conservatism
    d. Libertarianism

27. Which of the following is a consequence of World War II?
    a. It led to the creation of the League of Nations.
    b. It led to a major global outbreak of influenza.
    c. It made the US the only superpower in the world.
    d. None of the above

28. What consequences did the New Deal have?
    a. It established a number of federal agencies and programs that continue to function in the 21st century.
    b. It led to a third political party.
    c. It established a two-term limit in the White House.
    d. It led to the Great Depression.

29. Latitudinal lines are used to measure distance in which direction?
    a. East to west
    b. North to south
    c. Between two sets of coordinates
    d. In an inexact manner

30. Which political orientation supports cooperation between states as a means to improve the quality of life for all states, nations, and people?
    a. Fascism
    b. Conservatism
    c. Anarchism
    d. Internationalism

HiSET Practice Test #1

31. Which political orientation emphasizes a strong central government and promotes violence as a means of suppressing dissent?
    a. Communism
    b. Socialism
    c. Nationalism
    d. Fascism

32. Which of the following were characteristics of the Gilded Age?
    a. Social inequality
    b. Increasing urbanization
    c. Expanding industrialization
    d. All of the above

33. What determines the exchange rate in a floating or flexible exchange?
    a. The government
    b. Taxes
    c. The Federal Reserve
    d. The market

34. After the ratification of the Constitution, which power held by the states under the Articles of Confederation was ceded to the federal government?
    a. Power to levy taxes
    b. Power to establish courts
    c. Power to coin money
    d. Power to regulate trade

35. Which statement is true about inflation and purchasing power?
    a. As inflation decreases, purchasing power increases.
    b. As inflation increases, purchasing power decreases.
    c. As inflation increases, purchasing power increases.
    d. As inflation decreases, purchasing power decreases.

36. Which of the following motivated Christopher Columbus to sail across the Atlantic Ocean?
    a. A desire to establish a direct trade route to Asia
    b. A desire to confirm the existence of America
    c. A desire to prove the world was round
    d. A desire to spread Judaism

37. Which statement is true about goods and services?
    a. The quantity of goods and services matters more than their value.
    b. The value of goods and services matters more than their quantity.
    c. The quality of goods and services matters more than their production.
    d. The production of goods and services matters more than their quality.

38. Under Federalism, which is considered a concurrent power held by both the states and the federal government?
    a. Hold elections.
    b. Regulate immigration.
    c. Expand the territories of a state.
    d. Pass and enforce laws.

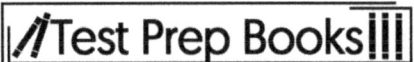

39. Which of the following characteristics best defines a formal region?
    a. Homogeneity
    b. Diversity
    c. Multilingualism
    d. Social mobility

40. Which check does the legislative branch possess over the judicial branch?
    a. Appoint judges.
    b. Call special sessions of Congress.
    c. Rule legislation unconstitutional.
    d. Determine the number of Supreme Court judges.

41. Which of the following sets includes a primary cause and effect of the American Revolution?
    a. A cause was the taxation of the colonies, and an effect was the civil rights movement.
    b. A cause was the Declaration of Independence, and an effect was the Constitution.
    c. A cause was the French and Indian War, and an effect was the Bill of Rights.
    d. A cause was the debate over slavery, and an effect was the Seven Years' War.

42. Which part of the legislative process differs in the House and the Senate?
    a. Who may introduce the bill
    b. How debates about a bill are conducted
    c. Who may veto the bill
    d. What wording the bill contains

43. Which of the following statements about the US Constitution is true?
    a. It was signed on July 4, 1776.
    b. It was enacted at the end of the Revolutionary War.
    c. New York failed to ratify it, but it still passed by majority.
    d. It replaced the Articles of Confederation.

44. Which of the following refers to the value of a good set by supply and demand rather than the actual value it represents?
    a. Commodity money
    b. Fiat money
    c. Bank money
    d. Reserve money

45. Which of the following is NOT included in the Bill of Rights?
    a. Freedom to assemble
    b. Freedom against unlawful search
    c. Freedom to vote
    d. Reservation of non-enumerated powers to the states or the people

46. The Silk Roads caused which of the following?
    a. Spread of Buddhism from India to China
    b. The devastation of European economies
    c. Introduction of the Bubonic Plague to the New World
    d. The Great War

47. Which political party was founded to advocate for the abolition of slavery?
    a. Constitutional Union
    b. Southern Democrat
    c. Republican
    d. Libertarian

48. Which of these is NOT a true statement about culture?
    a. Culture derives from the beliefs, values, and behaviors of people in a community.
    b. All people are born into a certain culture.
    c. Cultures are stagnant and cannot be changed.
    d. Culture can be embedded within families, schools, businesses, social classes, and religions.

49. What is NOT a common characteristic of an interest group?
    a. Seeks to influence public policy
    b. Employs lobbyists
    c. Regulates trade
    d. Benefits a specific segment of society

50. What caused the end of the Western Roman Empire in 476 AD?
    a. Invasions by Germanic tribes
    b. The Mongol invasion
    c. The assassination of Julius Caesar
    d. Introduction of Taoism in Rome

51. Which of the following is NOT a power of the mass media?
    a. Ability to shape public opinion
    b. Ability to regulate communications
    c. Ability to influence the importance of events in society
    d. Ability to determine the context in which to report events

52. Which form of government divides power between a regional and central government?
    a. Democracy
    b. Constitutional monarchy
    c. Federalism
    d. Feudalism

53. Which of the following statements most accurately describes the Mongol Empire?
    a. The Mongol army was largely a cavalry force.
    b. Mongol rulers did not tolerate other religions.
    c. Mongol rulers neglected foreign trade.
    d. The Mongol Empire is known for its discouragement of literacy and the arts.

54. Which of the following is not a characteristic of contractionary monetary policy?
    a. Increases the money supply
    b. Possibly increases unemployment due to slowdowns in economic growth
    c. Decreases consumer spending
    d. Decreases loans and/or borrowing

55. Which form of government most limits the civil liberties of the people?
   a. Authoritarianism
   b. Communism
   c. Socialism
   d. Federal monarchy

56. Which of the following was NOT a factor in the changing of the European societal structure during the beginning of the Renaissance?
   a. The effects of the plague
   b. The rise of the Catholic Church
   c. Fighting amongst religious sects
   d. Increased war throughout the 16th century

57. Which of the following are reasons that geography is important to the examination of history?

   I. Historians make use of maps in their studies to get a clear picture of how history unfolded.
   II. Knowing the borders of different lands helps historians learn different cultures' interactions.
   III. Geography is closely linked with the flow of resources, technology, and population in societies.
   IV. Environmental factors, such as access to water and proximity of mountains, help shape the course of civilization.

   a. I, II, and III only
   b. II, III, and IV only
   c. I, II, and IV only
   d. I, III, and IV only

58. How is economic growth measured?
   a. By the rise in the inflation of a country
   b. By the amount of reserves that a country holds
   c. By the amount of exports that a country has
   d. By the GDP of a country

59. Which of the following was NOT an important invention in the twentieth century?
   a. Airplanes
   b. Telegraph
   c. Television
   d. Computers

60. Which type of electoral system is considered the most proportionate?
   a. Majority
   b. Electoral College
   c. Plurality
   d. Single transferable vote

Answer Explanations #1

Language Arts: Reading

1. D: Extended metaphor. Metaphor is a direct comparison between two things, and extended metaphor is a lengthy, well-developed metaphor that usually extends over the length of the poem. In this poem, Keats forms an extended metaphor by drawing a comparison between the four seasons of nature and the "seasons" that humans experience from youth to old age.

2. A: Ponder. This question can be answered using context clues from the sentence: "Spring's honied cud of youthful thought he loves / To ruminate, and by such dreaming high / Is nearest unto heaven." Following the word "ruminate," it's restated as "such dreaming"; also, immediately before is the expression "youthful thought." Together, this sentence describes a young man pleasantly daydreaming. The only word related to thinking and daydreaming is "ponder," Choice A.

3. C: He spends less time thinking about beautiful things. This is a general comprehension question. The narrator describes a man in Autumn "contented so ... to let fair things / Pass by unheeded." In this case, "fair" is another word for "beautiful," and letting things "pass by unheeded" means "he doesn't pay attention to them." In contrast, a man in the Spring and Summer of life spends time appreciating and daydreaming about beautiful things.

4. A: Winter represents the end of man's life. This is a purpose question, but it also requires readers to understand that this poem is an extended metaphor. Since the narrator is developing an extended comparison between seasons and life, it's natural that winter should come last because it's the season of death, dormancy, and "pale" nature (unlike, say, Spring, which is a season of life and rebirth in nature).

5. C: People change as they move through different stages of life. This is an inference question asking readers to understand the narrator's perspective. Choices B and D both include an opinion or advice to the reader, while the tone of the poem is more neutral or purely descriptive (the narrator is simply describing the stages of life, rather than advising readers on how to behave). Choice C more closely agrees with the comparison that the narrator sets up in the poem; just as seasons change in nature, people also change throughout their lives.

6. B: He would postpone or avoid death. This is both a vocabulary and a comprehension question. Based on the poem's extended metaphor, readers can gather that Winter is a metaphor for the end of life; all people must pass through Winter or else they would never die. Looking at the poem's vocabulary, "mortal" refers to human's limited life span (the opposite of "immortal"), and "forego" means to turn something down.

7. A: "in the mind of man" (2). This is a fairly straightforward question about literary devices. Alliteration refers to repetition of a word's beginning sound, and Choice A is the only example of that ("mind" and "man" both start with the letter M).

8. B: The passage begins by giving the reader information about traditional birthing situations. Then, we are told that Mr. and Mrs. Button decide to go against tradition to have their baby in a hospital. The next few passages are dedicated to letting the reader know how Mr. Button dresses and goes to the hospital to welcome his new baby. There is a doctor in this excerpt, as Choice C indicates, and Mr. Button does put on clothes, as Choice D indicates. However, Mr. Button is not going to the doctor's office nor is he about to go shopping for new clothes.

9. A: The tone of the above passage is nervous and excited. We are told in the fourth paragraph that Mr. Button "arose nervously." We also see him running without caution to the doctor to find out about his wife and baby—this indicates his excitement. We also see him stuttering in a nervous yet excited fashion as he asks the doctor if it's a boy or girl. Though the doctor may seem a bit abrupt at the end, indicating a bit of anger or shame, neither of these

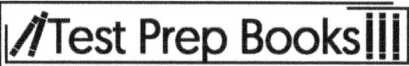

Answer Explanations #1

choices is the overwhelming tone of the entire passage. Despite the circumstances, joy and gratitude are not the main tone in the passage.

10. C: Mr. Button is dedicated to the task before him. Choice *A*, numbed, Choice *B*, chained, and Choice *D*, moved, all could grammatically fit in the sentence. However, they are not synonyms with *consecrated* like Choice *C* is.

11. D: The author describes a visual image—the doctor rubbing his hands together—first and foremost. The author may be trying to make a comment about the profession; however, the author does not "explain the detail of the doctor's profession" as Choice *B* suggests.

12. D: We know we are being introduced to the setting because we are given the year in the very first paragraph along with the season: "one day in the summer of 1860." This is a classic structure of an introduction of the setting. We are also getting a long explanation of Mr. Button, what his work is, who is related to him, and what his life is like in the third paragraph.

13. B: "Talk sense!" is an example of an imperative sentence. An imperative sentence gives a command. The doctor is commanding Mr. Button to talk sense. Choice *A* is an example of an exclamatory sentence, which expresses excitement. Choice *C* is an example of an interrogative sentence—these types of sentences ask questions. Choice *D* is an example of a declarative sentence. This means that the character is simply making a statement.

14. C: This passage can best be described as a narrative, which is a type of passage that tells a story. Choice *A*, expository, is a text organized logically to investigate a problem. Choice *B*, descriptive, is a text that mostly goes about describing something or someone in detail. Choice *D*, persuasive, is a text that is organized as an argument and meant to persuade the audience to do something.

15. D: To define and describe examples of spinoff technology. This is a purpose question—*why* did the author write this? The article contains facts, definitions, and other objective information without telling a story or arguing an opinion. In this case, the purpose of the article is to inform the reader. Choices *A* and *B* are incorrect because they argue for an opinion or present a position. Choice *C* is incorrect because the focus of the article is spinoff technology, not the history of space technology.

16. B: This organization question asks readers to analyze the structure of the essay. The topic of the essay is about spinoff technology, and the thesis statement at the end of the first paragraph offers the opinion, Spinoff technology proves that it is worthwhile to invest in scientific research because it could enrich people's lives in unexpected ways." The next two paragraphs provide evidence to support this opinion, making Choice *B* the best option. Choice *A* is the second-best option because the first paragraph gives a general definition of spinoff technology, while the following two paragraphs offer more detailed examples to help illustrate this idea. However, it is not the best answer because the main idea of the essay is that spinoff technology enriches people's lives in unexpected ways. Choice *C* is incorrect because the essay does not provide details of any specific moment in history. Choice *D* is incorrect because the essay does not discuss a popular misconception.

17. C: This reading comprehension question can be answered based on the second paragraph—scientists were concerned about astronauts' nutrition and began researching nutritional supplements. Choice *A* isn't true because it reverses the order of discovery (first NASA identified algae for astronaut use, and then it was further developed for use in baby food). Choices *B* and *D* are not uses of algae discussed in the article.

18. B: This vocabulary question could be answered based on the reader's prior knowledge, but the passage provides context clues for readers who've never encountered the word *neurological*. The next sentence talks about "this algae's potential to boost brain health," which is a paraphrase of "neurological benefits." From this context, readers should be able to infer that *neurological* relates to the brain.

Answer Explanations #1

19. D: This purpose question requires readers to understand the relevance of the given detail. In this case, the author mentions "costly and crucial equipment" before space suit visors, which are given as an example of something valuable. Choice *A* isn't correct because fashion is only related to sunglasses, not to NASA equipment. Choice *B* can be eliminated because it's simply not mentioned. While Choice *C* seems like it could be true, it's not relevant.

20. A: The central idea of this passage is to introduce certain insects that transition from water to air. Choice *B* is incorrect because although the passage talks about gills, it is not the central idea of the passage. Choices *C* and *D* are incorrect because the passage does not define insect breathing or invite readers to participate in insect preservation. Rather, the passage serves as an introduction to stoneflies, dragonflies, and mayflies and their transition from water to air.

21. C: To molt is to shed part or all of the outer shell, as noted in Choice *C*. Choices *A*, *B*, and *D* are incorrect. The word in the passage is mentioned here: "But it is advisable in connection with our present subject to dwell especially on some insects that remain continually under water till they are ready to undergo their final molt and attain the winged state, which they pass entirely in the air."

22. B: Notice how the first paragraph goes into detail describing how insects are able to breathe air. The second paragraph acts as a contrast to the first by stating, "[i]t is of great interest to find that, nevertheless, a number of insects spend much of their time under water." Watch for transition words such as "nevertheless" to help find what type of passage you're dealing with.

23: C: *Instars* are the phases between two periods of molting, and the text explains when these transitions occur. The preparatory stages are acted out in the water, while the last stage is in the air. Choices *A*, *B*, and *D* are all incorrect.

24. C: Overall, the author presents us with information on the subject. One moment where personal interest is depicted is when the author states, "It is of great interest to find that, nevertheless, a number of insects spend much of their time under water."

25. C: Their larvae can breathe the air dissolved in water through gills of some kind. This is stated in the last paragraph. Choice *A* is incorrect because the text mentions this in a general way at the beginning of the passage concerning "insects as a whole." Choice *B* is incorrect because this is stated of beetles and water-bugs, and not the insects in question. Choice *D* is incorrect because this is the opposite of what the text says of instars.

26. B: According to the passage, boatmen and scorpions have some way of protecting their spiracles when submerged. We see this in the second paragraph, which says "(boatmen and scorpions) which have some way of protecting their spiracles when submerged."

27. D: Criticize a theory by presenting counterevidence. The author mentions anti-Stratfordian arguments in the first paragraph, but then goes on to debunk these theories with facts about Shakespeare's life in the second and third paragraphs. Choice *A* is incorrect because the author is far from unbiased; in fact, the author clearly disagrees with anti-Stratfordians. Choice *B* is also incorrect because it's more closely aligned with the beliefs of anti-Stratfordians. Choice *C* can be eliminated because, while it's true that the author gives historical background, the purpose is using that information to disprove a theory.

28. B: "But in fact, there isn't much substance to such speculation, and most anti-Stratfordian arguments can be refuted with a little background about Shakespeare's time and upbringing." The thesis is a statement that contains the author's topic and main idea. As seen in question 27, the purpose of this article is to use historical evidence to provide counterarguments to anti-Stratfordians. Choice *A* is simply a definition; Choice *C* is a supporting detail, not a main idea; and Choice *D* represents an idea of anti-Stratfordians, not the author's opinion.

Answer Explanations #1

29. C: A rhetorical question is asked not to obtain an answer but to encourage readers to more deeply consider an issue.

30. B: This question asks readers to refer to the organizational structure of the article and demonstrate understanding of how the author provides details to support the argument. This particular detail can be found in the second paragraph where the author says, "even though he did not attend university, grade-school education in Shakespeare's time was actually quite rigorous."

31. A: This is a vocabulary question that can be answered using context clues. Other sentences in the paragraph describe London as "the most populous city in England" filled with "crowds of people." Choice *B* is incorrect because London was in Shakespeare's home country, not a foreign one. Choice *C* isn't mentioned in the passage. Choice *D* isn't a good answer because the passage describes London as an important city, not underdeveloped.

32. D: In Shakespeare's time, glove-makers weren't part of the upper class. Anti-Stratfordians doubt Shakespeare's ability because he wasn't from the upper class; his father was a glove-maker; therefore, in at least this example, glove-makers weren't included in the upper class. This is an example of inductive reasoning, using two specific pieces of information to draw a more general conclusion.

33. C: It's an example of a play set outside of England. This detail comes from the third paragraph, where the author responds to skeptics who claim that Shakespeare wrote too much about places he never visited, so *Romeo and Juliet* is mentioned as a famous example of a play with a foreign setting. In order to answer this question, readers need to understand the author's purpose in the third paragraph and how the author uses details to support this purpose. Choices *A* and *D* aren't mentioned, and Choice *B* is clearly false because the passage mentions more than once that Shakespeare never left England.

34. A: It's possible to learn things from reading rather than firsthand experience. This inference can be made from the final paragraph, where the author refutes anti-Stratfordian skepticism by noting that books about life in Europe could circulate throughout London. From this statement, readers can conclude the author believes it's possible that Shakespeare learned about European culture from books. Choice *B* isn't true because the author believes that Shakespeare contributed to English literature without traveling extensively. Similarly, Choice *C* isn't a good answer because the author explains how Shakespeare got his education without attending a university. Choice *D* can also be eliminated because the author describes Shakespeare's genius, and Shakespeare clearly isn't from Italy.

35. A: This is a straightforward question that requires readers to know that a first-person narrator speaks from an "I" point of view.

36. D: This can be inferred from the fact that the traveler must refer to his dictionary to understand those around him. Choice *A* isn't a good choice because the traveler seems to wonder why the driver needs to drive so fast. Choice *B* isn't mentioned in the passage and doesn't seem like a good answer choice because he seems wholly unfamiliar with his surroundings. This is why Choice *C* can also be eliminated.

37. B: This can be found in the first sentence of the third paragraph, which states, "I soon lost sight and recollection of ghostly fears in the beauty of the scene as we drove along." Also, readers should get a sense of foreboding from the first two paragraphs, where superstitious villagers seem frightened on the traveler's behalf. However, the final paragraph changes to delighted descriptions of the landscape's natural beauty. Choices *A* and *D* can be eliminated because the traveler is anxious, not relaxed or comfortable at the beginning of the passage. Choice *C* can also be eliminated because the traveler doesn't gain any particular insights in the last paragraph, and in fact continues to lament that he cannot understand the speech of those around him.

38. D: The answer to this reading comprehension question can be found in the second paragraph, when the traveler is "just starting for an unknown place to meet an unknown man"—in other words, a complete stranger.

Answer Explanations #1

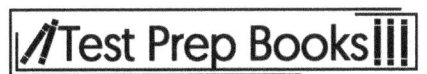

39. C: Answering this prediction question requires readers to understand foreshadowing, or hints that the author gives about what will happen next. There are numerous hints scattered throughout this passage: the villagers' sorrow and sympathy for the traveler, their superstitious actions, the spooky words that the traveler overhears, and the driver's unexplained haste. All of these point to a danger that awaits the protagonist.

40. A: As mentioned in the previous question, this sentence is an example of how the author hints at evil to come for the traveler.

41. A: Inferring is reading between the lines. Choice B describes the skimming technique. Choice C describes a questioning technique readers should employ, and Choice D is a simple statement regarding summary. It's an incomplete answer and not applicable to inference.

42. D: The correct answer is when an author chooses words or phrases that invoke feelings other than their literal meaning. Choice A refers to footnoting, which isn't applicable, and Choice C refers to a literary device. Choice B defines denotation, which is conceptually the opposite of connotation.

43. A: The purpose is to inform the reader about what assault is and how it is committed. Choice B is incorrect because the passage does not state that assault is a lesser form of lethal force, only that an assault can use lethal force, or alternatively, lethal force can be utilized to counter a dangerous assault. Choice C is incorrect because the passage is informative and does not have a set agenda. Finally, Choice D is incorrect because although the author uses an example in order to explain assault, it is not indicated that this is the author's personal account.

44. C: If the man being attacked in an alley used lethal force in self-defense against the man with a knife, it would not be considered illegal. The presence of a deadly weapon indicates malicious intent, and because the individual is isolated in an alley, lethal force in self-defense may be the only way to preserve his life. Choices A and B can be ruled out because in these situations no one is in danger of immediate death or bodily harm by someone else. Choice D is an assault and does exhibit intent to harm, but this situation isn't severe enough to merit lethal force; there is no intent to kill.

45. B: As discussed in the second passage, there are several forms of assault, like assault with a deadly weapon, verbal assault, or threatening posture or language. Choice A is incorrect because the author does not mention what the charges are on assaults; therefore, we cannot assume that they are more or less than unnecessary use of force charges. Choice C is incorrect because anyone is capable of assault; the author does not state that one group of people cannot commit assault. Choice D is incorrect because assault is never justified. Self-defense resulting in lethal force can be justified.

46. D: This statement most undermines the last part of the passage because it directly contradicts how the law evaluates the use of lethal force. Choices A and B are stated in the paragraph, so they do not undermine the explanation from the author. Choice C does not necessarily undermine the passage, but it does not support the passage either. It is more of an opinion that does not offer strength or weakness to the explanation.

47. C: Choice C is correct because it clearly establishes what both assault and lethal force are and gives the specific way in which the two concepts meet. Choice A is incorrect because lethal force doesn't necessarily result in assault. This is also why Choice B is incorrect. Not all assaults would necessarily be life-threatening to the point where lethal force is needed for self-defense. Choice D is compelling but ultimately incorrect; the statement touches on aspects of the two ideas but fails to present the concrete way in which the two are connected to each other.

48. A: Choice D is incorrect because while the passages utilize examples to help explain the concepts discussed, the author doesn't indicate that they are specific court cases. It's also clear that the passages don't open with examples, but instead, they begin by defining the terms addressed in each passage. This eliminates Choice B and ultimately reveals Choice A to be the correct answer. Choice A accurately outlines the way both passages are structured. Because the passages follow a nearly identical structure, Choice C can easily be ruled out.

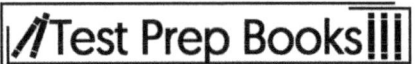

49. C: Choices *A* and *B* are incorrect because it is clear in both passages that intent is a prevailing theme in both lethal force and assault. Choice *D* is compelling, but if a person uses lethal force to defend himself or herself, the intent of the defender is also examined in order to help determine if there was excessive force used. Choice *C* is correct because it states that intent is important for determining both lethal force and assault and that intent is used to gauge the severity of the issues. Remember, just as lethal force can escalate to excessive use of force, there are different kinds of assault. Intent dictates several different forms of assault.

50. B: The example is used to demonstrate a single example of two different types of assault and then adds in a third type of assault in its conclusion. The example mainly provides an instance of "threatening body language" and "provocative language" with the homeowner gesturing threats to his neighbor. It ends the example by adding a third type of assault: physical strikes. This example is used to show the variant nature of assaults. Choice *A* is incorrect because it doesn't mention the "physical strike" assault at the end and is not specific enough. Choice *C* is incorrect because the example does not say anything about the definition of lethal force or how it might be altered. Choice *D* is incorrect because the example mentions nothing about cause and effect.

Language Arts: Writing

1. B: Move the sentence so that it comes before the preceding sentence. For this question, place the underlined sentence in each prospective choice's position. Leaving the sentence in place is incorrect because the father "going crazy" doesn't logically follow the fact that he was a "city slicker." Choice *C* is incorrect because the sentence in question is not a concluding sentence and does not transition smoothly into the second paragraph. Choice *D* is incorrect because the sentence doesn't necessarily need to be omitted since it logically follows the very first sentence in the passage.

2. D: Choice *D* is correct because "As it turns out" indicates a contrast from the previous sentiment, that the RV was a great purchase. Choice *A* is incorrect because the sentence needs an effective transition from the paragraph before. Choice *B* is incorrect because the text indicates it *is* surprising that the RV was a great purchase because the author was skeptical beforehand. Choice *C* is incorrect because the transition *furthermore* does not indicate a contrast.

3. B: This sentence calls for parallel structure. Choice *B* is correct because the verbs *wake*, *eat*, and *break* are consistent in tense and parts of speech. Choice *A* is incorrect because the words *wake* and *eat* are present tense while the word *broke* is in past tense. Choice *C* is incorrect because this turns the sentence into a question, which doesn't make sense within the context. Choice *D* is incorrect because it breaks tense with the rest of the passage. *Waking*, *eating*, and *breaking* are all present participles, and the context around the sentence is in past tense.

4. C: Choice *C* is correct because it is clear and fits within the context of the passage. Choice *A* is incorrect because "We rejoiced as 'hackers'" does not explain what was meant by hackers or why it was a cause for rejoicing. Choice *B* is incorrect because it does not mention a solution being found and is therefore not specific enough. Choice *D* is incorrect because the meaning is eschewed by the helping verb had to rejoice, and the sentence suggests that rejoicing was necessary to "hack" a solution.

5. A: The original sentence is correct because the verb tense and the meaning both align with the rest of the passage. Choice *B* is incorrect because the order of the words makes the sentence more confusing than it otherwise would be. Choice *C* is incorrect because "We are even making" is in present tense. Choice *D* is incorrect because "We will make" is future tense. The surrounding text of the sentence is in past tense.

6. B: Choice *B* is correct because there is no punctuation needed if a dependent clause ("while traveling across America") is located behind the independent clause ("it allowed us to share adventures"). Choice *A* is incorrect because there are two dependent clauses connected and no independent clause, and a complete sentence requires at least one independent clause. Choice *C* is incorrect because of the same reason as Choice *A*. Semicolons have the

Answer Explanations #1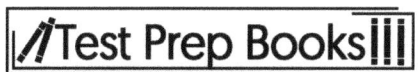

same function as periods; therefore, there must be an independent clause on either side of the semicolon. Choice D is incorrect because the dash simply interrupts the complete sentence.

7. C: The rule for *me* and *I* is that one should use *I* when it is the subject pronoun of a sentence and *me* when it is the object pronoun of the sentence. Break the sentence up to see if *I* or *me* should be used. To say "Those are memories that I have now shared" is correct, rather than "Those are memories that me have now shared." Choice D is incorrect because *my siblings* should come before *I*.

8. D: Choice D is correct because Fred Hampton becoming an activist was a direct result of him wanting to see lasting social change for Black people. Choice A doesn't make sense because "In the meantime" denotes something happening at the same time as another thing. Choice B is incorrect because the text's tone does not indicate that becoming a civil rights activist is an unfortunate path. Choice C is incorrect because "Finally" indicates something that comes last in a series of events, and the word in question is at the beginning of the introductory paragraph.

9. C: Choice C is correct because there should be a comma between the city and state, as well as after the word "Illinois." Commas should be used to separate all geographical items within a sentence. Choice A is incorrect because it does not include the comma after "Illinois." Choice B is incorrect because the comma after "neighborhood" interrupts the phrase, "the Maywood neighborhood of Chicago." Finally, Choice D is incorrect because the order of the sentence designates that Chicago, Illinois is in Maywood, which is incorrect.

10. C: The paragraph is incorrect as-is because it is too long and thus loses the reader as it changes focus halfway through. Choice C is correct because if the new paragraph began with "While studying at Triton," we would see a smooth transition from one paragraph to the next. We can also see how the two paragraphs are logically split in two. The first half of the paragraph talks about where he studied. The second half of the paragraph talks about the NAACP and the result of his leadership in the association. If we look at the passage as a whole, we can see that there are two main topics that should be broken into two separate paragraphs.

11. B: The BPP "was another activist group that ..." We can determine this answer by using context clues. We know that the BPP is "similar in function" to the NAACP. Previous sentences describe the function of the NAACP as an activist group, so we can assume that the BPP is also an activist group.

12. A: Choice C is incorrect because it misplaces the apostrophe. While Choice D contains proper construction of a possessive, it changes the name of the organization from *the Black Panther Party* to *the Black Panther Parties*. Choice B also changes the name of the organization, and it doesn't use a possessive form. Choice D is incorrect because, again, the word "parties" should not be plural; instead, it is one unified party.

13. C: Choice C is correct because the passage is in the past tense and *enabled* is a past tense verb. Choice A, "enable," is present tense. Choice B, "are enabling," is a present participle, which suggests a continuing action. Choice D, "will enable," is future tense.

14. D: Choice D is correct because the conjunction "and" is the best way to combine the two independent clauses. Choice A is incorrect because the word "he" becomes repetitive since the two clauses can be joined together. Choice B is incorrect because the conjunction "but" indicates a contrast, and there is no contrast between the two clauses. Choice C is incorrect because the introduction of the comma after "project" with no conjunction creates a comma splice.

15. C: The word "acheivement" is misspelled. Remember the rules for "*i* before *e* except after *c*." Choices B and D, "greatest" and "leader," are both spelled correctly.

16. B: Choice B is correct because it provides the correct verb tense and verb form. Choice A is incorrect; Hampton was not "held by a press conference"—rather, he held a press conference. The passage indicates that he "made the gangs agree to a nonaggression pact," implying that it was Hampton who was doing the speaking for this

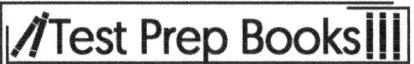

Answer Explanations #1

conference. Choice *C* is incorrect because, with this use of the sentence, it would create a fragment because the verb *holding* has no helping verb in front of it. Choice *D* is incorrect because it adds an infinitive ("to hold") where a past tense form of a verb should be.

17. A: Choice *A* is correct because it provides the most clarity. Choice *B* is incorrect because it doesn't name the group until the end, so the phrase "the group" is vague. Choice *C* is incorrect because it indicates that the BPP's popularity grew as a result of placing the group under constant surveillance, which is incorrect. Choice *D* is incorrect because there is a misplaced modifier; this sentence actually says that the FBI's influence and popularity grew, which is incorrect.

18. B: Choice *B* is correct. Choice *A* is incorrect because there should be an independent clause on either side of a semicolon, and the phrase "In 1976" is not an independent clause. Choice *C* is incorrect because there should be a comma after introductory phrases in general, such as "In 1976," and Choice *C* omits a comma. Choice *D* is incorrect because the sentence "In 1976." is a fragment.

19. C: Choice *C* is correct because the past tense verb "provided" fits in with the rest of the verb tense throughout the passage. Choice *A*, "will provide," is future tense. Choice *B*, "provides," is present tense. Choice *D*, "providing," is a present participle, which means the action is continuous.

20. D: The correct answer is Choice *D* because this statement provides the most clarity. Choice *A* is incorrect because the noun "Chicago City Council" acts as one, so the verb "are" should be singular, not plural. Choice *B* is incorrect because it is perhaps the most confusingly worded out of all the answer choices; the phrase "December 4" interrupts the sentence without any indication of purpose. Choice *C* is incorrect because it is too vague and leaves out *who* does the commemorating.

21. B: Here, a colon is used to introduce a quotation. Colons either introduce explanations or lists. Additionally, the quote ends with the punctuation inside the quotes, unlike Choice *C*.

22. A: This passage is predominantly in the present tense, and the author is describing education as it currently is, so Choice *A* is the correct answer. Choice *B* is incorrect because the subject and verb do not agree; the singular subject "Education" should be paired with the singular verb "provides." Choice *C* is incorrect because the passage is in present tense, and "Education will provide" is future tense. Choice *D* doesn't make sense when placed in the sentence.

23. D: The possessive form of the word "it" is "its." The contraction "it's" denotes "it is." Thus, Choice *A* is wrong. The word "raises" in Choice *B* makes the sentence grammatically incorrect. Choice *C* adds an apostrophe at the end of "its." While most nouns indicate possession with an apostrophe, adding 's to the word "it" indicates a contraction.

24. C: The word *civelized* should be spelled *civilized*. The words *distinguishes* and *creatures* are both spelled correctly.

25. B: Choice *B* is correct because it provides clarity by describing what *myopic* means right after the word itself. Choice *A* is incorrect because the explanation of *myopic* comes before the word; thus, the meaning is skewed. It's possible that Choice *C* makes sense within context. However, it's not the best way to say this because the commas create too many unnecessary phrases. Choice *D* is confusingly worded. Using "*myopic focus*" is not detrimental to society; however, the way Choice *D* is worded makes it seem that way.

26. C: The passage's second paragraph can be divided into two paragraphs because it is about two separate topics. The paragraph's first main focus is education addressing the mind, body, and soul. This first section, then, could end with the concluding sentence, "The human heart and psyche ..." The next sentence should start a new paragraph

Answer Explanations #1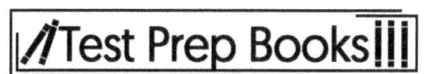

with "Education is a basic human right ..." The rest of this paragraph talks about what education is and some of its characteristics.

27. A: Choice A is correct because the phrase *others' ideas* is both plural and indicates possession. Choice B is incorrect because *other's* indicates only one "other" that's in possession of "ideas," which is incorrect. Choice C is incorrect because no possession is indicated. Choice D is incorrect because the word *other* does not end in *s*.

28. D: This sentence must have a comma before *although* because it is connecting two independent clauses. Thus, Choices B and C are incorrect. Choice A is incorrect because the second sentence in the underlined section is a fragment.

29. C: Choice C is the correct choice because the word *their* indicates possession, and the text is talking about *their students*, or the students of someone. Choice A, *there*, describes where something is located. Choice B, *they're*, is a contraction and means *they are*. Choice D is not a word.

30. B: Choice B uses all punctuation correctly in this sentence. In American English, single quotes should only be used if they are quotes within a quote, making Choices A and C incorrect. Additionally, punctuation should go inside quotation marks (with a few exceptions), making Choice D incorrect.

31. B: Choice B is correct because the conjunction *and* is used to connect phrases that are to be used jointly, such as teachers working hard to help students identify salient information and to think critically. The conjunctions so, but, and nor are incorrect in the context of this sentence.

32. A: Choice A has consistent parallel structure with the verbs *read*, *identify*, and *determine*. Choices B and C have faulty parallel structure with the words "determining" and "identifying." Choice D has incorrect subject/verb agreement. The sentence should read, "Students have to read ... identify ... and determine."

33. D: The correct choice for this sentence is that "they are ... shaped by the influences." The prepositions "for," "to," and "with" do not make sense in this context. People are *shaped by*, not *shaped for, shaped to,* or *shaped with*.

34. A: To see which answer is correct, it might help to place the subject, teachers, near the verb. Choice A is correct: "Teachers ... must strive" makes grammatical sense here. Choice B is incorrect because "Teachers ... to strive" does not make grammatical sense. Choice C is incorrect because "Teachers must not only respect ... but striving" does not use parallel structure. Choice D is incorrect because it is in past tense, and this passage is in present tense.

35. C: Choice C is correct because it uses an em dash. Em dashes are versatile. They can separate phrases that would otherwise be in parentheses, or they can stand in for a colon. In this case, a colon would be another decent choice for this punctuation mark because the second sentence expands upon the first sentence. Choice A is incorrect because the statement is not a question. Choice B is incorrect because adding a comma here would create a comma splice. Choice D is incorrect because this creates a run-on sentence since the two sentences are independent clauses.

36. B: The best place for this sentence given all the answer choices is at the end of the first paragraph. Choice A is incorrect; the passage is told in chronological order, and leaving the sentence as-is defies that order, since we haven't been introduced to who raised George. Choice C is incorrect because this sentence is not an introductory sentence. It does not provide the main topic of the paragraph. Choice D is incorrect because again, it defies chronological order. By the end of paragraph two we have already gotten to George as an adult, so this sentence would not make sense here.

37. D: Out of these choices, a semicolon would be the best fit because there is an independent clause on either side of the semicolon, and the two sentences closely relate to each other. Choice A is incorrect because putting a comma between two independent clauses (i.e., complete sentences) creates a comma splice. Choice B is incorrect; omitting

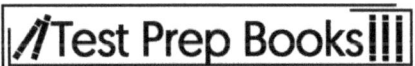

punctuation here creates a run-on sentence. Choice C is incorrect because an ellipsis (...) is used to designate an omission in the text.

38. B: This is another example of parallel structure. Choice A is incorrect because the verbs in the original sentence are "growing," "depleting," and "results," the last of which has a different form than the first two. Choices C and D add "depletes" and "grows," both of which abandon the "-ing" verbs.

39. C: Choice C is correct because it keeps with the verb tense in the rest of the passage: past tense. Choice A is in present tense, which is incorrect. Choice B is present progressive, which means there is a continual action, which is also incorrect. Choice D is incorrect because "was returning" is past progressive tense, which means that something was happening continuously at some point in the past.

40. C: The correct choice is the subordinating conjunction, *when*. We should look at the clues around the phrase to see what fits best. Carver left his money *when he died*. Choice A, *because*, could perhaps be correct, but *when* is the more appropriate word to use here. Choice B is incorrect; *although* denotes a contrast, and there is no contrast here. Choice D is incorrect because *finally* indicates something at the very end of a list or series, and there is no series at this point in the text.

41. A: There should be no change here. Both underlined sentences are complete and do not need changing. Choice B is incorrect because there is no punctuation between the two independent clauses, it is considered a run-on. Choice C is incorrect because placing a comma between two independent clauses creates a comma splice. Choice D is incorrect. The underlined portion could *possibly* act with a colon. However, it's not the best choice, so omit Choice D.

42. D: Choice D is correct. The text before this underlined phrase talks about the difference between "discovery" and "exploration," so making a decision on what term to label Columbus would be the best choice. The other three choices may be true to the historical narrative of Columbus; however, they do not fit within the surrounding text.

43. B: This question seeks to determine the best introductory word for the main point of the following sentence. Choice B is correct; the word "Rather" indicates something unexpected. "Rather" fits in this sentence because it is "unexpected" that Leif Erikson first came to the New World and not Columbus. Choice A is incorrect; "Nevertheless" means "all the same," and does not fit with the sentiment of this sentence. Choice C is incorrect because "Finally" is used to indicate the last point in a series, and we do not have a listed series here. The word "Suddenly" is used to indicate something that has happened quickly or unexpectedly. Thus, Choice D is incorrect.

44. C: Choice C is correct; the underlined phrase consists of part of an independent clause and a dependent clause ("Depending on which historian you read.") The dependent clause cannot stand by itself. Thus, the best choice is to connect the two clauses with a comma. Choices A and D do not work because you must have two independent clauses on either side of a period as well as a semicolon. Choice B is incorrect because an exclamation point is used to show excitement and does not fit the tone here.

45. A: There should be no change. The sentence fits perfectly before the current one because in question is who raised Leif. Choice B is incorrect because this narrative is in chronological order, and by the end of the second paragraph, Leif is already an adult. Choice C wouldn't work because the sentence is not an introductory sentence. Rather, it shares the details of Leif's childhood. Finally, Choice D is incorrect because there is already a transition, "Instead," to lead into the next sentence.

46. C: To find out the best answer, try out each answer choice. Choice A is incorrect; it might make sense that Leif is "later trying to return home." However, the next sentence says "Leif with the intention of taking supplies," and is not grammatically correct. Choice B is also incorrect because we would have the same problem with "Leif with the intention of taking supplies." Choice D is not a good answer choice because it inverts words that are otherwise clear with Choice C, "Leif later tried to return home with the intention of taking supplies."

Answer Explanations #1

47. B: The most appropriate verb for this sentence is Choice *B*, "Leif consulted." Choice *A* is in present tense and therefore does not fit with the rest of the passage. Choice *C* is incorrect because "consulting" is present progressive tense and also does not fit with the consistent past tense of the passage. Choice *D*, "Leif was consulted with a merchant," doesn't make sense. Leif can consult with a merchant or be consulted by a merchant.

48. D: Choice *D* uses the correct punctuation. American English uses double quotes unless placing quotes within a quote (which would then require single quotes). Thus, Choices *A* and *C* are incorrect. Choice *B* is incorrect because the period should go outside of the parenthesis, not inside.

49. C: Choice *C* is correct. The subject and verb agree with each other (accounts describe), and there is no apostrophe because no possession is being shown. Choices *B* and *D* are incorrect because there is no possession— "accounts" is simply plural. Choice *A* is incorrect because the subject and verb do not agree with each other (accounts describes).

50. D: Choice *D* is correct because the interrupting phrase, "seventeen years later," is separated by commas. Choice *A* is incorrect because putting a period between "later" and "The" causes the first sentence to become a fragment. Choice *B* is incorrect because of the same reason: the semicolon should have an independent clause on either side of it, and the first half of the sentence is not an independent clause. Choice *C* needs commas to separate the interrupting phrase or else the words become mashed together, causing confusion.

51. C: A complex sentence joins an independent or main clause with a dependent or subordinate clause. In this case, the main clause is "The restaurant is unconventional." This is a clause with one subject-verb combination that can stand alone as a grammatically complete sentence. The dependent clause is "because it serves both Chicago style pizza and New York style pizza." This clause begins with the subordinating conjunction *because* and also consists of only one subject-verb combination. Choice *A* is incorrect because a simple sentence consists of only one verb-subject combination—one independent clause. Choice *B* is incorrect because a compound sentence contains two independent clauses connected by a conjunction. Choice *D* is incorrect because a compound-complex sentence consists of two or more independent clauses and one or more dependent clauses.

52. A: Parallelism refers to consistent use of sentence structure or word form. In this case, the list within the sentence does not utilize parallelism; three of the verbs appear in their base form—*travel*, *take*, and *eat*—but one appears as a gerund—*going*. A parallel version of this sentence would be "This summer, I'm planning to travel to Italy, take a Mediterranean cruise, go to Pompeii, and eat a lot of Italian food." Choice *B* is incorrect because this description is a complete sentence. Choice *C* is incorrect, as a misplaced modifier is a modifier that is not located appropriately in relation to the word or words they modify. Choice *D* is incorrect because subject-verb agreement refers to the appropriate conjugation of a verb in relation to its subject.

53. C: In this sentence, the modifier is the phrase "Forgetting that he was supposed to meet his girlfriend for dinner." This phrase offers information about Fred's actions, but the noun that immediately follows it is Anita, creating some confusion about the "do-er" of the phrase. A more appropriate sentence arrangement would be "Forgetting that he was supposed to meet his girlfriend for dinner, Fred made Anita mad when he showed up late." *A* is incorrect as parallelism refers to the consistent use of sentence structure and verb tense, and this sentence is appropriately consistent. *B* is incorrect as a run-on sentence does not contain appropriate punctuation for the number of independent clauses presented, which is not true of this description. *D* is incorrect because subject-verb agreement refers to the appropriate conjugation of a verb relative to the subject, and all verbs have been properly conjugated.

54. B: A comma splice occurs when a comma is used to join two independent clauses together without the additional use of an appropriate conjunction. One way to remedy this problem is to replace the comma with a semicolon. Another solution is to add a conjunction: "Some workers use all their sick leave, but other workers cash out their leave." *A* is incorrect as parallelism refers to the consistent use of sentence structure and verb tense; all

313

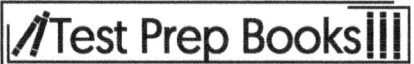

Answer Explanations #1

tenses and structures in this sentence are consistent. *C* is incorrect because a sentence fragment is a phrase or clause that cannot stand alone—this sentence contains two independent clauses. *D* is incorrect because subject-verb agreement refers to the proper conjugation of a verb relative to the subject, and all verbs have been properly conjugated.

55. D: The problem in the original passage is that the second sentence is a dependent clause that cannot stand alone as a sentence; it must be attached to the main clause found in the first sentence. Because the main clause comes first, it does not need to be separated by a comma. However, if the dependent clause came first, then a comma would be necessary, which is why Choice *C* is incorrect. Choices *A* and *B* also insert unnecessary commas into the sentence.

56. A: The affix *circum–* originates from Latin and means "around" or "surrounding. It is also related to other words that indicate something round, such as *circle* and *circus*.

57. C: A style guide offers advice about proper formatting, punctuation, and usage when writing for a specific field, such as journalism or scientific research. The other resources would not offer similar information. A dictionary is useful for looking up definitions; a thesaurus is useful for looking up synonyms and antonyms. A grammar book is useful for looking up specific grammar topics. Thus, Choices *A*, *B*, and *D* are incorrect.

58. B: A word's origin is also known as its *etymology*. In addition to offering a detailed list of a word's various meanings, a dictionary also provides information about a word's history, such as when it first came into use, what language it originated from, and how its meaning may have changed over time. A thesaurus is for identifying synonyms and antonyms, so Choice *A* is incorrect. A style guide provides formatting, punctuation, and syntactical advice for a specific field, and a grammar book is related to the appropriate placement of words and punctuation, which does not provide any insight into a word's origin. Therefore, Choices *C* and *D* are incorrect.

59. C: The main idea of a piece is its central theme or subject and what the author wants readers to know or understand after they finish reading. Choice *A* is incorrect because the primary purpose is the reason that a piece was written, and while the main idea is an important part of the primary purpose, the above elements are not developed with that intent. Choice *B* is incorrect because while the plot refers to the events that occur in a narrative, organization, tone, and supporting details are not used only to develop plot. Choice *D* is incorrect because characterization is the description of a person.

60. A: The passage describes a situation and then explains the causes that led to it. Also, it utilizes cause and effect signal words, such as *reasons*, *factors*, *so*, and *as a result*. Choice *B* is incorrect because a compare and contrast order considers the similarities and differences of two or more things. Choice *C* is incorrect because spatial order describes where things are located in relation to each other. Finally, Choice *D* is incorrect because time order describes when things occurred chronologically.

Mathematics

1. B: The product of two irrational numbers can be rational or irrational. Sometimes the irrational parts of the two numbers cancel each other out, leaving a rational number. For example, $\sqrt{2} \times \sqrt{2} = 2$ because the roots cancel each other out. Technically, the product of two irrational numbers is a complex number, because real numbers are a type of complex number. However, Choice *D* is incorrect because the product of two irrational numbers is not an imaginary number.

2. A: The relative error can be found by finding the absolute error and making it a percent of the true value. The absolute error is $36 - 35.75 = 0.25$. This error is then divided by 35.75—the true value—to find 0.7%.

3. B: The car is traveling at a speed of 5 meters per second. On the interval from 1 to 3 seconds, the position changes by 10 meters. This is 10 meters in 2 seconds, or 5 meters in each second.

4. B: The first step is to make all exponents positive by moving the terms with negative exponents to the opposite side of the fraction. This expression becomes:

$$\frac{4b^3 b^2}{a^1 a^4} \times \frac{3a}{b}$$

Then the rules for exponents can be used to simplify. Multiplying the same bases means the exponents can be added. Dividing the same bases means the exponents are subtracted. Thus, after multiplying the exponents in the first fraction, the expression becomes:

$$\frac{4b^5}{a^5} \times \frac{3a}{b}$$

Therefore, we can first multiply to get:

$$\frac{12ab^5}{a^5 b}$$

Then, simplifying yields:

$$12 \frac{b^4}{a^4}$$

5. B: There are two zeros for the function: $x = 0, -2$. The zeros can be found several ways, but this particular equation can be factored into:

$$f(x) = x(x^2 + 4x + 4) = x(x+2)(x+2)$$

By setting each factor equal to zero and solving for x, we find two solutions. On a graph, these zeros can be seen where the line touches the x-axis.

6. C: The terms "whole numbers" and "natural numbers" include all the ordinary counting numbers (1, 2, 3, 4, 5, …), and sometimes zero depending on the definition used, but no negative numbers. The term "integers" includes all those numbers, their negatives, and zero. So – 4 is not a whole number or a natural number, but it is an integer. It is also rational because it can be written as a ratio of two integers ($-\frac{4}{1}$); all integers are rational. It is a real number because it does not have an imaginary component (symbolized by the letter i); all integers are real numbers.

7. D: This problem involves a composition function, where one function is plugged into the other function. In this case, the $f(x)$ function is plugged into the $g(x)$ function for each x value. The composition equation becomes:

$$g(f(x)) = g(2) = (2)^3 - 3(2)^2 - 2(2) + 6$$

Simplifying the equation gives the answer:

$$g(f(x)) = 8 - 3(4) - 2(2) + 6$$

$$g(f(x)) = 8 - 12 - 4 + 6$$

$$g(f(x)) = -2$$

Answer Explanations #1

8. A: The volume of the sphere is 288π cubic meters. Using the formula for sphere volume, we see that:

$$\frac{4}{3}\pi r^3 = 288\pi$$

We solve this equation for r to obtain a radius of 6 meters. The formula for surface area is $4\pi r^2$, so:

$$SA = 4\pi 6^2 = 144\pi \text{ square meters}$$

9. D: This system of equations involves one quadratic equation and one linear equation. One way to solve this is through substitution.

Solving for y in the second equation yields:

$$y = x + 2$$

Plugging this equation in for the y of the quadratic equation yields:

$$x^2 - 2x + x + 2 = 8$$

Simplify the equation:

$$x^2 - x + 2 = 8$$

Set this equal to zero and factor:

$$x^2 - x - 6 = 0 = (x - 3)(x + 2)$$

Solving these two factors for x gives the zeros:

$$x = 3, -2$$

To find the y-value for the point, plug in each number to either original equation.

$$(3)^2 - 2(3) + y = 8$$

$$9 - 6 + y = 8$$

$$3 + y = 8$$

$$y = 5$$

$$(-2)^2 - 2(-2) + y = 8$$

$$4 + 4 + y = 8$$

$$8 + y = 8$$

$$y = 0$$

Solving each one for y yields the points $(3, 5)$ and $(-2, 0)$.

10. D: This problem can be solved by using unit conversion. The initial units are miles per minute. The final units need to be feet per second. Converting miles to feet uses the equivalence statement $1 \text{ mi} = 5{,}280 \text{ ft}$. Converting minutes to seconds uses the equivalence statement 1 min = 60 s. Setting up the ratios to convert the units is shown in the following equation:

$$\frac{72 \text{ mi}}{90 \text{ min}} \times \frac{1 \text{ min}}{60 \text{ s}} \times \frac{5{,}280 \text{ ft}}{1 \text{ mi}} = \frac{380{,}160 \text{ ft}}{5{,}400 \text{ s}} = 70.4 \frac{\text{ft}}{\text{s}}$$

The initial units cancel out, and the new units are left.

11. D: The expression is simplified by collecting like terms. Terms with the same variable and exponent are like terms, and their coefficients can be added.

Since the two sets of parentheses are being added, the parentheses are actually not needed. Like terms can be added together even if they are in different sets of parentheses.

12. C: Because the triangles are similar, the lengths of the corresponding sides are proportional. Therefore, these two relationships exist:

$$\frac{30 + x}{30} = \frac{22}{14}$$

$$\frac{y + 15}{y} = \frac{22}{14}$$

Using cross multiplication on the first proportion results in the equation:

$$14(30 + x) = 22 \times 30$$

When solved, this gives:

$$x \approx 17.1$$

Using cross multiplication on the second proportion results in the equation:

$$14(y + 15) = 22y$$

When solved, this gives:

$$y \approx 26.3$$

13. A: Finding the product means distributing one polynomial onto the other. Each term in the first polynomial must be multiplied by each term in the second polynomial. Then, like terms can be collected. Multiplying the factors yields the expression:

$$20x^3 + 4x^2 + 24x - 40x^2 - 8x - 48$$

Collecting like terms means adding the x^2 terms and adding the x terms. The final answer after simplifying the expression is:

$$20x^3 - 36x^2 + 16x - 48$$

14. C: Finding the zeros for a function by factoring is done by setting the equation equal to zero, then completely factoring. Since there is a common x for each term in the provided equation, that would be factored out first. Then the quadratic that was left could be factored into two binomials, which are $(x + 1)(x - 4)$. Setting each factor equal to zero and solving for x yields three zeros.

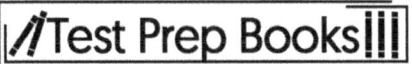

Answer Explanations #1

15. A: First, the sample mean must be calculated.

$$\bar{x} = \frac{1}{4}(1 + 3 + 5 + 7) = 4$$

The standard deviation of the data set is:

$$\sigma = \sqrt{\frac{\sum(x - \bar{x})^2}{n - 1}}$$

$n = 4$ represents the number of data points.

Therefore, $\sigma =$

$$\sqrt{\frac{1}{3}[(1 - 4)^2 + (3 - 4)^2 + (5 - 4)^2 + (7 - 4)^2]}$$

$$\sqrt{\frac{1}{3}(9 + 1 + 1 + 9)} = 2.58.$$

16. B: This problem can be solved by setting up a proportion involving the given information and the unknown value. The proportion is:

$$\frac{21 \text{ pages}}{4 \text{ nights}} = \frac{140 \text{ pages}}{x \text{ nights}}$$

Cross-multiply to get $21x = 4 \times 140$. Solving this leaves $x \approx 26.67$. Since this is not an integer, round up to 27 nights because 26 nights would not give Sarah enough time to finish.

17. D: Dividing rational expressions follows the same rule as dividing fractions. The division is changed to multiplication by the reciprocal of the second fraction. This turns the expression into:

$$\frac{5x^3}{3x^2y} \times \frac{3y^9}{25}$$

Multiplying across creates:

$$\frac{15x^3y^9}{75x^2y}$$

Simplifying leads to the final expression of:

$$\frac{xy^8}{5}$$

18. B: The technique of completing the square must be used to change the equation below into the standard equation of a circle:

$$4x^2 + 4y^2 - 16x - 24y + 51 = 0$$

First, the constant must be moved to the right-hand side of the equals sign, and each term must be divided by the coefficient of the x^2-term (which is 4). The x- and y-terms must be grouped together to obtain:

$$x^2 - 4x + y^2 - 6y = -\frac{51}{4}$$

Then, the process of completing the square must be completed for each variable. This gives:

$$(x^2 - 4x + 4) + (y^2 - 6y + 9) = -\frac{51}{4} + 4 + 9$$

The equation can be written as:

$$(x - 2)^2 + (y - 3)^2 = \frac{1}{4}$$

Therefore, the center of the circle is $(2, 3)$, and the radius is:

$$\sqrt{\frac{1}{4}} = \frac{1}{2}$$

19. D: Setting up a proportion is the easiest way to represent this situation. The proportion is $\frac{20}{x} = \frac{40}{100}$, and cross-multiplication can be used to solve for x. Here, $40x = 2{,}000$, so $x = 50$. The answer can also be found by viewing the two fractions as equivalent, knowing that 20 is half of 40, and 50 is half of 100.

20. B: We can try to solve the equation by factoring the numerator into $(x + 6)(x - 5)$. Since $(x - 5)$ is on the top and bottom, that factor cancels out. This leaves the equation $x + 6 = 11$. Solving the equation gives the answer $x = 5$. When this value is substituted back into the equation, it yields a zero in the denominator of the fraction. Since this is undefined, there is no solution.

21. B: The formula can be manipulated by dividing both the length, l, and the width, w, on both sides. The length and width will cancel on the right, leaving height, h, by itself.

22. C: The sample space is made up of $8 + 7 + 6 + 5 = 26$ balls. The probability of pulling each individual ball is $\frac{1}{26}$. Since there are 7 yellow balls, the probability of pulling a yellow ball is $\frac{7}{26}$.

23. B: The domain is all possible input values, or x-values. For this equation, the domain is every number greater than or equal to zero. There are no negative numbers in the domain because taking the square root of a negative number results in an imaginary number.

24. B: An equilateral triangle has 3 sides of equal length, so if the total perimeter is 18 feet, each side must be 6 feet long. A square with sides of 6 feet will have an area of $6^2 = 36$ square feet.

25. C: It may help to look at this problem as a fraction: $\frac{1.2 \times 10^{12}}{3.0 \times 10^8}$. We can calculate $\frac{1.2}{3} = 0.4$, and using the rules of exponents, we can see that $\frac{10^{12}}{10^8} = 10^{12-8} = 10^4$. This gives us an answer of 0.4×10^4, which is Choice A, but our answer is not yet in scientific notation because the first term, 0.4, is not between 1 and 10. We can rewrite 0.4×10^4, multiplying the first term by 10 and subtracting 1 from the exponent, which gives 4.0×10^3, Choice C.

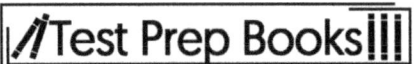

Answer Explanations #1

26. D: The slope from this equation is 50, and it is interpreted as the cost per gigabyte used. Since the g-value represents the number of gigabytes and the equation is set equal to the cost in dollars, the slope relates these two values. For every gigabyte used on the phone, the bill goes up 50 dollars.

27. B: The zeros of this function can be found by setting $f(x)$ equal to 0 and solving for x.

$$0 = x^2 + 4$$
$$-4 = x^2$$
$$\sqrt{(-4)} = x$$

Taking the square root of a negative number results in an imaginary number, so the solution is: $x = \pm 2i$

28. D: The formula for the volume of a cube is $V = s^3$, where V is the volume and s is the side length. Here, $s = 5$ cm, so $V = (5 \text{ cm})^3 = 125 \text{ cm}^3$.

29. B: The y-intercept of an equation is found where the x-value is zero. Plugging zero into the equation for x, the first two terms cancel out, leaving -4:

$$0^2 + 3(0) - 4 = -4$$

30. A: The definition of an even function is that $f(-x) = f(x)$. We can plug in $-x$ to our function to see what we get:

$$f(-2) = \frac{1}{2}(-x)^4 + 2(-x)^2 - 6$$

Since $(-x)^4 = x^4$ and $(-x)^2 = x^2$, we see that $f(-x)$ is equal to the original function, so our function is even.

The definition of an odd function is that $f(-x) = -f(x)$. We can calculate $-f(x)$:

$$-fx = -1\left(\frac{1}{2}\right)x^4 + 2x^2 - 6 = \left(-\frac{1}{2}\right)x^4 - 2x^2 + 6$$

This does not equal $f(-x)$ (which, remember, is the same as our original function), so our function is not odd.

31. A: This has the form $t^2 - y^2$, with $t = x^2$ and $y = 4$. It's also known that $t^2 - y^2 = (t + y)(t - y)$, and substituting the values for t and y into the right-hand side gives $(x^2 - 4)(x^2 + 4)$.

32. B: For the first card drawn, the probability of a king being pulled is $\frac{4}{52}$. Since this card isn't replaced, if a king is drawn first, the probability of a king being drawn second is $\frac{3}{51}$. The probability of a king being drawn in both the first and second draw is the product of the two probabilities:

$$\frac{4}{52} \times \frac{3}{51} = \frac{12}{2,652}$$

To reduce this fraction, divide the top and bottom by 12 to get $\frac{1}{221}$.

33. C: The equation $x = 3$ is not a function of x because it does not pass the vertical-line test: if any vertical line can intersect the equation's graph at more than one point, the equation is not a function. This test comes from the

Answer Explanations #1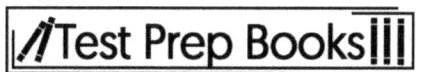

definition of a function, in which each x value in the domain must be mapped to no more than one y value. This equation is a vertical line, so the x value of 3 is mapped to an infinite number of y values.

34. D: If we roll a die twice, there are six possibilities for the first roll and six for the second roll, which gives $6 \times 6 = 36$ total possibilities. Now, how many ways are there to roll exactly one 6? We could get a 6 & 1, or 6 & 2, or 6 & 3, or 6 & 4, or 6 & 5. Furthermore, the 6 could come on the second roll; we could get a 1 & 6, or 2 & 6, or 3 & 6, or 4 & 6, or 5 & 6. Counting these up, we find a total of 10 different ways to roll exactly one 6. That means the event could happen in 10 out of 36 possible rolls, so the probability is $\frac{10}{36}$, which simplifies to $\frac{5}{18}$.

35. A: The function can be factored to identify the zeros. First, the term $3x$ is factored out to the front because each term contains $3x$. Then, the quadratic is factored into $(x + 3)(x - 2)$.

36. B: To solve this correctly, keep in mind the order of operations with the mnemonic PEMDAS (Please Excuse My Dear Aunt Sally). This stands for Parentheses, Exponents, Multiplication & Division, Addition & Subtraction. Taking it step by step, solve inside the parentheses first:

$$4 \times 7 + 4^2 \div 2$$

Then, apply the exponent:

$$4 \times 7 + 16 \div 2$$

Multiplication and division are both performed next:

$$28 + 8$$

Addition and subtraction are done last.

$$28 + 8 = 36$$

The solution is 36.

37. C: The formula for the area of the circle is πr^2, and 9 squared is 81. Choice *A* is not the correct answer because that takes the square root of the radius instead of squaring the radius. Choice *B* is not the correct answer because that is 2×9. Choice *D* is not the correct answer because that is simply the value of the radius.

38. A: If each man gains 10 pounds, every original data point will increase by 10 pounds. Therefore, the man with the original median will still have the median value, but that value will increase by 10. The smallest value and largest value will also increase by 10, so the difference between the two (the range) will remain the same.

39. B: The table shows values that are increasing exponentially. The differences between the inputs are the same, while the differences in the outputs are changing by a factor of 2. The values in the table can be modeled by the equation $f(x) = 2^x$.

40. C: To find the average of a set of values, add the values together and then divide by the total number of values. In this case, include the unknown value, x, of what Dwayne needs to score on his next test. The average must equal 90. Set up the equation and solve.

Answer Explanations #1

First, combine like terms:

$$\frac{78 + 92 + 83 + 97 + x}{5} = 90$$

$$\frac{350 + x}{5} = 90$$

Next, multiply both sides by 5:

$$(5)(\frac{350 + x}{5}) = (90)(5)$$

$$350 + x = 450$$

Lastly, subtract 350 from both sides:

$$350 + x - 350 = 450 - 350$$

$$x = 100$$

41. D: When a point is reflected over an axis, the sign of at least one of the coordinates must change. When it's reflected over the x-axis, the sign of the y coordinate must change. The x value remains the same. Therefore, the new ordered pair is $(-3, 4)$.

42. D: First, subtract $1,437 from $2,334.50 to find Johnny's monthly savings; this equals $897.50. Then, multiply this amount by 3 to find out how much he will have (in 3 months) before he pays for his vacation; this equals $2,692.50. Finally, subtract the cost of the vacation ($1,750) from this amount to find how much Johnny will have left: $942.50.

43. A: To calculate the range in a set of data, subtract the lowest value from the highest value. In this graph, the range of Mr. Lennon's students is 5, which can be seen physically in the graph as having the smallest difference between the highest value and the lowest value compared with the other teachers.

44. A: The slope is given by:

$$m = \frac{y_2 - y_1}{x_2 - x_1} = \frac{0 - 4}{0 - (-3)} = -\frac{4}{3}$$

45. B: The inscribed rectangle is 9×12 inches. First find the length of AC using the Pythagorean Theorem. So, $9^2 + 12^2 = c^2$, where c is the length of AC in this case. This means that $AC = 15$ inches. This means the diameter of the circle is 15 inches. This can be used to find the area of the entire circle. The formula is πr^2. So, $3.14(7.5)^2 = 176.6$ sq. inches. Then, subtract the area of the rectangle to find just the just the area of the shaded region. This is $176.6 - 108 = 68.6$.

46. A: If s is the size of the floor in square feet and r is the rate on Tuesday, then, based on the information given, $p = \frac{s}{4}$ and $r = \frac{s}{3}$. Solve the Monday rate for s, $s = 4p$, and then substitute that in the expression for Tuesday.

47. D: For an even number of total values, the median is calculated by finding the mean, or average, of the two middle values once all values have been arranged in ascending order from least to greatest. In this case, $\frac{83+92}{2}$ would equal the median 87.5, Choice D. Choice A is the lowest two values divided by 2, $\frac{78+83}{2} = 80.5$. Choice B is the first and third values divided by 2, $\frac{78+92}{2} = 85$. Choice C is the second and fourth values divided by 2, $\frac{83+97}{2} = 90$.

Answer Explanations #1

48. B: To simplify this inequality, subtract 3 from both sides:

$$3 - 3 - \frac{1}{2}x \geq 2 - 3$$

$$-\frac{1}{2}x \geq -1$$

Then, multiply both sides by -2 (remembering this flips the direction of the inequality):

$$(-\frac{1}{2}x)(-2) \geq (-1)(-2)$$

$$x \leq 2$$

49. B: Using the Pythagorean theorem, we can determine the length of the hypotenuse by plugging in the lengths of the sides $a^2 + b^2 = c^2$, or $3^2 + 4^2 = c^2 = 25$. We can then take the square root of 25 to $c = 5$. Choice A is not the correct answer because that is $3 + 4$. Choice C is not the correct answer because that is stopping at $3^2 + 4^2$ is $9 + 16$, which is 25. Choice D is not the correct answer because that is 3×4.

50. C: Kimberley worked 4.5 hours at the rate of $\frac{\$10}{h}$ and 1 hour at the rate of $\frac{\$12}{h}$. The problem states that her time is rounded to the nearest hour, so the 4.5 hours would round up to 5 hours at the rate of $\frac{\$10}{h}$.

$$(5 \text{ hours}) \times \left(\frac{\$10}{1 \text{ hour}}\right) + (1 \text{ hour}) \times \left(\frac{\$12}{1 \text{ hour}}\right) = \$50 + \$12 = \$62$$

51. C: The total percentage of a pie chart equals 100%. We can see that CD sales make up less than half of the chart (50%) but more than a quarter (25%), and the only answer choice that meets these criteria is Choice C, 40%.

52. B: Start by squaring both sides to get $1 + x = 16$. Then, subtract 1 from both sides to get $x = 15$.

53. B: We can use slope-intercept form, $y = mx + b$. We are told that the y-intercept (b) is 1, which gives us $y = mx + 1$. Now we can plug in the x and y values from our point, (1,2), to find the slope: $2 = m(1) + 1$, so m=1. This gives us $y = x + 1$.

54. A: The perimeter of a rectangle is $P = 2l + 2w$. We are told $P = 44$, so $2l + 2w = 44$. We are also told that the width is 2 cm less than the length: $w = l - 2$. Substituting this for w in the perimeter equation, we get $2l + 2(l - 2) = 44$, which is Choice A. Although it's not necessary to answer the test question, we could solve the equation to find the length and width. The equation simplifies to $4l - 4 = 44$, or $l = 12$, and since $w = l - 2$, we find $w = 10$.

55. D: The slope is given by the change in y divided by the change in x. Specifically, it's:

$$slope = \frac{y_2 - y_1}{x_2 - x_1}$$

The first point is $(-5, -3)$, and the second point is $(0, -1)$. Work from left to right when identifying coordinates. Thus, the point on the left is point 1 $(-5, -3)$ and the point on the right is point 2 $(0, -1)$.

Now we just need to plug those numbers into the equation:

$$slope = \frac{-1 - (-3)}{0 - (-5)}$$

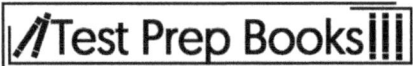

It can be simplified to:

$$slope = \frac{-1+3}{0+5}$$

$$slope = \frac{2}{5}$$

Science

1. A: Both types of cells are enclosed by a cell membrane, which is selectively permeable. Selective permeability means that it acts as a gatekeeper, allowing certain molecules and ions in and out while keeping unwanted ones at bay, at least until they are ready for use. Prokaryotes contain a nucleoid and do not have organelles; eukaryotes contain a nucleus enclosed by a membrane, as well as organelles.

2. D: The Celsius, or Centigrade, scale is based on a 100-degree difference between the freezing and boiling points of water; 0 °C is the freezing point of water, and 100 °C is the boiling point of water. The Fahrenheit scale was created by Daniel Gabriel Fahrenheit to attempt to avoid negative temperatures measured in everyday use. Daniel Fahrenheit set 100 °F equal to his internal body temperature. The Kelvin scale was created to set 0 as the complete absence of thermal energy, also known as absolute zero. The Rankine scale, which is commonly used in the aerospace industry, was created to be for Fahrenheit what Kelvin is to Celsius.

3. B: During telophase, two nuclei form at each end of the cell and nuclear envelopes begin to form around each nucleus. The nucleoli reappear, and the chromosomes become less compact. The microtubules are broken down by the cell, and mitosis is complete. The process begins with prophase as the mitotic spindles begin to form from centrosomes. Prometaphase follows, with the breakdown of the nuclear envelope and the further condensing of the chromosomes. Next, metaphase occurs when the microtubules are stretched across the cell and the chromosomes align at the metaphase plate. Finally, in the last step before telophase, anaphase occurs as the sister chromatids break apart and form chromosomes.

4. C: Elements are minerals formed by elements that occur naturally and aren't combined with other elements or substances. This group contains metals such as gold and nickel.

5. B: Potential energy is stored energy that an object has due to its position or shape. Kinetic energy is the energy involved in movement. Magnetic energy is the energy associated with a magnetic field. Nuclear energy is the energy contained within the nucleus of an atom.

6. D: Meiosis has the same phases as mitosis, except that they occur twice—once in meiosis I and once in meiosis II. During meiosis I, the cell splits into two. Each cell contains two sets of chromosomes. Next, during meiosis II, the two intermediate daughter cells divide again, producing four total haploid cells that each contain one set of chromosomes.

7. C: The mitochondrion is often called the powerhouse of the cell and is one of the most important structures for maintaining regular cell function. It is where aerobic cellular respiration occurs and where most of the cell's ATP is generated. The number of mitochondria in a cell varies greatly from organism to organism and from cell to cell. Cells that require more energy, like muscle cells, have more mitochondria.

8. C: Nitrogen is the most abundant element in the atmosphere at 78%. Carbon dioxide and water don't make up a large percentage. Oxygen makes up only 21% of the atmosphere.

9. A: Radio waves have the longest wavelength and shortest frequency on the electromagnetic spectrum. Gamma rays have the shortest wavelength and highest frequency. X-rays are similar to gamma rays and are on the same

Answer Explanations #1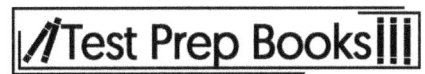

side of the electromagnetic spectrum. Microwaves are on the same end of the electromagnetic spectrum as radio waves, but they have shorter wavelengths and higher frequencies.

10. A: Photosynthesis is the process of converting light energy into chemical energy, which is then stored in sugar and other organic molecules. The photosynthetic process takes place in the thylakoids inside chloroplast in plants. Chlorophyll is a green pigment that lives in the thylakoid membranes and absorbs photons from light.

11. B: Viscosity is a physical measurement of a fluid's resistance to flow. In simpler terms, viscosity is the stickiness of a fluid. Out of the provided options, honey has the highest viscosity since there is resistance to its flow. Liquid water flows easily and does not hold shape well, meaning it is less viscous than honey. Likewise, alcohol flows well since it is not very viscous. Although viscosity is typically more relevant to liquids, gases do have measurable viscosity, which is less than that of fluids due to their lack of density.

12. C: The dew point is the temperature at which the water vapor in a sample of air at constant barometric pressure condenses into water at the same rate at which it evaporates. It isn't a measure of pressure.

13. B: Carbohydrates consist of sugars. The simplest sugar molecule is called a monosaccharide and has the molecular formula of CH_2O, or a multiple of that formula. Monosaccharides are important molecules for cellular respiration. Their carbon skeleton can also be used to rebuild new small molecules. Lipids are fats, proteins are formed via amino acids, and nucleic acid is found in DNA and RNA.

14. C: Work is a measurement of energy transfer that occurs when an external force is exerted on an object, making it move. Acceleration is the rate of velocity change. Synergy is an interaction of forces in which the combined force is greater than the sum of the individual forces. Pressure is the force exerted on a surface area.

15. B: The secondary structure of a protein refers to the folds and coils that are formed by hydrogen bonding between the slightly charged atoms of the polypeptide backbone. The primary structure is the sequence of amino acids, similar to the letters in a long word. The tertiary structure is the overall shape of the molecule that results from the interactions between the side chains that are linked to the polypeptide backbone. The quaternary structure is the complete protein structure that occurs when a protein is made up of two or more polypeptide chains.

16. D: DNA and RNA each contain four nitrogenous bases, three of which they have in common: adenine, guanine, and cytosine. Thymine is only found in DNA, and uracil is only found in RNA. Adenine interacts with uracil in RNA, and with thymine in DNA. Guanine always pairs with cytosine in both DNA and RNA.

17. B: The Coriolis effect is created by Earth's rotation. As wind moves toward the equator, the Earth's rotation also makes the wind move to the west. The Earth's axis and mountains don't play a part in the Coriolis effect.

18. A: The Big Bang theory explains how the universe was created from a large explosion, resulting in an expanding cloud of cosmic dust that clumped together to form stars and planets. Dark matter and life are found within the universe, and gravity is a universal law that helps explain how the Big Bang occurred.

19. B: Dominant alleles are considered to have stronger phenotypes and, when mixed with recessive alleles, will mask the recessive trait. The recessive trait would only appear as the phenotype when the allele combination is "aa" because a dominant allele is not present to mask it.

20. C: Dark storm clouds are considered nimbostratus clouds, which are located less than 2,000 meters above sea level. There are no atmospheric clouds in outer space.

21. D: Radiation can be transmitted through electromagnetic waves and needs no medium to travel. Radiation can travel in a vacuum. This is how the Sun warms the Earth, and this principle typically applies to large objects with

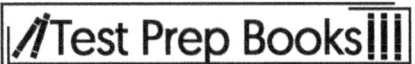

Answer Explanations #1

great amounts of heat or objects that have a large difference in their heat measurements. Choice A, convection, involves atoms or molecules traveling from areas of high concentration to those of low concentration, and they transfer energy or heat with them. Choice B, conduction, involves the touching or bumping of atoms or molecules in order to transfer energy or heat. Choice C, induction, deals with charges and does not apply to the transfer of energy or heat. Choices A, B, and C need a medium in which to travel, while radiation requires no medium.

22. A: Speciation is the method by which one species splits into two or more species. In allopatric speciation, one population is divided into two subpopulations. If a drought occurs and a large lake becomes divided into two smaller lakes, each lake is left with its own population that cannot intermingle with the population of the other lake. When the genes of these two subpopulations are no longer mixing with each other, new mutations can arise and natural selection can take place.

23. C: In the Linnaean system, organisms are classified as follows, moving from few and general similarities to comprehensive and specific similarities: domain, kingdom, phylum, class, order, family, genus, and species. A popular mnemonic device to remember the Linnaean system is "Dear King Philip Came Over For Good Soup."

24. D: Choice D is correct because the weight of an object is equal to the mass of an object multiplied by the acceleration of gravity. According to Newton's second law of motion, $F = m \times a$. Weight is the force resulting from a given situation, so the mass of the object needs to be multiplied by the acceleration of gravity on Earth: $W = m \times g$. Choice A is incorrect because, according to Newton's first law, all objects exert some force on each other, which is based on their distance from each other and their masses. This is seen in planets, which affect each other's paths and those of their moons. Choice B is incorrect because an object in motion or at rest can have inertia; inertia is the resistance of a physical object to change its state of motion. Choice C is incorrect because the mass of an object is a measurement of how much substance there is to the object, while the weight of an object is gravity's effect on the mass.

25. A: Fungal cells have a cell wall, similar to plant cells; however, they use oxygen as a source of energy and cannot perform photosynthesis. Because they do not perform photosynthesis, fungal cells do not contain chloroplasts.

26. A: Kepler's laws are:

    a. The orbit of a planet is elliptical in shape, with the Sun as one focus.

    b. An imaginary line joining the center of a planet and the center of the Sun sweeps out equal areas during equal intervals of time.

    c. The ratio of the square of the orbital period to the cube of the average distance from the Sun is the same for all planets.

These laws explain planetary motion created by gravity, such as the Earth's movement around the Sun. They don't have anything to do with how water, air, or sunlight move.

27. B: A decomposition reaction breaks down a compound into more basic components. Choice A is incorrect because a synthesis reaction joins two or more elements into a single compound. Choice C, an organic reaction, is a type of reaction involving organic compounds, primarily those containing carbon and hydrogen. Choice D, oxidation/reduction (redox or half) reaction, is incorrect because it involves the loss of electrons from one species (oxidation) and the gain of electrons to the other species (reduction). There is no mention of this occurring within the given reaction, so it is not correct.

28. A: Roots are responsible for absorbing water and nutrients that will get transported up through the plant. They also anchor the plant to the ground. Photosynthesis occurs in leaves, stems transport materials through the plant and support the plant body, and phloem moves sugars downward to the leaves.

29. C: The number of each element must be equal on both sides of the equation, so Choice C is the only correct option. $2\ Na + 2\ Cl$ does equal $2\ Na + 2\ Cl$ (the number of sodium atoms and chlorine atoms match).

In Choice A, $1\ Na + 2\ Cl$ does not equal $1\ Na + 1\ Cl$ (the number of chlorine atoms do not match).

In Choice B, $2\ Na + 2\ Cl$ does not equal $1\ Na + 1\ Cl$ (neither the number of sodium atoms nor chlorine atoms match).

In Choice D, $2\ Na + 4\ Cl$ does not equal $2\ Na + 2\ Cl$ (the number of chlorine atoms do not match).

30. D: Tropism is a response to stimuli that causes the plant to grow toward or away from the stimuli. Hydrotropism is a response to a change in water concentration. Phototropism is a reaction to light that causes plants to grow toward the source of the light. Thermotropism is a response to changes in temperature. Gravitropism is a response to gravity that causes roots to follow the pull of gravity and grow downward, but also causes plant shoots to act against gravity and grow upward.

31. C: The force that opposes motion is called *friction*. It also provides the resistance necessary for walking, running, braking, etc. In order for something to slide down a ramp, it must be acted upon by a force stronger than that of friction. Choices A and B are not actual terms, and Choice D is the measure of mass multiplied by velocity ($p = mv$).

32. C: Population dynamics look at the composition of populations, including size and age, and the biological and environmental processes that cause changes. These can include immigration, emigration, births, and deaths.

33. C: When the left side of the Moon is illuminated in the northern hemisphere, as it is in the given figure, it's in the waning phase. In contrast, when the right side of the Moon is illuminated, it's in its waxing phase. Gibbous describes a moon that's more than half-illuminated, and a crescent is less than half-illuminated.

34. D: An isotope of an element has an atomic number equal to its number of protons, but a different mass number because of the additional neutrons. Even though there are differences in the nucleus, the behavior and properties of isotopes of a given element are identical. Atoms with different atomic numbers also have different numbers of protons and are different elements, so they cannot be isotopes.

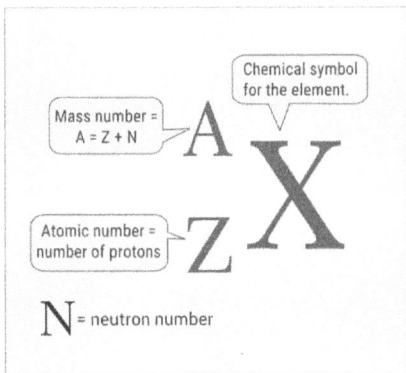

35. A: Ecosystems are maintained by cycling the energy and nutrients that they obtain from external sources. The process can be diagrammed in a food web, which represents the feeding relationship between the species in a community. A phylogenetic tree shows inferred evolutionary relationships among species and is similar to the fossil record. A pedigree chart shows occurrences of phenotypes of a particular gene through the generations of an organism.

36. D: Viruses are not classified as living organisms. They are neither prokaryotic or eukaryotic; therefore, they don't belong to any of the answer choices.

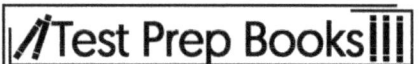

Answer Explanations #1

37. A: The neutrons and protons make up the nucleus of the atom. The nucleus is positively charged due to the presence of the protons. The negatively charged electrons are attracted to the positively charged nucleus by the electrostatic or Coulomb force; however, the electrons are not contained in the nucleus. The positively charged protons create the positive charge in the nucleus, and the neutrons are electrically neutral, so they have no effect. Radioactivity does not directly have a bearing on the charge of the nucleus.

38. D: DNA is replicated during the S-phase of interphase, which isn't considered part of mitosis. Mitosis is just the process of separation.

39. D: Ice (solid water) can be found in Saturn's rings. Liquid water may have recently been discovered on Jupiter's moons Europa and Callisto.

40. D: The law states that matter cannot be created or destroyed in a closed system. In this equation, there are the same number of molecules of each element on either side of the equation. Matter is not gained or lost, although a new compound is formed. As there are no ions on either side of the equation, no electrons are lost. The law prevents the hydrogen from losing mass and prevents oxygen atoms from being spontaneously spawned.

41. B: Solar eclipses should not be looked at directly. The rays of the Sun do not seem as bright as normal but can still cause damage to the eyes. A pinhole camera facing away from the eclipse allows the viewer to see a reflection of the eclipse instead of the actual eclipse. Choices A, C, and D all require looking directly at the solar eclipse.

42. B: A cell membrane is a phospholipid bilayer, with the lipid or fat portion (the tails) composing the middle. Lipids are hydrophobic or water-fearing. Think about how difficult it is to mix oil (a lipid) and water. The phosphate portion is hydrophilic or water-loving and composes the surfaces of the membrane. Cellulose is only found in plant cells, which have a cell wall instead of a cell membrane.

43. C: During a lunar eclipse, the Sun and Moon are on opposite sides of the Earth. They line up so that the Sun's light that normally illuminates the Moon is blocked by the Earth. This causes the Moon to become dim. Sunlight can still be seen, Choice A, and the Earth does not become dark, Choices B and D.

44. C: Draw the square by placing the parents' alleles first and then match them up accordingly in the gray boxes.

	Father G	Father g
Mother G	GG	Gg
Mother g	Gg	gg

45. C: Kingdom Protista contains all the single-celled eukaryotic organisms. Kingdom Monera and Domain Archaea contain prokaryotes. Choice D is just a level of the classification system.

46. D: An atom is structured with a nucleus in the center that contains neutral neutrons and positive protons. Surrounding the nucleus are orbiting electrons that are negatively charged. Choice D is the only correct answer.

47. C: The nucleus houses and regulates the genetic material within eukaryotic cells; it does not produce ATP. ATP is produced through oxidative phosphorylation in the mitochondria of eukaryotic cells. Chloroplasts are organelles

Answer Explanations #1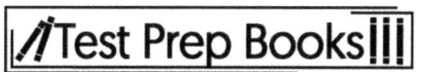

within plant cells that produce ATP. Cytosol is where glycolysis occurs, which is the breakdown of glucose to produce ATP and NADH.

48. B: The Moon does not produce harmful light rays that can damage the eyes, so lunar eclipses can be viewed directly. A telescope would allow the lunar eclipse to be magnified and seen more clearly. During a solar eclipse, the Sun's rays appear to be dim and easy to see directly, but they are still harmful to the eyes.

49. C: The integumentary system makes up the skin, which acts as a physical barrier against pathogens, infections, injuries, and sunlight. The muscular system is composed of the skeletal muscles of the body that facilitate movement. The endocrine system is composed of glands that produce hormones to regulate bodily functions. The lymphatic system is a network of vessels that helps maintain the balance of fluids within the body.

50. B: In the anaphase step of mitosis, sister chromatids are pulled apart toward opposite ends of a cell. In prophase, chromatin condenses to form chromosomes, spindles form on opposite ends of a cell, and the nuclear envelope breaks apart. In metaphase, the nuclear envelope completely disappears, and the chromosomes align at the center of a cell at a location known as the metaphase plate. In telophase, the separated chromosomes are enclosed to form two daughter cells.

51. B: Solar eclipses are viewed during the daytime because they involve viewing the Sun while it is out during normal daytime hours. Lunar eclipses, Choices *C* and *D*, are viewed at nighttime when the Moon is in the sky during its normal hours. The Moon is normally illuminated by the Sun that is on the other side of the Earth. When the Sun is on the other side of the Earth, it is nighttime for people looking at the Moon.

52. B: Models are representations of concepts that are impossible to experience directly, such as the 3D representation of DNA, so Choice *B* is correct. Choice *A* is incorrect because theories simply explain why things happen. Choice *C* is incorrect because laws describe how things happen. Choice *D* is false because an observation analyzes situations using human senses.

53. C: A diploid cell has two sets of chromosomes (one set inherited from each parent). Cells with more than one nucleus are referred to as multinucleated cells. A phospholipid bilayer (or cell membrane) is present in all types of cells. Prokaryotic cells are the only cells without a nucleus.

54. D: Volcanic activity can occur both at fault lines and within the area of a tectonic plate at points called hot spots. Volcanic activity is more common at fault lines because of cracks that allow the mantle's magma to more easily escape to the surface.

55. D: Ribosomes are small, round organelles found floating in the cell's cytoplasm but are primarily attached to the endoplasmic reticulum. Ribosomes are the sites where protein synthesis will occur, and they also contain ribonucleic acid (RNA). Choice *A* is incorrect since the nucleolus is the site where ribosomes are produced. Choice *B* is incorrect since mitochondria are the organelles where aerobic respiration occurs to produce adenosine triphosphate (ATP). Choice *C* is incorrect since the cytosol is the liquid matrix that suspends the organelles within the cell.

56. C: Jupiter is the largest planet in the solar system, and it is primarily composed of hydrogen and helium. Ammonia is in much lower quantity and usually found as a cloud within Jupiter's atmosphere.

57. A: Alveoli are sacs of lung tissue that specialize in transferring oxygen and carbon dioxide between blood and air inhaled into the lungs. Capillaries are the smallest blood vessels that facilitate the transfer of gases and nutrients between blood and tissues. The aorta is the largest artery that delivers blood from the heart to the rest of the body. Axons are nerve fibers that deliver action potentials away from the cell body of a nerve cell.

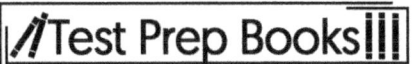

Answer Explanations #1

58. A: A control is the component or group in an experimental design that isn't manipulated—it's the standard against which the resultant findings are compared, so Choice A is correct. A variable is an element of the experiment that is able to be manipulated, making Choice B false. A constant is a condition of the experiment outside of the hypothesis that remains unchanged in order to isolate the changes in the variables; therefore, Choice C is incorrect. Choice D is false because collected data are simply recordings of the observed phenomena that result from the experiment.

59. C: A hypothesis is a statement that makes a prediction between two variables. The two variables here are the amount of poison and how quickly the rat dies. Choice C states that the more poison a rat is given, the more quickly it will die, which is a prediction. Choice A is incorrect because it's simply an observation. Choice B is incorrect because it's a question posed by the observation but makes no predictions. Choice D is incorrect because it's simply a fact.

60. B: The independent variable is the variable manipulated, and the dependent variable is the result of the changes in the independent variable. Choice B is correct because the amount of poison is the variable that is changed, and the speed of rat death is the result of the changes in the amount of poison administered. Choice A is incorrect because that answer states the opposite. Choice C is false because the scientist isn't attempting to determine whether the rat will die *if* it eats poison; the scientist is testing how quickly the rat will die depending on *how much* poison it eats. Choice D is incorrect because the cage isn't manipulated in any way and has nothing to do with the hypothesis.

Social Studies

1. B: Reconstruction was the Postbellum Era in which the United States tried to reinstate former Confederate states into the Union and rebuild the South through occupation. The Antebellum Era, Choice A, was the time frame that preceded the Civil War. The Progressive Era, Choice C, was the era of widespread reform in the late nineteenth and early twentieth century that set the stage for Prohibition. The civil rights movement, Choice D, is the era of U.S. history that witnessed desegregation, reaching its culmination in the mid-1960s under the presidency of Lyndon B. Johnson.

2. D: Federalism is the term that refers to the division of power between the federal and state governments. Republicanism, Choice A, is the concept of the election of the representatives by the citizens to carry out the citizens' will in governing the country. Choice B is the protection of individual rights enshrined in the Constitution. These include rights such as the freedom of speech and the freedom of religion. The separation of powers, Choice C, refers to the creation of the three branches of government.

3. B: Macroeconomics studies the economy on a large scale and focuses on issues such as unemployment, interest rates, price levels, and national income. Microeconomics, Choice A, studies more individual or small group behaviors such as scarcity or supply and demand. Scarcity, Choice C, is not correct because it refers to the availability of goods and services. Supply and demand, Choice D, is also incorrect because it refers to the quantity of goods and services that is produced and/or needed.

4. C: Alexandria became the capital. Jerusalem, Choice A, although the epicenter of Judaism and Christianity, did not host as many scholars as Alexandria during the Hellenistic period. Constantinople, Choice D, is incorrect because it was not yet created during the Hellenistic period. And Athens, Choice B, the former capital of Greek scholarship, is not the answer because scholarly culture shifted from Athens to Alexandria during this period.

5. C: Opportunity cost refers to the value of what is lost when one alternative is chosen over another. Economic systems refer to methods of organizing the production and distribution of goods in society. Supply and demand is an economic model for how prices are determined. Finally, inflation, Choice D, refers to how the cost of goods and services increases over time.

Answer Explanations #1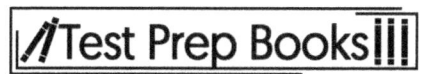

6. B: Cities and localities are led by the local mayor, who is an elected official selected by the people. Choices *A*, *C*, and *D* do not match the description provided.

7. D: Following his election during the Great Depression, Franklin Delano Roosevelt pledged a *New Deal* for the American people, inaugurating an era of social welfare and public works programs. The Great Society, Choice *A*, also set forth social welfare and public works programs, but under the presidency of Lyndon B. Johnson (LBJ). The War Against Poverty, Choice *B*, was a subcategory of LBJ's Great Society—it promised to declare war on poverty like any nation would declare war on a foreign threat. Progressivism, Choice *C*, brought about reforms much like the New Deal, but during the early twentieth century, prior to the Great Depression and FDR's administration.

8. A: A free market does not involve government interventions or monopolies while trading between buyers and suppliers. However, in a command market, the government determines the price of goods and services. Gross and exchange markets refer to situations where brokers and traders make exchanges in the financial realm.

9. A: Renaissance scholars and artists sought to emulate classical Greek and Roman culture. They translated Greek and Roman political philosophers and literature. They also copied classical architecture. Europeans had little direct contact with China until the 13th century, which was long after the Zhou Dynasty collapsed, making Choice *C* incorrect. The Renaissance Era occurred within the continent of Europe and drew from other European styles, so nations of northern Africa and the Middle East, such as ancient Egypt and the Ottoman Empire, had little to no inspiration on Renaissance scholars and artists at that time. Therefore, Choices *B* and *D* are incorrect.

10. C: The United States is largely considered to be a representative democracy. The people elect representatives who are then tasked with passing laws and governing according to the will of the people who elected them. A democracy, Choice *A*, is truly government for and by the people, with frequent elections and direct and indirect involvement in governing by the people. A direct democracy, Choice *B*, is one in which the people vote on all of the laws directly and select all of their leaders. Choice *D*, socialist democracy, is a theory of government that combines free and fair elections and representative government with some form of publicly owned programs and social safety nets, such as free public education and welfare programs.

11. A: Most scholars already knew the world was round by 1492. On the other hand, the arrival of Europeans in North and South America introduced deadly diseases that killed millions of native peoples. Europeans had developed immunity to diseases such as smallpox, while Native Americans had not. In addition, Europeans introduced a number of new plants and animals to the New World, but they also adopted many new foods as well, including potatoes, tomatoes, chocolate, and tobacco. Finally, Europeans tried to convert Native Americans to Christianity, but Native Americans did not completely give up their traditional beliefs. Instead, they blended Christianity with indigenous and African beliefs to create new syncretic religions.

12. D: Thematic maps create certain themes in which they attempt to illustrate a certain phenomenon or pattern. The obvious theme of a climate map is the climates in the represented areas. Thematic maps are very extensive and can include thousands of different themes, which makes them quite useful for students of geography. Topographic maps, Choice *A*, are utilized to show physical features; conformal projections, Choice *B*, attempt to illustrate the globe in an undistorted fashion; and isoline maps, Choice *C*, illustrate differences in variables between two points on a map.

13. C: Power is the ability of a ruling body or political entity to influence the actions, behavior, and attitude of a person or group of people. Authority, Choice *A*, is the right and justification of the government to exercise power as recognized by the citizens or influential elites. Similarly, legitimacy, Choice *D*, is another way of expressing the concept of authority. Sovereignty, Choice *B*, refers to the ability of a state to determine and control their territory without foreign interference.

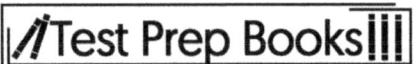

14. A: Devastated by World War II, Britain and France were unable to maintain their empires. Japan and Germany were also weak, which left only the United States and USSR as superpowers. The Russian Revolution had occurred during World War I, in 1917, making Choice *B* incorrect. Ideological and economic conflict between the US and the USSR led to the start of the Cold War shortly after World War II ended, making Choice *C* incorrect. Choice *D* is also incorrect; the death of Franz Ferdinand marked the beginning of World War I.

15. D: Behaviors of firms is not an indicator of economic growth because it refers to the behavior that firms follow to reach their desired outcome. GDP, unemployment, and inflation are all indicators that help determine economic growth.

16. B: Latitudinal and longitudinal coordinates delineate absolute location. In contrast to relative location (Choice *C*), which describes a location as compared to another, better-known place, absolute location provides an exact place on the globe through the latitude and longitude system. Cardinal directions (north, south, east, west), Choice *A*, are used in absolute location, but coordinates must be added in order to have an absolute location. Absolute location is far more precise than simply finding the hemispherical position on the globe (Choice *D*).

17. A: Nationalism remains a powerful force to this day. Nationalism drove conflict in Ireland, Spain, Yugoslavia, and elsewhere. However, the end of the Cold War removed many of the political barriers that had prevented interaction between the western and Communist blocs. In addition, religious fundamentalism became an increasingly common response to the rapid changes that occurred during the late twentieth and early twenty-first centuries. There was also a rise in cultural and economic globalization, as well as in environmentalism.

18. D: Sovereignty is the feature that differentiates a state from a nation. Nations have no sovereignty, as they are unable to enact and enforce laws independently of their state. A state must possess sovereignty over the population of a territory in order to be legitimized as a state. Both a nation and a state must have a population, Choice *C*. Although sometimes present, a shared history and common language are not requirements for a state, making Choices *A* and *B* incorrect.

19. D: In his book, *The Prince*, Niccolo Machiavelli advocated that a ruler should be prepared to do whatever is necessary to remain in power, including using violence and political deception as a means to coerce the people of a state or eliminate political rivals. John Locke, Choice *A*, contributed and advocated liberal principles, most prominently the right to life, liberty, and health. Jean-Jacques Rousseau, Choice *B*, heavily influenced the French Revolution and American Revolution by advocating individual equality, self-rule, and religious freedom. Karl Marx, Choice *C*, wrote that the struggle between the bourgeois (ruling class) and the proletariat (working class) would result in a classless society in which all citizens commonly owned the means of production.

20. A: Carolina is divided into two separate states—North and South. Maine was part of Nova Scotia and did not become an American territory until the War of 1812. Likewise, Vermont was not one of the original Thirteen Colonies. Canada remained a separate British colony. Finally, Florida was a Spanish territory. Therefore, by process of elimination, *A* is the correct list.

21. C: Federal Reserve. The Federal Reserve is the bank of banks. It is the central bank of the United States and controls the value of money. A commodity is the value of goods such as precious metals. While the Central Reserve and Bank Reserve may sound like good options, the term *bank reserve* refers to the amount of money a bank deposits into a central bank, and the Central Reserve is simply a fictitious name.

22. B: Britain was not defeated in the French and Indian War, and, in fact, disputes with the colonies over the new territories it won contributed to the growing tensions. All other options were key motivations behind the Revolutionary War.

23. B: Thomas Hobbes is considered the father of social contract theory. In his book *Leviathan*, Hobbes advocated for a strong central government and posited that the citizens of a state make a social contract with the government

Answer Explanations #1

to allow it to rule them in exchange for protection and security. John Stuart Mills, Choice A, is most commonly associated with the political philosophy of utilitarianism. Aristotle, Choice C, believed that man could only achieve happiness by bettering their community through noble acts, while Immanuel Kant, Choice D, promoted democracy and asserted that states could only achieve lasting global peace through international cooperation.

24. A: Closed market operations. Monetary policies are sustained by assuring bank reserves, adjusting interest rates, and open market operations. Closed market operations do NOT uphold monetary policies.

25. C: Abraham Lincoln was elected president as part of the new Republican Party, and his plans to limit and potentially abolish slavery led the southern states to secede from the Union.

26. C: Conservatism emphasizes maintaining traditions and believes political and social stability is more important than progress and reform. In general, Socialism, Choice A, seeks to establish a democratically elected government that owns the means of production, regulates the exchange of commodities, and distributes the wealth equally among citizens. Liberalism, Choice B, is based on individualism and equality, supporting the freedoms of speech, press, and religion, while Libertarian ideals, Choice D, emphasize individual liberties and freedom from government interference.

27. D: World War I led to the League of Nations, Choice A. There was also a major influenza outbreak after World War I, Choice B. The USSR and US both emerged as two rival superpowers after World War II. It was thus a bipolar, rather than unipolar, world. The tension and mistrust between the US and USSR eventually led to the Cold War, which ended in 1991.

28. A: The New Deal introduced a number of programs designed to increase regulation and boost the economy. Many of them remain in effect today, such as the Social Security Administration and the Securities and Exchange Commission. The New Deal also led to the Republican and Democratic parties to reverse their ideological positions on government intervention. It did not lead to a third party, Choice B. President Franklin D. Roosevelt was actually elected to four terms in office, and the official two-term limit was not established until the 22nd Amendment was ratified in 1951. Until then, the two-term limit had been an informal custom established by President George Washington when he left office in 1797. Thus, Choice C is incorrect. Choice D is also incorrect. The Great Depression led to the New Deal, not the other way around.

29. B: Lines of latitude measure distance north and south. The equator is zero degrees, and the Tropic of Cancer is 23.5 degrees north of the equator. The distance between those two lines measures degrees north to south, as with any other two lines of latitude. Longitudinal lines, or meridians, measure distance east and west, even though they run north and south down the globe. Latitude is not inexact, in that there are set distances between the lines. Furthermore, coordinates can only exist with the use of longitude and latitude.

30. D: Internationalism promotes global cooperation and supports strong unity between the states in order to achieve world peace and improve quality of life for all global citizens. Fascism, Choice A, values the strength of a state over all foreign powers and emphasizes the state over individual liberties, and Fascists typically establish an authoritarian government and consider violence necessary to suppress dissent and revitalize a struggling nation. Conservatism, Choice B, is focused on maintaining the traditions and political institutions within a single country. Anarchism, Choice C, favors a completely free society ruled by a government composed of only voluntary institutions.

31. D: Fascism considers a strong central government, martial law, and violent coercion as necessary means to maintain political stability and strengthen the state. Neither the politics of Communism, a society in which the people own the means of production, nor Socialism, a society in which the government owns the means of production, promote violence but instead advocate a classless society that eliminates the class struggle. Thus, Choices A and B are incorrect. Nationalism, Choice C, emphasizes preserving a nation's culture, often to the

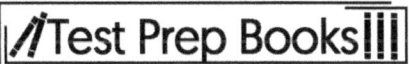

exclusion of other cultures, but violence is not officially promoted as a means for suppressing dissent, as is the case with Fascism.

32. D: Mark Twain called the late 1800s the Gilded Age because the appearance of extreme wealth covered up massive social inequality. While many wealthy industrialists became very rich, many workers worked in poor conditions for low wages. The onset of the Second Industrial Revolution led to an expansion of the chemical, telecommunications, and metallurgical industries. Urbanization also increased during this period as workers crowded into cities in search of work.

33. D: The market, through supply and demand, determines the exchange rate with a flexible or floating exchange rate. The government, Choice A, is not the correct answer because it is involved in fixed exchange rates to help keep exchange rates stable. Taxes, Choice B, is also incorrect because they create government revenue. The Federal Reserve, Choice C, is the bank of banks.

34. C: Under the Constitution, the power to coin money is designated exclusively to the federal government, but both the states and the federal government maintain the power to collect taxes from the citizens under their jurisdictions and establish courts lower than the Supreme Court, though states may only establish regional courts within their states. The states reserve the right to regulate trade within their states (intrastate), while the federal government maintains the power to regulate trade between states (interstate).

35. B: As inflation increases, purchasing power decreases. As more money is printed, the monetary value of the dollar drops and, in turn, decreases the purchasing power of goods and services. So, as inflation increases, consumers are not spending as much, and the value of the dollar is low.

36. A: King Ferdinand and Queen Isabella agreed to support Columbus' mission because he promised to establish a direct trade route to Asia that would allow European merchants to bypass Middle Eastern middlemen. Columbus had no idea that America existed, Choice B, and he believed he had landed in India when he arrived in the Caribbean. That's why he mistakenly called the natives *Indians*. It is a common myth that Columbus sought to prove experts wrong by showing them the world was round, not flat. Most European thinkers already knew the world was round, making Choice C incorrect. Choice D is also incorrect; Christopher Columbus practiced the Christian faith, not Judaism.

37. B: The number of goods and services produced does not determine economic growth—the value of the goods and services does. For example, a real estate agent who sells 10 houses valued at $200,000 each would earn the same commission as an agent who sells one house valued at $2,000,000. Even though one sold more homes, the value of ten houses adds up to the same amount as the single home that the other realtor sold.

38. D: Both the states and the federal government may propose, enact, and enforce laws. States pass legislation that concerns the states in their state legislative houses, while the federal government passes federal laws in Congress. Only states may hold elections and determine voting procedures, even for federal offices such as the president of the United States, and only the federal government may expand any state territory, change state lines, admit new states into the nation, or regulate immigration and pass laws regarding naturalization of citizens.

39. A: Homogeneity, or the condition of similarity, is the unifying factor in most formal regions. Regions have one or more unifying characteristics, such as language, religion, history, or economic similarities, which make the area a cohesive formal region. A good example is the Southern United States. In contrast, diversity and multilingualism, Choices B and C, are factors that may cause a region to lose homogeneity and be more difficult to classify as a region. Also, social mobility, Choice D, is a distractor that refers to one's ability to improve their economic standing in society and is not related to formal regions.

40. D: The Constitution granted Congress the power to decide how many justices should be on the court, and Congress first decided on six judges in the Judiciary Act of 1789. The Constitution granted the power to appoint

Answer Explanations #1

judges and to call special sessions of Congress to the president. Only the Supreme Court may interpret the laws enacted by Congress and rule a law unconstitutional and subsequently overturn the law.

41. C: The Declaration of Independence occurred during the American Revolution, so it should therefore be considered an effect, not a cause. Similarly, slavery was a cause for the later Civil War, but it was not a primary instigator for the Revolutionary War. Although a single event can have many effects long into the future, it is also important to not overstate the influence of these individual causes; the civil rights movement was only tangentially connected to the War of Independence among many other factors, and therefore it should not be considered a primary effect of it. The French and Indian War (which was part of the Seven Years' War) and the Bill of Rights, on the other hand, were respectively a cause and effect from the American Revolution, making Choice C the correct answer.

42. B: The process by which the House and Senate may debate a bill differs. In the House, how long a speaker may debate a bill is limited, while in the Senate, speakers may debate the bill indefinitely and delay voting on the bill by filibuster—a practice in which a speaker refuses to stop speaking until a majority vote stops the filibuster or the time for the vote passes. In both the House and the Senate, anyone may introduce a bill. Only the president of the United States may veto the bill, so neither the House nor Senate holds that power. Before the bill may be presented to the president to be signed, the wording of the bill must be identical in both houses. Another procedural difference is that the number of amendments is limited in the House but not the Senate; however, this does not appear as an answer choice.

43. D: The Constitution was signed in 1787; the Declaration of Independence was signed in 1776. It was successfully ratified by all the current states, including New York. Finally, the Articles of Confederation were established at the end of the American Revolution; the Constitution would replace the articles years later due to issues with the government's structure.

44. B: Fiat money. Commodity money, Choice A, refers to a good that has value, such as a precious metal. Bank money, Choice C, is money that is credited by a bank to those people who have their money deposited there. The term reserve money, Choice D, does not refer to anything.

45. C: The first ten amendments to the Constitution are collectively referred to as the Bill of Rights. The Founding Fathers did not support universal suffrage, and as such, the Bill of Rights did not encompass the freedom to vote. The Fifteenth Amendment provided that the right to vote shall not be denied on the basis of race, color, or previous condition of servitude, and women did not receive the right to vote until passage of the Nineteenth Amendment. The other three answer choices are included in the Bill of Rights: the freedom to assembly is established in the First Amendment, the freedom against unlawful search is established in the Fourth Amendment, and the reservation of non-enumerated powers to the states or the people is established in the Tenth Amendment.

46. A: The Silk Roads were a network of trade routes between Asia and the Mediterranean. Merchants and Pilgrims traveled along the Silk Roads and brought new ideas and technologies, as well as trade goods. For example, Buddhism spread from India to China. Chinese technologies also spread westward, including gunpowder and the printing press. The Silk Roads also spread the Bubonic Plague to Europe, but it did not arrive in the New World until Columbus landed there in 1492.

47. C: The Republican Party emerged as the abolitionist party during the Antebellum Period and succeeded in abolishing slavery after the North's victory in the Civil War. The Constitutional Union Party supported slavery but opposed Southern secession, while the Southern Democrats supported slavery and secession. The Whig Party splintered in the 1850s as a result of tension over slavery, leading to the creation of the Republican Party and Constitutional Union Party.

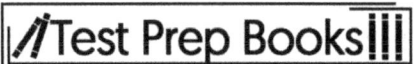

48. C: Each statement about culture is correct except for Choice *C*. Cultures often will adapt to the settings in which they are found. Improvements in technology, changes in social values, and interactions with other cultures all contribute to cultural change.

49. C: While interest groups attempt to influence the legislation and organizations that regulate trade, they do not possess the authority to enact or enforce laws necessary to regulate trade. However, they may influence policy through the use of petitions, civil suits against the government, and by the practice of lobbying, in which paid lobbyists put pressure on lawmaking bodies. Interest groups form due to a common connection between the members of a group attempting to bring about change that benefits a specific segment of society, such as teachers or pharmaceutical corporations.

50. A: Large numbers of Franks, Goths, Vandals, and other Germanic peoples began moving south in the 5th century AD. They conquered Rome twice, and the Western Roman Empire finally disintegrated. The Mongol invasion, Choice *B*, pushed westward in the 13th century, long after the western Roman Empire was gone. The assassination of Julius Caesar, Choice *C*, led to the end of the Roman Republic and the birth of the Roman Empire. Taoism never spread to Rome, making Choice *D* incorrect.

51. B: The mass media does not have the ability to regulate communications. The mass media has the ability to shape public opinion, making Choice *A* incorrect. Mass media selects which events to report on and thereby influences the perceived importance of events in society and determines the context in which to report events, making Choices *C* and *D* incorrect. Only the federal government may regulate communications through agencies such as the Federal Communications Commission (FCC).

52. C: Federalism divides power between regional and federal governments, and it is the form of government upon which the United States is structured, according to the Tenth Amendment. While a constitutional monarchy, Choice *B*, is typically divided between a monarch, the head of state, and a legislative body, usually a parliament, power is not reserved to the regional government. A democratic government, Choice *A*, is a government ruled by the people and does not specify division of powers. Feudalism, Choice *D*, is an economic system popular in medieval Europe where the monarchy granted the nobility land in exchange for military service, and the nobility allowed serfs to live on their land in exchange for labor or percentage of crops.

53. A: The Mongols were a nomadic people who trained as horsemen from a young age. They used their highly mobile army to build a huge empire in Asia, the Middle East, and Eastern Europe. Mongol rulers were relatively tolerant of other religions because they wanted to reduce conflict within their empire, making Choice *B* incorrect. They also encouraged trade because they produced few of their own goods, making Choice *C* incorrect. The Mongol rulers also encouraged literacy and appreciated visual art, making Choice *D* incorrect.

54. A: In contractionary monetary policy, the money supply is decreased. All of the other choices are characteristics of contractionary monetary policy.

55. A: An authoritarian government is ruled by a single party that holds complete control over the powerful central government. Authoritarian governments limit political freedom and civil liberties to diminish any opposition. Communism, Choice *B*, is one in which the class struggle between the ruling and working classes is eliminated because the means of production belongs to the people. Similarly, Socialism, Choice *C*, is classless, but in this type of government, the government owns the means of production and is often democratic. Unlike a regular monarchy, a federal monarchy, Choice *D*, is a federal government in which political power is divided between the monarch (head of state) and regional governments, resulting in checks and balances of power.

56. B: The rise of the Catholic Church, Choice *B*, was not a change in the societal structure because it was already established. As the medieval period ended in Europe and the Renaissance began, deep and systemic changes happened in Europe. The plague wiped out nearly half of the European population, Choice *A*, changing work and

Answer Explanations #1

home life. Fighting occurred amongst Protestants and Catholics in many European countries, Choice *C*. Due to these religious differences, war ravaged the area, Choice *D*.

57. C: Historians make use of maps in their studies to get a clear picture of how history unfolded, knowing the borders of different lands helps historians learn different cultures' interactions, and environmental factors, such as access to water and the proximity of mountains, help determine the course of civilization. The phrase "Geography is closely linked with the flow of resources, technology, and population in societies" is a characteristic of economics.

58. D: The GDP is used to measure an economy's growth. The inflation of a country doesn't tell us anything about their growth. A country may hold a lot of money in reserves, but this does not tell us if they are growing or not. The same can be said for having a lot of exports. It doesn't indicate that an economy is necessarily growing.

59. B: Out of the four inventions mentioned, the first telegraphs were invented in the 1830s, not in the twentieth century. In contrast, the other inventions had considerable influence over the course of the twentieth century.

60. D: Proportional electoral systems reflect the divisions in an electorate proportionately in the elected body. In single transferable vote systems, voters rank individual candidates by their preference, and the top candidates' votes are transferred to the second-place candidate, and so on, once a candidate receives the minimum votes to win a seat in the election; thus, the single transferable vote system is the most proportionate electoral system. The Electoral College is the method of electing the President of the United States Although the Electoral College apportions a number of electors to each state according to the number of congressional seats in the state, it is not a proportional electoral system. To win a majority vote, a candidate must receive over 50% of the vote, so the minority's preferences are not proportionally reflected in the body. Similarly, a plurality only requires the highest percent of votes among any number of candidates, which often results in most voters voting *against* the winning candidate.

HiSET Practice Tests #2, #3, and #4

To keep the size of this book manageable, save paper, and provide a digital test-taking experience, the 2nd, 3rd, and 4th practice tests can be found online. Scan the QR code or go to this link to access it:

testprepbooks.com/online387/hiset

The first time you access the tests, you will need to register as a "new user" and verify your email address.

If you have any issues, please email support@testprepbooks.com.

Index

Absolute Error, 70
Absolute Monarchy, 220
Acceleration, 152, 153, 155, 156, 157, 158
Accuracy, 69
Activation Energy, 165
Acute Angle, 85
Acute Triangle, 77
Addition, 196
Addition Rule, 94
Adjacent Angles, 85
Algebraic Expressions, 98, 101
Alliteration, 303
Allusion, 21, 255
Alternate Exterior Angles, 86
Alternate Interior Angles, 85
American Psychological Association Style (APA), 58
American Revolution, 196, 198
Angle, 73, 74, 76, 77, 78, 80, 82, 85
Angle-Angle-Angle (AAA), 74
Angle-Angle-Side (AAS), 74
Angular Momentum, 158
Antecedent, 48
Antoine Lavoisier, 164
AP Stylebook, 58, 59
Area, 58, 67, 68, 79, 80, 82, 83, 84, 117, 156, 199, 215, 244, 276, 280, 282, 316, 319, 321, 322
Area of a Square, 79
Area of a Trapezoid, 79
Area of a Triangle, 79
Aristocracy, 219
Associative Property, 64
Assumption, 16, 25
Asymptote, 101, 115, 116
Atmosphere, 26, 45, 159, 175, 176
Authoritarian State, 219
Auxiliary (Helping) Verbs, 47
Bar Graph, 19, 20, 89
Bathymetry, 240
Bicameral, 210, 214
Biochemical Rocks, 167
Boston Massacre, 198
Boston Tea Party, 198
Box Plot, 86, 88
Bryan Garner, 59
Buffer, 166
Business Cycle, 223, 224
Cartesian Plane, 89

Catalysts, 165
Caucuses, 216
Causal, 197
Causally Related, 197
Cause, 14, 39, 88, 160, 161, 203, 221, 224, 255
Cause and Effect Order, 25, 273
Cause and Effect Structure, 39
Cell, 38, 66, 165, 273, 274
   Cells, 160
Center of Dilation, 73
Chance, 95
Chart, 89
Chemical Reactions, 164
Chemical Rocks, 167
Chicago Manual of Style, 58, 59
Choices, 14, 16, 303, 304, 306, 307, 308, 309, 311, 312, 313
Chronological Order, 25
Chronology, 198
Circle, 80, 81, 83, 84, 85, 91, 277, 280, 282, 318, 319, 321, 322
Circle Graph, 91
Claim, 251, 253, 269, 271, 306
Clastic, 167
Clauses, 39, 41, 42, 43, 52, 54, 308, 309, 311, 312, 313, 314
Climate, 208
Climate Change, 208
Closed Form, 25
Clouds, 20, 175
Coefficient, 98, 102, 106, 107, 111, 115, 118, 164, 319
Coenzymes, 165
Cofactors, 165
Colloquial Language, 26
Colon, 54, 310, 311, 312
   Colons, 54
Commutative Property, 64
Compare and Contrast Order, 25, 273
Comparison-Contrast Paragraph Structure, 39
Complex Numbers, 63, 64
Complex Sentence, 39, 43, 313
Composite Number, 64
Compound, 43, 47, 93, 94, 164, 313
Compound Event, 93, 94
Compound Sentences, 43
Compound-Complex Sentence, 43
Conclusion, 13, 25, 29, 32, 257, 273, 306

Conclusions, 194, 198
Conduction, 159
Congruent, 73, 74
Conjugate, 64
Conjunction, 41, 52, 309, 313
   Conjunctions, 41
Connotation, 14, 15, 21, 46, 255, 307
Consecutive Interior Angles, 86
Constitutional Convention, 204
Constitutional Monarchy, 220
Consumer Price Index (CPI), 223
Context, 13, 14, 29, 37, 40, 58, 120, 194, 208, 255, 303, 304, 306, 308, 309, 310, 311
Continental, 202
Convection Current, 159
Conversion Factor, 68, 70
Coordinating Conjunction, 41, 43
Coordinating Conjunctions, 41
Coplanar, 85
Correlated, 197
Corresponding Angles, 85
Crescent, 199
Crowned Republic, 220
Dashes, 54
Declaration of Independence, 196
Deductive Reasoning, 17
Degrees, 72, 73, 74, 80, 85, 93, 159, 240
Delegates, 204, 210, 216
Demand, 221
Democracy, 199, 204, 207, 208, 215, 219
Denotation, 14, 15, 46, 307
Density, 84, 152, 244
Dependent, 18, 19, 42, 43, 54, 91, 92, 93, 94, 95, 110, 215, 220, 308, 312, 313, 314
Descriptive Writing, 39
Desert
   Deserts, 175
Detrital Rocks, 167
Diction, 14, 15, 25, 26, 30
Dictionary, 14, 46, 57, 58, 70, 253, 272, 306, 314
Difference of Squares, 98
Dilation, 73
Dimensional Analysis, 67
Direct Democracy, 219
Direct Primaries, 208
Discriminant, 108
Displacement, 152
Distributive Property, 64
Domain, 113, 114, 120, 121, 122, 123, 278, 319
Drag, 156, 157

Economic System, 218
Economics, 220, 227
Economy, 26, 200, 205, 218, 221, 222, 223, 224, 225
Ecosystem
   Ecosystems, 160, 207
Effect, 196, 197, 198
Effects, 201, 214, 267, 268
Electoral College System, 215
Electoral Process, 216
Electors, 215, 217
Electric Energy, 160
Electrical Current, 160
Electrostatics, 160
Ellipsis, 54, 65, 312
Endpoints, 84
Energy, 152, 159, 160, 161, 165, 194, 207
Enzymes, 165
Equiangular Polygons, 76
Equilateral Triangle, 77, 319
Ethnic Group, 201
Evidence, 13, 17, 29, 31, 37, 38, 45, 194, 249, 274, 305
Exclamation Point, 53, 312
Executive Branch, 204, 207, 209, 210, 212, 220
Exponents, 65, 100
Extreme Values, 113
Fact, 14, 21, 25, 32, 49, 59, 97, 152, 194, 196, 199, 239, 252, 257, 258, 263, 266, 274, 305, 306, 308, 332
Factor, 64, 68, 71, 73, 99, 100, 101, 117, 222, 272, 317, 321
Factors, 196, 198
Families, 43, 47, 202, 203, 263, 273
Federal Courts, 211, 212
Federalism, 219, 220
Figurative, 20, 21, 25, 44
Figurative Language, 20, 21
Figure of Speech, 44, 46, 47
   Figures of Speech, 44, 46
First-Person Narrator, 306
Flexible, 25
Foliated Rocks, 167
Force, 46, 152, 153, 154, 155, 156, 157, 161, 200, 203, 205, 206, 255, 256, 257, 307, 308
Formulas, 69, 82, 105, 119
Fossil, 159, 167
Fractional Exponents, 65
French and Indian War, 198
Full Rotation, 85

Index

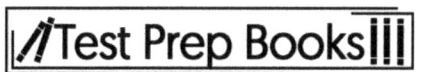

Function, 25, 47, 51, 101, 102, 103, 105, 113, 114, 115, 116, 117, 118, 120, 121, 122, 124, 208, 209, 215, 259, 261, 275, 278, 279, 280, 281, 309, 315, 317, 320, 321
General Election, 217
General Order, 25
Generalization, 194
Generalizations, 29, 30, 202
Geology, 167
Glossaries, 58
Government, 207, 209, 214, 215, 218, 225
Graphs, 19, 120
Gravity, 155, 156, 157, 158, 175
Gross Domestic Product (GDP), 221, 222, 223, 224
Groups, 18, 19, 54, 59, 63, 64, 69, 165, 202, 204, 205, 207, 216, 222
Growth, 196
Heart, 263, 265, 310
Heat, 159
Hemispheres, 240
Heterogeneous, 165
Histogram, 86
Historical Narrative, 196
History, 21, 22, 33, 58, 202, 204, 207, 208, 209, 249, 251, 302, 304, 314, 337
Homogeneous, 165
House of Representatives, 210, 211, 214, 218
Hypabyssal Rocks, 167
Hyperbole, 21, 47
Hypotenuse, 74, 81, 82, 283, 323
Hypotenuse-Leg (HL), 74
Idiom, 44
Igneous Rocks, 167
Imagery, 26
Immigration, 197
Indefinite Pronouns, 48
Independent Clause, 41, 42, 43, 52, 54, 308, 309, 310, 311, 312, 313
Induction, 160
Inductive Reasoning, 17
Inferences, 13, 16, 17, 29
Inflation, 223, 224
Inflection, 54
Inspiration, 200
International Date Line, 240
International System of Units (SI), 152
Interquartile Range (IQR), 88
Intersecting Lines, 85
Intrusive, 167
Inverse, 65, 67, 107, 112, 113, 115, 121, 122, 123

Irony, 16, 31, 47
Irrational Numbers, 64, 65, 274, 314
Isaac Newton, 153
Isosceles Triangle, 74, 77
Joules, 159
Judicial Branch, 211, 212
Kidneys, 48
Kingdom, 220
Latitude, 240
Least Common Denominator (LCD), 100
Legislative Branch, 210, 214, 217, 220
Like Terms, 98, 317
Line, 19, 20, 25, 30, 45, 63, 65, 71, 73, 74, 80, 82, 84, 85, 86, 89, 91, 92, 93, 103, 104, 105, 110, 111, 115, 118, 122, 124, 125, 154, 156, 157, 158, 161, 205, 221, 240, 246, 247, 282, 284, 285
Line Graph, 19, 20, 91, 92
Line Plot, 89
Line Segment, 73, 74, 80, 84
Linear, 26, 92, 98, 104, 109, 110, 111, 112, 115, 116, 120, 123, 124, 158
Literally, 44
Logarithmic Function, 115
Longitude, 240
Macroeconomics, 221, 222
Magma, 167
Magnetic Energy, 161
Magnetic Forces, 160, 161
Magnitude, 67, 152, 154
Main Idea, 13, 22, 37, 38, 40, 198, 304, 305, 314
Mass, 66, 70, 84, 152, 153, 154, 155, 156, 158, 175, 176, 204, 206, 207
Maximum Value, 102, 113
Mean, 14, 30, 44, 51, 57, 64, 70, 74, 87, 88, 89, 96, 97, 247, 250, 253, 255, 318
Median, 87, 88, 96, 97, 280, 283, 321
Meridians, 240
Metamorphic Rocks, 167
Metamorphism, 167
Metaphor, 20, 246, 303
Method of Least Squares, 93
Metonymy, 47
Mexican-American War, 194
Microeconomics, 220, 221
Mineral, 167
Modals, 47
Mode, 88, 96, 97
Modern Language Association Style (MLA), 58
Modifiers, 47, 49
Moment of Inertia, 158

Momentum, 154, 155, 156, 158
Monarch, 47, 220
Monarchy, 220
Monomial, 98
Mood, 26, 30, 45, 46, 254
Motive, 17
Multiple, 32, 43, 55, 57, 64, 74, 95, 109, 110, 199, 200, 202, 204, 205, 206, 209, 241
Nation, 201, 202, 203, 205, 206, 207, 208, 209, 210, 214, 221, 222
National, State, and Municipal Elections, 208
Natural Number, 63, 64
Negative Exponents, 66
New Left, 194
Non-Foliated Rocks, 167
Non-Linear, 26, 124
Non-Renewable, 159
Nonsense, 55
Non-Uniform Probability Model, 94
Nouns, 51
Nullification, 214
Numerical Order/Order of Importance, 25
Objective Pronouns, 48
Observation, 161
Obtuse Angle, 85
Oligarchy, 219
Ones, 198
Open Form, 25
Opinion, 31, 207, 249, 273, 303, 304, 305, 307
Order, 67
Order of Magnitude, 67
Organic Cofactors, 165
Origin, 69, 89, 120, 272, 282, 314
Outlier, 88, 97
   Outliers, 87, 96, 97
Oxford Comma, 58, 59
Parabolic Curve, 157
Parallel, 42, 59, 73, 74, 77, 85, 110, 311, 312, 313
Parallel Structure, 42
Parallelogram, 77
Parallels, 17, 240
Parliamentary System, 219, 220
Participles, 47
Particles, 47
PEMDAS, 64, 66, 321
Perimeter, 79, 80, 119, 284, 319
Periods, 53
Perpendicular Lines, 85
Personification, 21
Persuasive Texts, 46

pH, 165, 166
pH Scale, 166
Picture Graph, 90
Pie Chart, 91
Plane, 73, 85, 89, 102, 103, 107, 122, 158
Plutocracy, 219
Plutonic Rocks, 167
Point of View, 306
Polar, 159, 175
Polarization, 160
Political Institution, 209
Polygon, 75, 76, 79
Polynomial, 98, 99, 100, 101, 118, 317
Population, 97, 199, 203, 211, 215, 216, 239, 302, 337
Possessive Pronouns, 49
Precision, 69
Predictions, 30, 31, 97
Presidential System, 219, 220
Primary Elections, 216
Primary Sources, 243, 245
Prime [Greenwich] Meridian, 240
Prime Factorization, 64
Prime Numbers, 64
Probability, 86, 94, 95
Problem-Solution Structure, 38
Product Markets, 221
Pronoun, 48, 49, 51
   Pronouns, 47, 48, 51
Pronoun Reference, 48
Pronoun-Antecedent Agreement, 48
Proportional Relationship, 71
Prose, 26
Pun, 272
Purpose, 194
Pythagorean Theorem, 81, 82, 323
Question, 53
Question Marks, 53
Quotation Marks, 54
Radians, 85
Radiation, 159, 206
Random Sample, 97
Range, 54, 55, 58, 87, 97, 114, 120, 122, 123, 166, 249, 251, 280, 282, 322
Rate of Change, 124
Rational Expression, 100, 101, 109, 318
   Rational Expressions, 100, 101, 109, 318
Rational Numbers, 64
Ratios, 70, 71
Ray, 84
Real Numbers, 63

Index

Recall Elections, 208
Rectangle, 74, 78, 79, 83, 88, 119, 158, 284, 322
Rectangular Pyramid, 83
Red Herring, 30
Reference Materials, 57
Referendums, 208
Reflection, 73, 159
Refraction, 161
Regime, 219
Regression Lines, 92, 93
Relation, 13, 25, 70, 120, 219, 314
Relationship, 196, 197, 198
Relative Error, 70, 274, 314
Religion, 22, 33, 199, 200, 208, 219, 251
Remainder Theorem, 99
Renewable, 159
Representative Democracy, 219
Research, 245
Resistance, 198
Rhombus, 77
Right Angle, 78, 80, 85
Right Triangle, 74, 76, 81, 82, 153, 283
Rigid Motion, 73, 74
Rio Grande River, 197
Rotation, 73, 85, 158, 175
Run-on Sentence, 52, 311, 312, 313
Sample, 97, 277, 318, 319
Scale Factor, 71, 73
Scalene Triangle, 77
Scarcity, 221
Scatter Plot, 91
Scientific Method, 39
Scientific Notation, 66
Secondary Sources, 194, 198, 243, 245
Sediment, 167
Sedimentary Rocks, 167
Segregation, 204, 205, 207
Semicolons, 54, 308
Senate, 210, 211, 212, 213, 214
Sentence, 14, 15, 20, 21, 22, 30, 31, 37, 39, 40, 41, 42, 43, 44, 46, 47, 48, 49, 50, 51, 52, 53, 54, 59, 252, 255, 258, 259, 260, 261, 262, 264, 265, 266, 267, 268, 269, 270, 271, 272, 273, 303, 304, 306, 307, 308, 309, 310, 311, 312, 313, 314
Sentence Fragment, 51, 52, 314
Sequence, 198
Sequence Structure, 38
Side-Angle-Side (SAS), 74
Side-Side-Side (SSS), 74
Simile, 20
Simple Event, 93, 94
Simple Sentence, 42, 43, 313
Single Solution, 110
Size, 272
Skewed, 88, 310
Skewed to the Left, 88
Skewed to the Right, 88
Skewness, 88
Slavery, 196, 197
Slope, 20, 93, 104, 105, 111, 116, 124, 278, 282, 285, 320, 322, 323
Solar System, 175
Solution, 194
Spatial Order, 25, 273
Square, 63, 64, 65, 67, 78, 79, 80, 81, 84, 88, 99, 102, 103, 107, 108, 109, 110, 155, 157, 276, 278, 316, 318, 319, 321, 323
Square Root, 63, 65, 88, 102, 107, 108, 109, 319, 321, 323
Stance, 194
Standard Deviation, 88, 277, 318
State, 13, 40, 47, 56, 165, 203, 204, 207, 208, 211, 214, 215, 216, 217, 218, 219, 220, 267, 273, 307, 309
Statistics, 86, 97
Strata, 167
Structure, 25, 38, 42, 161, 209
Style, 25, 26, 45, 58, 59, 203, 271, 272, 273, 313, 314
Style Manual, 58
Subject, 15, 16, 23, 26, 32, 33, 40, 42, 43, 45, 49, 50, 119, 194, 207, 243, 245, 272, 311, 313, 314
Subordinate Clause, 41, 52, 313
Subordinating Conjunction, 41, 42, 43, 312, 313
Substitution, 81, 110, 164, 316
Suffix, 47, 56, 57
Summarizing, 198
Summary Order, 25
Sun, 53, 175, 178
Supplementary Angles, 85
Supply, 221, 223
Supporting Details, 22, 25, 37, 38, 314
Supreme Court, 208, 211, 212
Surface Area, 82
Symmetric, 88, 116, 118, 120
Synecdoche, 47
System of Equations, 110, 111, 113, 276
Tally Chart, 90
Temperature, 72, 84, 93, 159, 165, 176
Tenth Amendment, 214

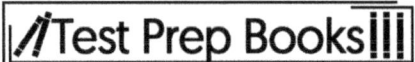

Term, 55, 58, 64, 89, 98, 107, 159, 208, 210, 218, 219, 222, 223, 224, 255, 269, 312, 317, 319, 321
Terms, 196, 245
Textual Evidence, 13
Theme, 22, 23, 39, 308, 314
Thesaurus, 58, 272, 314
Thesis Statement, 22, 31
Three Laws of Motion, 153
Tone, 15, 25, 45
Topic, 22, 26, 29, 31, 37, 39, 45, 194, 196, 304, 305, 311
Torque, 158
Transformation, 73, 167
Transitions, 25, 39
Translation, 73
Trapezoid, 77
Two-Party System, 215
Tyranny, 198
Unemployment, 222, 223
Uniform Probability Model, 94
Unit Rates, 70
Urinary System, 48
Vaccine, 15
Vector, 152, 154
Velocity, 152, 153, 154, 155, 156, 157, 158
Venn Diagrams, 39
Verb, 40, 42, 43, 47, 48, 49, 50, 51, 56, 271, 272, 308, 309, 310, 311, 312, 313
Vertex, 83, 85, 118
Vertical Angles, 85
Volume, 82, 83
Voter Initiatives, 208
Voting, 205, 207
Weight, 29, 92, 155, 280
Whole, 196
William Strunk, 59
Wind, 194
Zeros of a Function, 99, 103

Dear HiSET Test Taker,

Thank you for purchasing this study guide for your HiSET exam. We hope that we exceeded your expectations.

Our goal in creating this study guide was to cover all of the topics that you will see on the test. We also strove to make our practice questions as similar as possible to what you will encounter on test day. With that being said, if you found something that you feel was not up to your standards, please send us an email and let us know.

We would also like to let you know about other books in our catalog that may interest you.

ACT

This can be found on Amazon: amazon.com/dp/1637758596

SAT

amazon.com/dp/1637759738

GED

amazon.com/dp/1637752369

ACCUPLACER

amazon.com/dp/1637756356

We have study guides in a wide variety of fields. If the one you are looking for isn't listed above, then try searching for it on Amazon or send us an email.

Thanks Again and Happy Testing!
Product Development Team
info@studyguideteam.com

Online Resources

Included with your purchase are multiple online resources. This includes the practice tests in an interactive format and a convenient study timer to help you manage your time.

Scan the QR code or go to this link to access this content:

testprepbooks.com/online387/hiset

The first time you access the page, you will need to register as a "new user" and verify your email address.

If you have any issues, please email support@testprepbooks.com.

Thank you for letting us be a part of your studying journey!

www.ingramcontent.com/pod-product-compliance
Lightning Source LLC
Chambersburg PA
CBHW040928240426
43667CB00026B/2984